$ 93.50

CONSTRUCTS FOR UNDERSTANDING JAPAN

Japanese Studies
General Editor: Yoshio Sugimoto

Images of Japanese Society: *Ross E. Mouer and Yoshio Sugimoto*
An Intellectual History of Wartime Japan: *Shunsuke Tsurumi*
A Cultural History of Postwar Japan: *Shunsuke Tsurumi*
Beyond Computopia: *Tessa Morris-Suzuki*
Constructs for Understanding Japan: *Yoshio Sugimoto and Ross E. Mouer*

Forthcoming
Japanese Models of Conflict Resolution: *S. N. Eisenstadt and E. Ben-Ari*
Enterprise Unionism in Japan: *Hirosuke Kawanishi*
Group Psychology of the Japanese in Wartime: *Toshio Iritani*

CONSTRUCTS
FOR
UNDERSTANDING
JAPAN

edited by

Yoshio Sugimoto and Ross E. Mouer

Kegan Paul International
London and New York

First published in 1989 by Kegan Paul International Limited
PO Box 256, London WC1B 3SW

Distributed by
John Wiley & Sons Ltd
Southern Cross Trading Estate
1 Oldlands Way, Bognor Regis
W. Sussex PO22 9SA, England

Routledge, Chapman and Hall Inc
29 West 35th Street
New York, NY 10001
USA

The Canterbury Press Pty Ltd
2/71, Rushdale Street
Scoresby, Victoria 3179
Australia

The publishers gratefully acknowledge the assistance of the
Utah Foundation in the publication of this volume

Produced by Worts-Power Associates.

Set in Times
by Wessex Typesetters
(Division of The Eastern Press Ltd)
Frome, Somerset
and printed in Great Britain by
Dotesios Printers Ltd
Trowbridge, Wiltshire

ISBN 0 7103 0209 6

Contents

List of Abbreviations   vii
List of Figures   vii
List of Tables   viii
Notes on the Editors   x
Notes on the Contributors   xi
A Note on Japanese Names   xii
Preface   xiii

Introduction   Cross-currents in the Study of Japanese
               Society
               Yoshio Sugimoto and Ross Mouer   1

PART ONE: THE EXPRESSION OF INDIVIDUAL SELF-
INTEREST

1   A Theory of Social Exchange as Applied to Japan
    Harumi Befu   39
2   Arc, Circle and Sphere: Schedules for Selfhood
    David W. Plath   67
3   Some Conditions for QC Circles: Long-term
    Perspectives in the Behaviour of Individuals
    Koike Kazuo   94
4   Friendship in Cross-cultural Perspective
    Reiko Atsumi   130

v

PART TWO: INSTITUTIONS AND STRUCTURED
INEQUALITY

5 A Multi-dimensional View of Stratification: a
   Framework for Comparative Analysis
   Ross Mouer and Yoshio Sugimoto   157
6 The Transition of the Household System in Japan's
   Modernization
   Kawamura Nozomu   202
7 Resolving Social Conflicts: a Comparative View of
   Interpersonal and Inter-group Relations in Japan
   Susan J. Pharr   228
8 Interest Groups and the Process of Political Decision-
   making in Japan
   Sone Yasunori   259
9 Japanese Industrial Relations: an External Perspective
   Solomon B. Levine   296

PART THREE: METHODOLOGICAL HORIZONS

10 The *Emic–Etic* Distinction and Its Significance for
    Japanese Studies
    Harumi Befu   323
11 The Role of Typologies in Understanding Japanese
    Culture and Society: From Linguistics to Social Science
    J. V. Neustupný   344

Index   381

List of Abbreviations

ASC   *Asahi Shinbun*, morning edition
ASY   *Asahi Shinbun*, evening edition
JT   *The Japan Times*
MSC   *Mainichi Shinbun*, morning edition
MSY   *Mainichi Shinbun*, evening edition
NKSC *Nihon Keizai Shinbun*, morning edition

List of Figures

A   Third-Level Comparisons in Cross-Cultural
      Research   17
1.1   Correlation of Mean Instrumental and Expressive
      Values Assigned to 20 Exchange Acts by 138 Male
      Respondents   48
1.2   Cognitive Structure in which Various Resources are
      Seen in Terms of their Relationship to Particularism
      and Concreteness   49
3.1   A Comparison of Age–Wage Profiles for Blue-
      Collar Male Employees in Japan and Selected
      European Countries   109
3.2   A Comparison of Age–Wage Profiles for White-
      Collar Male Employees in Japan and Selected
      European Countries   110
3.3   The Percentage Distribution of Male Employees by
      the Length of Continuous Employment in the Same
      Firm: a Comparison of Japan and Selected European
      Countries   113
5.1   A Two-Dimensional Distribution of the Labour
      Force   166
6.1   Three Types of Family Structure   206
6.2   A *Dōzoku* Consisting of Ten Households   207
6.3   The Idea of the *Dōzoku* Relationships: the Branch
      Families of the Main Family (*Honke*) after Fourteen
      Generations   208

6.4	Order of Succession to the Japanese Throne	213
6.5	Nakane's Two Principles of Stratification	219
6.6	Four Types of Society	220
6.7	Types of Relationships	220
6.8	Focus of Attention in *Ie Shakai* Theories	225
8.1	Expansion of Groups and Organizations since 1900	285
11.1	Hierarchy of Interrelated Principles and Features	348
11.2	A Tree Diagram of the 'Self-Interest' Type	350

List of Tables

A	Distribution of *Emic* Concepts in Two Dimensions	16
1.1	Mean Expressivity and Instrumentality Values of 20 Exchange Acts as Evaluated by 138 Males	47
3.1	Views of American and Japanese Workers on the Organization of Work and Supervisor Communications with Workers under His Supervision	97
3.2	Views of American and Japanese Workers on Job Security and Redundancy owing to the Introduction of New Technology	98
3.3	A Comparison of the Attitudes of Japanese and American Workers concerning Union-Organized Strikes	99
3.4	Percentage of Workers Involved in Small-Group Activities by Firm Size according to the Presence or Absence of a Labour Union	103
3.5	Evaluations of the Effectiveness of Small-Group Activities by Firm Size	103
3.6	Worker Responses to Question No. 16 on the Acceptance of Supervisory Authority: a Comparison of Japanese and American Workers	121
3.7	Responses to Question No. 20 concerning Promotion Decisions: a Comparison of American and Japanese Workers	122

5.1	Types of Rewards	163
5.2	The Relative Solidarity of Persons in a Category Defined by an Agent of Stratification	168
5.3	National System of Commendations	172
8.1	The Support Groups of HOC MPs who Represent Large-Scale Organization by Political Party	266
8.2	Successful Candidates from the Various Ministries and Sources of Support	269
8.3	Okabe's Votes and Expenditures of Land Improvement Enterprises by Prefectures	270
8.4	Percentage Composition of the General Accounts Budget: 1955–78	273
8.5	Annual Expenditures which Require Re-examination	276
8.6	Membership in Various Types of Organizations in Six Countries	284
8.7	Year in which Japanese Groups and Organizations were Founded	285
8.8	Influences on Political Decisions	287
8A(1)	A Typology of *Shingikai*	290
8A(2)	Classification of *Shingikai* by Member's Background and by Ministry Affiliation, 1974	291
8B(1)	Classification of *Shingikai* by Member's Background and by Ministry Affiliation, 1984	292
11.1	A Typology of Types	364
11.2	Some Japanese Reference Strategies	370

Notes on the Editors

SUGIMOTO, Yoshio: Professor of Sociology and Dean of Social Sciences at La Trobe University, Melbourne. Author of *Popular Disturbance in Postwar Japan* (Asian Research Service, 1981), and *Chō-kanri rettō Nippon* (The ultra-controlled Japanese archipelago) (Kōbunsha, 1983) and co-editor of *Democracy in Contemporary Japan* (Hale and Iremonger/M. E. Sharpe, 1986) and *The Japanese Trajectory: Modernization and Beyond* (Cambridge University Press, 1988).

MOUER, Ross E.:   Senior Lecturer in Japanese Studies, Monash University, Melbourne. Co-author of *Labor Policy in Japan* (Japanese Studies Centre, 1986) and co-editor of *Japan's Impact on the World* (Japanese Studies Association of Australia, 1984).

The editors co-authored *Images of Japanese Society* (Kegan Paul International, 1986) and *Nihonjin wa 'Nihon-teki' ka* (Arguments about the nature of Japanese society) (Tōyō Keizai Shinpō-sha, 1982) and co-edited *Kojin Kanjin Nihonjin* (Individual self-interests and interpersonal relations in Japanese society) (Gakuyō Shobō, 1987), and *Nihonjinron ni kansuru 12-shō* (Twelve chapters on theories of Japanese society) (Gakuyō Shobō, 1983).

Notes on the Contributors

ATSUMI, Reiko: Senior Lecturer, School of Modern Asian Studies, Griffith University, Brisbane, Australia.

BEFU, Harumi: Professor of Anthropology at Stanford University. Author of *Japan: an Anthropological Introduction* (Chandler, 1971) and *Ideorogii to shite no Nihon bunka-ron* (Theories on Japanese culture as ideology) (Shisō no Kagaku-sha, 1987).

KAWAMURA, Nozomu: Professor of Sociology at Tokyo Metropolitan University. Author of *Nihon shakaigaku-shi kenkyū* (A historical study of Japanese sociological theories) (Ningen no Kagaku-sha, 2 vols, 1973/75), *Nihon bunka-ron no shūhen* (On theories of Japanese culture) (Ningen no Kagaku-sha, 1982), and *Chishiki shakaigaku no shosō* (Aspects of the sociology of knowledge) (Shiraishi Shoten, 1987).

KOIKE, Kazuo: Professor of Management at Hōsei University, Tokyo. Author of *Understanding Industrial Relations in Japan* (Macmillan, 1988), *Shokuba no rōdō kumiai to sanka* (Labour unions and their participation in firms) (Tōyō Keizai Shinpō-sha, 1977), and *Nihon no jukuren* (Skill formation in Japan) (Yūhikaku, 1981).

LEVINE, Solomon B.: Professor of Business and Economics at the University of Wisconsin. Author of *Industrial Relations in Postwar Japan* (University of Illinois Press, 1958). Co-author of *Human Resources in Japanese Industrial Develop-*

ment (Princeton University Press, 1980). Co-editor of *Workers and Employers in Japan* (Princeton University Press, 1974).

NEUSTUPNÝ, J. V.:   Professor of Japanese Studies at Monash University, Melbourne. Author of *Post-Structural Approaches to Language* (University of Tokyo Press, 1978), *Gaikokujin to no komunikeishon* (Communicating with foreigners) (Iwanami Shoten, 1981), and *Communicating with the Japanese* (*The Japan Times*, 1987).

PHARR, Susan J.:   Professor of Government at Harvard University. Author of *Political Women in Japan* (University of California Press, 1981).

PLATH, David W.:   Professor of Anthropology at the University of Illinois. Author of *The After Hours* (University of California Press, 1964). Co-author of *Sensei and His People* (University of California Press, 1969). Editor of *Aware of Utopia* (University of Illinois Press, 1971), *Adult Episodes in Japan* (Brill, 1975), *Work and Lifecourse in Japan* (State University of New York Press, 1983).

SONE, Yasunori: Professor of Political Science at Keiō University, Tokyo. Author of *Kettei no seiji keizaigaku* (Political economics of decision-making) (Yūhikaku, 1984). Co-author of *Manjô itch to tasûketsu* (Unanimous consensus and majority rule) (Nihon Keizai Shinbun-sha, 1980), and co-editor of *Sekai seiji no naka no Nihon seiji* (Japan in world politics) (Yūhikaku, 1983).

A Note on Japanese Names

The Japanese convention that family name precedes personal name is generally followed in this book. However, those Japanese who either live in the West or have chosen to adopt the opposite (Western) convention of personal name followed by family name in their writings in English are identified accordingly. In the table of contents, for example, Atsumi, Befu and Sugimoto are listed in Western order, but all other Japanese names are in Japanese order, surname first. Uncertainty may be resolved by reference to the Notes on Contributors and the index, where all persons named in the text are listed in alphabetical order according to their family names.

Preface

This volume has emerged from the International Colloquium on the Comparative Study of Japanese Society. Held at Noosa Heads in Queensland from 29 January to 6 February 1982, the colloquium brought together participants from eight countries to discuss about thirty papers. The participants came with a common sense of dissatisfaction with the 'group model' or 'consensus-oriented theories' as a means of understanding Japanese society. The papers and discussion focused on alternative approaches for conceptualizing Japanese society and on methodological issues in the comparative study of Japanese society.

Unfortunately, it has not been possible to incorporate the full breadth of intellectual activity which characterized the colloquium.[1] Only eleven papers were selected through a two-tiered system of referring and editing. Those chosen focus on the expression of individual self-interest, on social institutions and the structuring

---

1 For a fuller account of the colloquium, see 'Toward the Comparative Study of Japan', *Center News*, vol. 7, no. 2, June 1982, 2–4; 'Tokushusei to Dōjini Fuhensei mo' (Studying the Similarities as Well as the Differences), *Mainichi Shinbun* (evening edition: 17 March 1982), 4; 'Nihon Shakai no Hikaku Kenkyū – Nuusa Kokusai Kaigi kara' (The Comparative Study of Japan – Notes from the Noosa International Colloquium), *Kyōto Shinbun* (12 March 1987), 11; 'Toward the Comparative Study of Japan – or, Dancing the Noosa Tango', *The Australia–Japan Foundation Newsletter*, vol. 2, no. 1, April 1982, 14–16.

of inequality, and on aspects of methodology relevant to the development of Japanese studies as a distinct academic activity. Although the papers were initially drafted in the early 1980s, most have been considerably reworked. The introduction seeks to explain the continuing relevance of the papers in terms of the development of Japanese studies in the late 1980s.

Illness and personal disruptions have delayed the publication of this volume beyond any reasonable period of time. The editors thank the contributors for their patience while this project 'simmered on the back burner' and for bearing with the often repeated demands for rewriting. The generosity of various funding agencies is also appreciated. Without the financial assistance of the Japan Foundation, the Australia–Japan Foundation, the Utah Foundation, Griffith University and the Australian National University, neither this volume nor the colloquium would have been possible. Finally, a special note of thanks must go to Griffith and La Trobe Universities and to the Japanese Studies Centre in Melbourne for various forms of institutional support which was central to the smooth running of the colloquium and the preparation of the manuscript.

Yoshio Sugimoto and Ross Mouer
Melbourne, October 1987

Introduction
Cross-currents in the Study of Japanese Society

Yoshio Sugimoto and Ross Mouer

1 The changing tides

As the seasons change, so do the winds which blow on Japanese
studies. Studies on the nature of Japanese society are exposed to
changes in the intellectual climate. Sometimes the change is abrupt,
marked by the opening of the country or the end of a war. At
other times the drift has been on a steady current; imperceptible
perhaps, but just as surely moving Japan from one climatic zone
to another. As our images of Japanese society have inevitably
been part of the Japanese landscape while also being shaped by
the intellectual environment in Japan and abroad, it is not
surprising that they too have changed with the seasons.

These shifts in our visions of Japanese society have become
more apparent during the 1980s. In addition to the growing
awareness of the ideological setting in which internationalization
and current research on Japan are occurring, a number of meta-
theoretical discussions have underlined various ways in which the
study of Japanese society has been shaped by changes in Japan's

1

political and economic position in the world over the last half century. The writings of Glazer (1975), researchers at the Nomura Sōgō Kenkyūsho (1978), Lehmann (1978), Nagoya (1979), Minear (1980a, 1980b), Minami (1980), Yamagishi and Brinton (1980), Kawamura (1982), Sugimoto and Mouer (1980b, 1981, 1982a, 1982b, 1986, 1987), Lummis (1982a and 1982b), Lummis and Ikeda (1985), Neustupný (1982), Tsukishima (1984), Hamaguchi (1979 and 1985), Gill (1984, 1985a, 1985b), Gluck (1985), Shinbori (1985), Dale (1986), Befu (1987a) and Yamamoto (1987) – to mention but a few – form a *prima facie* case for considering the studies of Japanese society as social phenomena. These have not been the first attempts to systematize Japan's recent intellectual history. They have, however, shifted attention from the mass media to the activities of social scientists engaged in the study of Japan.

Although a definitive analysis is awaited, along with case studies in particular areas, the influence of this new scholarship has been felt in several ways. One is the move of scholars away from the blatant romanticism, naïve armchair speculation, the commercial orientation found in many best-sellers and the ideological myth-making which characterized earlier forms of *nihonjinron* in the 1970s. Another is in the increased willingness of writers to include in their accounts of Japanese society an analysis of the literature on Japanese society in a semi-meta-theoretical fashion. The introductory textbooks on Japanese society edited by Naitō *et al.* (1980) and by Fuse *et al.* (1982) provide such examples. Their discussions of Japanese society provide a sharp contrast to the purely descriptive accounts of sociologists in the older school (for example, Fukutake 1972 and 1981). A third is the appearance of a sociology-of-knowledge perspective in particular areas such as industrial relations (cf. Shimada 1984a, Kawanishi 1982 and Mouer 1987).

It would be unwise to see meta-*nihonjinron* as the only variable dampening the enthusiasm for *nihonjinron* among academics. Other factors include higher incomes. A more stable economic environment has lessened the need for academics to write popular fiction and best-sellers for supplementary income. Japan's improved status internationally has reduced the need to stress constantly the uniqueness of Japanese society in order to establish an acceptable national identity.

The vision of Japanese society which has been a major concern of much meta-theory is a genre variously referred to as '*nihonjinron*', '*nihon bunkaron*', 'the group model' and 'the consensus model'. Although these terms have been used rather loosely, they have nevertheless come to designate a fairly coherent image of Japanese society. The image consists of a theory or set of theories which portray Japanese society as having exceptionally low levels of conflict. In these descriptions, importance is attached to the unusually strong emphasis in Japanese culture on group membership and on consensus. The Japanese have been presented as lacking a strong ego, and as being exceptionally homogeneous culturally and socially. National culture has often been the major variable of first resort when explaining structures and behaviour which seem to set Japanese apart from people in other societies. Epistemologically, the paradigm has been cast outside the methodologies generally associated with social science. Depending heavily on intuitive insight and arguments supported largely by linguistic analogies and anecdotal illustrations, its advocates have tended to treat the West as a monolith.

Challenges to the national character approach can be traced to the early 1950s. There was then a world view which sought explanations of Japanese social phenomena in terms of the internal structuring of social inequality within Japan, and in terms of Japan's position in a hierarchically structured world system. Marxist and radical–liberal interpretations of Japanese society seemed to be an inevitable product of a scholarship zealously concerned with the 'democratization' of Japan (for instance, cf. Shimizu 1951 and Kuno 1952). However, even the most committed Marxist writers seemed unable to free themselves from notions of the authoritarian personality in the collective Japanese consciousness. It is not surprising, therefore, that these views of life in Japan began to give way with economic growth in the 1960s to 'modernization theories' which tended to view the world system in terms of uni-directional evolution. Culturally given social systems could be understood as being holistic entities with an ordered position in the convoy of mankind which was moving toward modernity. Modernization theory was persuasive. It allowed for the principle of cultural relativism and an emphasis on national culture to be accommodated within more universally conceived, though hierarchically structured, notions of convergence.

A second challenge to the notion of a determining national character appeared in the early 1970s. Buoyed initially by the student movement of the late 1960s, the views of conflict-theorists and anti-establishmentarians were given a further boost in the 1970s by the anti-pollution movements, the growing conspicuousness of various citizen movements, and the burgeoning of the reformist parties. It was a period when representations of this scholarship at academic discussions of Japanese life were often juxtaposed to the national culture paradigm, and debate occurred in a lively fashion. Although this literature has been largely beyond the horizon of the meta-theorists and awaits further study, its connection with a particular political viewpoint is unmistakable; its sudden decline in the late 1970s cannot be understood apart from changes in the political and economic climate, both internationally and domestically.

In the 1980s yet another wave of writings have criticized consensus-oriented explanations of Japanese society (for example, Lummis 1982a; Ogawa 1985; Kurihara 1982; Takabatake and Kurihara 1985; Sugimoto 1981 and 1983; Hidaka 1985; Tsurumi 1986 and 1987; and McCormack and Sugimoto 1986 and 1988). This current critique has moved beyond fairly straightforward concerns with open-conflict and outright exploitation to consider the prevalence of less visible forms of control in Japanese society. For example, widespread control has been particularly mentioned in discussions of education (Kamata 1984; Oyama and Takano 1986). Attention has been directed to issues of neo-nationalism. Of particular concern is the way Japanese conceptualize dealings with the outside world. 'Soft-authoritarianism' and 'friendly fascism' have been used as terms for discussing internal developments within Japanese society.

There has also been a renewed interest in the Emperor system as a cornerstone in establishment-oriented ideology. The perfunctory role of the Emperor in the day-to-day running of Japan's political bodies may have induced a tendency to dismiss him as an old fatherly figure in the backdrop of Japan's political life. Yet a growing number of observers are coming to attach special significance to the Emperor and his family in terms of their continuing symbolic importance in the minds of many Japanese. The ideology associated with the maintenance of the imperial institution has been seen as a barrier to improving the status of *burakumin* (Irokawa 1984) and as a hindrance impeding the women's movement (Kanō 1979). Kan (1984) argues that the association of the Emperor with the notion of cleanliness inevitably builds into the culture a hierarchy of purity – a view which leads Kan to conclude that the position of the Emperor is maintained by reference to that which is contaminated.

The case against the consensus model, which is often formulated in terms of national character stereotypes, continues to build, though the progress appears in bursts and starts. In discussing the current status of the literature on Japanese society, however, it would be misleading to suggest that *nihonjinron* is now simply receding from academic writing. The publication of *nihonjinron* continues to be well-received even in the late 1980s (Hamaguchi and Kumon 1982; Takeda 1984; Amanuma 1987; Hendry and Webber 1986; Doi 1985 and 1986; Morita 1987). The academic consultants listed by the editors of Time-Life books in their recent volume (1986) also suggest that the view of Japan embodied in *nihonjinron* will be around for some time. Hall (1987) indicates that many of 'today's Japanologists' are serving to cover over some of the important realities shaping life in Japan by making cultural excuses for Japan, a contribution to a breakdown of international communications by what he refers to as the 'mutual understanding industry'. Johnson (1987) suggests that the continuing emphasis on Japan's cultural uniqueness now goes beyond being a healthy push for a modicum of 'cultural relativism' and constitutes little more than a form of Japanese racism. The emphasis on cultural uniqueness as the major variable explaining these several phenomena has a long tradition extending back to the prewar period, as Kawamura (1982), Sugimoto and Mouer (1986), Dale (1986), Yamamoto (1987) and others have argued. It is not surprising, then, that the literature articulating that viewpoint has continued to evolve. The work of Nakane and Doi, and the later manifestations of that genre in the work of Reischauer and Vogel, are now being left behind. Three thrusts in particular deserve attention in the 1980s.

One reassertion of the *nihonjinron* perspective can be found in the mammoth work of Satō, Kumon and Murakami (1979). Later summarized by Murakami (1984), the emphasis is on the emergence of the *ie* as a social and cultural norm in Japanese society. In the argument that there is a fundamental continuity in Japanese culture and social structure between the prewar and postwar periods, the American occupation is treated as being somewhat irrelevant to the democratization of Japan. The logical development of the *ie* or *mura*-type approach to human organization is seen as Japan's

5

own form of democracy. However, the line between (1) the emphasis on prewar Japanese-style democracy and progressive social policies as important legacies in the postwar period – a theme taken up briefly some time ago by Nakayama (1975: 69–75 and 89–90), for example, and now articulated more fully by Dower (1987) – and (2) the tendency to justify the status quo in Japan by referring to cultural antecedents and treating them as given (a point raised in this volume by Kawamura) is thin. In praising the relationship between the government and industry and Japanese-style management as sources of Japan's postwar economic growth, the postwar development of Japanese society is seen as having been almost inevitable given Japanese culture and social structure. The suggestion is that such arrangements were successful in the Japanese setting precisely because they were uniquely Japanese. The view of Japanese society as a large *mura* or *ie* connects closely with the image of Japan as a fairly homogeneous middle-class society, having neither marked social inequalities nor strong 'horizontal' class consciousness. The possibility of Japan having moved in other directions is not considered. The assumptions of unusual homogeneity, consensus and group-orientations are basic to this view of Japanese society.

A second development can be found in the work of Hamaguchi (1977, 1982 and 1985). His emphasis has been on the 'contextual orientation' of the Japanese, an emphasis which sets the Japanese psychology apart from that of Westerners. He argues that an entirely new paradigm is required in the social sciences if Japanese society is to be properly understood. He argues that Japanese have a different frame of reference – that they begin thinking in social terms by referring to their relationship with others (cf. Hamaguchi *et al.* 1987). This is seen as contrasting with the Western individual, whose basic concern begins with himself or herself as the starting point for social action.

Here, too, the links with *nihonjinron* are obvious. The same sweeping supra-cultural stereotyping of the West appears, although it is interesting to note that the concept of '*kanjinshugi*' (contextualism), which is seen as being central to the 'Japaneseness' (*nihon rashisa*) of the Japanese mind set, is constructed largely in terms of Hsu's notion of *jin*. Much of Hamaguchi's writings actually refer to *kanjinshugi* as a characteristic of '*tōyōjin*' (meaning 'Orientals' in general, but indicating primarily Chinese cultural norms). As a recent discussion (Hamaguchi *et al.* 1987) reveals, contextualism is a concept which defies definition in an operational sense, a problem similarly faced by Nakane's notion of *tateshakai* ('vertical and horizontal relationships') and Doi's concept of *amae* ('dependency').

Although Hamaguchi seems to concede that Western social scientists using Western paradigms (which inevitably rely on the concept of the individual as the starting point) can explain some behaviour in Japan, he argues that the diverse paradigms offered by the symbolic-interactionists, Marxists, Freudian psychology and Weberian sociology all revolve around the 'individual' as the unit of analysis. Hamaguchi therefore concludes that theories based on Western paradigms will never explain Japanese behaviour as adequately as a paradigm based on contextualism or interpersonal relationships. How contextually oriented paradigms will differ methodologically has not been adequately explained. As with much of the *nihonjinron*, the argumentation is largely intuitive. The end result is perhaps more sophisticated, but the emphasis is still on the need to use an ambiguously defined framework conceived largely in terms specific to the Japanese language to make comparative statements about the uniqueness of Japanese social structures and cultural norms.

The third wave of neo-*nihonjinron* can be found in the notion of '*nihon bunmeiron*' (theories of Japanese civilization). This approach is best seen in the series of international conferences on aspects of Japanese society and culture arranged by the Kokuritsu Minzoku Hakubutsukan (The National Museum of Ethnology) under the leadership of Umesao Tadao. While those conferences have been held in the Kansai area, the Society for the Comparative Study of Civilizations has emerged somewhat independently in the Kantō area.

New developments along these lines add two variations to the earlier literature associated with '*nihonjinron*'. First, they occur with a fairly explicit insistence that the unit of analysis ought to be the civilization. The shift from *bunka* (culture) to *bunmei* (civilization) as the unit of analysis is seen by some as placing the discussion of Japanese society in a wider context. Culture (including social values and national character) comes to be subsumed within a much broader range of concerns. Civilization includes not only culture but social organization, structures and institutions. Although '*bunmei*' is not defined, it would seem that the term is conceived so that different civilizations might be placed in some evolutionary hierarchy – a hierarchy in which Japan occupies a position near the top (Itō 1985). Moreover, by changing the unit of analysis to civilization, the difficulty of comparing Japanese society and culture with a monolithic conception of 'the West' seems to be overcome, for it is easier to argue that both Japan and the West are civilizations.

There is still plenty of room to debate how different *bunkaron* and *bunmeiron* are. While much of *nihon bunkaron* dealt with organizational and structural variables, *nihon bunmeiron* tends to focus on the cultural. This ambiguity can clearly be seen in a recent paper on the 'methodology of comparative *bunmeiron*' by Umesao (1985). One of the leading proponents arguing for the use of this unit of analysis in the comparative study of Japan, he argues that Japan should be studied as a civilization because it is different from the West. The difference he cites, however, is cultural – the alleged absence in Japan of the emphasis on the individual which is prevalent in the West (p. 23). The question of what constitutes a civilization and what the other civilizations might be tends to be overlooked. As with *nihonjinron*, the comparisons tend to be confined to comparisons of Japanese and Western civilizations. This can also be seen in the way 'civilization', 'nation', 'state' and 'culture' tend to be used interchangeably in Yano's efforts (1986a and 1986b) to distinguish between Japan's 'flow civilization' and the 'stock civilization' found in the West, and to justify Japan's pursuit of a different kind of 'internationalization'.

Although the label has changed, the paradigm seems to be largely the same. While it would be unfair to evaluate contributions of Umesao and Yano to the study of Japanese society on the basis of one essay, the example does illustrate the extent to which *nihonjinron* continues to influence the frame of reference utilized by those who claim they are opening new ground in the study of Japanese society by focusing on the comparison of civilizations.

2 Other cross-currents

It is within the context of these developments that the papers in this volume have significance. The products of a conference held at Noosa Heads (in Queensland, Australia) in January and February 1982, they address at least three issues that deserve attention in any appraisal of Japanese society. In searching for ways to move beyond the *nihonjinron* paradigm, while at the same time avoiding the pitfalls of narrowly defined conflict models, participants in the International Colloquium for the Comparative Study of Japanese Society considered the notion of personhood and the nature of interpersonal relations in the context of institutionalized power relations.

An important theme in the papers which form Parts One and Two of this volume is that many Japanese have a clear notion of self-interest. Although much has been made of the dichotomy between Western individualism and the group orientation or interpersonal contextualism of the Japanese, several papers in this volume suggest that the two might be complementary. In arguing that the social exchange model can be used to understand Japanese behaviour, Befu presents a framework in which there is a symbiotic relationship between the context in which interpersonal relations occur and the way in which the self-interests of the actors are identified. Plath's paper considers how the notion of life cycle connects with an individual's ideas about the timing or scheduling of behaviour. His presentation and the contributions to a volume he edited (1983) highlight the individual's capacity to reassess his or her own position on the sea of life and to change direction midway through life. There is in Plath's account a view of the individual Japanese as a coherent entity seeking to make sense of his or her existence as an integrated and rational whole within several given social contexts.

It is this ability to maintain sight of one's own interests in relation to the well-being of larger social entities which links the redirection accompanying mid-life crises with the individual's willingness to stay affiliated with a particular group. This view is often expressed in reference to life within work-related organizations. Kawamura's paper alludes to an intellectual climate in which employees come to believe that their fate at work is like that of the individual cast at sea in a lifeboat: should the firm go bankrupt, the boat will capsize, and all, including oneself, will drown.

It is not unreasonable, therefore, that Koike chooses to study his individuals within the context of an important group at work, the quality-control circle. In a carefully reasoned presentation, he tries to develop a structure logically linking the pursuit of self-interest with group activity. Koike emphasizes the institutional context in which the structuring of careers serves to tie individual rewards to the acquisition of firm-specific skills and to the productivity of a particular enterprise and a particular work group.

Koike is not the only observer to comment on how self-interest is maximized in the context of firm-specific career employment in the large-scale sector. Much has been written about the egoism of enterprise unions which have sought to protect the elitist interests of their memberships by excluding workers on the fringe (poorly paid part-timers and those working for sub-contractors) and by frustrating policies which would cut into their own incomes (for example, minimum-wage legislation and anti-pollution legislation). Kawanishi's account (1982) of the struggle between 'industrialism' and 'enterprisism' reveals how the latter emerged as the primary force determining the structures which would link the individual's fortunes to those of a specific group within society.

Common to the presentations by Plath and Koike is the emphasis on long-term planning. Although the link between a specific act of behaviour and self-interest may not be obvious, it nonetheless exists. It must be understood within the context of goals which are, at the time of behavioural choice, still only silhouetted on the horizon toward which one's ship is moving. Befu phrases this slightly differently, arguing that in Japanese society generalized exchange seems to be more prevalent than balanced exchange, and that the instrumental value derived from an exchange act correlates with the expressive value from that act. Befu points to the need in discussions of social exchange to specify more clearly the length of time involved when an individual calculates instrumental and expressive values.

Mouer and Sugimoto attempt to provide a framework for considering how individual self-interest may be aggregated with the self-interest of others. They present a model which might account for some important aspects of collective action while providing substance to the otherwise abstract notion of 'contextualism'. They argue that interpersonal relations are shaped considerably by the relative positioning of the actors in a complex matrix of inequality. They identify a number of dimensions in which inequality occurs. Pharr deals with three of their dimensions in her discussion of status-based conflict: ethnicity, gender and age. Sone's paper refers frequently to geography, occupation and several other variables in accounting for the distribution of power among a large variety of interest groups.

Social inequality is another theme highlighted by the social exchange and stratification models. Befu refers to unbalanced and negative exchange, an idea he has developed elsewhere (1974, 1987b) in more detail. For Mouer and Sugimoto, the creation and maintenance both of the inequalities associated with social class and of the status quo can be understood only by reference to criss-crossing hierarchies. This leads to the question of power relations. Debate concerning the nature of Japanese society has often centred on the extent to which behaviour is more regulated in Japan.

One approach to dealing with power confronts directly the question of influence. Sone does this in his examination of Japanese interest groups. He seeks to identify influential actors in terms of the rewards they might be expected to receive were they actually able to 'manipulate the system'. Although Sone's actors are clearly motivated by economic gain, Sone concludes that economic power is not so easily transformed back into political power. Given a corporatist balance between strategic sectors, his paper suggests that there may be a need to consider more carefully the distribution of power within various institutional sectors.

The question of power and control can also be approached indirectly. Atsumi argues that Japanese distinguish between friend-ship and *tsukiai*. The former is seen as occurring more or less as the result of free choice; the latter is formed in response to a sense of obligation bolstered by an awareness of sanctions.

From this distinction emerges a problem not adequately discussed either in this volume or elsewhere (for instance, in Smith's treatment (1983) of how tradition is created) – namely, the distinction between ideology and culture, and the impact of ideology on social behaviour. To what extent, for example, are social norms embodied in a 'politically neutral' culture transcending the interests of all identifiable groups within society? To what extent is the sense of obligation systematically associated with certain classes of people in a manner which consistently serves the interests of those in other classes?

Kawamura's chapter on the Emperor system and the ideology of the household system discusses an important metaphor which has often been used by representatives of the state and by business leaders to legitimize specific social arrangements in postwar Japan. For Kawamura the metaphor of the family continues to be conceived in a way that keeps the precept of the Emperor system alive. While recognizing that the family has changed greatly over the postwar years, Kawamura argues that the ideology continues to provide a convenient vocabulary shaping not only behaviour within the family setting, but also in other spheres such as work. For more concrete examples, one is left to read writers such as Kogawa (1986), who argues that the electronic media serve as a vessel in which an ideology based on the Emperor system is sustained. In arguing that Japanese feminists will face an uphill climb as long as the male-oriented Emperor system remains intact, Kogawa supports Kawamura's interpretation, as does the recent research by Kanō (1979), Irokawa (1982) and Kan (1984).

In most instances, the ways in which behaviour is systematically regulated by socio-political institutions are more obvious than the interconnections with 'exploitative ideologies'. For Pharr, the power relations between the status groups she studies are quite clearly institutionalized. Conflict occurs when the subordinate groups wish to renegotiate their relations with the superordinate group. Pharr tends to see attempts at renegotiation in terms of small rituals or token behaviour which symbolize the relationships. The symbols themselves are part of a larger institutional arrangement in which the power relations have evolved. Hence the conflict is between new radical ideologies justifying change and the vocabulary of the ingrained institutions which by its very existence establishes and maintains the status quo.

For Sone, the power relations are less clear. Sceptical of simplistic theories which posit the existence of an elitist monolith such as 'Japan Incorporated', he suggests that political power is diffused both by pluralistic alliances and by corporatist structures. There is a particular emphasis on the need to shift attention from the legislature to the administrative sphere. Sone argues that the very nature of power is changing in contemporary Japan as the realignment of interests has come to produce a much more complex matrix of criss-crossing stratifications. Nevertheless, at whatever level, there is a clear view of groups competing for a voice in the political processes.

In his treatment of industrial relations in Japan, Levine also eschews simple explanations for complex phenomena. He underlines the importance of having a broad grounding in the major institutions and a comprehensive knowledge of the full range of actors and their goals. The emphasis is similar to that found in the survey of labour policy provided by Ono and Mouer (1986). For Levine the first step is to gain an overview of industrial relations as a system with purposive actors. Such a framework allows for the systematic appraisal of Japan's industrial relations in comparative perspective. The end result is a shift from the common emphasis on the uniqueness of life-time employment, seniority wages, company welfare and enterprise unions to labour legislation, dualities in the labour market, the patterns of conflict and the interface between industrial relations and the politics of postwar Japan.

3 Navigational skills

A major shortcoming of *nihonjinron* past and present has been the absence of methodological considerations. At the risk of overgeneralization, one might add that this has been a burden borne by most involved in area studies. It has been common for those in area studies to sense a dilemma between knowing all there is to know about 'their' society and the need for methodological sophistication. While many accept a role as the rapporteur for that society, they also find themselves in a difficult position when asked, and expected, to make sweeping statements about their society, frequently placing it in comparative perspective. For nearly all who study a particular society and culture, their investigations are, implicitly or explicitly, a venture into the world of comparative studies. Whether the aim is to examine a global theory or to uncover a uniqueness, their investigations are invariably carried out with reference to more than the one society.

The debates on methodology and on the nature of 'science' in the social sciences have a long history. Although science is basically comparative, the frameworks for comparative analysis associated with most disciplines tend to have been developed for intra-societal comparisons of fairly small units. Groups or organizations are usually taken as being the largest unit of analysis for intra-societal comparisons, although widening the comparative framework to encompass civilizations has in some instances facilitated the comparison of institutions.

In the study of Japanese society, however, the assumption of cultural homogeneity seems to have obviated the need for careful intra-societal comparisons. Although the methodology is not well known, the survey finding of the Prime Minister's Office showing that 90 percent of all Japanese identify with the middle class or that Japanese have only a vertical consciousness seems to have become widely accepted as fact, and the number of social scientists seriously probing variation within Japanese society according to income, class or occupation has markedly declined over time. From the early 1960s onwards, the major works on Japanese society have shifted the search for variation from intra-societal comparisons to the discussion of how the responses of Japanese to such questionnaires compare across societies, cultures and civilizations. Of course, while Japan has constantly been compared with societies of the West, seldom has it been compared with Korea and other nearby societies.

Despite the emphasis on comparing Japanese society with other societies, very little attention has been given to the methodological problems posed by cross-cultural comparisons. Again, this may not be a problem unique to the study of Japan. Most area studies are organized on the premise that one is methodologically prepared for field work by studying a discipline and the language of the target population. It is assumed that the researcher will pick up practical hints in the field in an *ad hoc* manner. Although personal accounts by senior researchers are sometimes systematized for public debate, the usual practice is that newer-comers rely on 'the oral tradition'.

The editors of this volume have argued strenuously (1982a, 1984, 1986) that a fully fledged discussion of comparative methodology is necessary if Japanese studies is to develop as a discipline or paradigm. Although volumes on Japanese society continue to appear in rapid succession, few speak to the methodological issues involved. The exception would be those volumes which have emerged directly from doctoral research and explain a methodology specific to that research. Although methodological issues are occasionally mentioned in book reviews, methodology is seldom discussed as a feature which distinguishes Japanese studies as a 'discipline'.

One major exception might be Dore's comments (1966) in the volume he edited for the 'Princeton series'. He touches upon the difficulty of using Japan as a test case for examining modernization theory. However, his insights appeared as an afterthought in an introduction written after the volume was compiled, not as a keynote helping to inform or to direct the research. Another exception might be the handbook on field work compiled by Ward (1964), editor of another volume in the Princeton series. The papers in Part Three may be seen as contributions to informed debate in the area of methodology in Japanese studies.

The paper by Befu on *emic* (cultural-specific) and *etic* (universalistic cross-cultural) modes of analysis demonstrates clearly that the language barrier is more than a problem of translation. Befu argues that the use of language as a tool for analysis, for transcription and for communicating the results of one's research on one culture to persons in another often involves the imposition of categories from the one culture onto those of the other culture.

Although these points are directly linked with issues related to cultural imperialism and cultural relativism in the context of international relations, they are also of interest to those who wish to analyze intra-societal dynamics. Stratification and the existence of subcultures within Japanese society mean that the forms of language used by one sub-group in society are imposed upon other sub-groups within the society. Is it not possible to think of the language and concepts built into the colloquial language of women, persons in the Kansai area, and the Korean minority as containing a number of *emic* concepts which must be put aside in deference to the '*etic*' concepts of the more dominant sub-groups whenever they come into contact with members of those sub-groups (that is, men, persons from the Kantō area and 'ordinary' Japanese)?

Although the ways in which *emic* and *etic* approaches lead to very different visions of a given society have for some time been discussed by anthropologists, in the case of studying Japanese society it may be that the more fundamental distinction between, for example, those emphasizing conflict and inequality, on the one hand, and those emphasizing consensus and homogeneity, on the other, can be traced back to their disparate assessments as to the extent to which one set of linguistic concepts has been superimposed on all of Japanese society. No doubt perceptions as to how the processes of such superimposition occurred will also differ. The extent to which and the processes by which the *emic* concepts of one sub-group are superseded with the *etic*-cum-*emic* concepts of another sub-group, thereby elevating an *emic* term to serve as the standard medium for society-wide communication, would prove to be an interesting study for those interested in how cosmopolitan various sub-groups in Japanese society are toward other sub-groups. This is, interestingly, a context in which interpersonal values may come to the fore for close examination. The conflict of subcultures certainly highlights many differences in the ways in which interacting persons perceive not only one another but also an extensive array of other abstract actors including significant others.

From this perspective, the distinction between *emic* and *etic*

Table A   *Distribution of* Emic *Concepts in Two Dimensions*

		Society	
		Japan	Australia
Social class	The elite	JE *emic*	AE *emic*
	The masses	JM *emic*	AM *emic*

takes on an added significance. Table A suggests how sweeping references to the *emic* concepts of one society or another may greatly oversimplify the situation when Japanese and Australian societies are compared. Societies tend to be compared in terms of the *emic* concepts of their elites (that is, JE- and AE-type concepts). However, it is by making the three kinds of comparisons shown in Figure A that a true picture of the internal dynamics of a society can be fully grasped in comparative perspective.

Neustupný's paper on typologies reminds us that Japanese studies, like all academic endeavours, is conducted within paradigms. Academic argument depends upon a large number of assumptions being tied together by an interwoven logic. The use of certain categories at one level often implies the use of certain categories at other levels. Neustupný's paper calls for a strengthening of the logical linkage which binds together in a coherent whole the generalizations we make. His proposal for clearly identified levels of abstraction underlines the need for greater conceptual clarity. It is in terms of the approaches to the logical structuring of propositions about Japanese society that Neustupný writes of 'paradigms', a theme he has dealt with in the past (1980).

Figure A *Third-Level Comparisons in Cross-Cultural Research*

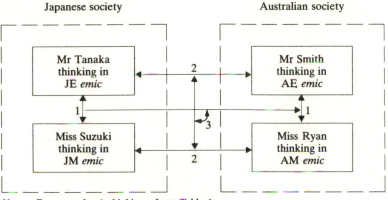

Note: For types of *emic* thinking refer to Table A.
Source: Adapted from Figure 13.3 in Sugimoto and Mouer (1986) (cf. pp. 357–9).

4 On the open seas: from 'Japan Incorporated' to 'Japan International'

The papers in this volume focus largely on the structure of Japanese society and culture without reference to the international dimension. At the Noosa Colloquium David Plath suggested that there might be a need to shift our attention from the internal dynamics of Japanese society in isolation to a broader consideration of Japanese society in its international context. He characterized this shift in problem consciousness as stepping beyond narrower concerns simply with how Japan functions as 'Japan Incorporated', in which the phenomena discussed was seen from the outside, to a broader interest in 'Japan International', in which the tangents linking the Japanese experience with our own come to centre stage.

From this perspective, we might see a move away from simple comparisons wherein national society or culture form the unit of analysis. Attention might instead be focused on points of contact between organizations or groups within two or more societies. This would allow smaller units to be compared, with due consideration being given to the stratified social context in which they have existed in the past. The tidal waves produced by international forces can easily drench the inhabitants living on an isolated

17

cultural island. Caught in the rip tides caused by internationaliz-ation, groups and organizations have become semi-detached and drawn out to sea. Torn from their cultural moorings, some groups flounder upon international seas while others do not. It is in this setting that the relative importance of culture can be compared with that of other factors. Different actors adopt different strategies to right their crafts. It is on the open seas of internationalization that we may catch a glimpse of the actors behaving 'on their own', even if momentarily, until help arrives and contact is re-established with their own culture.

Much of the debate on learning from Japan has, of course, focused on the question of Japan's cultural insularity. Are there tangents which will bring cultures increasingly into contact on this level? If so, to what extent will they free individuals from the operations of the state or the national society? With the heightened trade friction between Japan and other industrialized countries, international attention has focused increasingly on the degree to which the Japanese domestic market is closed to foreign countries. That the notion of reciprocity is given a central place in inter-national debate suggests that Befu's exchange model may have special relevance in understanding the behaviour of Japanese at the end of the twentieth century. The nation state is no longer the only international actor. Moreover, the Japanese business community abroad no longer consists only of *sararīman* from Japan's large trading companies. Increasingly, a diverse range of Japanese individuals are mingling with those from other cultures in all walks of life.

In the past the nation state, and the Japanese state more so than others, carefully regulated the traffic into and out of its harbours. It scrutinized carefully the coming and going not only of its citizens and those from other states, but also the flow of ideas and goods through its ports. Internationalization may not have dismantled that system, but it does seem inevitably to have resulted in a relaxation of various trade barriers; while many non-tariff barriers have been built into national ideologies and these have been internalized within the national cultures over time, the pressures against quotas on the exchange of goods, ideas and people will continue to mount.

Regardless of how we evaluate these developments, it is clear from the volume edited by Mannari and Befu (1985) that interna-tionalization has been, and will continue to be over the next few decades, an on-going process shaping and symbolizing social change in Japan. Students of Japanese society will need increasingly to incorporate the international dimension into their analyses of Japanese society. We might then enquire as to how Japan's internationalization will impinge not only upon Japanese society itself but also upon the study of that society.

'Internationalization'[1] has shifted the dominant ideology in Japan away from providing justifications for importing Western technology and ideas to supplying reasons for accepting a new role as an exporter of Japanese technology and ideas. While the word 'internationalization' suggests that there is a move toward more cosmopolitan values, it is also used to indicate a kind of neo-nationalistic push beyond the shores of Japan. This facet of internationalization is symbolized by the establishment of an increasing number of full-time Japanese schools for Japanese children overseas to maintain their 'Japaneseness', by the appearance of Japanese medical teams abroad exclusively for Japanese businessmen and their families, and by the mushrooming of Japanese tourist facilities designed specifically for Japan's international travellers. The trend is reminiscent of the American enclaves abroad which accompanied America's move into the international arena three or four decades ago. It is as though the 'Hilton hotel syndrome' is giving way to the '*karaoke* bar syndrome'.

The consequences of Japan's internationalization for our images of Japanese society and culture are twofold. Most prominent, perhaps, is the changing ideological hue. The upsurge of national awareness and a renewed pride in Japan as a dominant nation state on the world scene have recently been cited as evidence that 'neo-nationalism' is on the rise in Japan. Focused questions have

1 'Internationalization' is an interesting word. It seems to have been coined as an English equivalent for the Japanese word '*kokusaika*'. As a key word in the political culture in contemporary Japan, it has come to mean a variety of things. The term loosely refers to how Japan's international relations are changing in objective terms. The relations are defined not only by Japan's trade balances, but also by the demands placed on Japan as a result of those balances and by the increased involvement of Japanese in the day-to-day functioning of other societies. This set of meanings in the 1980s contrasts with the mind set of the 1950s and even the 1960s when the emphasis was still on transferring foreign technology into Japan and on 'opening Japan up' to foreign ideas.

been asked concerning the extent to which the cultural expression of this pride represents a re-emergence of the nationalism and ultra-nationalism which characterized the public ideology in Japan during the 1930s and the early 1940s.

The concern about the revival of prewar and wartime metaphysics is not entirely unfounded. Many prominent scholars in Japan, including many of the 'Kyōto school academics' who have been so vitally involved in the establishment of the government's International Centre for Japanese Studies, have become increasingly vocal in expressing the view that the Emperor system is the uniquely Japanese institution most worthy of the people's attention, support and respect (cf. Ueyama 1985). Many writers have attempted in recent years to portray Japan's ancient culture as the purest expression of 'Japaneseness', an essence which should not be contaminated by foreign influence (Umehara 1985). Yano's notion (1986b) of flow and stock civilizations rides high on the assumption that Japan continues to be able to move ahead 'with the times' because of its traditionally dynamic and classless social structure, whereas Europe is seen as being enfeebled and past its prime, indicative of the fact that the materialistically acquisitive culture of the West has outlived its usefulness. In business and political circles, the sentiment is high that Japan is used as a scapegoat to explain the decline of the international competitiveness of American commodities.[2] The 'Japan-bashing' now in vogue in the United States is dismissed as nothing but an extension of America's ethnocentric attempts to impose the unfair war trials and damaging social programmes on Japan during the occupation (Etō 1987).

Also conspicuous is the contempt with which other Asian countries are viewed. For example, Asians are chided for being lazy and for not having the Japanese work ethic (Hasegawa 1986). There is also the view that many Asians have a mistaken idea about their own histories. A large number of the parliamentarians in the Liberal Democratic Party maintain that the protests of Asian neighbours against some descriptions of Japan's wartime military activities in Japanese textbooks amount to intervention in the internal affairs of Japan. Arguments are being advanced by academicians that Japanese acts in China and elsewhere during

2 See, for example, the June 1987 issue of the influential monthly magazine *Bungei Shunjū*, which claimed, 'Warui no wa Amerika da' (Those who should be criticized are Americans).

the Fifteen Years' War were morally justified, and that the Chinese were actually 'blessed' by Japan's presence in their midst. They now claim that the 'Rape of Nanking' in 1937 is only a fantasy. The emphasis ought instead, they argue, to be focused on 'Japan's burden in Asia' and on Japan's contribution to China's development. 'After all', comment many Japanese visitors to Changchun in northeast China, 'the functional buildings which one can see today are really the ones which the Japanese themselves built over a half century ago'.

This sense of superiority and arrogance towards the rest of the world is reflected in a kind of persecution complex. As international criticisms of Japanese economic and political policies increase, it is instructive to note that this sense of paranoia seems to increase in proportion to popular ethnocentricism and the dissemination of an official doctrine which promotes neo-nationalism as a coherent way of providing self-justifications and self-rationalizations for the policies which Japan's political leadership are adopting in the face of Japan's 'internationalization'.

The publicity given to Nakasone's remarks on intelligence in September 1986 drew attention to the frequency with which such views are expressed in Japan. Many commentators have begun to ask about the extent to which such views represent the outlook of more than a small handful of Japanese. Nakasone's remarks revealed not so much a slip of the tonuge as a documented sequence of such phraseology which suggests that there is, at least in some quarters of Japanese society, a very strongly ingrained racism. For that reason, it is argued, his comments were taken for granted by the Japanese public. Startling to many foreign observers was not the fact that racism existed in Japan, but the extent to which many Japanese seemed unable or untrained to recognize that Nakasone's remarks had any racist implications at all. Moreover, both the political establishment and the mass media in Japan were painstakingly slow to concede that such implications were there. The affair appears to have brought attention to the depth of the folk belief that Japanese 'uniqueness' is biologically based.

No doubt, this naïvety is the basis for many best-sellers advocating the uniqueness of the Japanese brain (for example, Tsunoda 1978) and many other 'bio-sociological' theories of Japanese behaviour, such as Sabata's theory (1966) that there is a relationship between the herbivorous habit of the Japanese and their thought patterns. The biological reductionist assumption about the 'Japanese character' also manifests itself in the *ketsueki-gata* boom, the popular fad in which personality is attributed to blood type (Iwami 1986). It is in this intellectual climate that the anti-Semitic literature (for example, Uno 1987a and 1987b, Kubota 1987 and Miyazaki 1987) has served to deflect attention from the conflict of economic and social interests by suggesting that the trade friction between Japan and the United States and the ensuing economic trouble in Japan has resulted from a Jewish conspiracy (cf. Katō 1987). The rise of neo-nationalism is thus intimately connected with racism and sowing the seeds of racial hatred. Dale (1986) and others may not be exaggerating the case in suggesting that 'some of the nationalist ideas are awfully close' to Nazism in being not only chauvinistic but racist as well (Buruma 1987: 27).

When this 'new' outburst is considered along with a more carefully documented study of Japanese textbooks over a much longer period, one begins to discern a different trend in Japanese society. To borrow the vocabulary of Garner (1977: 3–9), the ideological trappings point to the fact that internationalization may not be the 'historic change' or 'fundamental transformation' it is made out to be. Although the cycle has taken nearly fifty years to repeat itself, what we may have is nothing more than a 'recurrent change'. The spread of middle-class consciousness and the many other 'epic-making changes' associated with Japan's modernization, even Westernization, and the fruits of rapid econ-omic growth may become superficial, while the continuities may emerge as fundamental in the revised characterization of Japanese society in the neo-nationalistic terms associated with *nihonjinron*.

This would also be the warning of Dower (1986): the legacy of racism from the Fifteen Years' War is still with us. It will continue to shape the perceptions of the Japanese held by Japanese and by non-Japanese alike. The symbols of racial difference are so powerfully part of the colonial and post-colonial experience, and of the occupation and post-occupation experience, that they are easy to conjure up again as internationalization brings the national interest of the Japanese state into conflict with the interests of other states. Yet research agendas in Japan are such that the efforts of individuals to replace notions of racial differences with assumptions of racial equality are not supported by basic research. The consequences of this fact require special consideration when we evaluate our images of Japan.

While no serious student of Japan would confuse the 1930s with the 1980s, Japan's internationalization causes us to reconsider the question as to what is central and peripheral to being Japanese in contemporary Japan. To recast C. Wright Mills's distinction between 'personal troubles' and 'public issues' (1957: 8–11), it seems that a critical mass is reached whereby what was previously perceived as personal views suddenly take on new meaning as social statements. The ideology of racism and/or cultural superiority challenges us to look beyond official explanations and the official *emic* vocabulary of one sub-group in Japan. There is not only the problem of basing our generalizations on changes in the *emic* vocabulary of just the one sub-group, but also that of the independence of social sciences from the social milieu which produces them.

This brings us to another way in which Japan's internationalization may be affecting overseas scholarship on Japan. It is now a trite cliché that the victor writes history. Yet the power generated by Japan's massive trade surpluses can be seen not only in the rewriting of Japan's textbooks for social studies at the secondary level but also in the structuring of social science at the more abstract level. As Befu hints in Chapter 10, there may be no truly *etic* concepts; the best we have are the *emic* concepts of the most influential society which may be superimposed on world society as a kind of lingua franca. But the lingua franca of an era tends to symbolize an international hierarchy; to maintain the hierarchy the universal concepts that might exist in the language are mythicized. They are at the same time presented as *etic* while also being made even more *emic* so that language's rightful owner can control the dialogue and set the agenda. As the authors argue elsewhere (Sugimoto and Mouer 1986: chapters 7 and 15), one can see in the emphasis on Japan's uniqueness not only a kind of psychological preparation for Japan's 'internationalization' in terms of how it provides a national identity for Japanese; one can also see in the state's utilization of *nihonjinron* as ideology a power dimension. The dissemination of 'Japanese management' is a good example.

As long as the word 'Japanese' can be attached to that style of management, homage will be paid to the high priests who live in Japan. By selling Japanese-style management as economically rational, the *emic* is transformed into the *etic*, and the *etic* back into the *emic*. Few students of colonialism or imperialism would

23

deny the psychological power which the appearance of being *etic* and of embracing a universal rationality gave to concepts such as 'modernization' and 'development'. Moreover, in retrospect it is easy to see in the use of such concepts the underlying ethnocentric assumptions of the industrialized West.

Undoubtedly those who see Japan as being misunderstood will protest that another ethnocentric extrapolation has been made when it is suggested that Japan too will use its heyday in the same way as did many Western nations.

However, the setting of agenda for the study of Japan is occurring in a fairly obvious manner. The proliferation of Japanese foundations funding social science and the channelling of their funds into Japanese studies raises serious questions for those wishing to study Japanese society. The issue of ideological control aside, the recent injection of funds into Japanese studies means that Japanese studies is becoming big business. To the extent that Japanese studies require a comparative or cross-cultural perspective, the costs are immense and considerable organization is required. In the past Japanologists tended to work on their own, content largely with describing Japanese society and perhaps speculating about the comparative significance and uniqueness of the phenomena they observed. Most careful comparative work on Japan involved only two societies at best or, if a number of societies were involved, an artful weaving of facts garnered from a thorough reading of secondary sources. However, this is changing. The injection of some of Japan's economic surplus into Japanese studies means that scholars will be able to go beyond simply describing Japan as a case study.

The new wealth in Japanese studies raises several serious questions for the student of Japanese society. One is the growing systematization of our images of Japan in educational institutions and various media. The result is the increased willingness of interested parties to project official interpretations into that social science which is concerned with understanding Japanese society. During the early 1980s various official bodies, or organizations sanctioned by official bodies, conducted surveys on the state of Japanese studies abroad. So many of the mail surveys came with explanations that the surveying body was interested in promoting '*the* correct understanding of Japan' (*nihon no tadashii rikai*). The assumption in most of those explanations, of course, was that there was one correct understanding.

The role of the Ministry of Education in establishing the International Centre for Japanese Studies in Kyōto immediately raises questions about the extent to which such a centre will be 'allowed' to engage in 'objective' research. Even the most rudimentary enquiry into the record of the Ministry will reveal its very high profile in directing the content of textbooks for Japanese school children, in promoting the translation into English of conservative or even nationalistic scholarship on Japan, in systematically removing conflict-oriented interpretations from the education and cultural system, and in centralizing its control over all facets of Japanese education. The Ministry's attitude seems to have been that it alone will decide what is truth and damn the views of those in the other countries whose histories it is redefining. The 'Hidaka Incident' also raises serious questions about the role of other branches in the Japanese government in regulating the activities of anti-establishment academicians (cf. McCormack 1985 and 1987). It is also interesting to note the title applied to one of the published research reports using the kind of survey just mentioned above: 'Chinichika no Tanjō' (The Birth of the Japan Expert) (Shinbori 1986). It is interesting to note, however, that the volume is not about all experts, but about those whose views are rather favourable toward Japan. Cynical observers have noted that the word '*shinnichika*' (person who is close to Japan – that is, pro-Japanese) should have been used instead of '*chinichika*' (person who knows about Japan). The choice of words implies the subtle but extremely significant use of nuance which should not be overlooked in appraising government-sponsored research.

Large-scale funding has also meant large-scale Japanese studies. During the 1960s the study of Japan was markedly shaped by the sponsorship of the Ford Foundation, Fulbright Fellowships and other establishment-oriented schemes in the United States. The production of the 'Princeton series' on the modernization of Japan was not merely a shot in the arm for Japanese studies which contributed greatly to improved scholarship on Japan. It was also the story of how a considerable amount of energy available for Japanese studies in the United States became 'locked' into a single orientation. It was a vehicle by which a somewhat self-appointed priesthood formed a fairly comprehensive network which strongly influenced decisions concerning research funding and personnel selections in the field for another one or two decades. To be sure, in the American experience, the economies of scale could be seen in research, as in the factory. But just as size may have been one factor building complacency into several American industries, so too has size and bureaucratic control served to restrict creative exploration in America's social sciences.

Today the money for Japanese studies is being supplied increasingly by Japanese sources: the Ministry of Education, the Japan Foundation, the Toyota Foundation, the Suntory Foundation, the Mitsui Scholarships, the Mombushō Scholarships, the Japan Airlines Scholarships, the Japanese government's gifts of one million dollars each to ten universities in the United States, the funds to the Australia–Japan Research Centre at the Australian National University and to Thammasat University in Bangkok, the Nissan Corporation for the Institute at Oxford, the Mitsubishi Corporation for its chair at Harvard, and the Japanese Government again for the International Centre for Japanese Studies established in Kyōto. It would be naïve to think that these funds have been given without careful attention having been paid to the ideological orientations of the recipients. The fact that the funds are made available through large, centralized bureaucratic bodies means that huge funds can easily be channelled in specific directions and seriously disadvantage small producers of Japanese studies. In the academic supermarket the commercialization of research tends to heighten the importance attached to the packaging of ideas (as opposed to the ideas themselves).

Given the strong interest which the Japanese establishment has in images of itself, it seems inevitable that, as in the American case, Japan's massive flows of income cannot but work towards the commercialization of Japanese studies. Few of the above-mentioned bodies which distribute the research for Japanese studies give any public account of how their decisions are made. Sometimes, however, we are given a glimpse. One of the foundations, for example, limits applicants for its scholarships to unmarried males in their twenties. It does not take too much imagination to speculate about how research problems for Japanese studies might be shaped by this selection of participants. Persons most oriented to the values of Japan's large firms will tend not to ask questions about the status of women in the secondary labour market, about minority issues or about the state of welfare for the aged. The blossoming of Japanese studies is not a campaign to let the proverbial 'one hundred flowers' bloom.

Given the dominant role of establishment-oriented bodies in

structuring Japanese studies, it might be good to return to consider the distinction between competing *emic* approaches with Japanese society. Concepts are not simply descriptive labels; they contain understandings of the entire society. If one aim of social science is to go beyond official understandings and Japanese studies is to be part of that tradition, then it is necessary to consider carefully the relationship between the society's *etic* concepts and the notion of false consciousness. As the establishment parades its *emic* concepts as *etic* concepts for understanding Japanese society not only in academic arenas but also in textbooks and in the mass media, it becomes increasingly necessary for social scientists to examine carefully the self-fulfilling functions of such demonstrations.

One often hears the comment these days that Japan is the world's richest nation but that few Japanese actually feel that way although they read figures verifying the fact everyday in the newspapers. So too do Japanese continue to be told how much they all belong to the middle class, while marketing research shows clearly how segmented their consumer behaviour really is. Perhaps internationalization will serve to bring these kinds of contradictions out into the open. Given that 'internationlization' and 'intermestication' were both coined in Japan, perhaps it is not too Westernly ethnocentric to predict that fundamental changes will result from the current transformation which is now troubling not only the guardians of Japanese society but also many who study it from afar.

References

Amanuma, Kaoru
  1987 *'Ganbari' no Kōzō* (The Structure of *'Ganbari'*) (Tokyo: Yoshikawa Kōbunkan).
Befu, Harumi
  1987a *Ideorogii to shite no Nihon Bunkaron* (Cultural Theories of Japan as Ideology) (Tokyo: Shisō no Kagakusha).
  1987b 'Weberian Bureaucracy and Japan: A Revisionist Proposal'. Unpublished paper.

Buruma, Ian
  1987 'A New Japanese Nationalism', *New York Times Magazine* (April 12), 23–38.
Dale, Peter
  1986 *The Myth of Japanese Uniqueness* (London: Croom Helm).
Doi, Takeo
  1985 *Omote to Ura* (The Revealed and the Unrevealed) (Tokyo: Kobundo).
  1986 *The Anatomy of Self: the Individual versus Society* (Tokyo: Kodansha International).
Dore, Ronald
  1967 'Introduction', in *Aspects of Social Change in Modern Japan*, edited by R. P. Dore (Princeton, NJ: Princeton University Press), 3–24.
Dower, John
  1986 *War Without Mercy: Race and Power in the Pacific War* (New York: Pantheon Books).
  1987 'The Legacies of the Lost War', a public address to the Fifth National Conference of the Japanese Studies Association of Australia (27 Aug.).
Etō, Jun
  1987 *Dōjidai e no Shisen* (A Contemporary Perspective) (Kyōto: PHP Kenkyusho).
Fukutake, Tadashi
  1972 *Gendai Nihon Shakairon* (A Theory of Modern Japanese Society) (Tokyo: Tokyo Daigaku Shuppankai).
  1981 *Nihon Shakai no Kōzō* (The Structure of Japanese Society) (Tokyo: Tokyo Daigaku Shuppankai).
Fuse, Tetsuji; Iwaki, Sadayuki; and Kamata, Toshiko (eds)
  1982 *Nihon Shakai no Shakaigaku teki Bunseki* (The Sociological Analysis of Japanese Society) (Kyōto: Akademia Shuppankai)
Garner, Roberta Ash
  1977 *Social Change* (Chicago: Rand McNally).
Gendai Shisō Henshūbu (eds)
  1984 *Nippon no Nekko* (The Fundamental Roots of Japan), a special issue of *Gendai Shisō* (July) (Tokyo: Seidosha).
Gill, Robin
  1984 *Omoshiro Hikaku Bunkakō* (A Lighthearted Comparative Analysis of Cultures) (Tokyo: Kirihara Shoten).
  1985a *Han Nihonjinron* (Against *Nihonjinron*) (Tokyo: Kosakusha).
  1985b *Nihonjinron Tanken: Yuniiukusabyō no Kenkyū* (An Investigation into 'Themes of the Japanese': Research into the Compulsive Concern with a Nation's Uniqueness) (Tokyo: TBS Buritanika).

Glazer, Nathan
1975 'From Ruth Benedict to Herman Kahn: the Postwar Japanese Image in the American Mind', in *Mutual Images: Essays in American Japanese Relations*, edited by Akira Iriye (Cambridge, Mass.: Harvard University Press), 138–68.

Gluck, Carol
1985 *Japan's Modern Myths: Ideology in the Late Meiji Period* (Princeton, NJ: Princeton University Press).

Hall, Ivan P.
1987 'Stop Making Excuses for Japan's Insularity', *Wall Street Journal* (6 July).

Hamaguchi, Eshun
1977 *'Nihon-rashisa' no Saihakken* (A Rediscovery of 'Japaneseness') (Tokyo: Nihon Keizai Shinbunsha).
1982 *Kanjin Shugi no Shakai: Nihon* (Japan: The Contextual Society) (Tokyo: Tōyō Keizai Shinpōsha).
1985 'A Contextual Model of the Japanese: Toward a Methodological Innovation in Japanese Studies', *Journal of Japanese Studies*, vol. 11, no. 2 (Summer), 289–321.

Hamaguchi, Eshun; and Kumon, Shunpei (eds)
1982 *Nihon-teki Shūdan-shugi* (Japanese Groupism) (Tokyo: Yuhikaku).

Hamaguchi, Eshun *et al.*
1987 'Nihonron no Paradaimu Tenkan' (Paradigm Shift in the Theories on Japan) and 'Kokusai-teki Bunmyaku ni okeru Nihonron' (Theories on Japan in the International Context), in *Kojin, Kanjin, Nihonjin* (Individuals and Interpersonal Relations in Japanese Society) (Tokyo: Gakuyō Shobō), chs. 1 and 2.

Hasegawa, Keitarō
1986 *Sayonara Ajia* (Good-bye to Asia) (Tokyo: Nesco Shuppan).

Hendry, Joy; and Webber, Jonathan (eds)
1986 *Interpreting Japanese Society: Anthropological Approaches*, Occasional papers of the *Journal of the Anthropological Society of Oxford*, no. 5 (Oxford: JASO).

Hidaka, Rokurō
1985 *The Price of Affluence* (Tokyo: Kodansha International).

Irokawa, Daikichi
1982 *Tennō-sei to Minshū* (The Emperor System and the Masses) (Tokyo: Tokyo Keizai Daigaku Irokawa Kenkyū Shitsu).

Itō, Shuntarō
1985 *Hikaku Bunmei* (Comparative Civilizations) (Tokyo: Tokyo Daigaku Shuppaukai).

Iwami, Kazuhiko
1986 ' "Ketsueki-gata Bumu" no Kenkyū' (A Study of the 'Blood-

type Boom'), mimeographed paper (Suita, Osaka: Faculty of Sociology, Kansai Daigaku).

Johnson, Chalmers
1987   Interview broadcast as part of 'Four Corners', ABC Television, Channel 2 (Brisbane: 10 Aug.).

Johnson, Sheila
1986   *Amerikajin no Nihonjin kan* (American Attitudes Toward Japan, 1941–1985) (Tokyo: Saimaru Shuppankai).

Kamata, Satoshi
1984   *Kyoiku Kojo no Kodomotachi* (Children in the Education Factory) (Tokyo: Iwanami Shoten).

Kan, Takayuki
1984   *Gendai no Buraku Sabetsu to Tennō-sei* (The Emperor System and the Discrimination Against the Burakumin in Contemporary Japan) (Tokyo: Akashi Shoten).

Kanō, Miyoko (ed.)
1979   *Josei to Tennō-sei* (Women and the Emperor System) (Tokyo: Shisō no Kagakusha).

Katō, Shūichi
1987   'Nihon ni okeru "Han-yudaya Shugi" ' (Anti-Semitism in Japan), *ASY* (15 June), 7.

Kawamura, Nozomu
1982   *Nihon Bunkaron no Shūhen* (Some Arguments on Theories of Japanese Culture) (Tokyo: Ningen no Kagakusha).

Kawanishi, Hirosuke
1982   'Nihon ni okeru Rōdō Kumiai Kenkyū no Genjō to Kadai' (The State of Research on Labour Unions in Japan: Some Key Issues), *Chiba Daigaku Kyōyōbu Kiyō*, 122–47.

Kogawa, Tetsuo
1986   *Denshi Kokka to Tennō-sei* (The Emperor System and the Electronic State) (Tokyo: Kawade Shobō Shinsha).

Kubota, Masao
1987   *Yudaya o Ayatsuru Rokkufera Teikoku no Yabō* (The Ambitions of the Rockefeller Empire which Manipulates the Jews) (Tokyo: Tokuma Shobō).

Kuno, Osamu (ed.)
1952   *Nihon no Mondai* (Issues in [Contemporary] Japan), vol. II in *Iwanami Kōza Kyōiku* (Iwanami Lectures on Education) (Tokyo: Iwanami Shoten).

Kurihara, Akira
1982   *Kanri Shakai to Minshū Risei* (Control Society and Mass Rationality) (Tokyo: Shinyōsha).

Lehmann, Jean-Pierre
1978   *The Image of Japan: From Feudal Isolation to World Power*

1850–1905 (London: George Allen & Unwin).

Lummis, C. Douglas
1982a   *A New Look at the Chrysanthemum and the Sword* (Tokyo: Shohaku-sha).
1982b   *Uchinaru Gaikoku* (The Social Construction of Foreign Realities) (Tokyo: Jiji Tsūshinsha).
1984   'Japanese Critiques of Technological Society', *Canadian Journal of Political and Social Theory*, vol. 8, no. 3 (Fall), 9–14.

Lummis, C. Douglas; and Ikeda, Masayuki
1985   *Nihonjinron no Shinsō* (The Underlying Assumptions of the Theories on the Japanese) (Tokyo: Haru Shobo).

Mannari, Hiroshi; and Befu, Harumi (eds)
1983   *The Challenge of Japan's Internationalization: Organization and Culture* (Tokyo: Kodansha International and Kwansei Gakuin University).

McCormack, Gavan
1985   'Foreword', in Rokuro Hidaka's *The Price of Affluence* (Ringwood, Melbourne, Australia: Penguin Books), 1–8.
1987   'Random Notes from the Outgoing President', *Japanese Studies Association of Australia Newsletter*, vol. 7, no. 2 (June), 15–19.

McCormack, Gavan; and Sugimoto, Yoshio (eds)
1986   *Democracy in Contemporary Japan* (Sydney: Hale and Iremonger; New York: M. E. Sharpe).
1988   *The Japanese Trajectory: Modernization and Beyond* (Cambridge: Cambridge University Press).

Mills, C. Wright
1959   *The Sociological Imagination* (New York: Oxford University Press).

Minami, Hiroshi
1980   *Nihonjinron no Keifu* (The Development of 'Nihonjinron') (Tokyo: Kōdansha).

Minear, Richard
1980a   'Orientalism and the Study of Japan', *Journal of Asian Studies*, vol. 30, no. 3 (May), 507–17.
1980b   'The Wartime Studies of Japanese National Character', *Japan Interpreter*, vol. 15, no. 1 (Summer), 36–59.

Miyazaki, Masahiro
1987   *Yudaya ni Kodawaru to Sekai ga Mienaku Naru* (When You Are Obsessed with the Jews, You Find it Difficult to See the World) (Tokyo: Futami Shobō).

Morita, Akio
1987   *Made in Japan* (New York: Dutton).

Mouer, Ross
1987   'Nihon ni okeru Rōshi Kankei Kenkyū no Genjō' (The State

of Industrial Relations Research in Japan), *Jōsai Daigaku Daigakuin Kenkyū Nenpō*, no. 3 (March), 103–18.

Mouer, Ross; and Sugimoto, Yoshio
1981   *Japanese Society: Stereotypes and Realities* (Melbourne: Japanese Studies Centre).
1982a   *Nihonjin wa 'Nihonteki' ka* (How 'Japanese' are the Japanese?) (Tokyo: Tōyō Keizai Shinpōsha).
1984   'Kuni o Koeru "Hikakushugi" no Shiten' (For an International Perspective in International Comparisons), *Shiso no Kagaku*, no. 43 (Feb.), 20–9.

Mouer, Ross; and Sugimoto, Yoshio (eds)
1982b   *Nihonjinron ni kansuru Junishō* (Twelve Chapters on the Theories of the Japanese) (Tokyo: Gakuyō Shobō).

Murakami, Yasusuke
1984   '*Ie* Society as a Pattern of Civilization', *The Journal of Japanese Studies*, vol. 10, no. 2 (Summer), 281–367.

Nagoya, Tokimasa
1979   *Nihongaku Nyūmon* (An Introduction to Japanese Studies) (Tokyo: Shinseikaisha).

Naitō, Kunji, Chikazawa, Kei-ichi, and Nakamura, Masao (eds)
1980   *Nihon Shakai no Kiso Kōzō* (The Basic Structure of Japanese Society) (Kyōto: Akademia Shuppankai).

Nakayama, Ichirō
1975   *Industrialization and Labour-Management Relations in Japan*, translated by Ross Mouer (Tokyo: The Japan Institute of Labour).

Neustupný, J. V.
1980   'On Paradigms in the Study of Japan', *Social Analysis*, nos. 5/6 (1980), 20–8.
1982   *Gaikokujin to no Komyunikēshon* (Communicating with Foreigners) (Tokyo: Iwanami Shoten).

Nomura Sōgō Kenkyushō (Nomura Research Institute)
1978   *Nihonjinron: Kokusai Kyōchō Jidai ni Sonaete* (Theories of the Japanese: the Groundwork for an Era of International Cooperation). A special issue of *Refarensu* (no. 2).

Ogawa, Yō-ichi (ed.)
1985   *Kyodai Kigyōtaisei to Rōdōsha* (The Big Business System and Workers) (Tokyo: Ochanomizu Shoten).

Omae, Ken-ichi
1986   *Shin Kokufuron* (The New 'Wealth of Nations') (Tokyo: Kōdansha).

Ono, Tsuneo, and Mouer, Ross
1986   *Labor Policy in Japan: a Survey of Issues in the 'Eighties* (Melbourne: Japanese Studies Centre).

Oyama, Hiroshi; and Takano, Norinari (eds)

1986   *Kodomo no Jinken to Kanri Kyōiku* (Controlled Education and the Human Rights of Children) (Tokyo: Akebi Shobō).
Sabata, Toyoyuki
1966   *Nikushoku no Shisō* (The Thought Patterns of the Meat-Eaters) (Tokyo: Chūō Kōronsha).
Satō, Seizaburō; Kumon, Shunpei; and Murakami, Yasusuke
1979   *Bunmei to shite no Ie Shakai* (*Ie* Society as a Pattern of Civilization) (Tokyo: Chūō Kōronsha).
Shimada, Haruo
1984a   'Japanese Industrial Relations – a New Model? A Survey of the English-language Literature', in *Contemporary Industrial Relations in Japan*, edited by Taishirō Shirai (Madison, Wis.: University of Wisconsin Press), 3–28.
1984b   *Furiiranchi wa Mō Kuenai: Amerika Sangyō Shakai Saisei no Kōzō* (No More Free Lunches: a Plan for the Revival of Industrial Society in Contemporary America) (Tokyo: Nihon Hyōronsha).
Shimizu, Ikutarō (ed.)
1951   *Sekai to Nihon* (Japan and the World), vol. I in *Iwanami Kōza Kyōiku* (Iwanami Lectures on Education) (Tokyo: Iwanami Shoten).
Shinbori, Michiya
1986   *Chinichika no Tanjō* (The Birth of the Japan Specialist) (Tokyo: Tōshindo).
Smith, Robert
1983   *Japanese Society: Tradition, Self, and the Social Order* (Cambridge: Cambridge University Press).
Sugimoto, Yoshio
1981   *Popular Disturbance in Postwar Japan* (Hong Kong: Asian Research Service).
1983   *Chō-kanri Rettō Nippon* (The Ultra-controlled Japanese Archipelago) (Tokyo: Kōbunsha).
1986   ' "Nihon Minzokuron" e no Mittsu no Ryūho' (Three Reservations about 'Japanese Ethnic Uniqueness'), *MSY* (19 Nov.), 4.
Sugimoto, Yoshio; and Mouer, Ross
1980a   'Competing Models for Understanding Japanese Society: Some Reflections on New Directions', *Social Analysis*, nos. 5/6 (Dec. 1980), 194–204.
1986   *Images of Japanese Society: a Study in the Structure of Social Reality* (London: Kegan Paul International).
Sugimoto, Yoshio; and Mouer, Ross (eds)
1980b   *Japanese Society: Reappraisals and New Directions*. A special issue of *Social Analysis*, nos. 5/6 (December).
1987   *Kojin, Kanjin, Nihonjin* (Individuals, Interpersonal Relations

and Institutions in Japanese Society) (Tokyo: Gakuyō Shobō).

Takabatake, Michitoshi; and Kurihara, Akira
1985   'Nihongata Kanri Shakai no Kōzō – Ika ni shite Norikoerareruka' (The Structure of the Controlled Society, Japanese Style: How to Overcome the Phenomenon), *Sekai*, no. 470 (Jan.), 39–58.

Takeda, Kiyoko (ed.)
1984   *Nihonbunka no Kakureta Katachi* (Archetypes of Japanese Culture), a collection of lectures by Katō Shūichi, Kinoshita Junji, and Maruyama Masao (Tokyo: Iwanami Shoten).

Tanaka, Yuki
1987   'Review Essay: Purity vs. Contamination – a Cultural Link Between the Burakumin and the Emperor', *The Japanese Studies Association of Australia Newsletter*, vol. 7, no. 2 (June), 8–14.

Time-Life Books
1986   *Japan* (Amsterdam: Time-Life Books).

Tsukishima, Kenzō
1984   *'Nihonjinron' no Naka no Nihonjin* (A Historical Survey of how the Japanese have been Portrayed in Theories of the Japanese) (Tokyo: Dainihon Tosho).

Tsunoda, Tadanobu
1978   *Nihonjin no Nō* (The Brain Structure of the Japanese) (Tokyo: Taishūkan).

Tsurumi, Shunsuke
1985   *An Intellectual History of Wartime Japan, 1931–1945* (London: Kegan Paul International).
1987   *A Cultural History of Postwar Japan 1945–1980* (London: Kegan Paul International).

Ueyama, Shunpei
1985   *Tennō-sei no Shinsō* (The Structure Underlying the Emperor System) (Tokyo: Asahi Shinbunsha).

Umano, Shūji
1987   *Nippon ni Bōkoku no On ga Kikoeru* (Hearing the Sounds of National Decay in Japan) (Tokyo: Keizaikai).

Umehara, Takeshi
1985   *Nippon no Shinsō* (The Structure Underlying Japan) (Tokyo: Kōsei Shuppansha).

Umesao, Tadao
1985   'Hikaku Bunmeigaku no Hōhō' (A Methodology for the Comparative Study of Civilization), in *Toshika no Bunmeigaku* (The Civilizations Approach to Urbanization) (Tokyo: Chūō Kōronsha), 7–24.

Umesao, Tadao, and Moriya, Atsumi (eds)
1985   *Toshika no Bunmeigaku* (The Civilizations Approach to Urbanization) (Tokyo: Chūō Kōronsha).

Uno, Masami
  1987a *Yudaya ga Wakaru to Nihon ga Miete Kuru* (When You
    Comprehend the Jews, You Can See Japan) (Tokyo: Tokuma
    Shoten).
  1987b *Yudaya ga Wakaru to Sekai ga Miete Kuru* (When You
    Comprehend the Jews, You'll Be Able to See the World) (Tokyo:
    Tokuma Shoten).
Ward, Robert E. (ed.)
  1964 *Studying Politics Abroad: Field Research in the Developing
    Areas* (Boston: Little, Brown & Co.).
Yamagishi, Toshio, and Brinton, Mary C.
  1980 'Sociology in Japan and Shakai-Ishikiron', *American Sociologist*,
    vol. 15, no. 4 (Nov.), 192–207.
Yamamoto, Haruyoshi
  1987 *Gendai Shisō no Shōten* (The Foci of Contemporary Thought)
    (Tokyo: Keisō Shobō).
Yano, Tōru
  1986a 'Our Internationalization or Yours?' *Japan Times* (28 Sept.
    1986), 6.
  1986b 'Japan: Civilization in a Hurry', *Japan Times* (29 Sept. 1986),
    8.

Part One

The Expression of Individual Self-interest

Chapter One
A Theory of Social Exchange as Applied to Japan

Harumi Befu

1 Introduction

An adequate 'theory' of Japanese society should provide a model
of the Japanese person, a model of Japanese social relations and
a model of Japanese collectivity. It should also provide some basic
ground rules or a framework according to which these models can
be interrelated or integrated. Though a good deal has been written
about groups in Japan, and although one might point to Japanese
concepts such as *'jinkaku'* or *'seishin'* as examples of how Japanese
conceptualize personhood, few social science treatises have discussed the way Japanese conceive of the individual or the person as
a cultural concept. Social exchange theory has offered considerable
insight about interpersonal relations, and might be useful in linking
individual and collective behaviour.

　Given the fact that social exchange theory has provided a kind
of 'paradigm' for viewing the human condition in the English-
language literature, it is perhaps surprising that such a theory has
not been used to analyze Japanese society. Exceptions might be

the few fragmentary attempts by Lebra (1969, 1972 and 1975) and Befu (1967, 1968, 1976, 1977a and 1977b). However, neither Befu nor Lebra has used social exchange theory to develop an integrated model of interpersonal relations in Japan. Moreover, in spite of increasing interest in social exchange theory in Japan (Blau 1974; Hashimoto 1973; Hayakawa 1972 and 1973; Inuzuka 1974), the interest is primarily in introducing to Japanese readers exchange theories developed in the West. Thus, the understanding of Japanese society from the perspective of social exchange is still in its infancy. This paper discusses the possibility of understanding social relations in Japan in terms of social exchange.

Social exchange theory is presented here as a concept to explain interpersonal relations, which are seen as having an existence apart from that of the collectivity. Without a model of social relations entirely apart from one which explains collective behaviour, it is difficult to explain various kinds of common phenomena such as kinship relations, friendship, or the *tsukiai* relationship discussed by Atsumi in Chapter 4.

The discussion begins with a brief survey of some major concepts in exchange theory. It then considers some ideas on the instrumental and expressive meaning of social exchange and introduces some findings from an empirical study conducted in Kyōto. It concludes by considering briefly the relevance of social exchange theory for the study of Japanese society.

2   Concepts in exchange theory

A   Exchange resource
The theory of social exchange is predicated upon the idea that each person in society possesses certain resources and that persons act as members of society by exchanging these resources. The individual's (or the collectivity's) 'resources' are not limited to money, objects and other material things. They include intangibles such as knowledge and information which have an instrumental value. Respect, affection and other types of esteem relevant to an individual's psychological well-being are also resources.

B   Social and cultural contexts
An actor needs a stage, props, a costume and so on in order for

his offer to be taken seriously. By the same token, to participate in social exchange a social actor needs more than an abstract scenario. In order for an appropriate bargain to be struck an offer to exchange must be communicated in a culturally acceptable manner. Offers which do not accord with the social and cultural context will have a hollow ring.

The 'context' is defined by the values, norms and patterns which are peculiar to a given culture and social milieu. This context may be regarded as a *constant*. The context stands in contradistinction to the *variables* which constitute the model. To take an example from American society, in order to construct a model of the American family system one cannot ignore the educational, economic or political institutions of American society. Even though these institutions are 'outside' the family institution, one cannot understand the dynamics of the American family system unless one understands the role they play in American society.

C   The actors
Four types of actors participate in exchange transactions.

1. Individuals   The most common exchange acts are conducted between individuals who are members of a given society. Greeting one's boss, and sending gifts to one's wedding intermediary (*nakōdo*) are examples in which both parties to the exchange are individuals.

2. Entities Without Physical Existence   Some types of exchange involve an alter which does not have physical existence. Deities and ancestors are such entities. In her analysis of the behaviour of followers of *Tenshō Kōtai Jingū Kyō*, Lebra (1972) used the framework of social exchange. Followers believed that the spirit of a dead person may be saved through the prayers of the living; in exchange, the sacred spirit of the dead would help to cure the illness of the living. As long as the human actor believes that the dead person is capable of engaging in exchange acts, social exchange is said to occur even though the alter is dead.

Exchange with deities and spirits of this sort is not limited to Japan. Foster (1963) has observed that in some Indian villages in Mexico one prays for the blessing of Santos. By offering sacrifices, they believe he will cure a child's illness. When a villager's expectations are not met, he might prod Santos by threatening to cut off the offerings.

Exchange with imaginary alters is very often seen in psychological experiments. In experiments to verify hypotheses of social exchange theory, subjects need only believe that their exchange partners exist (for example, in another room). Once the assumption is accepted, the subject enters into an exchange relationship with this imaginary partner. Exchange is possible only in so far as the actor believes in exchange with the alter and believes that the alter is capable of responding within the framework of exchange existing in the actor's beliefs.

3. Corporate Bodies   Exchange may occur between corporate bodies. The well-known though complicated example of cross-cousin marriage is provided by Lévi-Strauss (1949). Here the exchange occurs between kinship groups. In Japan the household is not the only corporate body which engages in exchange. Village communities, business organizations and schools may also participate in social exchange. When such collectivities are the actors, the theoretical premises are somewhat different from those which apply when exchange occurs among individuals. Due to the complexities which are introduced when dealing with corporate bodies as an actor in exchange, the discussion in this paper is limited to a consideration of exchanges between non-corporate bodies.

It is not perfectly clear how the individual level relates to that at the corporate level. This issue was the focus of considerable debate in the 1950s and the 1960s. Although there is insufficient space to deal with this controversy here, Lévi-Strauss led those favouring an approach which called for exchange phenomena to be analyzed at the group level, whereas American anthropologists such as Homans and Schneider (1955) favoured an analytical approach which focused attention on exchange between members of the groups.

4. 'Society'   One often hears the expression in Japan that one is 'indebted to *seken*' or that one should 'pay back one's debt to the society to which he owes his existence'. Japanese often feel they are recipients of resources from an unspecified social unit which is not a group or an individual. Moreover, *'seken'* is conceived as an entity which can also exercise social sanctions (for example, cf. Inoue 1977). Accordingly, in thinking about social exchange in Japan, it is useful to view *'seken'* as a unit of exchange somewhat different from corporate bodies and dead or imaginary persons. One may also think of other terms for *'seken'*, such as *'shakai'* or '*yononaka*'. They all refer to 'society', 'the community' or 'the people' as an abstract collective.

D   The norm of reciprocity and customary rules of exchange

Gouldner (1960) has defined 'the norm of reciprocity' as a universal norm. According to him, the norm of reciprocity prescribes that an individual who has received assistance from another should return an offer of assistance or should at least avoid harming his benefactor. Obviously the norm is expressed differently in different societies. In Japan expressions such as '*onkei ni azukaru*', '*ongaeshi*', and '*orei*' indicate the notion of indebtedness and reciprocation.

While the norm of reciprocity denotes a generalized ethical principal that one should reciprocate a favour done, the term 'customary rules of exchange' refers to the social expectations concerning each specific type of social exchange in a particular society. For example, in Japan one must refer to local custom to know the amount which should be given to one's marriage intermediary (*nakōdo*) or the amount to give as a funerary gift (*kōden*). One might regard the rules of exchange as concrete formulations of the norm of reciprocity.

E   Strategies of exchange

'Strategies of exchange' refers to the set of thought processes by which an individual chooses to engage in social exchange. The customary rules of exchange often provide for some latitude in their application. For example, an appropriate gift to a tutor who has taught one's son can be selected from among different kinds of gifts, and its value can also vary a great deal.

To develop a good strategy, actors must be familiar with both the norm of reciprocity and the customary rules of exchange. They must also differentiate among various exchange acts in terms of costs and benefits. In short, one must know what and how to give to another in order to maximise the resources he or she receives in return. Giving another person a resource of great value will not necessarily result in a great return. Depending on the alter or depending on the exchange resource to be given, there are occasions when a gift of the smallest value may bring a large return. In some situations an exchange act which is outside this latitude may be considered to have the greatest strategic effect. For example, acts of exchange which exist outside the range of customarily defined rules are often labelled as a form of bribery, collusion or corruption.

F   Ideals and behaviour

The norm of reciprocity and rules of exchange are ideals. One criticism of theories emphasizing Japanese groupism is that 'groupism as an ideology' and 'groupism as group behaviour' are confused. There also seems to be an assumption that the people behave according to the idealized group model. In exchange theory, a clear distinction must be made between rules and behaviour. People do not always act according to the rules.

Norms involving *on* and *giri* are defined as cultural ideals, and Japanese etiquette books are replete with rules of exchange. According to the rules, one must show gratitude to persons who have done a favour or give gifts at *obon* and at the end of the year to a marriage intermediary. Norms and rules are important in *orienting* the behaviour of societal members, but they do not determine behaviour in a strict manner. While this orientation surely affects the individual, his actual behaviour is also determined by his orientations toward other norms and ideals and by his self-interested 'strategic' considerations. Empirically observed behaviour often does not correspond to any single ideal or norm concerning social exchange, although it may be guided or influenced by such abstract concepts.

3   Instrumentality and expressivity in social exchange

As stated above, anything from money to the expression of affection may serve as an exchange resource. It is possible to distinguish between two types of utility associated with exchange resources. One is the material use to which the resources can be put. For example, if the resource is money, it can be used to purchase other things one needs. The value of the other type is that the very act of giving the resource provides immediate psychological satisfaction to the receiver. Inviting a friend to a dinner party may obligate the friend to reciprocate at a later date. To the extent that this consideration is paramount, the dinner party is instrumental; it is an investment of resources with the expectation of a future return. However, many invitations are made simply as an expression of 'friendship'; there is enjoyment in the present act regardless of whether there is a 'return' in the future. From this perspective, the invitation is an *expressive act*. Thus, a given *act* may not be purely instrumental or purely expressive; most exchange acts in fact have both instrumental and expressive aspects in varying proportions.

The instrumental and the expressive value attached to the same exchange act will vary enormously depending on the situation. Gifts of money vary in amount. The value of a cigarette given to a friend who happens to be without one may vary depending upon the friend's need and other factors defining the situation. The love expressed towards one's lover and the affection shown to a neighbour would differ in intensity. The same type of exchange act may have different degrees of instrumentality and expressivity depending upon who the actor is and his relationship with the other party. For example, an automobile given by a wealthy parent to his son may not have as much instrumental or expressive value as the same given by a working-class father to his son.

Theoretically the expressive and/or instrumental value of an act could be either positive or negative. Acts with a negative value would be those which involve material or psychological damage for one of the parties to the exchange. Because the concept and theory of negative exchange has not yet been well developed, the discussion in this paper will be confined largely to exchanges bringing positive value to both parties.

A   Some empirical data from Japan

There is no necessary or logical relationship between the instrumental value and expressive value of exchange acts. In abstract terms various patterns can be conceived in the relationship between the two. To gain some insight into the relationship between these two types of value, an empirical study was conducted in Kyōto in 1970.[1] A random sample of 138 married men and 172 married women in the city of Kyōto was chosen to examine the relationship

1   The survey was carried out by Nagata Yoshioki, Kurita Yasuyaki and the present author. It was financially supported by the US National Science Foundation, the Center for Research in International Studies of Stanford University and S. Guggenheim Foundation.

45

between the instrumental value and the expressive value of various acts of exchange. The respondents were asked to evaluate the frequency with which twenty types of exchange acts occurred in Japanese society. The respondents were also asked to indicate on a scale from '1' to '5' how much instrumental value and how much expressive value each act provided to particular types of individuals. The Japanese words '*bengido*' and '*shinmitsude*' were used in the survey to capture the idea of instrumentality and expressivity; the first means roughly 'utility' or 'usefulness'; the second suggests 'intimacy' or 'affective closeness'. The individuals to be considered (called 'alter types') were defined as being a social superior, an equal or a subordinate; they were also defined as being a work-related acquaintance, a kinsman or a neighbour. An alter type could thus be defined as fitting one of nine categories. Respondents were asked to evaluate the meaning of a particular exchange act from the point of view of someone in one or another of the nine categories.

Although the results were somewhat different for males and females and also depending on whether the alter was socially superior, equal or subordinate, the amount of variation was small and is not important to the discussion in this paper. Accordingly, the findings presented in Table 1.1 and Figure 1.1 are for the male respondents for acts done toward a social superior. Several conclusions may be drawn.

First, the respondents did not differentiate as much among the acts in terms of their instrumental value as in terms of their expressive. The mean scores had a narrow range between 1.7 and 3.2 for the instrumental value, whereas they ranged from 2.0 to 4.5 for the expressive value.

Second, the instrumental value of an act is generally lower than its expressive value. We cannot automatically assume that the instrumental and expressive scales are seen in the same way by each respondent, even though both had the same numerical scale ranging from 1 to 5. However, it would seem that Japanese value an act for its expressivity more than for its instrumentality, even when an act's instrumental value appears to be obvious as in the providing of financial aid.

Third, there is a positive curvilinear correlation between the expressive value and the instrumental value. At the lower levels (with mean values below 3.0) the two scores are fairly similar. At the upper levels, however, the mean expressivity value is

Table 1.1 *Mean Expressivity and Instrumentality Values of 20 Exchange Acts as Evaluated by 138 Males*

Exchange Act	Mean Score for expressivity	Mean score for instrumentality
Providing financial aid	4.5	3.2
Serving as a guarantor for a person	4.1	2.9
Giving a seasonal gift such as a mid-year or an end-of-the-year gift	4.0	2.4
Helping someone with his/her house-cleaning or moving	4.0	2.4
Giving a gift on a personal occasion such as a birthday or a wedding	4.0	2.3
Giving a gift to someone after returning from a trip	4.0	2.1
Sending a gift on a special business occasion (such as starting a new job or starting a new business)	3.8	2.6
Informing a person of something he/she would benefit from	3.5	2.3
Giving a gift to someone because he/she had an accident or illness or some such mishap	3.5	2.3
Treating a person to a dinner	3.5	2.3
Taking a gift to someone when visiting him/her	3.3	2.1
Providing confidential advice on family problems and work-related problems	3.2	2.4
Introducing someone to a doctor	3.0	2.1
Speaking up for a person when he or she is criticized by others	3.0	2.1
Simply listening to complaints	3.0	2.1
Extending words of concern when misfortune (such as accidents or illness) occurs	2.9	2.0
Informing someone of recent developments in one's own personal life such as a change in one's job or in one's address	2.9	2.0
Sending a New Year's greeting card	2.3	1.8
Taking the initiative in greeting a person	2.1	1.7
Seeing a person willingly who has come to visit	2.0	2.1

considerably above the mean instrumental value. In other words, the relative disparity between the expressive and instrumental values assigned to an act increases as the overall importance of the act increases.

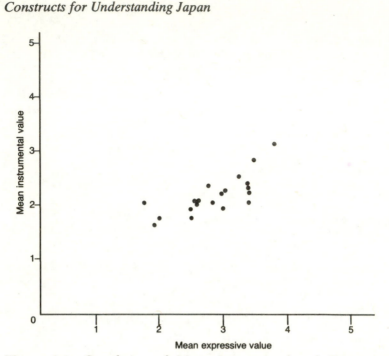

Figure 1.1 *Correlation of Mean Instrumental and Expressive Values Assigned to 20 Exchange Acts by 138 Male Respondents*

While this positive correlation may seem obvious, it is entirely possible to conceive of a society in which the two variables are negatively correlated. Although we do not have data for a similar sample of Americans which have been collected in exactly the same manner, the data provided by Uriel Foa (1971) – an American psychologist – allow an indirect comparison. Foa considered six types of exchange resources: love, service, material goods, money, information and status. His concern was with finding the types which were likely to be exchanged. As a result he discovered that resources which share similarities tend to be exchanged more readily. Foa found a relationship among the six categories in terms of concreteness and particularism (Figure 1.2).

The Kyōto survey also provided other data on the relationship between instrumentality and expressivity. Respondents were asked to think of particular individuals (such as a relative or a superior at work), and then to indicate the extent to which the respondent felt intimacy (*shinmitsudo*) (an expressive value) toward that

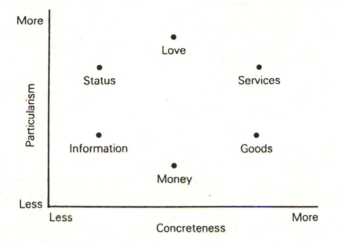

Figure 1.2 *Cognitive Structure in which Various Resources are Seen in Terms of Their Relationship to Particularism and Concreteness*

person and also the extent to which he or she received some benefit (*bengido*) (an instrumental value) from that person. The results revealed the same positive correlation between instrumentality and expressivity that was found with regard to the twenty exchange acts. In other words, toward the person to whom one shows high expressivity one also expresses high instrumentality. We also asked respondents to indicate the degree of instrumentality and expressivity which the respondent believed the alter held toward the actor. This also yielded a positive correlation between expressivity and instrumentality.

To generalize, it may be that in Japanese society those with whom one has an affective relationship are also the ones with whom instrumental exchanges occur. As a contrast, it may be, if Foa's analysis (1971) allows interpretation, that in the United States those who share an affective relationship tend to avoid instrumental relationships, and that instrumental relationships tend to develop when intimacy is absent.

Qualifying remarks are in order, however. In the Kyōto survey respondents were asked to select for instrumental and expressive evaluation relatives, friends, work-related people and neighbours – persons who are outside one's immediate family. Intra-familial exchange relationships need not be the same as those outside the family. Had the sample been composed so that it included both family members and non-family members, the findings might have shown differences between the exchange patterns between family members and those which occurred when extra-family relationships were involved. For this reason, it is unwise to generalize from the above findings about all Japanese human relationships.

B Bribery

In the above survey we investigated the relationship between instrumentality and expressivity in normal human relationships. There are patterns of exchange in Japanese society which are not represented here. One example is bribery. Bribery is highly instrumental in that through a gift of money and other material resources one tries to obtain resources which cannot be obtained through socially sanctioned means. In Japan, the behaviour of a government official receiving compensation other than his salary for the performance of his assigned duties constitutes the crime known as 'bribery'. At the same time, however, it is generally acknowledged that certain minimum customary gift-giving toward government officials must be condoned if it is of a customary nature. For this reason, prosecutors often concentrate only on the more flagrant violations. Where the giver and the receiver of a bribe have not maintained a relationship which would warrant giving and receiving of a gift of a certain value and kind, the transaction is regarded as a bribe.

If we are to interpret this in terms of expressivity and instrumentality, we would say that a bribe has an instrumental value and a range of expressive values which can be used to imply a certain level of intimacy in the past relationship between the briber and the bribed. The job of the judge is to make a decision as to whether or not such a past relationship has existed between the parties to bribery. Bribery is said to occur when the social relations implied by the value of the gift (that is, the bribe) are absent. It is for this reason the act is considered to be a bribe and the bribe-giver is judged to be guilty.

C Three types of social exchange

Sahlins (1965) proposed a model involving three types of exchange: generalized exchange, balanced exchange and negative exchange. Although he did not define each type clearly, his three types suggest that there is a need to distinguish between several types of exchange. By 'generalized exchange' Sahlins means exchange in which there is no requirement or expectation that the gift or favour be returned immediately with something of exactly the same value. When this type of exchange occurs, the amount or value of the social debt is not specified. In other words, repayment may be made over a long period of time in the form of material or psychological support. Even though there may also be an instrumental aspect to the exchange, the emphasis in generalized exchange tends to be on the expressive value of the relationship.

By 'balanced exchange' Sahlins referred to transactions which tended to be balanced even though there might be short time-lags. When this kind of exchange is occurring, the 'balance sheet' at any point in time tends to show that each partner has received something roughly equivalent to what he or she has given to the other party. In balanced exchange the emphasis tends to be on the instrumental value of the relationship.

Balanced exchange lends itself more readily to exchange measurement. This is because the very instrumentality of the act requires that both parties somehow be able to quantify the flow of resources. The resources used in balanced exchange can often be translated into some monetary standard. Expressive resources, being imponderable, are obviously much more difficult to quantify. How much affect has been given or received, when 'love' or 'praise' is involved, is a relatively vague matter of 'more or less'.

4 Balanced exchange and generalized exchange

These two kinds of exchange are ideal types; empirical cases of exchange would lie somewhere between the two extremes. Some exchange phenomena (as might be found within the family) tend to be closer to one ideal type (that is, generalized exchange) while other behaviour (as might be found in market exchange) tends to be closer to the other ideal type (namely, balanced exchange). As a case study of social exchange in the Japanese context, a novel on organizational life is introduced to illustrate some aspects of balanced exchange in Japan. First, however, it is useful to consider the position of balanced exchange and the applicability of exchange theory in that context.

A 'Intermediate organizations' and social exchange

It was suggested above that the relationships in some social groups, such as the family, are characterized primarily by generalized exchange, while the relationships in other situations, such as a market, are characterized primarily by balanced exchange. Between these two extremes various social organizations may be schools, business firms, clubs, the world of entertainers or the *yakuza*. Here the term 'intermediate organization' is used to refer not to the size of an organization but to its intermediate position on the continuum between balanced and generalized exchange.

There is a tendency in the literature on social exchange to interpret exchange acts solely in terms of their instrumental value and in terms of resources such as money and other material goods which are immediately associated with instrumental behaviour. The tendency has led some to argue that exchange theory does not really apply in organizations where expressive exchanges are important. This view is based on the misunderstanding that expressive resources are not amenable to exchange analysis. It is wrong to assume that persons who emphasize the sentimental or emotional side of things are incapable of exchange. Sentimentality and affection are themselves important resources which may be offered for exchange. One may say that in generalized exchange, the emphasis on expressive exchange overshadows and conceals the true extent to which instrumental exchange also takes place.

In our discussion of the Kyōto survey, we noted that the instrumental value and the expressive value of an act generally correlate positively. When a gift-giving act is perceived to have a high expressive value, it is also perceived to have a high (though not quite as high) instrumental value. Similarly for the evaluation of persons: those who are rated high on the expressive scale are also rated high (though not quite as high) on the instrumental scale. Thus, when expressivity is a salient feature in a relationship, it is likely that instrumentality will also be part of the exchange relationship.

The relative saliency of expressivity is probably due to the fact that in Japanese culture, as *tatemae* (that is, in public) it is not in good taste to speak of one's relationship with another person in instrumental terms whereas it is quite proper to emphasize the expressive aspects. According to those who argue for the group orientation of Japanese society, all groups – including, of course, intermediate types – stress expressive solidarity. From this perspective, it is said that Japanese groups are incapable of being analyzed as an exchange system. Such a claim, however, ignores the Japanese penchant for holding up *tatemae* in front of others so as not to show the *honne* (or the hidden agenda on which the instrumental motives for group participation appear). This fact is particularly important in understanding work situations in Japan.

Much is written about the importance of affect in Japanese work situations. Nearly all recent literature on Japanese management emphasizes the importance of affective relationships in Japan's industrial relations. The importance of expressive values may be seen in the commitment to work, in loyalty to the company, and in the dispensing of *amae*. In one way or another, much of the literature argues that the well-being of the Japanese company depends on a fluid exchange of affect. In fact, some argue that such human relationships have provided the essential ingredient or dynamic catalyst which accounts for the high productivity of Japanese firms.

This emphasis, however, has sometimes led to a basic misunderstanding and to conceptual confusion. From the literature, one almost gets the impression that expressive exchange is more important in Japanese companies than instrumental exchange. Obviously, no business organization can subordinate its instrumental goals to expressive (or 'pattern maintenance') goals. As the Kyōto survey suggested, the instrumental value of an exchange resource increases as its expressive value also increases. Given the high positive correlation between the two, an organization such as a business firm which promotes the exchange of highly expressive values in the company situation is likely to be facilitating exchange of high instrumental values as well. In short, instrumental goals of a company are achieved because the exchange of affect is insured in the work situation.

This discussion raises an interesting question concerning the relative importance attached to expressive, or generalized exchange in Japanese organizations compared to the weight given such exchange in organizations in other countries. Certainly the common view of Japan seems to be that this is the case, and that emphasis serves to remind us that at least in Japan such exchange is a crucial prerequisite for instrumental or balanced exchange to occur. We may then ask, when comparing the nature of social exchange in intermediate organizations in Japanese and American societies, 'Is there in Japan more of a predominance of expressive or generalized exchange over instrumental or balanced exchange than is the case in the United States?' There are also questions about the sources of variance within each society. For example, one tends to think of small groups as being characterized by generalized exchange, and large organizations as being characterized by balanced exchange.

In concluding, a couple of points require underlining. First, the preceding discussion does not argue that expressive exchange *causes* instrumental exchange. The Kyōto study does not reveal causality; it merely points to correlation. Second, even if some cross-cultural differences were found, the predominance of generalized exchange would not imply that instrumental exchange is unimportant. In most intermediate organizations, the exchange of instrumental resources is unquestionably important. Although their importance may not be readily apparent in face-to-face situations and therefore not easily observed by the social scientists, the fact that instrumental exchange is camouflaged by expressive exchange does not mean that the former does not exist.

The truth of the statement can be seen indirectly in a number of ways. One is the extent to which instrumental or balanced exchange is hidden in the popular culture. As an example, one might cite any number of popular novels. In the next section the author considers a volume with which he is familiar: Yamazaki Toyoko's *Shiroi Kyotō* (The Great White Tower) (cf. Befu 1977a and 1977b).

B *Shiroi Kyotō* as an example of balanced exchange

Bribery is a type of exchange in which instrumental values seem to be more predominant than expressive values. With the predominance of instrumental values comes balanced exchange. In *Shiroi Kyotō*, a novel by Yamazaki Toyoko, balanced exchange with an emphasis on instrumental values is depicted as central to human relations in Japan. The hero of this story, Zaizen Gorō, is an associate professor in the School of Medicine at Naniwa University in the Kansai area of Japan. He engages in an intensive campaign to obtain promotion to full professorship. It is a campaign in the framework of social exchange.

The immediate goal both for Zaizen and for the other two factions which oppose his promotion is to obtain a majority of the votes from the full professors. Each faction offers to each faculty member certain resources in exchange for his vote. For example, the local medical association, which consists largely of Naniwa alumni, provides financial support for Zaizen's election campaign. Members of the association expect, in return, that Zaizen will give them preferential treatment at the University Hospital by securing, for example, beds for their patients in normally crowded wards. An assistant professor in Zaizen's department supports Zaizen, eyeing Zaizen's support for his own promotion to associate professorship in the future. A lecturer in the department likewise supports Zaizen as a means of obtaining his own promotion to assistant professorship.

Others support Professor Kikuchi, a candidate from another university who has been proposed for the chair in opposition to Zaizen. This support flows from the fact that Kikuchi is supported by a Professor Funao, a nationally known medical professor at the prestigious Tōkai University in Tokyo who wields enormous power in the profession. By supporting Kikuchi, Funao is taking advantage of an opportunity to expand his power base in the Kansai area. In order to obtain votes for Kikuchi, Funao freely distributes resources he controls to certain faculty members. For example, to Professor Nozaka he promises a position on the board of directors of the Plastic Surgeon's Association of Japan. To Professor Kamiya he promises approval for the research grant proposal Kamiya has submitted to a particular research committee on which Funao sits.

In these various transactions, little importance is attached to the expressive values of exchange. Each resource exchanged has only an instrumental value. Since Japanese social and cultural norms – *tatemae* – place a value on the exchange of resources for expressive purposes, it is not surprising that Japanese tend to look down on such instrumental exchange. Cutting through the rhetorical *tatemae* of outward and formal propriety, Yamazaki's novel shows the naked self-centredness of the protagonists. By portraying, or even celebrating, the 'unrespectable' as heroes, Yamazaki's novel in some ways underscores the dual emphasis placed on instrumental and expressive values when individuals engage in social exchange. Because public emphasis is placed on expressivity and on the toning down (or hiding) of the instrumental aspects of social exchange in the day-to-day interaction of most Japanese (at least as *tatemae*), it often appears on the surface that acts predominate in expressivity in many of these intermediate organizations. In fact, however, instrumentality is always an important consideration, and both instrumental resources and expressive resources are always being exchanged to maintain an equilibrium in exchange relationships.

5 Vertical exchange and horizontal exchange

In the discussion so far, a clear distinction has not been made between (1) situations in which the actors are on a roughly equal footing and (2) situations in which one party is clearly in a superior position and the other is clearly in a subordinate position. However, human relationships between equals (horizontal relationships) and those between persons having unequal status (vertical relationships) are very different in most societies. Accordingly, some attention ought to be paid to this distinction of social exchange relationships. One important difference is that exchange is balanced in kind in horizontal relationships whereas in vertical relationships such a balance is not maintained.

Although temporary imbalances may occur in horizontal relationships, there is an obligation to return one's 'debt' and, once the return is made, the balance is restored. Even before the balance is restored there is a realization that the imbalance is temporary and that the relationship between the two is basically egalitarian. The maintenance of a balance is further facilitated by the fact that the resources exchanged are generally of the same kind. The receiver of resources has the capacity (in the instrumental or in the expressive sense) to return the same kind of resource that he or she received. If a friend receives a gift, he or she has the obligation to return a gift of similar value at a similar occasion. And the friend usually has the ability to do so. For example, if a wedding takes place in A's family, A's friend B would send a wedding gift to A's family. Later, if a wedding takes place in B's family, A would send a gift of similar value to B's family. Horizontal relationships are found not only in social relations in which expressivity predominates (such as in friendship) but also in relationships where instrumentality dominates (such as in the economic marketplace). When one purchases merchandise, one pays an equivalent value in cash for that merchandise.

In vertical relationships the resources which the superordinate gives to his subordinates often differ from the resources the subordinate is expected to return. The resources given to a subordinate are often those which the subordinate does not possess and is unable to return. For example, if a professor finds a job for a student, the debt cannot be returned to the professor by finding him a job since he already has one. Also, the professor–student relationship consists in the professor imparting knowledge to his student. The very imparting of knowledge in a one-directional fashion is what defines the relationships as vertical. In vertical relationship the subordinate lacks the resource which the superior has provided, and thus must return a different kind of resource to pay back his 'debt'. Usually, the subordinate has a greater need for the resource which the superior has than the superior has for whatever the subordinate can provide. This relates to the fact that the vertical relationship is basically one of inequality; it is a power relationship.

Power, in exchange theory, may be defined as the probability of controlling of another person's action by dispensing resources which that person needs. A balance is struck between the power holder and his subordinate as the former supplies needed resources to the subordinate while in return obtaining the latter's compliance to an extent commensurate to the value of the resource given. Although power as defined here may be exercised within or outside bureaucracy, the consequences are different in each case. First of all, outside bureaucracy, the resources for exercising power which an individual possesses are by and large personal assets: the individual's wealth, supernatural power, connections, knowledge, ability or charisma. One dispenses these personal resources to those who wish them in exchange for their services.

The theory of bureaucracy suggests that specific rights to exercise power (that is, authority) are attached to positions within the system. Corporations and government offices also provide employees with resources such as a salary and fringe benefits; in exchange, it expects such employees to obey the orders of the supervisors who manage the corporation at various levels. In short, as an ideal type, the management of bureaucratic organization is made possible through the exercise of 'bureaucratic power' which inheres in the *office* of the manager, rather than in his *person*. The office-holder (namely, the manager) uses the delegated power inherent in the office to control employees who are compensated not with the personal resources of the office-holder, but with the resources of the corporation which are given in return for control over his time and resources (that is, for his 'giving up' certain rights for delineated periods under stipulated conditions).

Although this view of bureaucracy is commonly accepted in the West, this theory of bureaucracy does not quite apply to Japanese bureaucracy either in the government or in private business. In Japanese society, exercise of power within bureaucracy relies a great deal on personal resources of the superior or the supervisor. When the head of a department or a section performs his duties (exercises his bureaucratically given power), subordinates do not obey simply because they receive salaries. Subordinates respect the superior and obey his commands because, in addition, the superior gives his personal resources to his subordinates. This means taking subordinates to bars for drinks, inviting them to his home, or serving as a confidant when a subordinate has personal problems. Such a supervisor would be respected and is considered to be a *jinkakusha* (a person of character and individual integrity).

In other words, Japanese bureaucracy functions more efficiently when the superior and the subordinates enter into a generalized exchange. On this point, it should be noted that to use one's own personal resources within the bureaucratic setting and to exercise power through generalized exchange contradicts the ideal often associated with European bureaucracy and the notions of rationality, as enunciated by Weber (1947).[2]

6 Conclusion – toward a social exchange model of Japanese society

The preceding sections have discussed the social exchange model with some reference to Japanese society. In the remaining pages some characteristics of Japanese society are discussed in terms of the exchange model.

A Relationship between instrumentality and expressivity

As we saw in the results of the Kyōto survey, resources which have a high expressive value also tend to have a high instrumental value. It should be noted with regard to the findings of that study, however, that the instrumental value associated with each resource was not as high as the expressive value. While there may have

2   For a discussion of the relationship between bureaucracy and the Japanese-style exchange, see Befu (1974; n.d.).

been some problems in operationalizing the two concepts, it would seem that in Japanese society social norms proscribe that instrumentality may be freely expressed, even though the intent to use or to take advantage of an alter through an exchange relationship may be built into all exchanges since the expressive and instrumental values appear to coincide. On the other hand, there are no proscriptions against expressing feelings of intimacy toward another person.

Japanese human relations seem to start from exchanges involving resources with low instrumental and expressive values; they develop as the exchange relationship expands to incorporate resources with higher values in both dimensions. As exchange acts accumulate, the expressive value of the relationship increases, along with its instrumental value. In Japanese thinking, to do whatever is useful for another person (in other words, to share resources with a high instrumental value) is to express intimacy or affect. At the same time, to express intimacy or affect is to demonstrate one's willingness to offer instrumental resources.

In conventional thinking, especially from the point of view of arguments about 'Japanese groupism', Japanese social relationships are said to be emotional and to be dominated by *amae*. Further, the exchange of instrumental values is not seen as being part of 'Japanese social relationships'. As a contrast, instrumental exchange has been regarded as an integral part of social relationships in the West. In characterizing Japanese society, there is a tendency to pick phenomena which contrast with Western society and regard them as 'Japanese'. It seems that the tendency to regard Japanese social relations as primarily emotional or expressive is predicated upon the view that Western societies are instrumental and Japanese society is the opposite. However, no intermediate group, whether in Japan or in the United States, will be wholly expressive. This is especially true with regard to the Japanese business organizations in which Western writers seem to be most interested in recent years. Japanese groups seem to be characterized by a balance of expressivity and instrumentality rather than by the predominance of the expressive orientation.

The question of how this compares with the situation in other societies invites frequent speculation, although as yet there is no careful comparison in this regard. It is commonly held by many Japanese, however, that in American society instrumental exchange and expressive exchange tend to be kept separate.

Japanese say that Americans are 'dry'. What they mean is that instrumental exchange need not be accompanied by expressivity and that it is not contrary to social norms for individuals to engage in instrumental exchange without any emotional or affective input.

It is also pointed out that in American society outside the bureaucracy or employment structure there is a value or a norm which discourages one from expecting a return from the person to whom one has provided instrumental resources. This view is consistent with the Christian notion of charity and altruism, although it is well to remember that Americans, too, distinguish between *tatamae* and *honne* of all sorts. What may appear to be altruism at one level may in fact involve expectations of return at the *honne* level.

The fact is that, even with the Christian tradition, much behaviour is carried out by Americans only after careful consideration has been given to the returns. However, the *tatamae* or ideology most frequently expressed in American society suggests that there is a high value in helping another person because the other person needs help or because one wants to help and not because one expects some kind of personal gain from doing so.

Herein may lie one important difference between Japanese and American social relations. In Japan the ideal may be that emotionality predominates, whereas in reality most acts have a strong instrumental aspect as expressivity and instrumentality go hand-in-hand. In America, the ideal may be that one offers instrumental resources without the expectation of there being any return, but in real life one often does expect return from another. In other words, the American approach to exchange is first to deny that there is to be an exchange, and then to expect it.

This does not mean that in Japanese exchange acts instrumentality and expressivity are always correlated. We have examined a portion of *Shiroi Kyotō* by Yamazaki as an extreme example of instrumental predominance. In order to bring out the extent to which some Japanese openly engage in instrumentally oriented exchange, the author describes exchanges at the level of *honne*, an approach which in this case expresses what Japanese regard as the seamy side of human relations. Since in the *tatamae* of Japanese society emotionality is important, the nearly complete absence of emotion makes *Shiroi Kyotō* a study in social criticism. In the 'face-to-face ideology', expressive resources are regarded with approval and instrumental resources with disapproval. For this reason Japanese and foreigners alike tend to think of Japanese society as being emotional or expressive. However, to achieve Japan's high level of economic growth, instrumental concerns have had to be important.

B Conditions of generalized exchange

A second characteristic associated with Japanese patterns of social exchange is that they tend to be relatively weighted toward generalized exchange when compared with American patterns of exchange. In the American family, children are often assigned garden work, the washing of cars, and house cleaning, for which they are paid a pre-determined amount of money. In primary groups in Japan, such as the family, such balanced exchange is relatively rare. Moreover, generalized exchange, which is emphasized within the family, tends to be extended into secondary, intermediate groups in Japan, whereas in the United States balanced exchange which is emphasized within the family, tends to be extended into secondary groups.

To analyze Japanese society from the point of view of social exchange is to characterize social relations in Japan as a series of transactions. The perspective presented in this paper is different from that in which Japanese society is characterized in terms of a certain type of group. There are individuals who belong to the 'Japanese group' and there are others who do not. If Japaneseness is to be characterized in terms of 'groupness', there are many Japanese who are not very 'Japanese'. However, there are few, if any, members of Japanese society who do not maintain Japanese social relations. In this sense models of Japanese society based on the notion of exchange have a distinct advantage over the group model in that they will be likely to apply to many more 'Japanese' and to a much wider range of social phenomena.

C Social exchange and the understanding of Japanese society

Analysis of social phenomena requires attention at several levels. One is the level of the individual, or the person. How a person is socially defined in a given culture varies a great deal, contrary to the common-sense notion that an individual is an individual. We have too readily applied the Western conception of the individual to other cultures, assuming that persons in other cultures have the same kinds of desires and aspirations, such as wanting to see self-interest protected at all costs, yearning for 'independence' and so on. We need a thorough study of the concept of the person in Japan. There would be great value in analyzing more thoroughly Japanese concepts such as *seishin, jinkaku*, and *otona*.

Another level of analysis is that of groups and institutions. A great deal of work has focused in Japan on this level, not to say that enough has been done. The study of Japanese groups, family and economic institutions and the like have been the mainstay of the sociology of Japan.

A third level is intermediate between the individual and groups and institutions. This is the level on which we have focused in this paper. Very little work has been done to elucidate the relationship of the person to the larger society. Social exchange is not necessarily the only perspective available for this purpose; but it is one which will help us to understand a great many phenomena. I have tried to indicate some of the ways in which it might do so.

As I have suggested elsewhere (1977a and 1977b), a careful examination of the internal dynamics of group behaviour – or, rather, the behaviour of individual members of a group – gives one a stronger realization that labels such as 'group consensus', 'group solidarity' and 'the concerted action of the group' provide a crude and often inaccurate description or summary for a whole series of individual transactions among members of a group. Much of their behaviour is motivated by self-interest, rather than by loyalty or dedication to the group. Often such transactions can be best analyzed in the framework of social exchange.

To illustrate this, we can return to *Shiroi Kyotō* discussed above. Most of the factions would in the end vote as blocs at the faculty meeting to decide the next full professor. Considered by itself, this fact might lead those interested only in the 'group' phenomena of Japanese to conclude very mistakenly that Japanese blindly and unthinkingly behave according to the dictates of the group. In a similar fashion, the bloc voting of members of the Liberal Democratic Party in the Diet may also be the result of a complicated series of exchange transactions on the part of individual Diet members. Without investigating these transactions, one would have little understanding of Japanese politics.

Social exchange as a theoretical framework should thus add an important dimension to the understanding of Japanese society, and should allow us to open our eyes to phenomena which we have ignored in the past. No claim is made, of course, that the social exchange model will provide a theoretical panacea, or that it would explain everything that needs to be explained. The cultural conception of the person is a relevant and separate dimension for social research. So too is the structure of social organizations and institutions. Taken together with other studies of these phenomena, however, the perspective of social exchange should provide us with a more holistic comprehension of Japan.

References

Abegglen, James C.
1958   *The Japanese Factory* (Glencoe, Ill.: The Free Press).
Befu, Harumi
1967   'Gift-giving and Social Reciprocity in Japan', *France-Asie/Asia*, no. 188, 161–77.
1968   'Gift-giving in a Modernizing Japan', *Monumenta Nipponica*, vol. 23, no. 3–4, 445–56.
1974   'Power in Exchange', *Asian Profile*, vol. 2, no. 6 (Dec.), 601–22.
1976   'Shakō' (Social Intercourse), ch. 12 in *Nihonjin no Seikatsu*, vol. IV of '*Kōza Hikaku Bunka*' (Lecture Series on Comparative Culture) (Tokyo: Kenkyūsha), 271–305.
1977a   'Rikoteki Nihonjin – Shiroi Kyotō no Kōkanron-teki Bunseki' (Self-centred Japanese: a Social Exchange Analysis of *Shiroi Kyotō*), *Kikan Jinruigaku*, vol. 8, no. 3, 198–231.
1977b   'Power in the Great White Tower', in *The Anthropology of Power*, edited by R. D. Fogelson and R. N. Adams (New York: Academic Press), 77–87.
1984a   'Civilization and Culture: Japan in Search of Identity', in *Japanese Civilization in the Modern World*, edited by Harumi Befu, Tadao Umesao and J. Kreiner, *Senri Ethnological Studies* (no. 16), 59–76.
1984b   'Ethnicity-ron no Kokusai Kankeiron e no Kōken: Nihon Bunkaron to no Kanrensei o Chūshin to Shite' (Contribution of Ethnicity Theory to International Relations Theory: in Relation to Nihon Bunkaron), *Mimpaku Tsūshin*, no. 25, 2–9.
1984c   'Amerika shakai to Nikkeijin' (American Society and the Japanese American), *Mimpaku*, vol. 8, no. 7, 2–7.

Constructs for Understanding Japan

1984d   'Ideorogii to shiteno Nihon Bunkaron' (Nihon Bunkaron as an Ideology), *Shisō no Kagaku*, no. 43, 6–19.

1984e   'Nihon no Kokusaika o Ureu' (My Concerns over Japan's Internationalization), *Shisō no Kagaku*, no. 43, 82–9; no. 45, 110–17; and no. 46, 94–103.

1984f   'Nihon Bunkaron wa Taishū Shōhizai' (Nihon Bunkaron is a Consumer Product), *Kikan Jinruigaku*, vol. 15, no. 1, 119–26.

1984g   'Amerika ni Okeru Yōshi Engumi Igo no Shomondai' (Problems after Adoption in the US), *Atarashii Kazoku*, no. 5, 49–56.

1984h   'Amerika ni Okeru Yōshi Engumigo no Mondai to Taiō' (Problems and Meeting Problems after Adoption in America), *Sodateru*, n.s., no. 19, 1–9.

1984i   'Social and Cultural Background for Child Development in Japan and in the United States', in *Child Development in Japan and the United States*, edited by Harold Stevenson and Kenji Hakuta (San Francisco: Freeman), 13–27.

1985   'Review of *Work and Lifecourse in Japan*, edited by David W. Plath', *Journal of Japanese Studies*, vol. 11, no. 2, 435–41.

n.d.   'Weberian Bureaucracy in Japanese Civilization', to be published in *Senri Ethnological Studies*.

Forthcoming   'Nihon Bunkaron: A Japanese Worldview', to be published in a Festschrift for Elman Service, edited by Thomas Harding.

Blau, Peter M. (trans.)

1974   *Kōkan to Kenryoku* (Exchange and Power), (Tokyo: Shin'yōsha).

Clark, Gregory

1977   *The Japanese Tribe* (Tokyo: Simul Press).

Doi, Takeo

1971   *Amae no Kōzō* (The Structure of Amae) (Tokyo: Kōbundō).

1973   *The Anatomy of Dependence* (Tokyo: Kodansha International).

Foa, Uriel

1971   'Interpersonal and Economic Resources', *Science*, vol. 171, no. 3969: (29 Jan.), 345–51.

Foster, George M.

1963   'The Dyadic Contract in Tzintzuntzan, II', *American Anthropologist*, vol. 65, no. 6 (December), 1280–90.

Gergen, Kenneth

1969   *The Psychology of Behavior Exchange* (Reading: Addison-Wesley).

Gouldner, Alvin W.

1960   'The Norm of Reciprocity', *American Sociological Review*, vol. 25, no. 2 (April), 161–78.

Hamaguchi, Eshun
1977 *'Nihon Rashisa' no Sai-Hakken* (Rediscovering 'Japaneseness')
(Tokyo: Nihon Keizai Shinbunsha).
Hashimoto, Shigeru
1973 'Kōkan Riron no Kenkyū' (A Study in Exchange Theory), *Meiji
Gakuin Ronshū*, no. 206, 43–57; and no. 211, 89–100.
Hayakawa, Kōichi
1972 'Shakai-teki Kōkan no Shomondai' (Problems in Social
Exchange), *Shakaigaku Ronsō*, vol. 54, 60–72.
1973 'Shakai-teki Kōdō To shakai-teki Kōkan' (Social Behaviour and
Social Exchange), *Nihon Daigaku Jinbun Kagaku Kenkyūjo Kiyō*,
vol. 15, 117–33.
Homans, George C.; and Schneider, David M.
1955 *Marriage, Authority and Final Causes* (Glencoe, Ill.: Free
Press).
Inoue, Tadashi
1977 *Sekentei no Kōzō* (The Structure of *Sekentei*) (Tokyo: Nihon
Hōsō Shuppan Kyōkai).
Inuzuka, Sen
1974 '"Kōkan Riron" – Sono Keifu to Seikaku' ('Exchange Theory':
Its Historical Antecedents and its Character), *Shakaigaku Hyōron*,
vol. 24, no. 4, 2–18.
Kahn, Herman
1970 *The Emerging Japanese Superstate* (Englewood Cliffs, N.J.:
Prentice-Hall).
Lebra, Takie
1969 'Reciprocity and the Asymmetric Principle', *Psychologia*,
vol. 12, 129–38.
1972 'Reciprocity-based Moral Sanctions and Messianic Salvation',
American Anthropologist, vol. 74, no. 3 (June), 391–407.
1975 'An Alternative Approach to Reciprocity', *American
Anthropologist*, vol. 77, no. 3 (Sept.), 550–65.
Lévi-Strauss, Claude
1949 *Les structures élémentaires de la parenté* (The Elementary
Structures of Kinship) (Paris: Press Universitaire de France).
Matsumoto, Y. Scott
1960 'The Individual in Contemporary Japan', a special issue of
American Philosophical Society Transactions, no. 60.
Mitchell, Douglas D.
1976 *Amaeru: The Expression of Reciprocal Dependency Needs in
Japanese Politics and Law* (Boulder, Col.: Westview Press).
Nakane, Chie
1971 *Japanese Society* (Berkeley, Cal.: University of California
Press).

Rohlen, Thomas P.
   1974   *For Harmony and Strength* (Berkeley, Cal.: University of
   California Press).
Sahlins, Marshall D.
   1965   'On the Sociology of Primitive Exchange', in *The Relevance of
   Models for Social Anthropology*, edited by Michael Banton (New
   York: Praeger), 139–236.
Thibault, John W.; and Kelly, Harold H.
   1967   *The Social Psychology of Groups* (New York: Wiley).
Vogel, Ezra
   1979   *Japan as Number One: Lessons for America* (Cambridge, Mass.:
   Harvard University Press).
Weber, Max
   1947   *The Theory of Social and Economic Organization* (Glencoe,
   Ill.: Free Press).

Chapter Two
Arc, Circle and Sphere: Schedules for Selfhood

David W. Plath

1 The timing of biographies

The channels that shape the time-bent current of biography are shifting around us. Post-modern societies have entered an era of radical change in the demography of the human life cycle, in the standardizing of its stages, and in the values imputed to ageing and maturity. Not only are more people living into adulthood and high age; mass longevity has stretched out the life expectancy of relationships. People not only need to anticipate living longer, they have to be prepared to live together longer. The four-generation family, once a remote human possibility, may soon be common.

Not only has paid employment come to be the test of personal maturity, but compulsory education and compulsory retirement segregate the youngest and the oldest from the labour force. Society is being ordered around a new structure of age classes, with new forms of class struggle and alienation.

Not only is death being called irrelevant, a life-cycle transition to nowhere; but faith in the progress of technology has weakened the worth of any form of maturity that fails to keep up to date. Old age has become a cultural nightmare, for it places a fearsome strain upon any group's heritage of ideas that link personal effort to reward.

In short, we have come into a new historical phase in the timing of human biographies. People must learn to reconcile their personal tempos of growth with the demands imposed by the rhythms of succession in a four-generation society and the rhythms of production in a high-technology economy. For more than a decade there have been indications that ideas regarding lifecourse are changing. To decipher the mass media these days one has to have a vocabulary that was unknown a generation ago. Routinely, the media are informing us about a whole new range of phenomena, beginning with adult diseases and moving on through dual-career marriage, the empty nest syndrome, *ikigai, kōrei shakai*, lifelong learning, life-cycle planning, mid-life crisis and *raifu wāku* to the rise of senior power. Fresh phrases appear monthly, often enough as *gairaigo* in Japanese.

There are native Japanese terms for the lifecourse – traditional words such as *shōgai* or *isshō* – that seem, to this outlander, semantically adequate. And Japanese Buddhist thinkers went to virtuoso lengths in elaborating their conception of a wheel of death-and-life. Why, then, the fad for '*kana*-nizing' English phrases such as *raifu saikuru*? Is it just another example of showing off one's foreign vocabulary? Or could those who utter the words *raifu saikuru* be hinting at something more: hinting that traditional ideas may not be good enough in a greying population, in a milieu where support-for-seniors is needed on a scale never dreamed of in Confucian philosophy?

In the scholarly arena, too, there is a mood of reappraisal, a hundred flowers of doubt about the standard concepts for explaining human ontogeny and the standard methods for studying it. There is no agreement yet on any new theory, not even a widely shared set of ideas and techniques. But there is a shared sense of problem, of a need for new perspectives on how people grow and change across the biographical chain of years. This search for a lifecourse outlook has sparked a flurry of academic writing and conferencing in recent years in the North Atlantic countries. I detect less of the same elsewhere, but that may only reveal an outsider's lack of information. At any rate, lifecourse thinking in

Euro-America has, by and large, been an extension of the Western heritage of intellectual fascination with the individual as a monad entity.

It is here that Japan can serve as a strategic case for comparative study. So near to the West in the production rhythms of its industrial economy, next door in the career rhythms of its large-scale institutions, Japan stands apart in its heritage of schedules for human cultivation. By examining Japan we may be able to advance our general understanding of the potential for healthy ageing in a post-industrial world.

The group model of Japanese society points to ways in which the currents of biography may differ from those in the West. It also exaggerates the differences, and so distorts our view of the pace and problems of ordinary personal development. By positing a timeless basic personality that is born fused with the basic culture (that is, not born free), that is congenitally over-attached to society, the group model obfuscates our understanding of the dynamics of the individual's long-term planning for self-preservation. Personal integrity is dissolved into a property of group solidarity; biographical movement is swallowed by organizational process. Some of the reports on lifetime employment, for example, lead me to conclude that on his retirement day the typical *shain* would not be able to write an autobiography: he could only produce a job résumé.

Clichés usually have a component of truth. The group model itself is due for recall to the factory, but perhaps we can salvage some of its parts. For instance, I do find evidence that in Japan – in loose and sweeping contrast to Euro-America – people tend to measure their personal development on a longer scale of years. Or that they seem more attuned to a need for mutual aid in exploiting opportunities for growth. Or that they view self-realization more in terms of situational response than of autonomous unfolding. These vague phrases need to be made more precise, to be rewritten without constant reference to 'the West' as a baseline. But perhaps they can be used as starting points – hypotheses, if you wish – for controlled comparative enquiry. By using a general perspective on the lifecourse, then, we may be able to advance our understanding of what is special about the human biography in Japan.

I am going to sketch some themes in lifecourse thinking in Euro-America. Then I will consider three concepts that, it seems to me, could be used for the framing of comparative research. I will call these unit-ideas *'arcs'* (trajectories of action), *'circles'* (clusters of intimates who grow older together), and *'spheres'* (visions of self-completion). The words are drawn from geometry, to suggest the need to keep one's analytic cool. But I also mean them, when put together, to suggest the frictional heat of human behaviour. My image is of a person steering himself along a path (arc), his actions shaped by those around him (circle), as he strives to realize an ideal of wholeness (sphere).

2   The lifecourse outlook

Scholarly discussions of lifecourse in Euro-America these days have a note of optimism. No one is prophesying a great leap out of the grooves laid down by biology and history, or an unchaining of mankind from the wheel of death-and-birth. But the human stuff is seen as being much more malleable, plastic, more open to continuing growth, more rich in reserve potentials than was usual for many of the founding fathers of modern psychological and social science. I see a marked difference here from the views that held sway earlier in our century when, for example, the psychologist who studied intelligence found that it deteriorated inexorably with age; or when Freud declared (or so it is alleged) that psychotherapy would be a waste of effort with anybody older than forty-five; or when gerontology was the dismal science of the day, defining itself as the study of human decay.

In any wave of rethinking, people usually know better what they want to reject than what they want to advocate. If a battery of new concepts for lifecourse development is not yet to hand, a lot of older concepts – for example, 'basic personality', 'deep structure' or 'normative control' – are under attack, regarded as shop-worn, or declared to have been rather poor predictors. Today's impulse is to emphasize change more than constancy, nurture more than nature, the pull of spirit more than the push of matter. Whatever the ultimate limits to human growth, says the lifecourse mood, scholars in the early industrial epoch held too gloomy a vision of the possibilities for human growth. Indeed, a comparative study launched at Harvard in 1979 – Japan is one of its six cases – forthrightly calls itself the Project on Human Potential (n.d. and 1981).

Lifecourse thinking also puts an accent on the self as an agent in its own development. The person is seen to have powers greater than previous theory granted to select and to modify, on the one hand, the normative pressures associated with roles, and, on the other, the carry-over effects of child training. He is seen as organizing himself along the lifecourse by distant goals more than by immediate roles. Today the possible trajectories of development are assumed to be much more numerous and diverse than was allowed for in the standard life-cycle models that posit a fixed sequence of stages of change. There is also new attention to the cumulative effects of experience and of inter-experience. Relations between, say, a mother and son when she is twenty and he is five are not believed to forecast very well how the two will interact when she is eighty and he is sixty-five. Individuals not only age with the decades; despite apparently similar experiences they may continue to grow more and more unique, less and less like their peers. The *new* gerontology of the 1980s postulates that there is less similarity among a group of seventy-year-olds than among a comparable group of twenty-year-olds. Accordingly, research techniques that were standardized upon sophomores in a classroom may go flaccid when used to tap salient dimensions in the personalities and life experiences of senior adults. Lifecourse enquiry has to become more ethnographic, more adapted to the real-time settings of growth, than was permitted by the scientific habits of an earlier psychology.

The overall trend of this re-thinking is not peculiar to the lifecourse outlook; it lines up with tendencies elsewhere in the human sciences today. Examples from psychology are the reaction against concepts of a timeless unconscious or an over-fixed basic personality; from sociology and anthropology they include the reaction against over-socialized concepts of the individual. The trend in lifecourse studies has its counterpart in trends of research on cognition and symbolism, on social networks and social interaction, or on narrative interpretation and cultural phenomenology.

What is special to the lifecourse perspective is its attempt to grasp biography as a whole, so to speak, to perceive patterns in a person's growth and development from cradle to grave. Like other calls for holism, this one has to be taken as an announcement of intentions more than of results. But at the very least the lifecourse outlook is prodding scholars to be cautious about investigating only one stage of life and then projecting long-term trends of development on the basis of what has been observed over a brief interval. Although no empirical study that I know of has actually been able to incorporate and frame the full sweep of the biographical span, a few longitudinal research archives approach that ideal. The Terman study of gifted children, the Oakland-Berkeley growth study, and the Grant study at Harvard have runs of data that now extend from childhood well into the middle years.

One effect of all this is to make the study of lifecourse development less a subject for personality and more a subject for social psychology, a problem of the actions of the self in a sequence of social settings. If social ecology is the study of human action in environments defined by space, perhaps the lifecourse prerspective gives us the beginnings of a social chronology, the study of selfhood in environments defined by time. Such a study seems particularly desirable today, when mass longevity is beginning to transform the whole social chronology of the life cycle much as mass productivity transformed the whole social ecology of property during the Industrial Revolution.

3 Scheduling selfhood

One of the central themes of lifecourse enquiry, then, is the timing of life events. The aim is to explain why a person changes into something different just when he does. Perhaps the development of an organism as a separate entity can be described well enough using a biological model of stages and transitions within the individual. But the development of a social animal has to be described in terms of a collective fabricating of selves, a 'rhetoric of maturity' (Plath 1980) that takes account of how much we shape each other's biography. This is particularly true for the symbol-stuffed animal that is *Homo sapiens*.

The human self is at once an *individual*, a mortal centre of initiative and integrity, and a *person*, a moral actor in society's dramas. Aware of morality, human beings live under a social imperative: to own themselves responsible for a line of consistency in their conduct, connecting behaviour in past settings to their behaviour in future ones. Aware of mortality, we live under an existential imperative: to sustain hope that despite the probability of decline and the certainty of death we nevertheless may achieve

our fair share of the rewards that can come to those who struggle
to be human. While breath remains, we stumble along in limbos
of becoming, trying to reconcile our thrust as a person with our
thrust as an individual (cf. Allport 1955; Burridge 1979).

As we wrestle with these imperatives we preserve the self by
feeding it, so to speak, upon nurturing others and nourishing ideas.
The most significant nurturing others, from a lifecourse point of
view, are our consociates, the people whose lives run close and
parallel to ours, who grow older with us. Here lifecourse enquiry
links up on the micro-social level with studies of interaction, of
networks, of support, or of cycles in family relationships (Hill and
Mattessich 1979). And on wider levels it can link up with studies
of factors that frame the micro-level contexts of action – the
pattern of age stratification in the social system (Riley 1976), or
historical trends that shift the structure of opportunities given to
different age cohorts (Hareven, ed. 1978; Elder 1980).

The most nourishing ideas that we feed upon are those contained
in our cultural schedules, ideas that help us plot where we are in
the confused currents of time so that we can project where we yet
may go. An earlier era might have called this a philosophy of life;
today's anthropologist would call it an ethno-theory of the life
cycle. Here lifecourse enquiry links up most immediately with
studies of age norms (Neugarten, Moore and Lowe 1968), or of
career timetables (Roth 1963), or of the 'cultural phenomenology'
of adulthood and ageing (LeVine 1978). More generally it can link
up with studies of life history (Langness and Frank 1981), or with
studies of cultural models of the person that individuals use in
making sense of their own lives (Geertz 1973; Hallowell 1955;
and Hareven 1978).

The assumption is that vitality in lifecourse development – as in
the snap of humour – is rooted in a keen sense of timing. A person
continues to monitor his position in time. He applies to himself
the battery of chronological measures available in his cultural
heritage; other people also apply these measures to him. His sense
of well-being and self-esteem will hinge upon how well he reconciles
where he temporally is with where he wants to be and where
others want him to be. So long as he continues to move through
the years 'on time', even when traumatic events and radical
changes occur in his life, he may be able to take them in stride.
This is the idea behind the 'predictable crises of adult life'
popularized in Gail Sheehy's *Passages* (1976). It is the unscheduled

crisis that is likely to prove emotionally devastating, possibly raising stress to the point where it results in illness (Neugarten 1979).

'Isn't it rich', goes one verse of the song *Send in the Clowns*, 'isn't it queer – losing my timing this late in my career'. If, as Freud saw it, slips of the tongue are the royal road into understanding the timeless human unconscious, then perhaps slips in timing may be the royal road into understanding the age-bound social scheduling of selfhood. At any rate, in lifecourse research, just as in other social research, it is as important to ask about how people cover their mistakes as it is to ask how they sustain their routines and achieve their successes.

'*Taimingu*' looks to be every bit as essential to self-esteem and self-realization in Japan as it does elsewhere. And the range of possibilities seems no less vast. Let me bracket that range by offering, as examples of the extremes, Yukiko on the one end and Yukio on the other. The reader is probably already familiar with them.

Yukiko is the third Makioka sister, the delicate snowflake of Tanizaki's novel *Sasameyuki*. More a patient than an agent in the shaping of her own life, Yukiko is almost incapable of taking any effective action even though she is over thirty and still single, a serious failure in the timing of marriage. Her family are obliged to mobilize themselves for 500 pages and five *miai* before they are able to correct the problem. Even at that, as she leaves for her wedding she is having attacks of diarrhoea.

At the other extreme is Yukio, the writer Mishima. His *seppuku* was a masterpiece of timing, and years of preparation went into it. For more than a decade he had rigorously toughened himself, proclaiming that after age forty-five the human body is odious. For several years he had trained a private army and had issued calls for a moral rearmament of the nation. He had produced, directed and played the leading role in a film on heroic *seppuku*. Whether or not he believed his 'coup' would succeed, he launched it in his forty-fifth year. As he left home on his way to the Eastern Army Headquarters, where the *seppuku* was staged, he put into the mail to his publisher the last instalment of his four-volume novel (and presumed life's masterwork) *The Sea of Fertility*. The date was 25 November, anniversary of the martyrdom of Yoshida Shōin.

Most Japanese lives are, of course, short of these extremes;

most people muddle along somewhere in the middle. It is their more ordinary or normal schedules of self-development that we particularly want to understand. The group model of Japanese society tends to favour the passive or Yukiko side of selfhood; a lifecourse approach can help balance the view by bringing out the active or Yukio side as well.

4 Arcs – and the growth of subjectivity

By an 'arc' I mean any sequence of connected movements along the timeline of biography. Some arcs are precisely shaped, measured and regulated, as in the linear programme that pushes a student through a series of schools and classes, or the corporation 'escalator' that the *sararīman* is said to ride during his years of employment. But many arcs, perhaps most, are more rubbery: roughly formed pathways, timetables, walks of life, *michi* or *dō*. 'Career' would almost do as a synonym for arc, so long as we understand the concept of a career in its broadest sense. I have learned to be careful with the word, however, because to some people it indicates first and foremost a line of paid employment. To them, speaking of a career of friendship is a contradicton in terms.

What matters most from a lifecourse point of view is that at any moment in time an individual is moving concurrently along several arcs; he is, as it were, marching concurrently to several different drummers. 'If one wishes to apply a timetable analysis to the whole of a person's life', writes Julius Roth (1963: 113),

> he must realize that each person is operating on a number
> of timetables simultaneously. . . . A man may be a parent
> concerned with measuring the development of his children
> in terms of the expectations about child development in his
> social group and at the same time be a professor measuring
> his success in his professional career by reference to the
> expectations of his occupational colleague group. . . . If the
> focus is on individual development, the interactions between
> timetables may be of more interest than the separately
> analyzed career timetables.

The group model of Japanese society obscures the bumping and grinding of timetables in interaction. It encourages us to analyze arcs in their singularity and in their situational separateness. We watch humanity moving past the door of the placement office. The scheduling of events shows up mainly as a problem of damping the turbulent flow of personnel through an organization. It is seen as an organizational problem. The only figure we see is that cheerful robot, the role-dedicated self. The problem of damping the flow of roles in terms of the individual's own scheduling needs slips into the shadows of our vision.

One of the great archetypes of rhythm known to common sense and everyday experience in any high-tech society is that of the commuter. The master beat of his life is the daily shuffle from home to workplace and back again – or, in the years of getting in step with this rhythm, between home and school. However else the routine may function, it segregates intimacy and work into different spaces, perhaps helping to reconcile family time and industrial time. By syncopating motions along different arcs, over the longer stretch we hope to coordinate the quick ripples of productive action with the slower waves of promotions and pay raises, and with the long tides of turnover as generation follows generation in the household.

By way of illustration, consider the junior executives in a public corporation in Tokyo, as reported by Skinner (1983). Most of the higher-ranking positions in the corporation are filled by outsiders from the national ministry that oversees the organization; few men ever reach the top from within. Most employees adjust to the situation in due course. They ordinarily remain loyal, diligent, even proud of their craft; it's just that they find their *ikigai* in aspects of the job other than the opportunities for promotion. A few men, however, retain hopes. And one way to judge a man's hopes, says Skinner, is to watch how long he remains in a low-rent corporation apartment. If he moves out and buys a house of his own fairly early, then he is betting that he will win promotion at least to middle rank. Only those of middle rank or higher will earn, over their working lives, enough money to pay off a mortgage.

For a second illustration, consider family planning, a timing problem than involves tough, intimate decisions about intervals of childbirth and reproduction activities. In a recent study of young salaried couples in Tokyo, Coleman (1983) shows how they carefully space births according to a calculus that takes into account not only the current supply of hands to provide child care but also the husband's long-range earning potential. More than a decade in the future, will the household be able to pay the college expenses of more than one child at a time? The phenomenon is a familiar one. But more often than not as I read studies of Japanese society I find the phenomenon being construed narrowly. It is taken as a problem of reconciling the arcs of movement of two or three persons within a single organization or social arena, most typically in investigations of the family cycle or of the linked careers of a *senpai* and his *kōai* at work.

The problem of how an individual synchronizes his arcs of development through different arenas is, of course, the heart-stuff of biography. In social research, on the other hand, individual dilemmas of timetable conflict do not seem to be taken as a key theme of analysis until the talk turns to 'women's two roles'. And then the tone of discourse frequently takes a turn for the polemic.

If there is ever an Olympic competition for role-dedication, the Japanese might indeed, as is so often alleged, win all the gold medals. This need not imply, as the group model does, that the typical *sararīman* deposits his mind in the corporation safe. I invite you to check this out with my chief consultant on salaryman life, Genji Keita (1972a, 1972b). The more arcs of conduct one examines in the plural, the further our analysis is moved from a single organization or arena, and the greater the need to use concepts of role detachment and self-centering. It is striking that the two most level-headed and sophisticated case studies dealing with arc-conflicts for the person in Japan are focused neither upon work nor upon family, but upon political involvement (Krauss 1973; Pharr 1981). That's an arc of conduct not readily subsumed under a single frame of institutional analysis.

Over-dedication to a role and its allied rhythms of conduct often leaves one tripping on one's own behavioural feet when one enters a new stage of life where the tempo is different. A cliché example is the housewife whose nest has emptied of children only to be filled instead with the constant presence of a pensioned husband. Vogel (n.d.) provides a poignant instance in the life history of a woman she calls Mrs Mieko Suzuki. When Vogel first got to know her, Mrs Suzuki was the classic *okusan*, a skilful household manager and cheerful caretaker of five children and a husband. She was vital and healthy:

. . . always charming and full of fun, never hurting anyone
nor leaving bad feelings in the relationship. Still, she never
let herself be pushed around or talked into doing something
she did not actually decide was in the best interests of her
family. Her purpose was clear. (p. 25)

But by the time Vogel met her again after a hiatus of several years
Mrs Suzuki's children were grown and gone, and her husband was
underfoot day and night.

She was almost toothless and quite emaciated, except for a
very protruding abdomen. Her hair was quite grey, uncurled
and pulled back into a neat but not very becoming knot.
She wore a simple western-style housedress, less elegant
and less flattering to her than her earlier kimonos, partly
because it revealed her skinny arms, her bow legs, and her
'pot belly'. Although she was only 58 years old, she looked
more like 80, certainly much older than her husband who
was 66. . . . Thirty years of raising five children was less
exhausting than four years of everyday care of her husband.
(p. 33)

Those who have a sense of role detachment, on the other hand,
have a reasonable likelihood of evolving new purposes and new
rhythms. The first time a Japanese man said to me, 'I died on 15
August 1945', I wondered if he had a morbid quirk of consciousness. After I had heard the same phrase from several men I began
to recognize it as a rather matter-of-fact idiom. For these men it
was a way of noting that defeat in the war had destroyed one of
the main arcs along which they forecast their lives, an arc leading
to death for the sake of the Emperor. However, as they would go
on to explain, they were able to return home, to pick up other
trajectories, to move on to marry, to support a family, to pursue
civilian occupations. Cook (1983) is conducting an extensive study
of the officers of the former Imperial army and navy. Surely they
should provide a prime example of Japanese role-dedication. Cook
reports that again and again they emphasize to him that they were
gunjin, men with a life-work, not mere 'careerists' grubbing for
pay and promotions. They were serving a cause, not just an
institution.

Perhaps every society has its flower children who are able to move through life in a timeless 'now'. But most of us seem to need long-range goals, master trajectories, so that we can set our shorter arcs of conduct into order. A lifecourse approach directs one to examine these larger timetables as they are conceptualized in Japanese religions, world-views and *jinseiron*; to ask about long-run promises of reward for short-run effort and denial; to discover how people apply these ideas to the scheduling of their lives. If 'deferred gratification' is the great virtue of the middle class, then it ought to be epidemic in a society where 90 per cent of the people identify themselves as being middle class. Japanese cultural conceptions of the lifecourse, then, should encourage a habit of judging the self and its progress against intervals of time that are somehow 'longer' than is usual in other countries.

I can think of tantalizing pieces of evidence that suggest the power of these longer timetables to shape Japanese motivation. Grossberg's (1981) study of attitudes toward dying among elderly people in rural Nara Prefecture suggests that many Japanese are much less disturbed by the thought of personal demise than by worries that their *ie*-line might cease. At the other end of the life cycle are Morsbach's investigations (Morsbach 1974, 1981; Morsbach and Okaki 1969; Morsbach, Yamamoto and Morsbach 1969) of the 'future biographies' written for him by schoolchildren. Compared with those written in the West, those written by Japanese depict fame or success coming to the author much later in life and only after great *kurō*; almost an anti-Cinderella complex. Somewhere in between is Lebra's questionnaire study (1973) of attitudes towards 'compensative justice and moral investment' on the part of Japanese, Koreans and (Hong Kong) Chinese. She remarks at one point in her report that 'Japanese may be as success-oriented as Chinese, but constrained by the priority of the inner quality of man over an external successful outcome and by a long-ranged view of a human career' (p. 289). Hints only, these little examples. But if 'it is goals rather than roles that organize career activity' (LeVine 1978:2) in a lifecourse perspective, and if my hunch is right that Japanese put the self and its goals on a wider scale in time (though perhaps narrower in space), then we may find that Japanese diligence is motivated by a rather strong self-awareness and subjectivity.

5 Circles – and the growth of dependability

As each of us cultivates a separate subjectivity, so too does each of us cultivate a separate circle of intimates who shape our life's tendencies as we shape theirs. If arcs make long-term continuity possible in our individual activities, circles do the same for our human relationships: they make long engagements possible (Plath 1980).

Neugarten (1976:16) describes the process as follows:

> An individual becomes a socio-emotional 'institution' with the passage of time. Not only do certain personality processes provide continuity, but the individual has built up around him a network of social relationships that supports and maintains him. The 'institutional' quality involves an individuated pattern of strategies for dealing with the changing world within and without, strategies that transcend many of the intra-psychic changes and (social) losses that occur.   (1965:16)

In recent lifecourse writings the buzz word for this phenomenon is 'convoy of social support', but the word support has to be construed in special ways. Others in a person's convoy or circle may not always provide him with 'support' in the usual sense of the word. But taken together, the others in a circle define the self as a unique person; no other human engages exactly the same set of partners. The circle thus assures the self of its 'capacity to be missed' in society and guarantees the self its 'improbabilities' and idiosyncrasies (Henry 1973:32). The death of a partner can take away an important element of one's own being. We may suffer as severely from the loss of a hated enemy as from the loss of a supportive friend.

Furthermore, partners to these long engagements are interdependent; the 'support' must flow both ways though it need not be in some balanced reciprocity. A person has to 'find himself' socially by integrating his circle, taking the evaluations and demands put upon him by his partners and bringing them into a workable coordination. From a scheduling point of view this means that he must synchronize his tempos of growth with theirs. He has a 'developmental stake' in his partners (Bengtson and Kuypers 1971) because if they get off-schedule in their life events he may be thrown off schedule in his. As Keith Brown would say, it takes three generations to produce one grandmother.

As an 'institution', then, a circle is a personalized institution, self-oriented and self-dependent. It is not a corporate institution like an *ie* or like Mitsui Shōji. It has no table of organization, no origin myth, no functions apart from its involvement in the course of one person's life. (In a limiting case it might evolve into a quasi-formal structure, as did Mishima's private army – which, apparently, disbanded after his suicide.) A person must continue to nurture his circle if it is to continue nurturing him. To be able to do this he must cultivate social skills that are not given at birth. He must acquire the ability to care for others in terms of what they need, not just selfishly in terms of what he wants. Others' needs and schedules hinge upon where *they* are – the 'developmental tasks' they are confronting – on their several stages of biography. So the self must gain not only in emotional capacity for caring, it must also gain in cognitive capacity for judging. It must understand the arcs of social chronology and where people fit into them. In a word, the self must mature in dependability.

The group model brings out some features of connectedness in Japanese social relations but fails to bring out this person-centred interdependence of a self and its partners maturing together, this developmental course of relationships. With its basic postulate of 'absolute dedication to a limited human nexus' the group model alerts us to pervasive themes in Japanese consciousness. Themes, for example, of humanity-as-relatedness (*ningen*), or of that 'craving for close contact' which is one of Doi's definitions of *amae* (1973:74). But once again the Yukiko image gets in the way; fascinated with the self as a fragile blossom, the group model fails to distinguish between normal hungers for human attention and pathological cravings for *kahogo*. Fascinated with the depths of dependency, the model never even deals with its reciprocal: somebody else has to have learned how to give personal attention before the actor being studied can begin to avail himself or herself of it.

A lifecourse approach can perhaps help us counteract these biases in the group model. It shows us a view of the self and its circle of partners engaged in long-term co-biography. Within this cluster, each partnership has its own arc of developmental opportunities. Not only is there shared experience; there is also a cumulative feeding back of experience into the relationships. Brothers may become best friends, a *yome* and a *shūtome* become colleagues. Partners come to play batteries of roles mutually, perhaps not relating as 'whole' persons but certainly relating in a discourse more rich and many-layered than that predicted by the clichés of role norms.

These arcs of co-experience are enormously diverse in onset, duration and outcome. Charting the galaxy of these co-experiences even for a short segment of one person's life is an exercise in social astronomy. Some relationships may be given at birth, but even these need to be cultivated in order to endure: witness the worries lately over the *jōhatsu mama* or the fears that the elderly are being discarded in a twentieth-century version of *obasuteyama*.

Partnerships that arise after birth need to be timed to begin in an appropriate season: the *kekkon tekireiki* is only the most often noted instance. There are, for example, optimal periods for cultivating protégés in one's craft, or for serving as a marital go-between. The *nakōdo* couple needs to be mature enough to stand as a model of a good, stable marriage but, at the same time, young enough to take a long-term interest in the success of the new marriage they are sponsoring.

Friendship is a particularly telling instance. Though a friendship could evolve at any time in life, the later it begins the less it can contain by way of co-experience. It could begin very early, the outgrowth of relations with a childhood playmate. But given the space-mobility of modern life – going away to school or in marriage or for employment – relations formed in childhood tend to be brittle. The critical season is in adolescence and early adulthood, when one is moving beyond the narrower arenas of home and neighbourhood and beginning to sharpen one's skill for nurturing new relationships. Afterward, amid the many demands of adult life, opportunities for striking up deep friendships will drastically diminish.

Kikuchi Kan's short story 'On the Conduct of Lord Tadanao' (1962) is an example of timing-failure in this regard. At one point in the story a *daimyō* realizes that nobody has ever treated him as a person, only as a lord:

> He had never known even the sympathy extended to a
> friend. From his childhood days numbers of page boys of
> his own age had been selected to keep him company. But

they had not associated with Lord Tadanao as friends. They
had merely offered submission.   (p. 130)

Friends can form a vital 'convoy of social support' when the self
must cope with the feelings of loneliness and uselessness that often
come in the later years. As the farmers of Suye told Embree
(1938:190) years ago, in old age '*dōnen* become closer than a wife'.

A few pages ago I suggested that perhaps Japanese conceptions
of human development measure the self against unusually long
spans of time. Might this also be so – and here is my second hunch
or hypothesis for comparative study – of Japanese conceptions of
the development of relationships?

Again I can only offer hints and impressions. But the Japanese
archetype of human growth (to put this oversimply for brevity's
sake) seems to give first priority to the cultivation of emotional
capacities for relatedness. What is special about that 'critter' called
Homo sapiens is not his capacity to 'know' – a notion that
perhaps has a Western bias – but his capacity for spontaneity,
responsiveness, tears and laughter, an ability to react to others.
Pelzel (1970) has pointed out that there are elements of such a
view already in the earliest Japanese mythology. In the primordial
worlds of the *Kojiki* and the *Nihongi* a lot of flora and fauna
also had human-like talents for sentience and spontaneity. This,
however, made for too much booming confusion. So civilization
was created, though not as in some origin myths by inventing
agriculture or discovering how to smelt iron; it was created by
damping the noise from the infra-human 'critters' and reserving
the lord's share of emotionality for humankind.

What is special about an individual of the species, then, is not
the ability to respond – that's built in – but what he learns to do
with that ability. His lifelong struggle as a person is to carry out
his obligations to others while augmenting – or at least not
diminishing – his ability to care for them responsively. The great
fear is that one may fail to elicit *ninjō* from others, and then be
blocked from cultivating one's own capacities for *ninjō* any further.
Moreover, mere physical death does not put an end to the need
for personal attention. The departed remain here spiritually, able
to continue daily rapport with family and friends. In this sense,
exclusion is a fate worse than death. For whether in this world or
another, without a circle of intimates to attend to one's human
integrity, it is in peril.

I am intrigued by pieces of evidence that can be culled from two recent studies that, in different ways, compare Americans and Japanese. The first study (Caudill and Schooler 1969) asked about reasons that are given for involuntarily placing a person in a mental hospital. What types of behaviour proved so threatening? The overall array of reasons is broadly similar on both sides of the Pacific. But Americans will cite, more often than Japanese do, 'bizarre ideas' or 'cognitive disorientation' as aberrations serious enough to require hospitalization. Japanese, on the other hand, will more often report that 'aggressive action' proved too upsetting.

In the second study (Kusatsu 1977), men in Japan and the United States were asked to rank their preferences for eighteen values (such as equality, pleasure, wisdom and so on). Again, there were many cross-cultural similarities: 'a world at peace', 'family security' and 'freedom' were among the top choices East and West. However, American men gave much higher priority than Japanese men did to 'national security', 'salvation', 'sense of accomplishment' and 'wisdom'. Japanese men saw much more significance in 'pleasure', 'an exciting life', 'mature love' and 'true friendship' (part II, p. 105). I wonder whether the American archetype, in short, urges the self to think straight and be secure, whereas the Japanese archetype favours a self that can feel human in the company of others? Such an extrapolation may be too sweeping a generalization. But even if it is only partly right, what might we predict – in broad comparison – about the difficulties that Americans and Japanese may have in adjusting to a world of mass longevity?

6   Spheres – and the growth of mastery

Along with a sense of timing and a circle of partners we also cultivate a 'sphere' of ideas and symbols that shape our feeling of being whole. This is a third long engagement, a dialectic between our life's events and the meaning we construe in those events. To borrow existentialist phrasing: across the years we move from the self we 'were' when the *monogokoro* of consciousness first appeared, on towards the self we are 'meant to be'. As arcs do for behaviour, and circles for relationships, spheres provide continuity for our identity.

With the growing of awareness each of us evolves a 'theory of oneself' (Brim, 1976). We take the life-giving myths, the nourishing ideas that are customary in our environment, and we customize or tailor them to our individual form. We spin a web of ideas that places the self within a world-view framed by our cultural heritage. Neither ideology nor religion in the public sense, though composed largely of collective representations in the public domain, this web of ideas is our personal philosophy of life.

If a circle assures us of the capacity to be missed socially, a sphere assures us that the self has something unique to be or to do in the world. 'There is a mission that only I can accomplish' was the way my interviewees in the Hanshin region would put it. Losing a piece of that sphere of significance, or finding part of it closed off, can be as painful as losing a friend. There is a sense in which these symbols of meaning become friends, as friends come to signify who we are. We have a developmental stake in both, a responsibility towards their integrity and preservation; although our dialogue with a circle of partners is a process quite different from our dialectic with a sphere of ideas.

As part of ordinary maturity and ageing we evolve an ever-better, more articulate 'theory': we reflect back over what we have experienced and put it into order mentally. We also tend to gain more confidence in it, increasing mastery of it, whether or not we ever formally deliberate on it. Lifecourse scholars speak of 'a stabilizing of age identity' (White, 1966) or a strengthening of 'integrity' (Erikson, 1955) as normal products of adulthood; Neugarten (1970: 78) refers to a 'conscious self-utilisation' that emerges in contrast to the 'self-consciousness of youth'. My middle-aged interviewees in the Hanshin used the word '*atsukamashisa*'. Without healthy self-mastery, on the other hand, growth is distorted, has no *marumi*, as seen in the pathologies of *amae* that are the subject of Doi's investigations. 'A man who has a *jibun* is capable of checking *amae*', writes Doi (1973: 19), 'while a man who is at the mercy of *amae* has no *jibun.*'

This growth of sophistication in the use of the local symbols, this expanding individuation, falls through the holes of any group model. The latter's concern is with socialization instead, with how people become more alike. But this leaves us with quite a problem. Japan's heritage of norms of social obligation may muffle the strength of individuation, whereas Japan's aesthetic heritage tends to encourage 'conscious self-utilization'. We see this, for example, in the prominence given to the acquisition of 'centering' or 'one-pointedness' in disciplines such as Buddhist meditation or the Tea Aesthetic or the martial arts. One finds such an array of different prescriptions for mastery in the domains and pathways of the symbol system as to defy simple summary. Some of the vocabularies are more manifestly artistic in their attention to the tangible expressions of mastery. Others are more evidently religious or spiritual or psychological in their attention to masterful states of being: offering what Rohlen (1978) has phrased as 'the promise of adulthood in Japanese spiritualism'.

There is a prodigious amount of research in the humanities on the material products of artistry and on articulations of the spiritual heritage. The difficulty, in terms of lifecourse analysis, lies in moving from these public recipes for mastery as collective representations to their fabrication into a sphere around the ordinary self. I can think of some studies that make a start in this direction; no doubt others will occur to the reader. An artist's work can be read, for example, as a commentary on his own life's events, as in the case study of three modern novelists provided by De Vos (1973: ch. 18). Morris (1975) has a fascinating monograph on 'noble failure' as a pattern of self-completion that he argues has been much admired and emulated through Japanese history. Lifton, Katō and Reich (1978: 15) scrutinize six famous figures from modern history, and ask whether the way a man died was an expression of the way that he organized how he lived, his 'means of perpetuating important cultural principles'. And in an earlier study, Lifton (1967) analyzed ordinary people – though in an extraordinary circumstance – asking how the survivors of Hiroshima have gone on to reformulate the meaning of death in their lives. Another study that is based on ordinary lives is Tsurumi's report (1970) on the *seikatsu tsuzurikata undō* and the women in it who 'compose' their lives by writing them out in compositions.

Ultimately, as we get nearer to a full version of lifecourse analysis, we may begin to track these arcs of self-symbol elaboration as they feed back into self-partner cultivation, showing how partners shape not only each other's experience but what that experience means as co-biography.

As with arcs and circles so with spheres: the Japanese traditions of self-mastery seem to encourage the long-range view. Rohlen (1978: 145) puts the case strongly:

What is significant in Japanese spiritualism is the promise itself, for it clearly lends meaning, integrity and joy to many lives, especially as the nature of adult existence unfolds. It fits the physical process of ageing. It recognizes the inherent value of experience. It gives strong witness to the importance of a lifelong effort to retain and develop personal integrity. . . . Here is a philosophy seemingly made for adulthood – giving it stature, movement, and optimism.

This brings me to my third theme for a comparative study. The Industrial Revolution dealt a double blow to Euro-American values favouring long-range self-completion. Secularism and scientism sapped the religious promise that one could come of age in an afterlife; faith in material progress stigmatized old age as obsolescence. 'Grey hair', in the words of an anonymous American writer early in our century, is 'an unforgivable witness of industrial inbecility' (quoted from Achenbaum 1978: 48). The new geronto-logy and the mood of lifecourse rethinking over the past decade may be an indication that the West is discovering new potentials for maturity as the potentials of progress grey with pollution. I think of examples such as a recent book with the title *Aging, Death and the Completion of Being* (Van Tassel 1979). Has the 'promise of adulthood' been durable enough that Japanese have escaped industrialism's shock to lifecourse optimism? Or are *pokkuri shinkō* and the unusually high rates of suicide among the elderly to be interpreted as signs that the shock has only begun to be felt?

7 Concluding remarks

The preceding discussion has advanced three arguments. The first argument is that lifecourse thinking in the West is dominated by an entity or particle model of development; we badly need a relational or field model. To borrow Hsu's phrasing (1971: 34), the West holds a Ptolemian view that puts the individual at the centre of the universe. What is wanted is a Galilean view, one that sees the self 'as part of a set of relationships with no assured starring role'. The locus of change then is 'not in the individual [personality] but in the circle of human beings, ideas and things in which he maintains intimacy'.

The second proposition is that much of the Japanese heritage of ideas about lifecourse is essentially Galilean. However, it has been phrased in idioms of aesthetics and spiritualism that are not all that easy to translate into the vocabulary of social science; indeed, it is an expression which could potentially inform if not transform that vocabulary. It seems to me that Ruth Benedict caught a good deal of this Galilean outlook in *The Chrysanthemum and the Sword*, but it was the notions of guilt and shame that caught her readers. As I count them, only four of the book's 300 pages deal with guilt and shame. For nearly half of the book what she offers is an exposition of Japanese forms of self-discipline, self-respect, and the dilemmas of virtue brought on by a never-ending need to reconcile the claims of others in one's circle of human attachments.

The third statement is that the structuralist models of Japanese groupism which have been in vogue for twenty years have not captured the Galilean outlook very well at all. I've used the cliché 'group model' in these pages as a device to help in presenting my own conceptual preferences. But this was not done in a silly spirit of demolition: structural models are of course powerful tools when one wants to explain some kinds of phenomena. Perhaps a creative theorist could manage to incorporate a Galilean dimension into the structuralist paradigm. Instead of starting with verticality or hierarchy – notions that are static – one might start with the concept of seniority. The slight change in orientation would lead one from a static to a dynamic structure and, perhaps, to the addition of a lifecourse time dimension to one's model of Japanese society.

There is an impulse behind the arguments: a concern with the challenge that mass longevity raises for our understanding of human co-biography. It is a concern underlined some time ago by Mills (1959: 165):

> The climax of the social scientist's concern with history is the idea he comes to hold of the epoch in which he lives. The climax of his concern with biography is the idea he comes to hold of man's basic nature, and of the limits it may set to the transformations of man by the course of history.

References

Achenbaum, W. Andrew
   1978   *Old Age in the New Land, The American Experience since 1970*
           (Baltimore, Md., and London: Johns Hopkins University Press).
Allport, Gordon W.
   1955   *Becoming* (New Haven: Yale University Press).
Baltes, Paul B. (ed.).
   1978   *Life-span Development and Behavior*, vol. I (New York:
           Academic Press).
Baltes, Paul B.; and Orville G. Brim, Jr. (eds)
   1979   *Life-span Development and Behavior*, vols. II and III (New
           York: Academic Press).
Bengtson, Vern L.; and Kuypers, J. A.
   1971   'Generational Differences and the Developmental Stake', *Aging
           and Human Development*, vol. 2, 249–60.
Brim, Orville G., Jr.
   1976   'Lifespan Development of the Theory of Oneself: Implications
           for Child Development', in *Advances in Child Development and
           Behavior*, edited by H. W. Rees and L. P. Lipsitt (New York:
           Academic Press), 241–51.
Burridge, Kenelm
   1979   *Someone, No One: an Essay on Individuality* (Princeton, NJ:
           Princeton University Press).
Caudill, William; and Schooler, Carmi
   1969   'Symptom Patterns and Background Characteristics of Japanese
           Psychiatric Patients', in *Mental Health Research in Asia and the
           Pacific*, edited by W. Caudill and T. Lin (Honolulu, Hi: University
           of Hawaii Press).
Coleman, Samuel C.
   1983   'The Tempos of Family Formation', in *Work and Lifecourse in
           Japan*, edited by David Plath (Albany, NY: State University of
           New York Press), ch. 9.
Cook, Theodore F., Jr.
   1983   'Cataclysm and Career Rebirth: the Prewar Military Elite', in
           Work and Lifecourse in Japan, edited by David Plath (Albany, NY:
           State University of New York Press), ch. 10.
De Vos, George A.
   1973   *Socialization for Achievement: Essays on the Cultural Psychology
           of the Japanese* (Berkeley and Los Angeles, Cal.: University of
           California Press).
Doi, Takeo
   1973   *The Anatomy of Dependence*, translated by John Bestor (Tokyo:
           Kodansha International).

Elder, Glen H., Jr.
  1980 'History and the Life Course', in *Biography and Society*, edited
        by Daniel Bertaux (Beverly Hills, Cal.: Sage Publications).
Embree, John F.
  1938 *Suye Mura, a Japanese Village* (Chicago, Ill.: University of
        Chicago Press).
Erikson, Erik H.
  1955 *Childhood and Society* (New York: W. W. Norton).
Geertz, Clifford
  1973 'Person, time and conduct in Bali', in *The Interpretation of
        Cultures* (New York: Basic Books), ch. 14.
Genji, Keita
  1972a *The Guardian God of Golf, and Other Humorous Stories*,
         translated by Hugh Cortazzi (Tokyo: The Japan Times).
  1972b *The Ogre, and Other Stories of the Japanese Salaryman*,
         translated by Hugh Cortazzi (Tokyo: The Japan Times).
Grossberg, John B.
  1981 'Formulating Attitudes Towards Death: a Study of Elderly
        Japanese Jodo Shin Buddhists', Doctoral dissertation. Urbana, Ill.:
        Department of Anthropology, University of Illinois at Urbana-
        Champaign.
Hallowell, A. Irving
  1955 'The Self and its Behavioral Environment', in *Culture and
        Experience* (Philadelphia, Pa.: University of Pennsylvania Press),
        ch. 5.
Hamaguchi, Eshun
  1979 *Nihonjin ni Totte Kyariā to wa* (The Meaning of Career for
        Japanese) (Tokyo: Nihon Keizai Shinbunsha).
  1980 'Nihonjin no Rentai-teki Jiritsu-sei' (The 'Associatedness' of
        the Japanese Self) *Gendai no Esupurii*, no. 160, 127–40.
Hareven, Tamara
  1978 'The Search for Generational Memory: Tribal Rites in Industrial
        Society', *Daedalus*, vol. 107, no. 4 (Fall), 137–49.
Hareven, Tamara (ed.)
  1978 *Transitions: the Family and Life Course in Historical Perspective*
        (New York: Academic Press).
Henry, Jules
  1973 'Personality and Ageing, with Special Reference to Hospitals
        for the Aged Poor', in *On Sham, Vulnerability and Other Forms of
        Self-Destruction* (New York: Vintage), ch. 2.
Hill, Reuben; and Mattessich, Paul
  1979 'Family development theory and life-span development', in
        Life-span Development and Behavior, vol. 2, edited by Paul B.
        Baltes and Orville G. Brim (New York: Academic Press), 162–204.

Hsu, Francis L. K.
1971 'Psychosocial Homeostasis and *Jen*: Conceptual Tools for
Advancing Psychological Anthropology", *American Anthropologist*,
vol. 73, no. 1 (Feb.), 23–44.
Kikuchi, Kan
1962 'On the Conduct of Lord Tadanao', translated by Geoffrey
Sargeant in *Modern Japanese Stories*, edited by Ivan Morris
(Rutland, Vt. and Tokyo: Tuttle), 102–37.
Kraus, Ellis S.
1974 *Radicals Revisited: Student Protest in Postwar Japan* (Berkeley
and Los Angeles, Cal.: University of California Press).
Kusatsu, Osamu
1977 'Ego Development and Sociocultural Process in Japan',
Keizaigaku Kiyō, no. 3, part I, 47–109; no. 3, part II, 74–128.
Langness, L. L.; and Frank, Gelya
1981 *Lives, an Anthropological Approach to Biography* (Novato,
Cal.: Chandler and Sharp).
Lebra, Takie S.
1973 'Compensative Justice and Moral Investment among Japanese,
Chinese and Koreans', *Journal of Nervous and Mental Disease*, vol.
157, no. 4 (Oct.), 278–91.
LeVine, Robert A.
1978 'Adulthood and Aging in Cross-Cultural Perspective', *Social
Science Research Council Items*, vols. 31/32 (March), 1–5.
Lifton, Robert J.
1967 *Death in Life: Survivors of Hiroshima* (New York: Random
House).
Lifton, Robert J.; Katō, Shūichi; and Reich, Michael
1978 *Six Lives Six Deaths; Portraits from Modern Japan* (New Haven,
Conn.: Yale University Press).
Mills, C. Wright
1959 *The Sociological Imagination* (New York: Oxford University
Press).
Morris, Ivan
1975 *The Nobility of Failure: Tragic Heroes in the History of Japan*
(New York: New American Library).
Morsbach, Helmut
1974 'How Adolescents View Their Future – a Comparison Between
Japan and Western Countries', *Proceedings of the 20th International
Congress of Psychology, 1972* (Tokyo: Science Council of Japan),
246.
1981 'Ganbare! – Socio-psychological Aspects of Persistence in
Japan', *Perspectives on Japan* (London Information Centre,
Japanese Embassy), vol. 3, 24–32.

Morsbach, Helmut; and Okaki, C.
  1969 'A Cross-Cultural Study of Future Expectations and Aspirations
        among Adolescent Girls', *Proceedings of the 8th International
        Congress of Anthropological and Ethnological Sciences* (Tokyo),
        381–5.
Morsbach, Helmut; Yamamoto, K.; and Morsbach, G.
  1969 'Future Planning: a Comparative Study between Japanese and
        American Boys', *Educational Studies* (International Christian
        University), vol. 14, 181–99.
Neugarten, Bernice
  1965 'Personality Changes in the Aged', *Catholic Psychological
        Review*, vol. 3, 9–17.
  1970 'Dynamics of Transition from Middle Age to Old Age:
        Adaptation and the Life-Cycle', *Journal of Geriatric Psychiatry*,
        vol. 4, 71–87.
  1979 'Time, Age, and the Life Cycle', *American Journal of Psychiatry*,
        vol. 136, no. 7 (July), 887–94.
Neugarten, Bernice; Moore, Joan W.; and Lowe, John C.
  1968 'Age Norms, Age Constraints, and Adult Socialization', in
        Middle Age and Aging, edited by Bernice Neugarten (Chicago, Ill.:
        University of Chicago Press), ch. 2.
Pelzel, John C.
  1970 'Human Nature in the Japanese Myths', in *Personality in
        Japanese History*, edited by Albert D. Craig and Donald H. Shiveley
        (Berkeley and Los Angeles, Cal.: University of California Press),
        ch. 1.
Pharr, Susan J.
  1981 *Political Women in Japan: the Search for a Place in Political
        Life* (Berkeley and Los Angeles, Cal.: University of California
        Press).
Plath, David W.
  1980 *Long Engagements; Maturity in Modern Japan* (Stanford, Cal.:
        Stanford University Press).
Plath, David W. (ed.)
  1983 *Work and Lifecourse in Japan* (Albany, NY: State University
        of New York Press).
Project on Human Potential
  n.d. *Project description* (Cambridge, Mass.: Harvard University,
        Graduate School of Education).
  1981 *Draft Summary of Bernard Van Leer Project on Human
        Potential, Workshop on United States and Japanese Perspectives on
        Potential*. Compiled by Lois Taniuchi, Merry White, and Susan
        Pollak (Cambridge, Mass.: Harvard University, Graduate School of
        Education).

Riley, Matilda W.
1976   'Age Strata in Social Systems', in *Handbook of Aging and the Social Sciences*, edited by R. H. Binstock and Ethel Shanas (New York: Van Nostrand), 189–217.

Rohlen, Thomas P.
1978   'The Promise of Adulthood in Japanese Spiritualism', in *Adulthood*, edited by Erik Erikson (New York: W. W. Norton), 129–47.

Roth, Julius A.
1963   *Timetables: Structuring the Passage of Time in Hospital Treatment and Other Careers* (Indianapolis and New York: Bobbs-Merrill).

Sheehy, Gail
1976   *Passages: Predictable Crises of Adult Life* (New York: E. P. Dutton).

Skinner, Kenneth A.
1983   'Aborted Careers in a Public Corporation', in *Work and Lifecourse in Japan*, edited by David Plath (Albany, NY: State University of New York Press), ch. 3.

Tsurumi, Kazuko
1970   *Social Change and the Individual: Japan Before and After Defeat in World War II* (Princeton, NJ: Princeton University Press).

Van Tassel, David D.
1979   *Aging, Death and the Completion of Being* (Philadelphia, Pa.: University of Pennsylvania Press).

Vogel, Suzanne
n.d.   'Woman as Mother, the Story of Mrs Suzuki', unpublished.

White, Robert W.
1966   *Lives in Progress* (New York: Holt, Rinehart and Winston).

Chapter Three
Some Conditions for QC Circles: Long-term Perspectives in the Behaviour of Individuals

Koike Kazuo

1   Introduction

It has often been posited that the Japanese worker is group-oriented. That assertion is examined in this paper. It is argued that the behaviour of Japanese workers can be better explained by reference to their economic interests. We will approach that assertion by examining behaviour which has been alleged to be the product of a group-orientation. By explaining the alleged group behaviour of workers with variables other than those associated with the notion of groupism, a basis will be established for criticizing the common assertions about the the group orientation of the Japanese worker.

Various kinds of behaviour can be observed at the place of work; this paper focuses on the activities which take place within QC circles. A QC circle is a small group formed by about ten individuals. The group considers and implements ideas about how production-related operations are organized on the shop floor.

The QC circle has come to be widely used at many places of work in present-day Japan, and is seen as being one source of Japan's economic competitiveness. Why focus on the activities of QC circles? Why not focus more directly on what workers are thinking? I wish to begin the discussion by considering these two questions.

A   Some observed similarities

Although it is possible to obtain the views of workers about a variety of matters directly by using an opinion survey, in order to bring out the features found in a particular country, some kind of international comparison is necessary. Although there are obviously great difficulties in making any international comparison, the difficulties are particularly pronounced when one relies only on written questionnaires. It is often the case that the same word in two languages actually means quite different things because of the extensive range of complex nuances which characterize most words. Moreover, even when respondents are referring to the same phenomena, they often use different words.

For these reasons, there are not very many comparative studies with usable results. Perhaps the study in the early 1960s by Whitehill and Takezawa (1968) is the only one which comes readily to mind with regard to the motivations and value orientations of Japanese and American workers. They administered surveys to about 1,000 production workers in four large, unionized firms each in Japan and in the United States. A written questionnaire of exactly the same thirty questions was administered to workers in both countries, and for that reason the study has provided us with a valuable set of data. In reporting on their analysis, the authors emphasized strongly the differences which exist between the thinking of the workers in each country.

However, if we put aside the interpretations of Whitehill and Takezawa and take a closer, dispassionate look at their data, the similarities between the two national samples are quite striking. Unlike the approach adopted by the two original authors, for this study the thirty questions were grouped into five categories: (1) those related to work, (2) those related to employment security, (3) those related to democracy on the shop floor, (4) those related to wages, and (5) those related to welfare benefits provided by the employer and to the workers' lives away from work.

The questions on which the views of American and Japanese

workers were most different are concentrated in the fourth and fifth categories. The questions in the fifth category can be broken down into two sub-groupings: (a) those concerning the workers' daily life style, and (b) the others concerned with welfare. The first asked about the role of one's supervisor when one got married. The other asked about whether a worker would give up his seat to his boss on a crowded bus. These questions yielded clear cross-cultural differences. Also, among the questions related to welfare was one which asked about the role of the company with regard to employee housing. One look at the answers suggests a big difference. In Japan many employees desired company housing whereas in America they look to the company for assistance in obtaining a housing loan. However, if we consider the differences in the housing situation in the two countries, can we really say that the difference in the way Japanese and American workers responded is so great? The important point is that in both countries it is expected that the company will assist the employee with one of his personal problems (namely, obtaining a home). On the basis of a difference in form only, can we say that the expectations of the Americans are not similar to those of the Japanese workers?

The fourth group of questions (concerning wages) deal with bonuses and family allowances. There are performance premiums in the USA for producing more than a set standard, but not the periodical lump-sum payments found in Japan. Also, family allowances are minimal in America, if paid at all. It is thus quite obvious that the answers to such questions will be different in the two countries. In general, the differences seem to appear when the questions are about the obviously different life styles or when they touch upon aspects of the systems or institutions which are different. However, this is different from saying that the value orientations of the workers in the two countries are different.

If we look at the questions concerning work and employment, we find that there is a surprising amount of agreement. In the next few paragraphs, the responses to one sample question each from groups (1), (2) and (3) are presented as examples which will show the extent to which such agreement exists.

Table 3.1 shows the responses to a question about decision making at work. It can be seen as being a question both about how work is carried out and about the relationship between a supervisor and those under his supervision. The most common proposition about work in the two countries is that in group-oriented Japan the supervisor would consult frequently with those under his supervision, whereas in individualistic America the lines of authority would be clearly defined and the supervisor would simply make the decision himself. However, a look at the results in the table shows that the distribution of answers was about the same in both countries. The largest number by far indicated that the supervisor should first consult with workers. The next largest group also said the supervisor should consult with the workers after the decision was made.

From the second group of questions about employment security is one on how the employment effects of new technology should

Table 3.1 *Views of American and Japanese Workers on the Organization of Work and Supervisor Communications with Workers under His Supervision*

When changes in work methods must be made, I think a supervisor should:	All respondents (%)		Subgroups: sex and age (%)							
	USA	Japan	USA				Japan			
			M	F	Y	O	M	F	Y	O
1 allow workers to decide for themselves what changes should be made and how to make them;	3	2	5	2	5	4	2	2	3	1
2 first ask workers for their suggestions regarding proposed changes, and then decide what to do;	66	73	73	60	74	72	74	72	77	72
3 first decide on the changes, and then ask for the cooperation of the workers;	22	21	16	27	15	17	21	21	17	24
4 decide himself what the changes shall be and put them into effect, since he is in charge of the work.	9	4	6	11	6	7	3	5	3	3

Notes: M = Male, F = Female, Y = Young, O = Old.
Source: Whitehill and Takezawa (1968), p. 180.

be dealt with when labour is made redundant (Table 3.2). It is often said that one manifestation of the Japanese worker's group orientation is lifetime employment and employment security.

However, the data in the Table 3.2 again show that there is very little difference at all between the two samples. In fact, one could say that American workers are more concerned with job security than their Japanese counterparts. In both samples, half of the respondents indicated that workers should be guaranteed employment until retirement, but a quarter of the American sample, contrasted against only 7 per cent of the Japanese sample, indicated that redundant workers should be given up to a year to find another job.

Table 3.2 *Views of American and Japanese Workers on Job Security and Redundancy owing to the Introduction of New Technology*

When a young production worker's job is taken over by a labour-saving machine, management should:	All respondents (%)		Subgroups: sex and age (%)							
	USA	Japan	USA				Japan			
			M	F	Y	O	M	F	Y	O
1 continue his employment, even if in maintenance or office work, until he retires or dies;	48	50	61	37	59	61	59	42	66	52
2 continue his employment, even if in maintenance or office work, for as long as one year so that he may look for another job;	25	7	18	31	17	19	7	7	6	7
3 continue his employment only when there is work available similar to his old job;	16	38	13	19	14	12	28	46	23	35
4 terminate his employment and help him find a job with another company.	11	5	8	13	10	8	6	5	5	6

Source: Whitehill and Takezawa (1968), p. 143.

As for the group of questions concerning industrial democracy at work and unionism, the question in Table 3.3 concerns union-organized strikes. It is often said that Japanese workers are closely tied to their firm and feel little loyalty for unions which go against the firm. But again, the findings suggest that there is very little difference between the two national samples. In both countries 29 per cent of the sample said they would actively support their leaders and go on strike even if they felt the strike was unjustified. The similarities also extend to the frequency with which the other answers were chosen.

Table 3.3 *A Comparison of the Attitudes of Japanese and American Workers concerning Union-Organized Strikes*

If the union calls a strike which you do not think is justified, and you have no fear of retaliation by the union or management, would you:	All respondents (%)		Subgroups: sex and age (%)							
	USA	Japan	USA				Japan			
			M	F	Y	O	M	F	Y	O
1 continue work and actively support management's position;	11	18	9	15	8	10	15	21	9	21
2 continue work but give no other support to management's position;	19	19	18	22	13	22	20	18	19	21
3 stop work but otherwise not actively participate in the strike;	41	34	39	46	39	39	31	37	32	31
4 stop work and actively support the position of your elected union representatives?	29	29	34	19	40	29	34	24	40	27

Source: Whitehill and Takezawa (1968), p. 332.

Whitehill and Takezawa argue that the similarities which appeared in their data were simply an accident. According to their view, the same answers are produced for very different reasons. However, the similarities are striking and cannot be ignored. Our next step is to look carefully for behaviour which is clearly different. Is there a difference in behaviour which arises out of a difference in social values such as the alleged groupism of the Japanese and the alleged individualism of Americans? Or is it possible that both groups of workers share the same values and ways of thinking about things, but that they behave differently because of some other intervening variable such as the objective conditions in which workers find themselves? This background to understanding and to interpreting behaviour, and answers to these kinds of questionnaires need to be considered very carefully.

B   Some 'Japanese' phenomena

Many phenomena have been said to be particularly 'Japanese' or said to be an expression of particularly Japanese groupism. Such phenomena can be sorted into three groups. One type consists of (a) allegedly Japanese phenomena which can be found in other societies if one takes the trouble to look, and (b) phenomena which did not exist in Japan in the past.

The 'three sacred treasures' (*sanshu no shingi*) are often cited as being the mainspring of industrial relations in Japan. The three are life-time employment, seniority wages and enterprise unionism. They provide a good example of this type of 'phenomena'. According to the familiar explanation, if the firm can guarantee the employee's daily living expenses through the seniority wage system and life-time employment, then there is a firm base for the enterprise union. This style of industrial relations is often put forth as a peculiarly Japanese trait. However, to draw such a conclusion, one would expect those arguing the case to have solid data, for example, on wages by age for a wide range of countries in Europe and North America. However, such data did not become available until the mid-1970s when the first results of the European Community's *Wage Structure Survey* (which has been administered only from 1972) were published. Nevertheless, even before those data became available, people were arguing (without any firm statistical basis) that seniority wages were a peculiarly Japanese phenomena. However, as the Economic Community data show, the so-called seniority wage curve associated with wage payments in Japan's large firms can also be found among white-collar males in Western Europe and is not peculiar to Japan. Elsewhere I have written about this in detail (Koike 1978a and 1981a). I will return to some of these points in the course of the discussion below.

There is a second category of phenomena alleged to be unique to Japan for which there is no comparative data. Although many such phenomena will join the first group as data does become available, it would still be premature at this stage to argue either way. Consider some of the notions about job definitions which are commonly found in discussions of work in Japan. There are many very important types of work where the division of labour is not completely clear. In order to fill the gaps which are left (that is, to get done the work which doesn't seem to fall into anyone's area of responsibility even after efforts have been made to allocate all possible tasks), it is argued that a certain amount of fluidity and flexibility is needed. In individualistic societies, it is difficult to find this kind of flexibility because each individual's job responsibilities are very clearly delineated. It is said that this kind of flexibility comes with an emphasis on groupism and with the focus on the overall efficiency of the group. However, unless the production process is extremely simple and straightforward, although the work processes may be broken down into component operations, any complication at all in the operations will mean that there are still areas where the responsibility for doing a particular task is not perfectly clear. No matter how one tries, it is impossible to predict all the eventualities, and one is forced in the end to accept that there will be uncertainty on the shop floor and that there will be occasions when a task must be performed by someone who had not been formally allocated that task (cf. Okamoto 1979 and Ishikawa 1981).

Accordingly, even in the most individualistic style organization, someone must possess the flexibility necessary for the overall production process to function smoothly. It may be that in Japan there is a slightly larger number of persons who possess this flexibility. However, neither this proposition nor the one which tries to explain such behaviour as a cultural trait have been properly investigated and must be recognized as being no more than interesting, though untested, hypotheses.

The third group of phenomena consists of those phenomena which, even after careful examination, seem to exist only or nearly exclusively in Japan. Although there may be one or two very limited examples of the phenomena in other industrialized countries, the occurrence of such phenomena is so much more frequent in Japan as to warrant the conclusion that the situation in Japan is qualitatively different. The prevalance of the QC circle would perhaps fall into this category of observed phenomena. For this reason, this paper's discussion of individualism alleged to exist among Japanese employees is centred on this phenomenon. By examining this phenomenon which is so commonly perceived as being evidence of Japanese uniqueness and group orientation, an effort is made to show ways in which the practices associated with QC circles may be understood as having emerged from a set of conditions which would link into more universally applicable explanations of behaviour.

2   Broadly conceived notions of 'skill'

A   QC circles as a large-firm phenomenon

Why have QC activities become so widely diffused in Japan? In looking for an answer to that question we must first consider carefully how such activities are actually distributed. We are still waiting for good data in this regard, but a fairly comprehensive survey was conducted by the Ministry of Labour in 1972 and 1977 which provides us with some idea of the situation [in private industry]. Published as *Rōshi Komyunikeshon Chōsa* (The Survey of Labour-Management Communications), the report provides a breakdown by firm size. The sample included some 5,000 private establishments having 100 or more employees. Some of the results are given in Tables 3.4 and 3.5. Although the survey asked about 'small-group activities', the activities covered are essentially the same as those found in QC circles and can therefore be referred to as QC activities without any serious difficulty. A number of conclusions can be drawn from the tables.

First, small-group activities are much more prevalent in the largest firms with over 5,000 employees (80 per cent) than in smaller firms with 100–299 employees (33.3 per cent). Moreover, as Table 3.5 shows, management's view of how effective such activities are in raising productivity also varies positively with firm size. Considering the results of the two tables together, it would seem that QC circles are effective in about 64 per cent of the large firms, but in only 15 per cent of the smaller firms.

In this regard, it is important to remember that the majority of Japanese workers are employed by firms with fewer than 100 employees. Those firms were not covered by this survey, but it is likely that the use of QC circles in these firms is even more limited. As far as I can tell, it would seem that QC activities were introduced into Japan's largest firms during the 1960s and then into a small proportion of Japan's medium- and smaller-sized firms during the 1970s. Accordingly, it would be difficult to generalize that the QC circle was a widespread phenomenon in contemporary Japan.

A second conclusion which can be drawn from Table 3.4 is that across all firm-size groupings the firms with labour unions were

Table 3.4 *Percentage of Workers Involved in Small-Group Activities by Firm Size according to the Presence or Absence of a Labour Union*

Enterprise size (number of employees)	Total	Firms with unions	Firms without unions
5,000–	77.2	77.4	67.3
1,000–4,999	58.5	59.1	53.6
300–999	42.9	43.9	39.1
100–299	33.3	34.6	41.7

Note: 'Small group activities' for the purpose of this survey are defined as follows: activities which occur spontaneously in small groups in which the members organize to promote quality control.
Source: Rōdōshō (Ministry of Labour), *Shōwa 52 Nen Rōshi Komyunikēshon Chosa* (The 1977 Survey on Communications among Labour and Management) (Tokyo: Rōdōshō, 1979).

Table 3.5 *Evaluations of the Effectiveness of Small-Group Activities by Firm Size (unit: percentages of establishments)*

Firm size (no. of employees)	Total	(A) Seen as being successful	(B) Somewhere in between	(C) Seen as being unsuccessful	(D) Don't know
5,000–	100.0	83.4	8.6	7.6	0.4
1,000–4,999	100.0	67.2	16.4	15.9	0.5
300–999	100.0	52.7	18.9	28.2	0.2
100–299	100.0	45.3	15.6	37.6	1.5

Note: This classification of each establishment was based upon the assessment of management.
Source: Same as for Table 3.4.

slightly more likely to have organized some kind of small-group activity for increasing production.

These two findings suggest that it may be necessary to reappraise earlier views concerning the operation of QC circles in Japan. Before moving further in that direction, however, it is first useful to consider the views which have thus far been expressed with regard to QC circles.

B Four necessary conditions for QC activities to be successful

When explaining the prevalence of QC circles in Japan, by far the most common approach has been to emphasize the connection with 'groupism' or loyalty to the firm. However, this kind of cultural explanation confronts the major difficulty of not being able to explain very well the above-mentioned patterns of variation. After all, the phenomenon is not found everywhere and where it does appear it does so in patterns. For the cultural explanation to be satisfying, the phenomenon would need to be spread much more evenly throughout a wider portion of Japan's enterprises.

Another approach is to argue that labour unions in Japan are very weak and that employees tend simply to follow the lead of management. This might be called the company union (*goyō kumiai*) (as opposed to enterprise union) hypothesis. To be sure, QC activities are often initiated by management. However, if those activities are an embodiment of management principles, and if we assume both that unions do not see the value of such activity and that they have a voice in the running of things within the enterprise, then we would expect to find such activities more strongly implanted in non-unionized firms. However, this would not accord with the data presented above in Table 3.4.

If we look at the actual workings of the QC circles, we will learn that a large proportion have to do with technical matters. In order for them to work, a high level of technical proficiency is necessary. It is unlikely that the desired change in technology can be introduced simply by being loyal to the firm, by being submissive to management or by possessing the right mental attitude. It is possible to think of four conditions which must be met before QC activities will be effective.

One is that the employees must already possess the technical knowledge relevant to fully understanding the production process. Another is that participants in the QC activities must have not only the ability but also the discretion to introduce and implement new ideas. Otherwise, the plans of the workers will remain simply as they are, as plans, rather than becoming reality. A third is that, in addition to having the knowledge and the authority to make changes, workers must have a reason for wanting to make the changes. Fourth, in close relationship to the third point, there needs to be some mechanism which will allow for the worker to benefit from his efforts. The discussion below begins by considering the first of these conditions in more detail.

C   The need to know the production process

QC activities are one approach to organizing the conduct of work on the shop floor. The goal is to devise better ways of performing concrete tasks. For QC activities to be successful, at least three types of technical knowledge are necessary.

The first consists of the techniques for discovering problems in the production process. They include the use of Pareto diagrams, fishbone diagrams, the use of check sheets, and other similar devices. These techniques are learned and utilized by those involved in QC circles in general, whether they be American or Japanese.

Second, in order to acquire these kinds of techniques, a certain reservoir of basic knowledge associated with minimal levels of literacy and numeracy is required. This kind of knowledge is taught primarily during the years of compulsory education. Among the advanced industrialized nations, there is not much difference in the way this kind of education is provided. It would be difficult to conclude (1) that Japanese are more likely than workers in other countries to receive the first two types of technical knowledge discussed here, or (2) that as a result of having such knowledge it is somehow easier in Japan than in other countries for firms to introduce QC activities.

The third type of knowledge necessary for QC circles to work is a thorough understanding of the production processes themselves. As an example, consider a group of ten workers who are operating a large machine. At first glance, the operation seems to be quite simple and straightforward; each person pushes the button required at his or her work station. However, to devise a better way of getting the job done with this kind of large machine the workers must have a fairly thorough knowledge about many aspects of the machine itself.

From among the many examples of QC activities, we can easily imagine one involving an automatic sausage-stuffing machine. What steps can be taken if the machine occasionally fails to stuff a sausage properly? The ultimate goal is to lower the percentage of faulty sausages, and the workers running the machine begin to look for the reason why the machine is 'malfunctioning'. As the first source of the problem, it is found that the sausages bend when they are heated and for that reason do not slip nicely into the skins. In order to correct the problem, changes are required which go beyond the group running the machine; something must be done at an earlier stage in the production process where the sausages are heated. In other words, a thorough knowledge of one's own machine is not enough; for workers to think of a solution, they must have a broader knowledge of the production process.

How does a worker obtain that kind of knowledge? It is impractical, if not impossible, to teach that kind of very specialized knowledge about a wide range of machines at school. Even at the special training centres which very large firms are able to set up, there is a limit to the amount of detail which can be taught about any one production process. At best, only the most fundamental knowledge is imparted. In any case, it is unlikely that workers will be taught about problems which have not yet been discovered, such as the way in which small adjustments in the temperature away from the accepted norm will affect the sausage.

One other possibility is that this knowledge is acquired 'on the job'. To ascertain that this is the case, we need to observe the way in which such skills are acquired. However, a means of directly measuring such skills has not yet been developed. The problem with quality indices is that they tend to be tautological. The only real solution is to develop proxy variables. As the first step in developing such a set of proxy variables, we might take a look at each individual's wages. It has been traditional that an individual's wages are seen as being a reflection of the individual's level of skill. Following along these lines, the next step is to consider carefully the extent to which seniority – merit-based wages (*nenkō chingin*) – are a peculiarly Japanese phenomenon.

D A look at the seniority-merit wage

At the present time the most common way of acquiring skills is through on-the-job training (OJT). According to this approach, one obtains his or her skill simply by doing the job. In plain terms such skills are acquired through experience. It would be hard to learn sophisticated techniques right from the start, but it is reasonable to expect that they will gradually be acquired. When sophisticated skills are involved we can posit that wages will continue to rise with experience until the skill is mastered. From this perspective we can use wages as a proxy variable for skill and test the notion that skill increases with experience. Because wage data are not broken down by years of experience, we have to use age groupings as the proxy variable for experience. Accordingly, if a young person gets a job and does not change his job very often, age will in a rough way reflect his or her years of experience. By looking at wage–age profiles in a number of countries, we can gain a better idea of the nature of skill formation in Japan. The test, then, becomes one of whether seniority-merit wages exist only in Japan. Although I have written on this matter elsewhere (Koike 1981a and 1978a), I wish to provide a brief summary here as background for understanding some of the arguments presented below.

As stated above, the European Community began to issue good comparative data from the mid-1970s. In judging the quality of such data, several considerations must be kept in mind. One is whether the data have been copied directly from the enterprise pay sheets. In obtaining this kind of data, written questionnaires and survey forms which rely on memory or less formal records invariably invite considerable bias. Another consideration is the size of the sample. Also important is the return rate; although the sample frame may be large, if the percentage of respondents returning the survey is small, there is room for bias. Finally, it should be noted that the inclusion of small firms in such surveys has often resulted in there being some bias. This is because the response rate and the sampling procedure itself are often in doubt. There may also be reservations about whether the records are accurately kept.

In the case of the surveys conducted by the European Community, pains have been taken to make sure that these problems were covered and the data can be said to be on par with those collected by the Ministry of Labour through its *Chingin Kōzō Kihon Chōsa* (The Basic Survey of the Wage Structure). It is a survey which is quite solid on all points mentioned above. Similar to the procedure adopted by the Ministry of Labour in Japan, the EC sample includes one-tenth of all enterprises with ten or more employees.

It should be noted, however, that there are some differences in how the Japanese and European surveys are conducted. The number of industries covered is larger in Japan. The EC data are for secondary industry (including mining and construction). However, if we take only the figures for manufacturing from both surveys, we obtain a fairly good comparison. A second difference is that the Japanese data is for firms (*kigyō*) with ten or more employees, while the European data is for places of work (*jigyōhō*) with ten or more employees. This is a crucial difference and would greatly undermine the value of comparisons in the tertiary sector, but in manufacturing the discrepancy is less of a problem and can perhaps be overlooked. Finally, the Japanese data provide much more detailed breakdowns and in terms of presentation are superior.

The important thing, however, is that good comparisons can be made by firm size and by age. Unfortunately, despite the similarities which at least make the basic comparisons possible, the European data give these breakdowns only for the entire sample as univariate distributions and do not provide two-dimensional tables giving, for example, the breakdowns by firm size and age together. It is, nevertheless, with these data that comparisons can be made.

E Seniority wages as a result of 'white collarization'

A comparison of the findings in the Japanese and European surveys yields the results given in Figures 3.1 – 3.2. Figure 3.1 compares the seniority wage curves for the various European countries with that for Japan. The comparisons are for male blue-collar workers only. The comparisons for male white-collar workers are given in Table 3.2 (page 98). Because we are interested in how wages rise with age and not in comparisons of the absolute wage levels in the different countries, all figures are pegged to an index of 100 which represents the average wages received by workers aged 20–24 years in each of the countries. In order to facilitate the visual presentation, the wage index is graphed on a logarithmic scale on the vertical axis. A look at the comparisons leads us to draw a number of interesting conclusions.

First, Japanese blue collar workers are paid more according to a seniority wage principle than are their European counterparts. Although a breakdown is not given for large firms by themselves in the data which are available for the European countries, it is clear from the Japanese data that the principle is particularly reflected in Japan's firms with over 1,000 employees. This would seem at least initially to give some credence to the commonly held

Figure 3.1 *A Comparison of Age–Wage Profiles for Blue-Collar Male Employees in Japan and Selected European Countries*

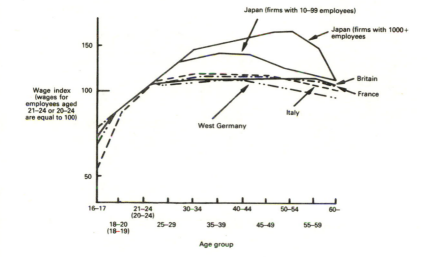

Notes: 1 The data are for male employees in manufacturing, except in Britain, where the data are for male employees in all industries.

2 The surveys from which the data are collected cover firms with ten or more employees, except in Britain, where all firms were surveyed.

Sources: 1 For Japan, the data were taken from *Shōwa 51-nen Chingin Kōzō Kihon Chōsa* (Survey of the Wage Structure: 1976) (Tokyo: Ministry of Labour, 1977).

2 For West Germany, France and Italy the data are from the European Community's *Structure of Earnings in Industry* (1972).

3 For Britain, the data are from the *New Earnings Survey* (1975).

perceptions about the uniqueness of Japan's seniority wage system. Even in the case of Japan's smaller firms with 10–99 employees, however, the curve seems to rise into the 30–40-year-old age bracket, whereas it flattens out much earlier in the case of the European countries.

Second, one must also note the sharp drop-off in the earnings of older workers in Japan. The wage rate is not simply a function of age or seniority, as some theorists would lead us to believe. Moreover, the drop-off also occurs for Japanese white-collar employees.

Third, the most noticeable finding is that the allegedly Japanese seniority wage profile seems to be quite widely applied to white

Figure 3.2   *A Comparison of Age–Wage Profiles for White-Collar Male Employees in Japan and Selected European Countries*

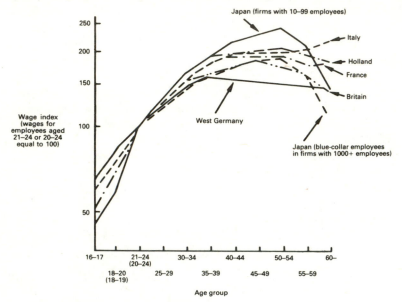

Notes: 1 The data are for male employees in manufacturing, except in Britain where the data are for male employees in all industries.
2 The surveys from which the data are collected cover firms with 10 or more employees, except in Britain, where all firms were surveyed.
Sources: 1 For Japan, the data were taken from *Shōwa 51-nen Chingin Kōzō Kihon Chōsa* (Survey of the Wage Structure: 1976) (Tokyo: Ministry of Labour, 1977).
2 For West Germany, France and Italy the data are from the European Community's *Structure of Earnings in Industry* (1972).
3 For Britain, the data are from the *New Earnings Survey* (1975).

collar workers in the European countries. Although the age–wage profile for Japan's white-collar employees has more curvature to it than do the curves for the European countries, it is not too different. Again, the drop-off after the peak is reached in the 50–60 age group is more pronounced for the Japanese samples. The point to be made when looking at Figure 3.2, however, is that the age–wage profile for blue-collar workers in Japan's large firms (with over 1,000 employees) is shown to be somewhat similar to the profiles found for white-collar employees in Europe's firms (with over 10 employees).

The similarities with regard to the white-collar workers (shown in Figure 3.2) are particularly important. The seniority wage system found in Japan's large firms is not unique to Japan. It is found among white-collar employees throughout Europe. What is unique to Japan is this kind of wage structure which is limited to white-collar workers in Europe, is also applied to blue-collar workers in Japan's large firms. In other words, the phenomenon to be explained as being different is the 'white collarization' of blue-collar workers in Japan's large firms [not the group orientation of Japanese workers]. If we are to think in terms of group orientations, then we should have to say that white-collar workers in Europe have the same group orientation. And, if we are to find an explanation other than value orientations for the white-collarization of blue-collar workers in Japan's large firms, it may be that it is the difference in blue- and white-collar orientations in this regard that need to be explained.

Unfortunately, we are unable to find a similar set of statistics for the American labour force. However, although much less of the necessary detail is given, the American census data do provide information on income by age group. With some estimating, we can gain a loose comparison which suggests that the situation for America's white-collar employees is about the same as that for such employees in Japan and Europe. The data also suggest that the situation for blue-collar workers would be somewhere between that found in Europe and Japan, perhaps a bit closer to the findings for Japan's blue-collar workers. What is important is that the white-collar curve is very similar to that in Japan and Western Europe, again reinforcing the view that the principle of seniority wages is not unique to Japan.

The overall conclusion to be drawn is that the wages of Japanese workers participating in QC activities are not too different from those paid to white-collar workers in many other countries. The next question to be asked, then, concerns the link between these wages and the skills of the workers who participate in the QC circles.

F   The 'white-collarization' of blue-collar workers in terms of labour turnover

The white-collarization of the blue-collar worker in Japan's large firms can also be seen in terms of the length of continuous employment at the same firm. It was argued above that skill can be conceived in terms of experience. Here it is useful to think in terms of experience obtained within the firm and experience gained outside the firm. When skill is acquired through OJT, the former type of skill is linked to the number of years an employee has been employed with the same firm. This is true because OJT has certain costs. The overall efficiency of workers not yet accustomed to the job is low. The number of poor-quality goods will increase. In order to lower the costs of such training, an effort is made to build in a progression so that the worker moves from simpler jobs to more complex jobs. For example, an employee might start work in an accounting section by doing the costing for some of the firm's less important products, and then gradually move into a position where he or she is doing the cost estimates for some of its main-line products. In this fashion, then, some of the costs of OJT (such as poor quality and lower efficiency) can be minimized. In designing this kind of programme, it is by far the easiest to do so if the entire progression occurs within a single firm. This is the reason why the length of employment is important in the implementation of OJT programmes.

The above-mentioned 1972 survey of the European Community also makes available for the first time good-quality data on years of employment for European workers. In Japan such data have been collected each year in the Ministry of Labour's *Chingin Kōzō Kihon Chōsa*. The findings in this regard are summarized in Figure 3.3. In looking at the comparisons, some light will also be thrown on the question of how unique life-time employment is to Japan.

If Japan is indeed characterized by life-time employment, then we would expect to find that the proportion of workers with only a few years' experience in the same firm would be fewer in Japan. A look at Figure 3.3 suggests that 12 per cent of the blue-collar workers in all Japanese firms had been employed for two years or less by their current employer. This figure is below that for any of the European countries, and therefore lends support to the common view of employment practices in Japan.

Of course, this matter can be looked at from another point of view by considering the proportion of workers who have worked at the same firm for a long period of time. Those in their present firm for over twenty years also represent 12 per cent of the Japanese sample. In this case, however, in most of the European countries a similar or a slightly larger proportion of the samples had worked at the same firm for this length of time. Italy and England provide exceptions, but it should be noted in the case of England that a category was not included for workers who had

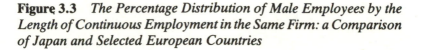

Figure 3.3 *The Percentage Distribution of Male Employees by the Length of Continuous Employment in the Same Firm: a Comparison of Japan and Selected European Countries*

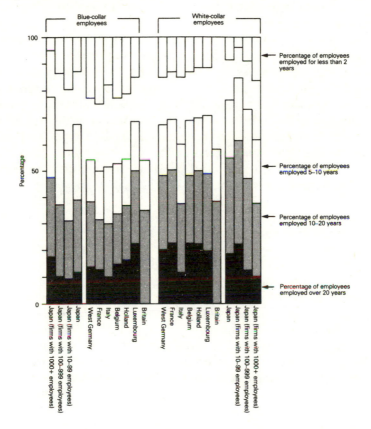

Notes: 1 The Japanese data are disaggregated for firms in different size groups. The European data are only for all firms with 10 or more employees.
2 The English data do not provide a breakdown for employees employed 20 years or more. Therefore, the upper category is 10 years or more.
Sources: Same as for Figure 3.1.

worked twenty years or more for the same firm. Luxembourg is also exceptional in that it provides a very high number of workers in this group. However, its population is too small to make a suitable comparison with the other countries. Nevertheless, the findings in Figure 3.3 suggest that it is difficult to conclude that life-time employment is peculiar to Japan.

At this stage some might wish to argue that life-time employment is a phenomenon associated with Japan's large firms. As expected, a look at the Japanese figures for the large firms only suggests that their blue-collar workers have on the average worked for a long period in their firm.

Here it is again interesting to look at the other half of the labour force, the white-collar employees. Again, we find that white-collar workers in all countries tend to have longer tenure with the same firm than do blue-collar workers. Japan's blue-collar workers in large firms have a tenure which is not very different from that of European white-collar workers. The conclusion in this regard as well, then, is that blue-collar workers in Japan's large firms have experienced 'white-collarization'. The next task, then, is to look more closely at this 'white-collarization' and consider its implications in terms of the processes of skill-formation.

G   Broadly defined careers

On-the-job training is a low-cost way of disseminating skills which is based on there being a progression of experiences from one related job to another. The systematic progression through a number of work experiences may be referred to as a 'career'. In thinking about a career, both its breadth and its depth may be considered as defining characteristics. Breadth refers to the number of related jobs involved in the concept of skill. To have broad skills, one must be able to cover most positions in the workshop and even some positions in workshops closely linked to one's own workshop. Depth refers to the range of positions of authority in the vertical hierarchy of status. The idea of depth concerns the extent to which employees can expect to work in a range of positions from that of the ordinary operative to that of being a leadman, a group leader or a foreman – or, if there is more depth to the career, to becoming a supervisor.

Of course, there are no good statistical data on this type of phenomenon. At the present time the researcher is simply left making his own individual enquiries, piecing together a picture one case at a time. Moreover, accurate records are seldom kept on 'intra-career' movement. In the case of Japan, wage rates are not always tied to a particular job, and personnel sections do not keep records of such 'minor' shifts. Up until now, attention has been given to job transfers, known as *haiten*, which have shifted workers to completely different sorts of unrelated jobs within the same plant, in which their previously acquired skills have little relevance. This type of transfer has been seen as being disadvantageous to the worker in terms of his or her career in many cases, has become the object of negotiations between unions and management, and has been recorded in written documents.

However, movement within the same workshop or among a cluster of related workshops has been seen as advantageous; it occurs as a matter of course and has not been taken up by the trade union as an issue for negotiation. To find out about the practices related to this kind of movement, the only approach is to interview older workers who have considerable experience at the workplaces concerned.

In the early 1970s, I had the opportunity to visit a number of large firms in chemicals and heavy manufacturing industry, and was able to make a comparison of the careers of blue-collar workers in the USA and in Japan. Following those interviews I was also able to gather some materials while holding further hearings with related persons. The findings from that research have previously been published (Koike 1977 and 1978b). To provide only the briefest of summaries, it can be concluded that practice of firms providing careers for blue-collar workers existed in both countries. A few of the younger workers would change companies, but once they had passed a certain point, they tended to settle into a career within the firm.

There did not seem to be great differences in the possibilities for promotion (that is, the depth of the career). To be sure, there were some differences. In America, for example, it was often the case that promotion to the position of foreman meant that a worker would have to leave the union, and it was not an infrequent occurrence that a worker would for that reason decline an offer of promotion to such positions. Nevertheless, the case was that the majority of foremen had been recruited from amongst the ranks, and in that regard it can be said that there is little difference.

The real differences between the two countries appeared with regard to the breadth of the careers. In Japan it seemed to be the case that workers tended to experience not only most of the important jobs in their own workshop, but also a number of jobs in workshops which were closely related in terms of the worker's skills. For example, one of the operators of a very large machine might be sent to work with the team of workers responsible for maintaining the machine. By working with maintenance, the worker would be able to learn a good deal about the way the machine was put together and how its parts were assembled.

This is the kind of knowledge referred to above as being essential for the functioning of QC circles. Moreover, one might go so far as to say that it is this type of knowledge which is what sets the technician apart from the ordinary worker. It is in this sense that we can talk about the 'white-collarization' of the blue-collar worker in Japan. 'White-collarization' thus refers to the processes and institutions which facilitate and support the acquisition of this broader understanding of the production process.

In the case of the American firms covered in this study, there were many instances where workers had not experienced all the main jobs even at their own workshop. Although some of the workers have had some experience at all of the jobs being done in their workshops, few had been sent outside of their own workshop to related workshops, and on this point the contrast with Japan is quite pronounced. In America, such job changes seem to be limited to times of emergency, such as when layoffs are occurring. The career of the American worker is clearly much more narrowly defined than that of his Japanese counterpart; consequently he has a much more restricted understanding of all the processes related to his own particular job. Japanese managers at American based factories often comment on this point. These managers are veterans from factories producing the same kinds of goods in Japan, and they are quite adamant in stressing how much broader the training received by Japanese workers is when compared with that of American workers.

In this regard, it would seem likely that American practices are closer to those found in Japan than are the practices followed in European firms. Although my own experience with Europe is quite limited, my impression is that on-the-job training is not highly evaluated in Europe and that the emphasis still tends to be on formal training. For this reason, the slope of the seniority wage curve discussed above is not as pronounced with Europe's blue-collar workers as it was with Japan's workers, or even the American workers.

It is also the case that the tendency to promote workers from within has become slightly stronger over time in Europe's large firms. If there is an opening for someone in one of the higher-paid positions, it is likely to be the practice in Japan that efforts will be made to fill the position with someone from within the firm who has previously worked in that workshop rather than hiring someone from outside. It is in this regard that we can talk about the internalization of the labour market in Europe's large firms. To be more precise, we should add that in Europe careers are much more likely to lack depth than in either America or in Japan.

To conclude, the feature which sets skill formation in Japan off from that in America and particularly in Europe is the breadth with which skill is defined in Japan. For this reason the Japanese worker is likely to have a much broader understanding of the various processes which impinge upon his job. Moreover, it is this kind of broad understanding which is critical to the successful functioning of QC circles.

However, it would be misleading to conclude that this broader notion of skill is peculiarly Japanese. There are many phenomena which can be easily explained if we recognize that the broad notion of skill is fairly common to white-collar work in most industrialized countries. The peculiarly Japanese phenomena are that blue-collar work in Japan's large firms is defined in broad terms characteristic of white-collar work in general, and that as a result there is a larger stratum of workers with these broad skills than is the case in other countries. Moreover, there is good reason to believe that even in Japan's smaller and medium-sized firms a small core of blue-collar workers have a similarly wide range of skills. The difference with the large firms, perhaps, is that the number of workers with such skills represents a smaller proportion of the blue-collar workforce in the smaller firms. For this reason, then, the seniority wage curve for blue-collar workers in the smaller firms is much flatter than is the case for blue-collar workers in the large firms (cf. Koike 1981b).

3 Democracy at work

A Workshop practices

The preceding section has touched upon the question of skills and their importance in initiating changes in the organization of the workshop which will produce improved efficiencies. However, even though workers may have the necessary skills and knowledge, unless they are given a certain amount of discretion with regard to these matters, change will not occur. Even if workers are able to come up with some good plans, they will have difficulty implementing their plans if they need always to be checking with superiors and trying to win them over. The need for independence in implementing changes, then, is a second prerequisite if QC circles are to function properly.

Another finding which emerged from the comparative study I made in the USA and Japan during the early 1970s was that in Japan movement within the shop was decided in accordance with practices developed within each shop. As stated above, the most important means of obtaining skills and knowledge relevant to the work process is to move around the shop and gain work experience at each work station. In Japan the process of rotation is not something which is decided through negotiations between labour and management. Nor is it decided by someone in the personnel section even within the same factory of the same company; the process of rotation varied from one workshop to another. At some workshops there is a system of systematic rotation which occurs at regular intervals; in others the process seems to be a more *ad hoc* arrangement. It is also the case in some workshops that a worker will be rotated through only a portion of the work stations, not all of them. The decision is made, at least nominally, by the foreman or supervisor, but in practice, the rotations are made according to a kind of tradition which has evolved over time within the shop. The important thing is that the practices at the shop level have evolved out of [informal] discussions among the workers themselves. The same thing can also be said about decisions concerning the movement of workers between closely related workshops.

On the other hand, in the American factories which I studied, it seemed to be the case that the rotation and promotion of personnel even within the same workshop was often decided through negotiations between the representative of the local union and management's representatives at the factory in question. Regardless of what was written in the contract, decisions were made strictly according to the accepted practice of seniority. In other words, when compared with Japan, the authority to make decisions was one level further up the hierarchy; whereas such decisions occurred on the shop floor in Japan, they occurred at the factory level in America.

The same thing can be said about the organization of work. At most American factories, it is often said in Japan, the work to be done is clearly laid out in a manual. The processes and the order in which the various operations are to be carried out are clearly laid down by the industrial engineers. Again, the decisions are made at the factory level. On the other hand, at workshops in Japan it is commonly said that no such manual exists. Actually, there are manuals and production standards documents which have been prepared by the production control division which exists at many of Japan's factories. However, no sooner is a manual made than the workers get together to make their own improvizations and go about getting the end product in the way they think is most suitable. Because such manuals are not followed, Japanese factories have come to place less emphasis on the production of such manuals.

In this regard the discussion with a certain supervisor at a large company was particularly revealing. Having done research in the area of industrial engineering, he was in an excellent position to comment on the efficiency of the factory operations. Having given a good deal of thought to the question of job rotation and the order of work operations, he sent his plans down to the shop floor. At first the plans were implemented according to his design. However, when he visited the shop floor some months later, the operations in no way resembled the procedures which had initially been implemented. During the intervening months, the original structures had been transformed by creative workers on the shop floor.

To summarize, decisions about the assignments and the rotation of workers and about the way work is organized tend to be made by workers at the shop level in Japan, whereas such decisions are made at the factory level in America. As a consequence, the discretion necessary for creative innovation at the shop floor can be said to exist in Japan, thereby fulfilling one of the necessary conditions for QC activities to be effective.

B Industrial democracy as seen in surveys of workers' attitudes in Japan and the United States

There were three questions in the survey by Whitehill and Takezawa which relate to the question of industrial democracy on the shop floor. One was presented above in Table 3.1. In that question workers had been asked about the desirability of foremen and supervisors being sensitive to the views of workers in their workshop. In that case we found that there was very little difference; workers in both countries felt that consultations were desirable.

The responses to the other two questions, however, suggest that there is a clear difference between Japanese and American workers. The responses summarized in Table 3.6 are to a hypothetical question concerning the worker's likely response to a change in work methods which seems 'unjustified' to the worker. In America, half the workers said they would obey the order because the superior had the authority to give the order; only one-fourth of the Japanese sample gave that answer. On the other hand, 59 per cent of the Japanese workers said they would resist the order, whereas only 46 per cent of the American sample would do so. Although the differences may appear to be rather small, the data suggest that Japanese workers might have slightly more freedom to express themselves. However, in interpreting the responses to this question, Whitehill and Takezawa seem to dismiss the findings simply as reflecting a kind of 'loyal insubordination' which comes from having first thought carefully about what was really in the best interests of management.

Table 3.7 involves a question about the authority of 'higher management' when it comes to promoting persons to supervisory positions. In America, two-thirds of the workers surveyed felt that management should decide on its own. Less than 10 per cent felt that agreement of subordinates who would be affected was necessary. In Japan much more emphasis was placed on the importance of agreement from below, and only 37 per cent felt that management should decide on its own.

This coincides with the results generated by other case studies. For example, in reporting on a study of forty firms in the 1950s Derber, Chalmers and Edelman (1965: 25) stated that none of the local unions had dealt with the issue of how supervisory personnel were to be selected. The results of a survey of Japanese factory unions in the mid-1950s show that the views of the workers in the shop involved were considered (Ōkōchi 1959).

To summarize, workers in Japan have considerable authority to make decisions regarding matters within their own shop. Such matters include the movement of personnel and the organization of work. For this reason we can conclude that the idea of worker participation and industrial democracy is firmly implanted among workers in Japan's large manufacturing firms. This is an important

Table 3.6 *Worker Responses to Question No. 16 on the Accept-ance of Supervisory Authority: a Comparison of Japanese and American Workers*

If I am unable to convince my supervisor that a change which seems justified to me should not be made in my work methods or assignments, I would:	All respondents (%)		Subgroups: sex and age (%)							
	USA	Japan	USA				Japan			
			M	F	Y	O	M	F	Y	O
1 resist his orders and refer the disagreement to the union;	39	34	38	43	41	35	32	35	34	29
2 resist his orders unless convinced by my co-workers that I am wrong;	7	25	5	8	1	9	20	30	22	18
3 obey his orders to avoid any unfavourable consequences;	4	15	5	3	6	4	17	14	16	18
4 obey his orders since, as supervisor, he must have the authority to give orders.	50	26	52	46	52	52	31	21	28	35

Notes: M = Male, F = Female, Y = Young, O = Old.
Source: Whitehill and Takezawa (1968), p. 185.

structure when it comes to promoting QC activities. This is not to argue that industrial democracy is more established in Japan than in other countries. Industrial democracy can occur in various ways on various levels. It may be that the power of unions and the ability of their leaders to speak out on various issues relevant to the well-being of the worker is better institutionalized in the United States. The focus of attention here has been only on the fact that Japanese workers seem to have more voice at the shop level.

4   Incentives and mechanisms providing rewards to workers

A   The structuring of careers within the firm
Although workers may have the ability and the discretion necessary to make innovations in how their work is organized, it is still not inevitable that they will do so. To choose to do so, the workers need to have some reason to do so. In other words, they need to

Table 3.7 *Responses to Question No. 20 concerning Promotion Decisions: a Comparison of American and Japanese Workers*

In deciding upon promotion to various supervisory levels, higher management should:	All respondents (%)		Subgroups: sex and age (%)							
	USA	Japan	USA				Japan			
			M	F	Y	O	M	F	Y	O
1 secure agreement from subordinates who will be affected;	6	38	6	7	8	4	29	46	34	24
2 secure agreement from the labour unions on all such decisions;	6	14	3	7	3	4	13	14	12	14
3 consult the labour union before making such decisions;	20	10	22	19	22	22	11	9	11	12
4 make such decisions carefully on the basis of its own judgement.	68	37	69	67	69	70	47	31	43	50

Source: Whitehill and Takezawa (1968), p. 308.

know either that they will profit from doing so or that they will be less well off by not doing so.

In economic terms, the incentive structure is provided by the establishment of internal labour markets. Internal labour markets provide the firm with one means of allocating jobs to employees and with a clear-cut structure for rewarding them. Plainly put, the system of internal labour markets is so structured that workers lose if they leave the firm and go elsewhere and they are rewarded for staying with the same firm for a long period of time. Within the firm, individuals are promoted over time and their wages increase accordingly. The career structure within firms may vary greatly from one firm to another in terms of breadth and depth. There would in reality be very few firms that had exactly the same career structure. For this reason, the skills and knowledge picked up within any given firm tend to be 'enterprise-specific'. To the extent that each career structure is unique to its firm, the cost of moving from one firm to another increases. To the extent that the career structures are deep and broad, the cost of moving from one firm to another increases. Finally, to the extent that the skill involved is a sophisticated one, the cost of moving from one firm to another increases. For this reason, it is the case in most industrialized societies that white-collar workers experience greater costs than blue-collar workers when changing from one company to another.

To the extent that the costs of moving from one firm to another are high, the employment prospects of the workers are more directly linked to the performance of the firm for which he or she works. To the extent that the firm prospers and grows, the chances for promotion are enhanced. If the firm does not do well, not only are the chances for promotion much more limited, but there is also a greater possibility that one will be laid off. With internal labour markets, the costs of being laid off for the worker are considerable; although one might actually be able to find another job, he or she would have to start all over again in terms of experience, and his promotion prospects would be greatly altered. To avoid the costs of being unemployed or of not being promoted, employees are motivated to work as hard as they can for the firm which is employing them. So that their own firm will not lose out to a competitor, workers are willing to put out a tremendous effort to raise levels of productivity and efficiency within their own firm. This is, I believe, where the worker's sense of motivation to make innovations can be found. This motivation is reinforced (a) to the extent that the career structures are deep and broad, and (b) to the extent that one has already invested his or her time in acquiring skills and knowledge specific to the firm in which they are working.

From the preceeding discussion it should be clear that this kind of motivation is not peculiar to Japanese workers. The career provided for blue-collar workers in Japan's large firms is fairly broad and deep. In this regard, it would seem that Japanese workers would be somewhat more motivated. However, in the case of America, if the financial position of the firm becomes precarious, layoffs will occur first among workers with the least seniority, whereas in Japan the layoffs will tend to occur more with those who have been with the firm for the longest period of time. In American firms which are unionized, the principle of seniority works to guarantee that workers who have been around the longest will be the most secure in their employment. In Japan, this is not the case, and there is a subtle process through which workers are motivated by a kind of 'anti-seniority' principle. In ' this regard, it could be argued that to the extent that a worker's career is protected by the seniority principle, his motivation to work is lowered. However, if a firm is really in very bad straits, and it is likely that the employment prospects of those with many years in the firm will be seriously affected, it is then likely that the motivation which flows from the second consideration (b) will be reinforced in the case of the United States. I would expect that the overall net effect on the absolute level of motivation which flows from the second consideration would in the end not be very different in Japan and in the United States.

From the limited enquiries I have made about the situation in Europe, internal labour markets and the corresponding career structures exist even for blue-collar workers in the large firms. However, the depth of such structure is much more shallow than in the case of either Japan or the United States. Accordingly, although the motivation which flows from consideration (a) may not be zero, it is likely to be somewhat lower than it would be in the other two countries. The number of persons in European firms with long tenures is fairly sizeable, and the employment guarantees for long-serving employees are not as strongly entrenched as in the United States. For this reason, the motivation which flows from consideration (b) must also be considerable. If the other conditions are provided, one would therefore expect QC circles to be effective in these countries as well.

B Participation, distribution and the role of trade unions

So that workers will continue to innovate over an extended period of time, some mechanism is required so that the improvements in productivity will benefit those who have come up with the innovations. To the extent that the unions have a voice in the running of things, their role relates to this point. Here we are talking specifically about their influence in two areas. One concerns management decisions affecting the organization of work on the shop level. The other concerns the mechanism by which additional gains from improved productivity will be distributed.

One interest of unions, then, is to ensure that workers have an opportunity to express their views to management. Assume that employees have cooperated with management to increase productivity and that as a result the profits of the firm have increased. If the profits are shifted to support the activities of another firm or simply to increase the consumption of the owner, the workers receive little return for their efforts. For them to get some benefit, some of the profits need to be reinvested in plant equipment which will enhance their employment prospects. For this reason, it is necessary that they be given some voice in deciding how the funds will be reinvested.

It seems common knowledge that the Western European countries have gone further than Japan in providing opportunities for labour to participate in management decision-making. Although there are mechanisms for employee representatives to sit on the management boards in many of the countries of Europe, Japanese firms have not yet come to provide for such participation. As an alternative, however, a system of consultations between management and union officials has become fairly widespread. Although more research is needed on the way these consultations actually operate, it would seem that they are of considerable importance in determining management policies. In terms of the comparison with Europe, there is also a need for more research to clarify the actual operations of management participation in those countries. The point to be made is that large firms in Japan are not without some effective means which guarantee that workers have some input into the decision-making processes of management. And saying this is not to say that there is not considerable room for improvement in the system of participation currently found in Japan's large firms.

The second area of interest to workers is that they receive the returns from the improvements in productivity directly in the form of better working conditions. This focuses attention on the question of distributive shares, and can be said to have traditionally been a major concern of the unions. The emphasis from this perspective is on negotiating with management concerning wages, dismissals, work assignments and transfers, promotions and various fringe benefits. Japan's enterprise unions have long been seen as having taken a weak stance on these kinds of issues. An examination of the carefully collected case studies of Nita (1981), however, shows clearly that the enterprise unions have effectively negotiated for these kinds of conditions. From my own research (1978a) I have the impression that the bargaining power of the American, British and Australian unions on these kinds of issues is immense, and that the Japanese unions are more in league with the unions found in Sweden and West Germany (in terms of the extent to which workers' organizations have an influence at the firm and factory level with regard to employment, transfers and wages).

In addition to the kinds of participation mentioned above, one might also mention the importance of being able to negotiate about the various conditions which surround the implementation of workshop innovations. This is an area where little participation occurs in present-day Japan. This may perhaps be due in part to the fact that Marxist ideology continues to have a small amount of influence in the Japanese union movement. Given this ideological orientation, there may be a built-in disinclination to cooperate positively in management-oriented strategies for promoting productivity. At the same time, the unions recognize the inevitable need for improved productivity and do not actively oppose such efforts. As a result, they give tacit approval, and for this reason there are few cases where the union has sought to make these activities a key issue in their negotiations with management.

5 Conclusions

It has been common in the literature on industrial relations in Japan for authors to emphasize how group-oriented the Japanese are, or how unique Japan is. To examine these assertions, the discussion in this paper has focused on QC activities as a representative practice commonly said to be unique to Japan. The analysis was concerned first with enumerating the conditions necessary for QC activities and second with considering the extent to which those conditions were peculiar to Japanese culture.

QC activities are an approach to workshop organization in which blue-collar workers make innovations in the way they conduct their work. QC activities are found in most large firms and in some medium-sized and smaller firms in Japan. The approach adopted in this paper was first to consider a few of the necessary conditions which must be met if QC activities are to be successfully implemented.

The minimal condition is that the workers have some minimal level of technical knowledge concerning the production process. This kind of skill is acquired through a wide range of experience. Workers experience a broad range of jobs not only within their own place of work, but also within closely related workshops.

Consequently, a 'total' understanding of the production processes relevant to operations within their own shop is obtained. Only with such a firm grasp of the fundamental production processes can workers come up with lasting innovations.

It needs to be stressed that this broad notion of skill is not particularly Japanese. We might be able to say, however, that Japan is the only country where a portion of blue-collar workers have such skills. Given that the patterns of tenure and wage payments for white-collar workers in industrialized societies seem to be common to those of the Japanese blue-collar employee, it is likely that white-collar workers in these countries possess a similarly broad type of skill. Although a broad grasp of the technical knowledge related to the production process is an attribute generally associated with industrial engineers in contemporary Japan, a proportion of the blue-collar stratum in Japan's large firms has come to possess this kind of knowledge. In other words, in Japan we can see the 'white-collarization' of some small, but very significant, portion of the blue-collar workforce. This means that Japan will have a slightly thicker layer of skilled blue-collar workers when compared with other industrialized societies. The point must be underlined that only a small number of blue-collar workers in Japan have this type of skill. They are concentrated mainly in the large firms.

The second condition facilitating the introduction of QC activities is the diffusion of authority regarding matters of work organization to the shop level. The preceding discussion suggested that Japanese workers had somewhat more discretion than their European and American counterparts in this regard.

The third condition for QC activities to be successful is that workers received some return for their efforts. This condition is illogically connected to the first condition. 'White-collarization' means that the longer an employee works for the same firm, the more skill he or she has and the greater the cost he or she will have to bear should the firm have financial difficulties. In Japan, in addition to a sizeable stratum of white-collar workers, a certain number of blue-collar employees in Japan's large firms are also working with these considerations in mind.

The fourth condition concerning participation is perhaps one which is less well met in Japan than the other three. Participation occurs, to be sure; workers have a say about management policies and unions negotiate with management in obtaining better wages for their members. For this reason one can say that there is probably enough participation for QC activities to be effective. However, one would probably have to conclude that the provisions for participation are somewhat insufficient in terms of promoting such activities over the long run; participation is less than what is needed. In particular, workers are somewhat behind in obtaining a voice about the running of the QC circles themselves.

If the relative success of QC activities can be explained in terms of the extent to which the above-mentioned conditions are fulfilled, then there is no need to draw out that curious variable known as 'groupism'. Rather, Japanese individuals will tend to behave in a way which maximises their own personal return. However, in so doing they tend to make a long-term assessment of things. If Japanese workers in deep careers behave with their long-term interests in mind, it is only logical that they would participate in QC circles. The above-mentioned conditions are not tied to the commonly cited cultural variables, and it would probably be difficult to explain QC activities using such concepts.

To reiterate the points made, QC activities have been successful in Japan because the number of workers who take a long-term view of things and who have a full understanding of the production processes account for a slightly larger proportion of the entire labour force in Japan than in other similarly industrialized countries. In all countries, such behaviour tends to be a character-istic of white-collar employees; in Japan such behaviour can also be found among a small number of the blue-collar workers who are employed by the large firms, and perhaps by a limited number of medium-sized and smaller firms. The key is the 'white-collarization' of blue-collar workers in Japan's large firms by giving them a very broad understanding of the production process. It is the presence of this very small segment of workers in the labour force which seems to account for the success of QC circles in Japan.

References

Derber, Milton; Chalmers, W. E.; and Edelman, Milton T.
  1965 *Plant Union–Management Relations: from Practice to Theory*
    (Urbana, Ill.: Institute of Labor and Industrial Relations, University
    of Illinois).
Ishikawa, Kaoru
  1981 *Nihon-teki Hinshitsu Kanri* (Japanese-style Quality Control)
    (Tokyo: Nihon Kagaku Gijitsu Renmei).
Koike, Kazuo
  1977 *Shokuba no Rōdō Kumiai to Sanka – Rōshi Kankei no Nichibei
    Hikaku* (Labour Unions at the Workshop and Participation: a
    Comparison of Industrial Relations in Japan and the United States)
    (Tokyo: Tōyō Keizai Shinpōsha).
  1978a *Rōdōsha no Keiei Sanka – Seiō no Keiken to Nippon* (Worker
    Participation in Management: the Experience of Western Europe
    and Japan) (Tokyo: Nihon Hyōronsha).
  1978b 'Japan's Industrial Relations: Characteristics and Problems',
    Japanese Economic Studies, vol. 7, no. 1 (Fall), 42–90.
  1981a *Nippon no Jukuren* (Skill Formation in Japan) (Tokyo:
    Yūhikaku).
  1981b *Chūshō Kigyō no Jukuren* (Skill Formation in Japan's Medium-
    and Small-sized Companies) (Tokyo: Dōbunkan).
Nita, Michio
  1981 'Tekko Rōshi Kyōgi no Seido to Jittai' (Institutions and Realities
    in Labour–Management Relations in the Iron and Steel Industry),
    Shakai Kagaku Kenkyū, vol. 32, nos. 5 and 6.
Okamoto, Yasuo
  1979 'Nihon Keiei ni okeru Shokuba Shūdan no Imi to Ishi Kettei
    Ruikei [ge]' (The Significance of Work Groups in Japanese
    Management and Different Approaches to Decision-making [II],
    Soshiki Kagaku, vol. 13, no. 1.
Ōkōchi, Kazuo *et al.* (eds).
  1959 *Rōdō Kumiai no Kōzō to Kinō* (The Structure and Functioning
    of Japan's Labour Unions) (Tokyo: Tokyo Daigaku Shuppankai).
Whitehill, Arthur M., Jr.; and Takezawa, Shin-ichi
  1968 *The Other Worker: a Comparative Study of Industrial Relations
    in the United States and Japan* (Honolulu: East–West Center Press).

Chapter Four
Friendship in Cross-cultural Perspective

Reiko Atsumi

1 Introduction

In a previous paper (Atsumi 1980) the author presented a framework for analyzing the personal relationships of Japanese. The
framework was constructed on the basis of how a sample of
male Japanese company employees perceived their own personal
relationships. Four types of relationships were identified: *tsukiai*
(obligatory non-kin relationship); friendship; *shinsekizukiai*; and
the intimate kin relationship. Two criteria were used to generate
these four types of relationships. One was whether their relationships were based on kin ties; the other was whether a feeling of
obligation (*giri*) or social necessity was present in the relationships.
Friendship was defined here as a non-kin relationship that has
developed from having similar interests, a mutual attraction and a
certain like-mindedness. It is a spontaneous relationship as opposed
to obligatory relationship (*tsukiai*). An individual's personal
relationships consist of these four types in one combination or
another. The nature of personal relationships varies not only

between individuals but also within a single individual according to one's life stage, various situational circumstances, values and attitudes towards life and towards a career. Although friendship and *tsukiai* may look alike in some of the outward behaviour, these two types of relationships were clearly differentiated in the mind of male company employees (Atsumi 1975 and 1980).

The present paper is concerned with friendship as one of the above four types of personal relationships – that is, non-obligatory non-kin relationships. Whether or not all non-obligatory non-kin relationships can be dealt with as one category of relationship depends on the meaning individuals attach to the relationships and on the role such relationships play in their personal life. The range and content of friendship vary from individual to individual. Some individuals have a limited number of close friendships; others maintain many sets of extended friendships. Yet these relationships all share certain characteristics to be categorized as friendship.

The objectives of this paper are three. The first is to identify essential properties or attributes of friendship which distinguish friendship from other types of personal relationships. The second is to investigate cultural backgrounds and social conditions which operate to produce different expectations and meanings with regard to friendship. Here the paper intends to demonstrate how certain cultural values encourage and facilitate or discourage and inhibit the development and maintenance of close friendship in a society. The third is to portray the future of Japanese friendship in the context of today's middle-class Japanese culture.

The discussion is important for several reasons. First, non-kin relationships seem to be playing an increasingly important role in modern industrial society, especially in contemporary Japan, although this does not necessarily undervalue the importance placed on kin-based relationships in Japan. Some non-kin relationships are *tsukiai*, such as those cultivated with colleagues and neighbours; others are friendships which have developed during school or university years, or through sharing a hobby or a common interest. Informal and fluid, these relationships seem to suit well the nature and pace of the life in contemporary Japan. Since one's social life, values and attitudes and psychological well-being are very much affected by the kind of personal relationships one maintains, it is worthwhile to examine the meaning and role of friendship in relation to those of other personal relationships in contemporary Japan. Such an examination is particularly meaningful in light of the rapid ageing of the Japanese population, since friendship along with intimate kin relationship will play an extremely important role in the later part of one's life.

Second, there is some evidence that friendship is valued in Japanese culture. Numerous novels and essays since the early Meiji period have focused on a theme of friendship. The attention given to friendship suggests that some features of Japanese culture and society encourage the formation, development and maintenance of close relationships with persons other than with family members. This is what Doi argues in his formulations of *'amae'* as a concept (Doi 1962: 136). Many of the male company employees interviewed by the author in the early 1970s (who were then in their thirties and forties) perceived their best male friends to be closer than their wives (Atsumi 1975). These men confided almost everything to these friends. We are not certain whether friendship is as important for other Japanese, as some accounts report that friendship with high intimacy and confidence is hard to establish among high-school students (for example, Rohlen 1983: 285). Of course, this could mean that the content and nature of friendship are changing in contemporary Japan. However, if the nature of friendship is actually changing, such changes are not likely to be isolated phenomena but a reflection of a broader change occurring in Japanese culture and society in general. It is hoped that this paper may provide a clue in this regard. In order to ascertain the exact nature of Japanese friendship, we first need to conceptualize clearly what friendship is. The author seeks to provide a preliminary framework for an empirical study investigating the friendship of Japanese men and women of different generations and different occupational categories. Lastly, by comparing friendship in Japan with that found in other societies an ultimate aim of this paper is to identify universal as well as unique features of Japanese culture.

In the next section the paper seeks to delineate the essential properties of friendship by surveying the available anthropological and sociological literature on friendship. Friendship in various other societies is compared with the friendship of male Japanese white-collar company employees (Atsumi 1975) and that of a sample of Japanese women interviewed by the author in the early 1980s.

2   Essential properties of friendship

Seldom is the concept of friendship clearly defined in the literature. Often the term has been used to mean many kinds of sociable or amiable relationships which are not based on kin ties. Nevertheless, the literature suggests that at least six basic properties can be identified as essential to friendship in a number of cultures. These are (1) equality in the relationship, (2) intimacy and confidence, (3) voluntary nature of the relationship, (4) a primacy of the affective dimensions over the instrumental dimensions, (5) mutual obligations and duties, and (6) durability of relationship. Each of these is discussed briefly below.

A   Equality in the relationship

Some degree of equality in social status and commonality of experiences seems to be required for establishment of friendship. Many studies have pointed out that the development of close friendship is usually limited to the individuals of the same sex who are age cohorts sharing the similar social status (Brandes 1973; Cohen 1961; Du Bois 1974; Foster 1976; Jacobs 1979; Kurth 1970; MacDougall 1981; Paine 1974; Piker 1968).

Equality in social status and background is seen as a basis for the friendship of elite Indonesian men (MacDougall 1981). These elite men form intimate friendships with men of a similar age and a similar educational background. A common mother tongue, the same religious orientation and political outlook further facilitate the development of friendship. Most of the friendships among elite Indonesian men were formed while they were studying at the same university, being away from their family and living in the same residence hall, or through sharing the same hardship during the revolution. Friendship based on equality is highly valued in stratified Indonesian society. A similar account is also reported on the friendship observed in a country town in Taiwan (Jacobs 1979).

Equality in relationship is considered important in Japanese friendship. A majority of Japanese company employees developed their friendship with a person with a similar social standing. Most of their friends were of the same sex and chosen from those who studied at the same school or university, from those who participated in the same extra-curricular activity, or from those who lived in the same dormitory or boarding-house. These lasting friends share compatible socio-economic backgrounds, a number of experiences and basic attitudes towards life.

B   Intimacy and confidence

Intimacy and confidence have been mentioned as essential properties of friendship in many studies. Intimacy means sharing private secrets. Friends can talk freely to each other and rely on each other with trust and confidence. According to Brandes (1973) it is taboo to maintain a posture of secrecy or privacy between true friends in a Spanish village. Friendship entails total personal involvement and commitment. This unqualified 'openness' of the heart between friends is shielded with the unusual 'closure' of the heart to others (Gilmore 1975, Paine 1974). Private secrets cannot be revealed to anyone else, even if requested by a close kinsman (Gilmore 1975: 318).

Intimacy and confidence unambiguously separate 'true friendships' from 'friendly relations' (Kurth 1970) and from acquaintanceship in middle-class American culture (Naegele 1958; Paine 1974). In his study of a Spanish village, Brandes (1973) found that a man's 'true friends' are distinguished from 'formal friends' (that is, 'age mates'). Gilmore (1975) reports that 'friends of trust' are distinguished from 'casual friends' among middle-class males in another Spanish community. Thai villagers (Foster 1976) also distinguish between 'friends to the death' and 'eating friends'.

Gilmore's 'casual friends' are those who participate in an exchange network in a bar, but are not allowed to come into one's home, which is part of one's private arena. In spite of the frequency of interactions between these 'friends' (long evening hours spent together almost daily in a village bar or tavern) and in spite of the obvious fun and pleasure derived from exchanging drinks and smokes, their relationship remains casual and superficial; it is not one of intimacy. In contrast, 'friends of trust' are 'friends sharing secrets'. Once the relationship has been established through the exchange of such information, there exists an 'unreserved surrender of the concealed private sphere of life' (Gilmore 1975: 317).

A parallel distinction can be drawn between *tsukiai* and the friendship of male white-collar company employees in Japan (Atsumi 1975, 1979 and 1980). Some Japanese company employees associate with their colleagues and other work-related people quite often after work, but the relationship is not very intimate because it is *tsukiai*. They eat and drink and/or play mahjong together after work. The frequency of association with *tsukiai* associates may be high, but it is not related to the degree of intimacy or confidence. Relationships with colleagues are not entirely free from the framework of work relationships even in off-work situations. In addition, those who are equal in rank are inherent competitors. Therefore, they do not reveal themselves or share private secrets with their colleagues or work-related people. Nor do they invite these people to their homes except for formal occasions. On the other hand, Japanese company employees may reveal themselves to friends who are not colleagues at work, and these friends may be invited to their homes.

A comparable situation is found with the personal relationships of full-time Japanese housewives. These women form casual and friendly relationships with their PTA associates, the mothers of their children, neighbours and the like. They see one another sometimes quite frequently out of necessity or obligatory feelings, but not out of mutual attractions. No intimacy or confidence develops in this type of relationship. On the other hand, intimacy and confidence is essential to their friendships, most of which are with a few former classmates. Salamon (1974) reports that these friends are perceived as being closer to them than even their family members.

Most friendships in Japan are formed through school and university life (Atsumi 1975; Embree 1939; Lebra 1984; Plath 1980; Salamon 1974 and 1975; Smith 1956), or through army life for those of the oldest generation (Plath 1980). Because close friendship is fostered by intensive shared experiences which involve the whole personality, it is difficult for many Japanese to make intimate friends after leaving school or university. Whether or not one can make a close friend later in one's life seems to depend on the availability of intensive shared experiences without the constraint of work or social obligation. For example, some of the full-time housewives interviewed by the author developed friendship with women whose children have gone to the same kindergarten. Their relationships started as casual acquaintance-ships, but blossomed into more intimate exchanges after their children finished kindergarten.

C   The voluntary nature of the relationship

All of the studies reviewed here have emphasized the voluntary nature of friendship. Friendship is not an ascribed relationship; friends are selected according to a person's free will. In this regard friendship can be differentiated from kin relationships and from some other types of relationships such as those which sometimes occur between age-mates. Kin relationships are based on the ties of blood, marriage and/or adoption. They are not formed on the basis of voluntary choice. Relationships between age-mates also are not voluntarily formed, although such relationships may develop into friendship. Of course, friendship is not the only relationship which is voluntarily formed. A business partnership, for example, can be contracted voluntarily. So, this criterion alone does not define a relationship as friendship. Relationships with co-workers and neighbours are not ascribed either, but the degree of free choice is more limited than is the case with friendship. One is often obliged to establish 'friendly' relationships with one's neighbours and/or workmates. This is another point that Japanese company employees stress in differentiating friendship from *tsukiai*. Friendship is a spontaneous relationship, whereas *tsukiai* is not (Atsumi 1975).

On the basis of the above it is doubtful whether we can classify as friendship most of what English working-class people call friendship. Most of these relationships are formed, in the case of men, between workmates who drop into a pub and have a drink together after work (Allan 1977 and 1979). Their relationships are framed by special circumstances (for example, they work in the same place or live in the same neighbourhood), and their place of interactions is confined to the same setting. This means that when the circumstances change, the relationship is likely to dissolve. If this is the case, the relationship is something other than friendship. The same can be said about the mateship of Australian men. The tradition of Australian mateship has grown out of men sharing hardship in Australia's early history. This solidarity relationship was considered essential for survival in the harsh environment, and mateship was aimed at strengthening the bonding of men (Bell 1973). In contemporary Australia mateship is still valued among trade unionists, army cohorts and those in sports. For the reason mentioned above, however, the relationship between mateship and friendship remains ambiguous.

D Affectivity versus instrumentality

The affective or emotional nature of close friendship is stressed by many researchers. Paine (1974), for example, assumes that human beings need affective relationships. The extent to which friendship satisfies this human need will vary, depending on the cultural values and the social conditions in each society. In some societies intimate kin relationships and/or affective conjugal bonds may well meet these human needs.

Both Du Bois (1974) and Wolf (1966) state that friendship can be classified according to the degrees to which affectivity/ expressivity and instrumentality are present in relationships. According to Du Bois, the relationship of 'exclusive friends' is primarily expressive or affective, whereas that of 'casual friends' is largely instrumental. However, available studies do not necessarily support this notion. Instrumentality exists to one degree or another in all friendships. In both Spanish and Thai communities instrumentality plays a crucial part in their exclusive friendships. Yuan (1975) notes that affectivity may be shown through exchanging material aids and assistance in some cultures, whereas in other cultures it is expressed mainly through non-material exchange such as conversations. In Wolf's 'emotional friendship' satisfaction of emotional needs is crucial, although it is not a feature of his 'instrumental friendship'. Nevertheless, even in the latter case, 'a minimal element of affect remains an important ingredient in the relation' (Wolf 1966: 13). If a relationship is predominantly instrumental and lacks an affective basis, it is probably best to conceptualize such relationships as being something other than friendship. This applies to Cohen's 'expedient friendship' (Cohen 1961), which is contractual and will be dissolved when the specific need for forming the relationship no longer exists. It is difficult to develop friendship without the basis of emotional compatibility even in communities where the mutual capability of providing economic assistance is an important criterion for forming a friendship (Brandes 1973, Gilmore 1975). This agrees with the conclusions found above in Befu's paper on social exchange; in such cases it is likely that economic interdependence buttresses the affective component of friendship (Brandes 1973: 753).

Affectivity is one of the criteria commonly used by Japanese company employees to classify their personal relationships (Atsumi 1975). They say friendship is made for its own sake, while *tsukiai* is cultivated to achieve a specific purpose, although this does not deny the existence of instrumental exchange between friends.

E   Mutual obligations and duties

It is said that one's willingness to assist close friends is unlimited (Kurth 1970), and that aid and assistance rendered from close friends should also be unconditional and without ulterior motives or self-interest. On the contrary, no such responsibilities, liabilities, privileges or rights are prescribed to 'casual friends' (Cohen 1961). Gilmore's 'casual friends' do not feel any responsibilities toward each other, and it is felt inappropriate to ask 'casual friends' for money or for the loan of important items (Gilmore 1975). Willingness to assist unconditionally, then, is the responsibility only of true friends. While this may sound as if the commitment of true friends becomes bondage, the fact is that true friends do not see it that way because they are happy to assist their friends.

In many pre-industrialized societies friendship seems to be formed primarily to secure various kinds of help and assistance (Brandes 1973; Foster 1976; Gilmore 1975; Wolf 1966). Cohen examined ethnographies of sixty-five societies and found the following seven areas in which friends can be of assistance to each other: (1) exchanging material and/or economic aids, (2) providing socio-political and emotional support, (3) serving as a go-between in love affairs and marriage arrangements, (4) meeting homosexual needs, (5) giving sponsorship in *rites de passage*, (6) providing support during mourning, and (7) exchanging children (Cohen 1961: 373). In some societies certain of the duties listed above may not be performed exclusively or even primarily by friends. Foster (1976) reports that kinsmen are first asked for economic assistance before friends are approached in Thai villages.

In Japan, white-collar company employees tend not to seek economic or material assistance from friends (Atsumi 1975). They believe that this kind of aid is more appropriately sought from intimate kinsmen, or through a professional organization, and that is what they do in practice. They carefully avoid lending or borrowing considerable amounts of money from a friend. The lending or borrowing of valuable items from a friend is also rare. This seems to hold true not only for friends but also with *tsukiai* associates, although it is all right to borrow small items such as books and small amounts of money for a short term. In this sense the absence of monetary or material exchange of significant value alone does not distinguish between friendship and *tsukiai*. Monetary exchanges are not practised between friends who are elite Indonesian men (MacDougall 1981) or between friends who are American housewives (Yuan 1975) either.

Many studies reviewed here indicate that the type of assistance most often sought exclusively from friends is spiritual and emotional support. Friends are obliged to give careful, honest, considered advice and opinions on personal matters. This sort of advice often influences the behaviour of Thai villagers (Foster 1976). In Japan as well, the male Japanese company employee seeks similar advice from his close male friends (Atsumi 1975). As a matter of fact, he may even consult one or two of his close male friends rather than his wife when he needs advice on personal matters involving career choice. This is an interesting contrast with Pleck's report (1975) on American men, who tended to obtain emotional support primarily from their wives or female friends. Personal and emotional support at a time of crisis (for example, upon a death in the family) is another type of assistance eagerly performed by friends (Gilmore 1975; Smith 1956).

F   Durability of relationship

Friendships are not immutable, but those with more intimacy and affectivity tend to be more durable. Foster (1976) reports that the friends in his study hoped that the relationship would last for a life-time. The term 'friend to the death' expresses this ideal very clearly. Yet, friendship can be terminated for a variety of reasons (Cohen 1961, Naegele 1958). This aspect of mutability of friendship clearly differentiates friendship from kin relationship and from what Cohen (1961: 352–3) labels 'inalienable friendship' (for example, fictive kinship and blood brotherhood). Kin relationships are based on publicly recognized ties of blood and marriage which involve a set of rights and obligations. A genealogically close kin relationship may at times become dysfunctional or inactive, but even in such a case those who are related by kinship cannot completely ignore a set of rights and obligations which binds their relationship. Friends are not bound by any publicly recognized rights and obligations, although this does not mean that nothing regulates friendship. What is permissible and desirable in a friendship relationship is formulated by a given culture. This is what Paine (1974) refers to as the 'rules of relevancy'. People learn these 'rules' through the process of socialization. These 'rules' are understood between friends, but are not protected by or fortified with legally or publicly established norms in the way that marriage and certain other types of personal relationships are. Therefore, friendship is a fragile relationship. As Naegele (1958) argues, friendship is easily revocable and reversible. Its durability depends on how each friend evaluates the other's conduct according to these 'rules'.

What, then, are the grounds for forming a durable friendship? In the Spanish community that Brandes (1973) studied, a series of culturally approved and formalized mechanisms operate to monitor and fortify friendship in an environment which is perceived as full of suspicion and distrust. One device is the requirement that one cannot give a vague response to a friend's greeting such as 'Where are you going?' A concrete answer as to where a person is going and for what purpose must be given to a friend. Formal requests must also be avoided among friends in the Spanish village community, because they tend to suggest that the other person is not as reliable or trustworthy as a close friend should be. In other societies other devices are employed. One is to emphasize supernatural sanction (Piker 1968). Another mechanism is to treat the friendship relationship as analogous to kinship (for instance, by forming pseudo-kinship and fictive kinship relations) (Eisenstadt 1956; Pitt-Rivers 1968). For both Japanese company employees (Atsumi 1975) and elite Indonesian men (MacDougall 1981), frequent face-to-face contacts or material exchange are not considered essential in maintaining friendship. According to Japanese company employees interviewed by the author, once a friendship is established, it continues unless friends experience an incident which upsets mutual trust. Although Paine (1974) states that the making and breaking of friendship in middle-class American culture is a matter of personal choice which cannot be socially controlled, his views need substantiation. Studies regarding this aspect of friendship in Japan are not available. There is a need for comparative studies which examine the conditions under which friendship is terminated.

In summary, friendship is a fairly durable relationship which is voluntarily established on the basis of trust and an affective bond between individuals who share similar socio-economic standing and experiences. The content of reciprocity between friends varies from one society to another, and may range from material aids and assistance to non-material communication and emotional and spiritual support. These properties differentiate friendship from other non-kin relationships and intimate kin relationships. Both friendship and intimate kin relationships are predominantly affective relationships, but in other respects they are quite distinct.

3 Friendship and socio-cultural variables

Does friendship of the kind delineated in the previous section exist in all societies? Is it valued to the same extent in all? If not, what socio-cultural variables account for the differential development and practice of friendship? This section attempts to answer these questions by examining the role of social and cultural background in a number of societies in which friendship flourishes.

Friendship seems to be an extremely important social institution in societies where formal social structures do not exist outside the household. Studies by Brandes (1973) and by Gilmore (1975) demonstrate the importance of friendship in Spanish communities where the nuclear family is the major and almost the only structural entity. Societies of this type are classified by Honigmann (1968) as 'atomistic' where the individual and his interests seem to be the primary concern of the people. In such societies interpersonal relationships between people seem to be characterized by strain, contention or invidiousness. Though it may sound contradictory, in this type of society friendship is highly valued as it provides an integrating force among villagers who perceive the outside world as being hostile and untrustworthy. In such a society a man must have a close friend to depend on in order to carry out the multiple functions of his everyday life satisfactorily and to counteract individual alienation. Furthermore, close friendship represents an ultimate value for villagers. For this reason, a person with friends is a person with an 'open personality'.

The picture of friendship drawn by Piker (1968) and Foster (1976) in their studies of 'loosely' structured Thai communities further illustrates the way in which villagers are left as individuals. Friendship is sought after by every villager not only for acquiring various forms of mutual assistance from friends but also for the meaning it carries for those who have friends, since friendlessness is considered by Thai people (Foster 1976) as fatal to the individual and as occurring as the result of a flaw in personality.

Few studies deal with friendship in pre-industrial societies where formal social structures other than the household predominate. However, we cannot conclude from this paucity of studies that friendship is not important in such societies. On the contrary, friendship was extremely valued among the gentry class in pre-revolutionary China where the patrilineal descent system was highly developed (Fried 1953). Friendship provided an invaluable outlet of emotions for Chinese who felt the pressures of kinship organization. Free exchange of ideas and emotions is not easy between kinsmen who are bound in formal rights and obligations. The same would apply to the traditional Japanese village where *dozoku* and other formal social organizations prevailed.

Friendship also seems to be particularly important in societies with high levels of social differentiation. In such societies various forms of contractual (for example, employer–employee, landlord–tenant) and professional (such as doctor–patient, shopkeeper–client) relationships as well as other instrumental relationships play a large part in the daily lives of people. Urban life in many industrialized societies is such that friendship provides a refuge from isolation, strain and various types of alienation. In friendship relationships, people are free from many of the demands of socially prescribed roles.

Contemporary Japanese society is certainly classified as having high levels of social differentiation, and as such Japanese people experience pressures and alienation similar to that experienced by their American or English counterparts. However, this does not mean that friendship among contemporary middle-class Japanese is the same as that among contemporary middle-class Americans or middle-class English. A close examination reveals that the nature of friendship among Japanese middle-class men and women is somewhat different from that reported for their middle-class American or English counterparts. First, the available literature indicates that friendships in America and England are shared by husband and wife (Allan 1977 and 1979; Babchuk 1965; Babchuk and Bates 1963; Bell 1981; Bott 1957), whereas in Japan they are reported as being sexually segregated (Salamon 1974 and 1975; Vogel 1963; Wimberly 1973a). In his study of friendship among American university students (200 white Americans aged from eighteen to twenty-six) Weinberg (1970) reports that most close friendships were established with a person of the same sex.

However, this seems to be replaced, at least in importance, by jointly established friendships after marriage. According to Babchuk and Bates (1963), a friend of one partner and his or her spouse often become friends of the couple soon after they are married. A couple now becomes an important unit in these friendships. Although each spouse may retain his or her individual friendships, their attention seems to shift to jointly established friendships. These friends exchange visits to one another's home, and participate in pastime activities such as a sport or a game.

A second difference seems to be in the nature of friendship maintained by middle-class Japanese men and their American counterparts. Several studies suggest that friendship with a high degree of intimacy and confidence is not very common between middle-class American men (Bell 1981; Levinson 1978; Lewis 1978; Pleck 1975); the opposite was true with Japanese company employees interviewed by the author. In one study only one-third of sixty-five middle-class American men said that they had a male friend to whom they could reveal everything (Bell 1981: 81). A study by Levinson (1978) who interviewed forty middle-aged men on the East-coast of America further confirms this tendency. Middle-class American men appear to seek intimacy more from women than from men (Pleck 1975). The Japanese men interviewed by the author provide a contrast. Moreover, in Japanese literature best friends portrayed are almost always of the same sex.

The two differences noted above may reflect differences between the ideals regarding marriage and masculinity in the middle-class Anglo-Saxon culture and those found in middle-class Japanese culture. First, in the Anglo-Saxon context companionship and shared experiences of a couple are stressed as being important in marriage; in Japanese context gender role segregation is seen as the ideal in marriage. Second, the ideal associated with American manhood appears to discourage the full development of emotionally close relationships between men. Lewis (1978) argues that the following four barriers limit intimacy between men: (1) competition, (2) homophobia, (3) an aversion to vulnerability and openness, and (4) the lack of role models. Although middle-class culture in contemporary Japan also tends to promote competition, the similarity seems to end there. As for female friendships, however, there seem to be some close parallels between the friendships of middle-class Japanese housewives (Salamon 1974 and 1975) and those of middle-class American housewives (Yuan 1975).

The friendship pattern of working-class English people is repor-ted to be situation-bound. Compared with their middle-class counterparts, their friends are chosen from a relatively narrow range of people coming mainly from among workmates and neighbourhood contacts (Allan 1979; Bott 1957). Friends of working-class English people are rarely invited to each other's home, which is different from the middle-class friendship pattern. This difference between middle-class and working-class friendship patterns is not necessarily a result of the economic differences between the two (for example, the size of the house), but rather appears to symbolize the difference in the meaning attached to kin relationships and that which is attached to friendship. In the English working-class culture only kin are permitted to enter the home, which is seen as being a private arena. In other words, friends are not expected to share the private aspects of one's own life. Another difference observed between the classes is that friendship is mostly segregated by gender among the working-class people. Even when a married couple develop friendship with a neighbouring couple, the wife becomes friends with the other wife and the husband with the other husband. No comparative data are available on Japanese or American blue-collar workers.

In one respect, then, the pattern of friendship maintained by middle-class Japanese seems similar to that found in the English working-class: they are both sexually segregated. This is, however, a rather limited similarity. In other respects the pattern of friendship is rather different. The friendships of middle-class Japanese do not appear to be situation-bound, as is the case among the English working-class. Furthermore, best friends (*shinyū*) are perceived as being even closer to oneself than family members by middle-class Japanese (Atsumi 1975; Salamon 1974). In addition, no economic or material help is exchanged or expected between Japanese friends, whereas such exchange is reported as being common among friends in the English working class. Japanese white-collar company employees consider friendship and economic relationships as being incompatible (Atsumi 1975). Japanese friends support each other, but their support is primarily in the emotional and psychological sphere. Close kin may also be able to provide emotional support, but not every middle-class Japanese has close relationships with kin, and close kin may not be the best people from whom one seeks emotional support for the reasons discussed in the previous section.

The foregoing discussion has focused on why friendship seems to develop in certain societies and on how the pattern of friendship is influenced by cultural values and the ideals of a society – specifically, values pertaining to marriage and conjugal relationships, to masculinity and to the role of kin relationships.

4   The future of Japanese friendship

Nation-wide research recently conducted by the Japanese government reported that Japanese youth (ages 15–24) listed 'obtaining friends' the thing they want to do most while young (Sōmu-chō 1985). In the same research 80 per cent of the young people interviewed rated 'friends' as one of the most important things in their life. This percentage exceeds the percentage of respondents who cited 'parents' (72 per cent) as one of the most important. Another survey among the young people (18–24) in eleven countries revealed that 96 per cent of the Japanese respondents answered that 'they have close friends' and that 90 per cent of those with close friends said that 'they are satisfied with their relationship with friends' (Sōrifu 1984). They also listed 'friends' as the first person to talk to 'when they have personal trouble and/or worries'. On the other hand, the youth of most other countries in this research cited 'mother' as the first person to talk to. The above findings indicate that close friendships are valued and cherished by the contemporary Japanese youth. Moreover, the results suggest that the type of friendship in Japan will continue to be between persons of the same sex and that it will be characterized by intimacy and by emotional and non-material exchange.

There are good reasons to accept these conclusions. This is particularly true if we are considering middle-class Japanese. Supporting evidence can be found in the fact that role segregation by gender continues to be accepted by middle-class culture in contemporary Japan.

Gender differentiation starts at secondary school (Rohlen 1983), and segregation by gender becomes conspicuous after graduating from that level. Ninety per cent of all junior college students are women, whereas more than three-quarters of the total students in four-year universities are men (Sōrifu 1985: 244). Furthermore, women concentrate in certain departments such as literature and home economics, while men predominate in departments such as law and engineering (Sōrifu 1985: 53). This trend of gender segregation in education is a mere reflection of what is considered desirable by the middle-class Japanese: the ideal and practice of segregated roles and activities by gender. Since a very high percentage of Japanese people make friends at school or at university (Sōrifu 1984), the current situation encourages the development of friendship between persons of the same sex.

These friends play a vital role for the psychological well-being of an individual even after he or she is married. In the Japanese urban middle-class families the husband's major and sole responsibility is to provide for his family; the wife's primary responsibilities are in the home and include the running of the household, managing family finances and looking after the welfare of the family (Fukaya 1979; Pharr 1976; E. Vogel 1963; S. Vogel 1978). The author's recent fieldwork revealed that the ideal of gender role segregation was so entrenched among middle-class families that even wives with full-time jobs outside the home tried hard to live up to the cultural norm. Although most middle-class Japanese families in the urban areas are nuclear in structure, they are quite different from the middle-class families in the West in that the Japanese husband and wife rarely share activities together (Vogel 1963; Wimberley 1973a). For example, most of the Japanese middle-class couples do not visit friends together or engage in a leisure activity together except for a short while until the arrival of the first child. Younger couples may sometimes go out together for shopping, or for eating together at a family restaurant on weekends, but they are almost always accompanied by their children. The wife in these cases is unlikely to turn to her husband for emotional support (Vogel 1963: 215), as her husband's work responsibilities increase along with the length of employment and he has a decreasing amount of time to spend at home (Atsumi 1975; Rohlen 1974; Vogel 1963). This pattern of segregation continues long after children reach their teens.

Here lies a strong need for women who are alone at home with children to seek close friendship with other women who are in similar circumstances. They may exchange visits to each other's home, or participate together in a cultural or leisure activity. The

146

essential function of these friendships is to provide companionship and sympathetic understanding of each other's circumstances and state of mind. When close friends live far apart, the telephone serves as an important means by which these emotional and personal exchanges are maintained (Salamon 1974 and 1975). This kind of non-material exchange with a close friend provides these women with genuine consolation, understanding and emotional support.

Similarly, Japanese husbands also need friends with whom they can relax and discuss openly their personal ambitions, concerns and problems. Their need to talk to a friend may not be as strong as in the case of their wives, since men have a job, co-workers to chat with and a number of culturally acceptable outlets for releasing stress and frustration. It is also the case that many of these middle-class men are involved in *tsukiai* activities of one kind or another and do not have the time necessary to see their close friends. Thus, the frequency of face-to-face contacts with friends tends to be low (Atsumi 1975 and 1980). None the less, their friendships appear to be indispensable to their personal well-being.

Is there any sign that changes will occur in these patterns of friendship in the near future? If it is changing, what sorts of changes are most likely to occur? Since the present pattern has been fostered and reinforced by the existing model of role segregation by gender, it may be useful to question first whether there is any sign of change in gender roles.

We can hypothesize that if there is a change in role segregation, there will be a change in the pattern of friendship as a natural consequence. At present no empirical data indicate such a change is occurring, although increasingly more married women are now engaged in work outside the home, as the recent labour statistics show.[1] This increase in the proportion of married women in employment, however, is largely the result of the increase of married women in part-time employment. For this reason, the increase of married women in employment will not necessarily lead to a change in the practice of role segregation by gender. After all, the majority of married Japanese women with children

1 In 1984 married women accounted for 59.2% of working women, whereas never-married female workers constitute 31.5% of the total female labour force. These percentages represent a reversal of the situation which existed in 1974 (Rōdōshō 1985).

prefer part-time employment to full-time employment; as long as they are not economically pressed, they will choose to conform to the role prescribed for women, and many of them fear that they could not fulfil the prescribed role properly if they were employed full time.

Would role segregation diminish if both the husband and the wife were employed full time outside the home? We can anticipate that some sort of adjustment would occur to accommodate with the full-time work role of the wife. For example, husband and wife might share domestic and child-rearing responsibilities inter-changeably and share more activities together. Such sharing of roles and activities would naturally provide married couples with more opportunities for joint friendship and for more frequent and intimate communication.

Presently available empirical data do not throw light on this issue, although the available material suggests that very little adjustment is being made among the middle-class families where both the husband and the wife are full-time employees. The majority of the married working women with children whom this author interviewed in 1985 faithfully followed the pattern of division of labour by gender, with a good deal of help from trusted kin such as a mother or a mother-in-law. A few of the husbands of these working women participated in some of the domestic work and shared some family responsibilities, but no appreciable difference was observed in their patterns of friendship. Further research is necessary before we can arrive at a conclusion concerning the above formulation.

A final question to be asked is whether the pattern of friendship described in this paper can also be found among other segments of Japanese population. There is a paucity of studies dealing with the life styles, values and attitudes of Japanese who do not belong to *sararīman* families. Wimberley (1973b) argues that the tradition of the *chōnin* (townsman) class in pre-industrial Japan is kept intact in the style and structure of the contemporary Japanese merchant families. This *chōnin* tradition is distinct from the *samurai* tradition which prevails in the *sararīman* families. In merchant families it is normal for a husband and a wife to work side by side, and to share many activities and responsibilities together. It is then possible that such couples develop common friends. A small sample of married women in family businesses were interviewed by the author in 1984 and lend support to this interpretation. Some of the husbands in the family business are actively engaged in domestic work and take primary responsibility for their children's education (for example, attending PTA meetings regularly). A majority of these couples enjoy shopping together, or taking trips together. Their friends are people in similar circumstances, and jointly made by a husband and wife, although female friends also see each other without the presence of their husbands. As these examples indicate, the friendship pattern of self-employed people seems to be different from that of the middle-class *sararīman* Japanese.

In conclusion, it is unlikely that intimate friendship with persons of the same sex will lose its importance among Japanese, even though more couples may cultivate joint friendships in the future. Japanese men and women seek emotional intimacy and personal gratification through frank communication with close friends. Such needs may be met partially by close kin relationships, but for the reasons stated before, there are limits on the extent to which kin relationships can adequately satisfy such needs. If the role segregation model is replaced by a jointly shared role model in the future, the quality of the conjugal relationship will change and Japanese husband and wife may become 'friends'. New conjugal relationships will probably come to fulfil the need currently being satisfied by close friends of the same sex. At present, there is little sign that such changes are occurring in the Japanese middle-class segment, and there appears to be no alternative. Indeed, it might be assumed that this type of close friendship will even increase in importance as people reach retirement. There is a need for empirical studies focusing on the functions and meanings of friendship of people at the later stage of life in a rapidly ageing Japanese society.

References

Allan, G. A.
    1977 'Class Variations in Friendships Patterns', *British Journal of Sociology*, vol. 28, no. 3 (Sept.), 389–93.

1979   *A Sociology of Friendship and Kinship* (London: George Allen & Unwin).

Atsumi, Reiko
1975   'Personal Relationships of Japanese White-Collar Company Employees', Ph.D. dissertation, University of Pittsburgh.
1979   '*Tsukiai*-Obligatory Personal Relationships of Japanese White-Collar Company Employees', *Human Organization*, vol. 38, no. 1 (Spring), 63–70.
1980   'Patterns of Personal Relationships in Japan – a Key to Understanding of Japanese Patterns of Thought and Behaviour', *Social Analysis*, nos. 5/6 (Dec.), 63–78.

Babchuk, N.
1965   'Primary Friends and Kin: a Study of the Associations of Middle Class Couples', *Social Forces*, vol. 43, no. 4 (May), 483–93.

Babchuk, N., and Bates, A. P.
1963   'The Primary Relations of Middle Class Couples: a Study of Male Dominance', *American Sociological Review*, vol. 28, no. 3 (June), 377–84.

Bell, Robert R.
1973   '*Mateship in Australia: Some Implications for Female–Male Relationships*', La Trobe Sociology Papers, no. 1 (Oct.).
1981   *Worlds of Friendship* (London: Sage Publications).

Bott, E.
1957   *Family and Social Network* (London: Tavistock Publications).

Brandes, Stanley H.
1973   'Social Structure and Interpersonal Relations in Navanogal (Spain)', *American Anthropologist*, vol. 75, no. 3 (June), 750–64.

Cohen, Yehudi A.
1961   'Patterns of Friendship', in Y. Cohen (ed.), *Social Structure and Personality* (New York: Holt, Rinehart & Winston), 351–86.

Doi, L. Takeo
1962   'Amae: a Key Concept for Understanding Japanese Personality Structure', in R. J. Smith, and R. K. Beardsley (eds), *Japanese Culture* (Chicago: Aldine Publishing Co.), 132–9.

Du Bois, Cola
1974   'The Gratuitous Act: an Introduction to the Comparative Study of Friendship Patterns', in E. Leyton (ed.), *The Compact: Selected Dimensions of Friendship* (Toronto: University of Toronto Press), 15–32.

Eisenstadt, S. N.
1956   'Ritualized Personal Relations', *Man*, vol. 56, no. 96 (July), 90–5.

Embree, John F.
1939   *Suye Mura – a Japanese Village* (Chicago: University of Chicago Press).

Foster, Brian L.
  1976 'Friendship in Rural Thailand', *Ethnology*, vol. 15, no. 3 (July), 251–67.
Fried, Morton. H.
  1953 *Fabric of Chinese Society: a Study of the Social Life of a Chinese Country Seat* (New York: Praeger).
Fukaya, Masashi
  1979 'Socialization and Sex Roles of Housewives', in M. I. White and B. Molony (eds), *Proceedings of the Tokyo Symposium on Women* (Tokyo: publisher unknown), 133–49.
Gilmore, David
  1975 'Friendship in Fuenmayor: Patterns of Integration in an Atomistic Society', *Ethnology*, vol. 14, no. 4 (Oct.), 311–24.
Honigmann, John J.
  1968 'Interpersonal Relations in Atomistic Communities', *Human Organization*, vol. 27, no. 3 (Fall), 220–9.
Jacobs, J. B.
  1979 'A Preliminary Model of Particularistic Ties in Chinese Political Alliances: *Kan-ch'ing* and *Kuan-hsi* in a Rural Taiwanese Township', *The China Quarterly*, no. 78 (June), 237–73.
Kurth, S. B.
  1970 'Friendships and Friendly Relations', in G. J. McCall *et al.* (eds), *Social Relationships* (Chicago: Aldine), 136–70.
Lebra, T. S.
  1976 'Sex Equality for Japanese Women', *The Japan Interpreter*, vol. 10, nos. 3–4 (Winter), 284–95.
  1984 *Japanese Women: Constraint and Fulfilment* (Honolulu: University of Hawaii Press).
Levinson, Daniel J.
  1978 *The Seasons of a Man's Life* (New York: Ballantine Books).
Lewis, Robert A.
  1978 'Emotional Intimacy Among Men', *Journal of Social Issues*, vol. 34, no. 1, 108–21.
Leyton, Elliott (ed.)
  1974 *The Compact: Selected Dimensions of Friendship* (Toronto: University of Toronto Press).
MacDougall, John J.
  1981 'Elite Friendship Ties and Their Political Organizational Functions – the Case of Indonesia', *Bijdragen*, no. 137, 61–89.
Naegele, Kaspar D.
  1958 'Friendship and Acquaintance: an Exploration of Some Social Distinctions', *Harvard Educational Review*, vol. 28, no. 3 (Summer), 232–52.

Paine, Robert
  1974 'An Exploratory Analysis in "Middle Class" Culture', in E.
    Leyton (ed.), *The Compact: Selected Dimensions of Friendship*
    (Toronto: University of Toronto Press), 117–37.
Pharr, Susan J.
  1976 'The Japanese Woman: Evolving Views of Life and Role', in
    L. Austin (ed.), *Japan – the Paradox of Progress*, 301–27.
Piker, S.
  1968 'Friendship to the Death in Rural Thai Society', *Human
    Organization*, vol. 27, no. 3 (Fall), 200–4.
Pitt-Rivers, J.
  1968 'Pseudo-kinship', in D. L. Sills (ed.), *International
    Encyclopaedia of Social Sciences*, vol. 8 (Crowell Collier and
    Macmillan), 389–93.
Plath, David W.
  1980 *Long Engagements* (Stanford: Stanford University Press).
Pleck, J.
  1975 'Male–Male Friendship: Is Brotherhood Possible?' in N. Glazer-
    Malbin (ed.), *Old Family/New Family* (New York: D. Van
    Nostrand), 229–44.
Rōdōshō, Fujin-Kyoku (Ministry of Labour, Women's Bureau)
  1985 *Fujin Rōdō no Jitsujō* (Facts on Women's Labour) (Tokyo:
    Ōkurashō Insatsu-kyoku).
Rohlen, Thomas P.
  1974 *For Harmony and Strength: Japanese White-Collar Organization
    in Anthropological Perspective* (Berkeley, Cal.: University of
    California Press).
  1983 *Japan's High Schools* (Berkeley, Cal.: University of California
    Press).
Salamon, Sonya Blank
  1974 'In the Intimate Arena: Japanese Women and Their Families',
    Ph.D. dissertation, University of Illinois.
  1975 'The Varied Groups of Japanese and German Housewives', *The
    Japan Interpreter*, vol. 10, no. 2 (Autumn), 151–70.
Smith, Robert J.
  1956 'Kurusu, a Japanese Agricultural Community', in J. B. Cornell
    and R. J. Smith, *Two Japanese Villages* (Ann Arbor, Mich.:
    University of Michigan, Center for Japanese Studies), Occasional
    Papers no. 5, 1–112.
Sōmūchō, Seishōnen Taisaku Honbu
  1985 *Seishōnen to Katsuryoku* (Youth and Vitality) (Tokyo:
    Ōkurashō Insatsu-kyoku).
Sōrifu, Seishōnen Taisaku Honbu (Prime Minister's Office, Youth Policy
    Office)

1984   *Nihon no Seinen* (Japanese Youth) (Tokyo: Ōkurashō Insatsu-kyoku).

1985   *Fujin no Genjō to Shisaku* (The Present Life Conditions of Women and Governmental Policies) (Tokyo: Gyōsei).

Vogel, Ezra F.

1963   *Japan's New Middle Class*, 2nd edn (Berkeley, Cal.: University of California Press).

Vogel, S. H.

1978   'Professional Housewife: the Career of Urban Middle Class Japanese Women', *The Japan Interpreter*, vol. 12, no. 1 (Winter), 17–43.

Weinberg, S. Kirson

1970   'Primary Group Theory and Closest Friendship of the Same Sex', in T. Shibutani (ed.), *Human Nature and Collective Behaviour* (Englewood Cliffs, NJ: Prentice-Hall), 301–19.

Wimberley, Howard

1973a   'Conjugal Role Organisation and Social Networks in Japan and England', *Journal of Marriage and the Family*, vol. 35, no. 1 (Feb.), 125–30.

1973b   'On Living with Your Past: Style and Structure Among Contemporary Japanese Merchant Families', *Economic Development and Culture Change*, vol. 21, no. 3 (April), 423–8.

Wolf, E. R.

1966   'Kinship, Friendship and Patron–Client Relationships in Complex Societies', in M. Banto (ed.), *The Social Anthropology of Complex Societies* (London: Tavistock Publications), 1–22.

Yuan, Ying-ying

1975   'Affectivity and Instrumentality in Friendship Patterns Among American Women', in D. Raphael (ed.), *Being Female* (The Hague: Mouton Publishers), 87–98.

Part Two

Institutions and Structured Inequality

Chapter Five
A Multi-dimensional View of Stratification: a Framework for Comparative Analysis

Ross Mouer and Yoshio Sugimoto

1 Introduction

Social inequality occurs in various forms in all complex societies. Not only is inequality ubiquitous, it is also patterned or structured in ways which seem to be rather universal. The general arrangements which determine who gets more or less income, power and status are fairly well known. More subtle are the ways in which sub-groupings and subcultures cut across each other. The relevance of structured inequality to our understanding of Japanese society is underlined in several ways.

Modern theories of sampling acknowledge the existence of important sub-groups within national populations. Techniques of random stratified sampling and procedures for weighting tabulations are utilized in the study of Japanese society and other complex societies because random sampling by itself seldom guarantees that a good cross-section of the population is studied. In attempting to obtain a representative sample, the most obvious considerations relate to (1) organizational affiliation – especially in the economic sector – and to (2) economic notions of class which derive essentially from some reference to occupation. Other variables to be considered include (3) gender, (4) age or generation, (5) geographic or spatial location, (6) educational background, and (7) ethnic, religious and language affiliations. While some might wish to question the relative importance of ethnicity, religion and language as differentiating factors in Japanese society, the above list includes those 'demographic variables' which are seen as being fairly universally important in segmenting most industrialized societies. Less universal factors, which might account for inequality or social cleavage of one sort or another in particular societies, could also be added to that list.

There is another reason for suspecting that consideration of social inequality might provide an important key for understanding Japanese society. As the symbolic interactionists and others suggest, an awareness of the social context is critical when interpreting social behaviour (and therefore the responses of subjects to questionnaires and interviews). Hence, knowledge of the hierarchies and power relations within societies is central to evaluating much of the data used in social science research. Whether explanations of behaviour are sought from the viewpoint of the individual (the approach taken by Koike and Plath in this volume) or on the level of interpersonal relations (an approach which Hamaguchi [1979 and 1985] claims has more validity when explaining behaviour in Japanese society), the basic question still concerns social inequality: 'Where am I in the social matrix?' and 'How is this relationship different from other relationships?'

Social inequality is also an important source of social tension. In making assessments about how just or democratic a society or a set of relationships might be, it must become a major consideration. Empirical studies of conflict in Japan show clearly that one or more of the variables mentioned above often delineate the lines of cleavage (for example, cf. Hane 1982, Najita and Koschmann 1982, Sugimoto 1981 and Koschmann 1978). In this paper, Pharr refers to gender, age and ethnic status. Much of the discussion of social change in Japan concerns shifts in the distribution of the population from one category to another. For these various reasons, it is not surprising that much attention is given to social inequality not only in textbooks produced in North America and Western Europe, but also in those produced in Japan itself. Moreover, it is a common theme in books which deal with Japanese society itself. Most empirical studies of Japanese behaviour point to the importance of factors associated with stratification.

While inequality is a universal phenomenon, it is not obvious that the patterns of inequality are the same in all societies. Nor is it obvious that the same patterns of inequality in two different societies will have the same consequences in terms of (1) the extent to which a people's life chances are delineated or (2) stratal consciousness and the formation of subcultures. Although there is a good deal of debate about the extent to which the distribution of income is more egalitarian in Japan than in other societies, and the extent to which more social mobility occurs in Japan than elsewhere, the purpose of this paper is not to resolve such issues. Nor is it to uncover an explanatory or causal model which will explain Japanese behaviour in linear fashion.

In line with Befu's discussion of the social exchange model in Chapter 1, the aim is to present a contextual framework which will allow us better to understand how certain aspects of Japanese behaviour are shaped by social structures. It might be viewed as the structural side of the more culturally defined exchange model. Alternatively, it could also be seen as a way of taking the concern with social exchange at the micro level and considering its implications at the macro level. However, the aim is simply to introduce a means of placing the study of Japanese society more clearly into a comparative perspective.

As the framework for conceiving of stratification in multiple dimensions has been explained elsewhere in some detail (Mouer and Sugimoto 1986: 273–374; and Sugimoto and Mouer 1982: 215–40), only a brief outline is presented in the following section. The discussion then proceeds to relate the Japanese cultural context to the model. The final section will consider the model's assumptions and its relevance for the study of Japanese society in general.

2   The multi-dimensional model of social stratification

Models of social stratification focus on the question, 'Who gets what?' The discussion below considers first a few basic assumptions which direct the enquiry and give it relevance. It then shifts to 'the what' and to 'the who'. It concludes by considering the general consequences of inequality in terms of social class.

A Assumptions

Over the last decade the most commonly cited model of Japanese society has been the 'consensus or group model'. For the most part, that label has been used as an umbrella to cover a variety of competing statements about the Japanese. However, it has also served as a useful appellation identifying a set of viewpoints with a discernible set of common assumptions as part of a larger paradigm for the study of Japanese society (Befu 1981a and 1981b; Neustupný 1981; and Sugimoto and Mouer 1986). While that model continues to enjoy widespread support among policy makers and the public at large and also among many scholars, over the past decade it has come to be criticized for methodological and empirical shortcomings and certain ideological biases. Even more fundamental have been the criticisms of the assumptions underlying that particular vision of society.

In moving away from explanations which rely on notions of consensus, highly integrated groups and homogenous actors, it is first necessary to examine the basic assumptions implicit in any 'new' view of how Japanese society functions. Three assumptions in particular delineate the stratification aproach from the 'consensus approach'.

1 Variation The first assumption is that there is considerable variation in behaviour and in thinking among Japanese, that such variation is patterned, and that Japanese society cannot be understood without a careful assessment of such variation. Variation in Japanese society is symbolized by the variety of consumer goods readily available in Japan, by the variety of life styles, and by the status/power/income differences which characterize interpersonal relations. As a corollary, it is premissed that Japanese society is and has been characterized by appreciable levels of social conflict, that the issues often concern inequalities and the size of distributional shares, and that the lines of cleavage often reflect the patterns of inequality in society.

2 Self-interest A second understanding basic to the stratification model is that individuals will seek to maximize their self-interest. Self-interest is defined as the acquisition of societal rewards or resources which include not only (1) economic profit or income, but also (2) power, (3) status and (4) knowledge or information. In order to maximize self-interest, individuals normally engage in some rational calculation. That individuals seek to maximize their self-interest does not mean that they are always successful in doing so. The assumption is about motivation.

Although this assumption may also be basic to Befu's exchange model, the principle of reciprocity is seen as being more problematic. Whereas the stratification model developed below does not explain inequality in terms of its 'ultimate origins', it does suggest that distributions of social rewards at one point in time will be strongly reflected in distributions at a latter point in time. The model does not require that self-interest be the only motivating force; nor does it deny the existence of altruist acts or instances of reciprocal exchange. It does, however, consider them problematic, suggesting that many times behaviour appearing to be altruistic or reciprocal can also be interpreted either (1) as satisfying some individual psychological need (that is, as the attempt to acquire status or some other form of psychic reward), or (2) as attempts to conceal the generation of surplus in the act of exchange.

3 Volition The third assumption concerns the way in which volition is shaped. Camus observed some time ago that individuals can will what they do but cannot will what they will. Similarly, we have come to eschew placing too much emphasis on the individual (a position which does not seem to have been seriously undermined by the bio-sociologists), as there is still little agreement on the nature of the outside forces which shape the human will. Unlike the holistic view of Japanese society, which posits that a fairly neutral culture determines behaviour by shaping the consciousness of individuals socialized in Japanese society, the stratification model utilizes the distinction between culture and ideology. The focus on power inequalities highlights the difference between ideas which simply spread of their own accord and those which are propagated by the state or by powerful persons to attain particular political outcomes. This suggests that while culture is important, so too are subcultures; that the differentiation between *etic* and *emic* concepts can also be made within a society where the concepts and vocabulary of one group of people are imposed upon persons in another group.

B   'The what' in social stratification: societal rewards and
     societal resources
'Self-interest' is conceived in terms of the societal rewards or social
resources which individuals acquire: the socially generated utilities
which are distributed in any given society. As in the exchange
model, these may have either consummatory or instrumental
value, and most rewards or resources will have both values in one
proportion or another.

The question of how best to define and categorize societal
rewards has long been one focus of debate. In this paper the three
dimensions associated with the Weberian tradition – income,
power and status – are utilized along with information as a fourth
category. The categories shown in Table 5.1 are suggestive, not
definitive. Each is discussed below.

1 Income   Income accrues to people in several forms: wages,
interest and rent are the components commonly discussed in
textbooks on economics. Among the four rewards, income seems
to be the most tangible. Perhaps for that reason, its distribution is
the most frequently used index of social inequality in empirical
studies. Moreover, it is commonly assumed that an individual's
income is a fairly good indicator of the amount of his or her other
social rewards.

2 Power   In the political arena, the relevant resource is power.
The essence of power lies in the ability to cause other people to
do things either against their will or in a manner contrary to their
'true self-interest'. Here too various sub-categories exist; they
include physical coercion and brute force, authority, influence and
persuasion.

3 Information   With the advent of the 'information age' or the
'information society', a large body of literature has paid attention
to the importance of information not only as an end in itself, but
also as an important resource which can be used to generate
upward social mobility. Knowledge, 'learning', sophistication,
common sense and perception all refer to the possession of
information. Clearly, some types of information will provide more
lasting satisfaction and value than others. Those who have access
to information are often able to generate further information.
They are also active in shaping the terms in which social dialogue
occurs. Furthermore, to some extent they are able to control the
quality and quantity of information others receive.

4 Status and prestige   The literature on social stratification com-

Table 5.1   *Types of Rewards*

Reward cluster	Examples of each kind of reward	Academic disciplines in which the reward is most studied
Economic rewards	salary pension environment employment security job safety public recreation facilities leisure bribes	economics urban planning conservation ecology engineering
Political rewards	charisma influence authority contacts guns and tanks army or police force votes publicity posters slush funds information and intelligence	political science sociology of social movements law & jurisprudence military history political sociology
Status (including psychological rewards)	status prestige honour esteem fame publicity recognition charisma friends conspicuous consumption	sociology in general psychology and psychoanalysis theology sociology of religion
Information-based rewards	knowledge specific skills social awareness technical know-how patents and copyrights inventions instruction and education industrial property intelligence access to mass media books, papers and manuscripts	education educational sociology sociology of knowledge communications theory journalism

Source: Mouer and Sugimoto (1986), pp. 296–7.

monly suggests that there be a rather open or 'catch-all' category for the various kinds of satisfaction people receive from being favourably evaluated by those around them, especially by 'significant others'. The idea of positive social evaluation is captured partially in terms like 'fame', 'honour', 'esteem', 'respect' and 'popularity'. 'Prestige' and 'status' are the more generic terms. Those who are ostracized from society are usually denied access to this resource.

5 Fungibility Much attention has been given to the phenomenon known as 'status inconsistency', the situation in which one receives disproportionately large or small amounts of one reward. Sports stars may have enormous income and prestige without yielding any significant power. However, as a general rule there will be in society at large a rather high correlation among the amounts of each reward which individuals receive. In this regard, numerous observers have noted the interrelatedness of rewards, some emphasizing the causal links. Lenski (1966: 45–6) and Dahrendorf (1969) for example, have suggested that one's access to power determines one's access to other rewards or resources. The Lynds (cf. Gordon 1958: 122–48) and Wessolowski (1969: 122–48) emphasized the primary importance of economic rewards. Warner (cf. Gordon 1958: 89–100) emphasized status as the starting point.

When referring to income, power, prestige and information *as societal rewards*, two comments should be made. First, reference is not made to all forms of utility. Persons working for themselves (doing yardwork, growing vegetables or building on their own land) create utility. However, the stratification model is concerned with utility which is created as a result of social interaction or which has consequences for such interaction. In this process, then, social exchange is fundamental. Second, the term 'reward', which is used in many textbooks on the subject, is often misleading in that it suggests a return for some merit. The model presented here is not clear on how rewards are acquired. Given that most rewards have instrumental aspects, and can be exchanged as resources, inequality can be passed from one generation to another. This means that there is a certain permanence to the patterns of inequality – a permanence which underlines the importance of ascribed relationships and facilitates the formation of class cultures and other subcultures.

C   The 'who' in social stratification: groups of people and the agents of stratification

The patterns of inequality can be drawn even more clearly by referring specifically to certain characteristics of the people who consistently receive disproportionately large or small allotments. While there are an endless number of ways in which differentiation occurs, the major characteristics which affect one's share of societal rewards in most societies were listed above: gender, age, spatial location and educational background. Occupation, industry and organizational size are particularly important in industrial societies. Ethnic identity, religious affiliation and family background are also important in many societies. There are other differentiating features about which trans-societal generalizations are more difficult: personality, intelligence, looks and so on. In this paper, variables which seem to influence the access which people have to societal rewards are referred to as 'agents of stratification'.

One's access to income, power, information and prestige is influenced considerably by the category to which he or she is affiliated in terms of each agent of stratification. For example, a well-educated, middle-aged male employed by a large firm in the city is likely to have a larger income than a younger, less-educated female working for a small subcontractor in a semi-rural environment. However, there are exceptions, and many of these can be accounted for by considering still other vectors in the distributive matrix.

The idea of a vector space can easily be understood if we consider a diagram with only two dimensions: occupation and firm size. Figure 5.1 shows how these two dimensions might be represented together to form a vector space. For occupation, five groups are given in rank order from that with the largest share to that with the smallest. For firm type, five groupings are given based on firm size. The model presented in Figure 5.1 suggests that in most cases the business executives and professionals in large firms are the best paid and that unskilled workers in very small firms receive the least.

Every individual can be located in one of the thirty boxes, the distance of each box from the origin representing the relative access to rewards. It should be noted that the size of the box is not meant to indicate the size of its population, and that the distances represented on the axes are not drawn to scale. Further, the exact locations of the intersections of the lattice formed in this fashion would no doubt be different if we considered the distribution of each reward separately. They would also vary from one society to another, although we would expect that by and large the ordering of the categories in any given dimension would be rather universal.

Figure 5.1 *A Two-Dimensional Distribution of the Labour Force*

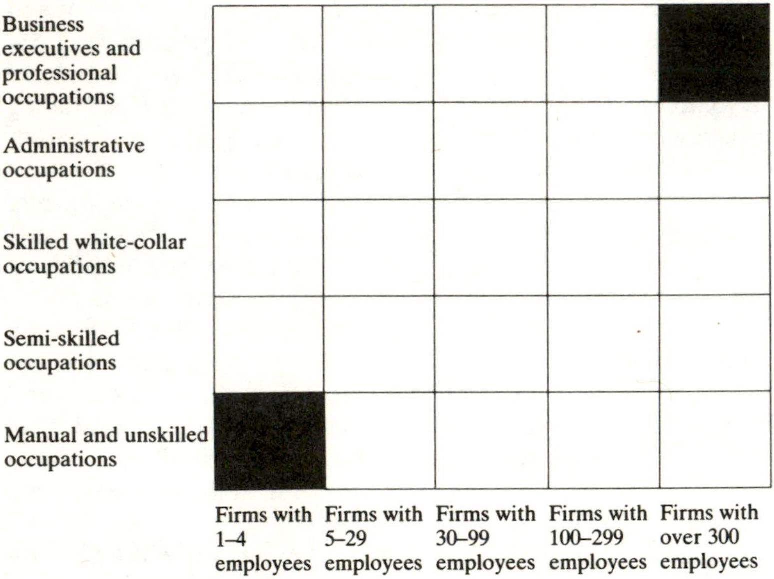

	Firms with 1–4 employees	Firms with 5–29 employees	Firms with 30–99 employees	Firms with 100–299 employees	Firms with over 300 employees
Business executives and professional occupations					■
Administrative occupations					
Skilled white-collar occupations					
Semi-skilled occupations					
Manual and unskilled occupations	■				

Source: Mouer and Sugimoto (1986), p. 286.

Some observers have attempted to assign primary importance to one particular agent of stratification. Such assertions have invited vigorous debate, and it would seem likely that the relative importance of different dimensions would vary from one society to another. For example, religion may be important in one society, but not in another. In most cases, these kinds of models do not include more than two types of groupings. The difficulties of visual presentation may have been one consideration limiting the development of more complex multi-dimensional models. Nevertheless, a framework with more dimensions would provide a better perspective on the complexity of Japanese society and the context in which social behaviour occurs.

D   The stratification model and the notion of social class

It is important to emphasize that differentiation alone does not always produce social stratification. First, differentiation may be random. Second, even when differentiation occurs in a systematic fashion, it may not be generally perceived. Social stratification begins to have a social significance when it is perceived as having consequences. One consequence, of course, is inter-generational linkage: the fact that distributions at one point in time seem to shape distributions at a later point in time. Another, more immediate consequence is the emergence of social classes.

Social stratification is a phenomenon which results from (1) the *objective fact* of systematic or structured differentiation being coupled with (2) the *subjective awareness* that one or more characteristics account for such differentiation. Among the various roles, traits and physical features which define the individual as someone fairly unique among thousands of human beings in the same society, certain ones have been shown repeatedly to correlate strongly with the individual's access to societal rewards. The same characteristics provide people with a common basis upon which they can communicate, associate and form groups. A sense of community is fostered by the common awareness that one shares with others characteristics which systematically give him or her a disproportionately large or small share of the societal rewards. In this way, the objective fact of differentiation links with the subjective dimension.

As individuals with similar distributions of societal rewards become more aware of their shared position in the overall structuring of inequality, their commonality takes on added significance. Groupings of such individuals develop communicative symbols and subcultures which serve to etch that commonality more permanently on the minds of those who constitute the society. As the number of characteristics shared by such a grouping come to embrace extensive patterns of language, life styles and ideology, the sense of group solidarity increases, and these groupings come to be recognized as 'social strata'. The most solidified strata are labelled 'social classes' in this chapter. The scheme developed here is shown in Table 5.2.

Defined in this fashion, the meaning of 'social class' is close to that given by Marx when he used the term '*Klasse für sich*', but without Marx's causative explanation. The main elements delineating class, then, are class consciousness, class conflict and

Table 5.2 *The Relative Solidarity of Persons in a Category Defined by an Agent of Stratification*

Kind of social amalgamation	Degree of cohesion and solidarity	Defining characteristics
No grouping	No cohesion; no solidarity	No systematic differentiation
Statistical grouping		Systematic differentiation 1 Systematic differentiation 2 Common awareness of differentiating trait(s)
Social stratum		1 Systematic differentiation 2 Common awareness of differentiating trait(s) 3 Common culture with others sharing the same trait(s) 4 Low mobility – some difficulty in changing trait(s) (inter- and intra-generationally)
Social class	Much cohesion; strong solidarity	1 Systematic differentiation 2 Common awareness of differentiating trait(s) 3 Common culture with others sharing the same trait(s) 4 Low mobility – considerable difficulty in changing trait(s) (inter- and intra-generationally) 5 Common sense of antagonism versus persons with dissimilar trait(s) 6 Quasi-organizational ties with those sharing the same trait(s)

class cohesion. On the other hand, 'statistical groupings' are close to the amalgamations referred to by Marx as *'Klasse an sich'*. Of interest here is Lenski's use (1966) of the term 'class'. Although the term is used by him to include less tightly knit amalgamations of people such as 'social groupings' or 'social strata' as defined in Table 5.2, he is none the less concerned very much with the social presence and the sense of becoming a group which people share. This concern is also found in Lenski's writings (1966) about the 'class struggle . . . between *age classes*' (p. 426) and 'the class system based upon sex' (p. 402). Parsons (1954: 328–9) too has it in mind when he writes about class as 'a plurality of kinship units' and 'class systems [which] . . . involve differentiations of family living'.

Most Japanese are very much aware of how the various kinds of societal rewards are distributed according to an individual's value in terms of the major stratification variables. Definite differences in patterned behaviour and thinking can be discerned among Japanese in different categories. Moreover, these differences produce stratal subcultures, as much in Japan as elsewhere. Each stratification variable tends to create these subcultures. Taken as a whole affiliation with one subculture in each dimension diffuses the individual's consciousness and retards the transformation of a sub-grouping delineated in any one dimension from being *Klasse an sich* into being a *Klasse für sich*. The interrelatedness of the rankings in one dimension (for example, the level of education) with those in another (such as occupation) mean that it is sometimes useful to think of social class as a catch-all or over-arching set of categories which make meaningful in the Japanese context references to the 'elites' and the 'masses', or to 'upper, middle and lower classes', or to 'the rulers' and to the 'ruled'.

The importance of a given stratification subsystem in generating its own form of class consciousness depends upon a number of factors. One is the extent to which the categories (or sub-groupings) used in conceiving of an agent of stratification account for overall dispersion in the distribution of societal rewards. This is the objective aspect of stratification and determines the relative importance of the subsystem in accounting for systematic differentiation. A second factor is the extent to which either some or all of the members in a particular subsystem grouping develop their own subculture and have a cohesive bond of solidarity. This is the subjective aspect of stratification and largely determines the amount of friction or tension produced by sub-groupings within a given subsystem. Finally, the importance of a given subsystem will depend upon the extent to which there is mobility between the various sub-groupings. Increased mobility will, on the objective level, reduce the importance attached to systematic differentiation in terms of access to societal rewards, while also weakening on the subjective level the individual's cohesive bonds with, and psychological commitment to, any given grouping.

The remaining sections of this chapter consider how the model might be cast in the Japanese setting. Elsewhere Mouer and Sugimoto (1986: 328–59) discussed the value which Japanese attach to income and power, and the way in which income, information and status may be used as power. Here attention is focused on the other two reward dimensions prestige and information.

3 Prestige and the Japanese concern with status

The Japanese concern with status and with their evaluation by others has frequently been cited in writings on Japan. Following on Benedict's analysis of 'shame' as a kind of negative measure of status, 'the loss of face', family honour and pride in one's company have received attention in the literature on Japan. The importance attached to status is also embedded in the language. For example, numerous expressions or proverbs underline the importance attached to status:

> (1) *mago nimo ishō*
>   (It is clothing and appearances that make the man.)
> (2) *keikō to narumo, gyūgo to naru nakare*
>   (Better to be the head of a lizard than the tail of a lion.)
> (3) *hito wa ichidai, nawa matsudai*
>   (One lives but a few years, one's [family] name will endure forever.)

There are also proverbs which express disdain for those who would value material comforts at the expense of having a fuller life:

> (1) *hana yori dango*
>   (Pudding before praise.)
> (2) *kotte wa shian ni atawazu*
>   (Too much diligence is harmful.)

Finally, there is also scorn for those who, at the other extreme, place too much emphasis on status and their own self-importance:

> (1) *kōman no hana*
>   (A nose which is better than anyone else's.)
> (2) *bushi wa kuwanedo takayōji*
>   (Even in poverty, the samurai will pose with airs.)

Taken together, these examples suggest (1) that status is perceived generally as being important for at least some Japanese, and (2) that there may be some variation in the importance attached to it. Overall, a survey of the several hundred *kotowaza* found in common dictionaries would probably suggest that status is seen as being important along with the other rewards. In other words, one cannot live on status alone, although at the same time one cannot really enjoy income and power without a certain measure of social approbation.

There is, of course, other evidence of the concern with status in Japan. Sometimes it comes in the form of enshrinement at Yasukuni Shrine, as the recent controversy concerning the burial and 'deification' of war criminals indicates; at other times it is seen in the amounts spent on wedding receptions or in the rush to buy a new 100,000-yen gold coin commemorating the sixtieth year of the current Emperor's rule.

As a taxonomy, Table 5.1 (page 163) suggests that it might be useful to think of each of the rewards in terms of a number of subcategories. In the Japanese context, four manifestations of the concern with prestige come readily to mind.

1. Awards   Japan is a society in which a large number of awards are given. These range from the awards given for outstanding achievement at school (*yūtōshō*) to the various decorations (*kunshō*) provided by the state, often in the name of the Emperor. Many firms have an established practice of giving the 'company president's award' (*shachōshō*) or 'branch head's award' (*shitenchōshō*) or other awards within particular sub-units of the organization. These are often given to entire units within the organization and are usually given weekly, monthly or annually, often as a reward for outstanding performance during a particular accounting period.

The bi-annual awarding of official medals in the spring and the fall (a practice begun in 1964) is widely publicized in all the newspapers and often on television. Moreover, the recipients are given graded awards, like first class honours, second class honours and so forth. The government also established a system of 'living national treasures' (*ningen kokuhō*) in the 1950s for outstanding artists both in the performing arts and in the traditional handicrafts. However, although particular awards have been introduced in the postwar period, the 'modern' system of awards itself was established in the Meiji period, in part to symbolize Japan's status as a modern nation state (cf. Naka 1973). Table 5.3 gives a very simple summary of various awards which are conferred by the state in

Table 5.3 *National System of Commendations*

Type	Awards	Comments	Year established
Kunshō	1 Daikun-i Kikuka Shōkeishi (Supreme Order of the Chrysanthemum)	Highest awards given by the state	1877
	2 Daikun-i Kikuka Daijushō (Grand Cordon of the Supreme Order of the Chrysanthemum)		1888
	1 Kyokujitsu shō (Order of the Rising Sun)	Men only	1875
	2 Hōkan shō (Order of the Precious Crown)	Women only	1888
	3 Zuihō shō (Order of the Sacred Treasure) *each order has 8 ranks*	Men and women	1888
Tokubetsu Kunshō	1 Kinshi Kunshō (Order of the Golden Kites)	Members of the armed forces (abolished in 1947)	1890
	2 Bunka Kunshō (Order of Culture)	Comes with a stipend	1937
Hōshō (Medals of Merit)	1 Kōju Hōshō (Red Cordon of Merit)	For saving a life	1881
	2 Rokujō Hōshō (Green Cordon of Merit)	For virtuous conduct	1881
	3 Ranju Hōshō (Indigo Blue Cordon of Merit)	For contributions to social welfare	1881
	4 Konju Hōshō (Navy Blue Cordon of Merit)	For the public donations of funds	1918
	5 Ōju Hōshō (Golden Cordon of Merit)	For contributions in business and industry	1955
	6 Shiju Hōshō (Purple Cordon of Merit)	For the development of the arts and science	1955

present-day Japan (cf. Sōrifu Shōkunkyoku 1986).

Although there appears to be no systematic study of all the awards and commendations available in Japanese society, the use of awards to motivate people seems to be extensive. Within the government alone, there are hundreds of prizes. The system branches out through various semi-official bodies into the private sector. The Ministry of Labour, for example, annually awards prizes for various activities. In the area of industrial safety there are (1) the Labour Minister's prize for having made the most improvement in safety (*shinpo shō*) which is awarded to seventy to eighty business enterprises each year, (2) the Minister's prize for the firm with the most outstanding safety record (*yūryō shō*), (3) another one for making efforts on behalf of safety (*doryoku shō*), and (4) one for meritorious service in the area of safety (*kōrō shō*). The ministry also awards (5) individual prizes for 'virtuous behaviour' in the area of safety (*zenkō shō*) (for example, for saving someone's life or for other brave acts to prevent a major disaster) and (6) smaller annual awards for the best poster, the best photograph, the best comic, the best essay and even, in one instance in 1954, for the best safety song lyrics which have promoted industrial safety and the prevention of occupational illness. In addition, the ministry annually nominates people for (7) the Prime Minister's Certificate of Commendation (the *Naikaku Sōri Daijin Hyōshō*), (8) the Medals of Merit (*hōshō*), and (9) various other decorations (*jokun*) which are awarded outside the ministry (on the early postwar period, cf. Nihon Sangyō Anzen Rengōkai 1963: 276–339; for a more recent update, cf. Chūō Rōdō Saigai Bōshi Kyōkai 1985: 38–59). Firms often compete for the enterprise prizes and offer various forms of incentives within their organizations to obtain good safety records.

Outside the ministry, various semi-official or quasi-autonomous bodies have been established to promote the various activities of the ministry. One such body is the Japan Council of Organizations for Young Workers (Nihon Kinrō Seishōnen Dantai Kyōgikai). The council was established in 1970 with the passage of the Young Workers' Welfare Law (Kinrō Seishōnen Fukushi hō), and consists of twenty-one national youth organizations. Each year it recommends its most outstanding affiliate and forty-seven youth clubs (one from each prefecture) for the Labour Minister's Medal of Commendation. Each of the organizations has its own programme and its own incentive schemes which involve various kinds of awards (cf. Nihon Kinrō Seishōnen Dantai 1986).

Prizes abound in many other areas of endeavour. In the world of literature and writing, the Akutagawa Prize, the Naoki Prize, the Osagari Jirō Prize, the Mainichi Publication Culture Prize, the Suntory Arts Prize and the Japan Essayists' Grand Prize are but a few of the best-known prizes. One list of literary prizes mentioned nearly 100 such awards (Kinokuniya Shoten: no date), including the Kanebō Misesu Juvenile Literary Prize said by the prestigious

173

Nihon Keizai Shinbun (11 Sept. 1986) to be highly esteemed by housewives. In the music world, there is the Japan Grand Record Prize and many others, plus the honour of being in the annual Red-White Song Competition which is held every New Year's eve by NHK. Nor should the prestige which accompanies the Demming Award (for quality control or small group activities to raise productivity) or the Avon Grand Prize (for outstanding contributions to society and to the 'development' of Japanese women) be overlooked as a motivating force in Japanese society. In addition to the Emperor's Cup, and a whole slew of prizes for the winner of each *sumō* tournament, there are the Fighting Spirit Prize, the Technique Prize and the Distinguished Performance Prize. In baseball, Japan has its own MVP awards (in fact, there was even an MVP of the Week award for each league in 1986), the triple crown and various other lesser awards. There are few fields in Japan in which someone is not awarded a prize.

Japanese are also inveterate competitors for national prestige in the international sweepstakes. The successful holding of the Olympic Games in Tokyo (1964), the World Exhibition in Osaka (1970) and the Sapporo Winter Olympics (1972) caught the imagination of many Japanese and were fully celebrated as international events by the coverage on Japan's national public broadcasting station. Coverage of the recent Asiad in Korea and the media rationalizations for Japan's dropping to third in the medal count indicate the importance attached by many Japanese to the nation's performance in that arena. The conferring of the Prime Minister's Award on Nakano Kōichi (professional cyclist) and on Murofushi Shigenobu (hammer thrower) for their success in international sports also points to the value placed on excellence at this level. Media reports on the Nobel Prize winners, human rights awards, the Harrison Prescott Eddy Medal and the Order of Aquira Azteca also serve to keep the matter of international prestige uppermost in many Japanese minds. As for the prestige it derives by offering prizes to foreigners, Japan offers not only its various official orders, but also the Japan Foundation Prize, the KICA Prize, the Japan Friendship Award, Zenkoku Yūgigyō's Pachinko Culture Award, assorted prizes in tennis and golf, and a host of other honours, their esteem bolstered by monetary reward as well.

2 Conspicuous consumption   Style also seems to be appreciated in Japan. One tangible expression of style comes in the form of parading consumer goods. There are many goods in Japan, from artwork to clothing and furniture, which have much more than a utilitarian value. As Tanaka's novel, *Nantonaku Kursuitaru* (Crystal Always), indicates, brand names seem to be particularly important in all fields of consumer marketing in Japan, and to a certain extent people are known by the labels of the goods they purchase. As Ejiri (1986) and others argue, private 'brandism' is a useful technique in target marketing a particular socio-economic group within the population, because brands identify their purchasers as being in a certain status group or from within a particularly well-thought-of group or sub-stratum within Japanese society.

Such labels are not just the mark of a particular income level; they also suggest discernment, taste and personal sophistication. Possession of these goods and the manner in which they are displayed can be a source of considerable social prestige and envy. In Japan, there is the phrase, '*kakko ii!*' There is also a sense of bad taste, and the possession of valued goods alone will not necessarily bring a favourable appraisal. There are social norms which specify the conditions under which these kinds of goods should be conspicuously displayed.

This concern seems also to be carried to the grave. At death people pay large sums for *kakko ii* posthumous names (*kaimyō*) which will mark the location of their graves. To have the posthumous title '*in*' after one's name indicates that one is of the highest status; '*den*' and '*kyo*' come a little below that in the hierarchy of status; '*shi*' (the character for '*samurai*'), which once indicated a fair amount of status in the secular world, is at the bottom of the titles when it comes to afterlife. In everyday life, people often refer to this status system as '*inden kyoshi*'.

3 'Qualifications' In many areas, Japanese like having a status-based ranking. Such rankings are provided in flower arranging, tea ceremony, and Japanese dancing; they are also found in *judō*, *kendō*, *igo* and *shōgi*. A good handicap in golf and a recognized level of English-language proficiency (as ascertained in a national test) provide status in a similar manner. The rankings do not necessarily reflect actual abilities, although in awarding a ranking enough attention is given to performance criteria enough of the time to allow all holders of a rank to enjoy the kudos associated with having the commensurate skill.

The desire to display a *kanban* (shingle) carries over into the world of work. The obvious examples, of course, can be found in the traditional professions. The examinations for entering the medical and legal professions are good examples. Once the examination is passed and the qualification is received, doctors and lawyers have enough status from the qualification that they can continue to practise long after their skills are out of date. However, there is also, to be sure, a skill or knowledge component which cannot be overlooked, and clients will distinguish between practitioners on the basis of their ability. Within the profession, there are laurels for the more proficient as the novel cited in Chapter 1 by Befu (*Shiroi Kyotō*) clearly suggests.

However, the concern with qualifications can be found much more widely among the population. The use of two kinds of '*shi*' – one being the suffix for *bengoshi* (lawyer) and the other for *ishi* (doctor) and *kyōshi* (teacher) – and other professional-sounding titles has spread to the renaming of many less skilled occupations to give them a (more) professional appearance. Examples include '*chōrishi*' for '*itamae*' (cook), '*hanbaishi*' for '*ten-in*' or '*serusùman*' (salesperson or salesman), and *eigo gaido tsuyakushi* for *eigo no gaido* (English-speaking guide). These 'titles' cannot be understood apart from the state-sponsored system of examinations and certification; they tend to require the accumulation of knowledge and tend to fuse status with set amounts of information.

This orientation has been reinforced in the vocational area by the implementation of a national system of examinations and licensing. Newspapers in Japan frequently carry the advertisements of schools which will prepare students in particular examinations. The General Correspondence Education Centre (Sōgō Tsūshin Kyōiku Sentā), for example, offers correspondence courses in over 200 subjects – some in language and 'hobby-like activities', but the vast majority in vocationally oriented skills. However, this process is not unique to Japan.

The attempt to 'professionalize' in order to achieve greater status (as well as income and influence) follows a similar path in many countries (cf. Larson 1977). One step is to change the name of the occupation or skill involved; another is to restrict employment in the area to persons with such a certificate. The formation of an association also serves to heighten the prestige attached to a qualification. The *iemoto* system is one way of providing that additional prestige, and in many areas it is not unusual to find several *iemoto* competing with each other for status.

4 Popularity   Pop stars, movie stars and other entertainers are able to gauge their level of popularity in the ratings. Figures are also available on the number of best-sellers sold and on the number of records sold to provide interested persons with a quantified measure of their relative prestige in the industry.

The study of status frequently leads to a consideration of the imperial family. Many of the state honours mentioned above are conferred in the Emperor's name. The Emperor's Cup in horse racing and in *sumō* and the use of the imperial family in presenting other awards reinforce a consciousness in which the Emperor and the royal family are at the apex of the status hierarchy. This is one aspect of the Emperor system dealt with in the paper by Kawamura. In the media, criticism of the imperial institution and 'inside revelations' about the life of the imperial family are taboo. This contrasts with what happens in England.

4   Knowledge and the Japanese concern with information

In recent years reference has frequently been made to the 'information age' and the 'information society' (cf. Hamaguchi 1986). Part of the concern with information may reflect a belief in technology-related progress. Itō's discussion (1985) of *'bunmei'* (civilization) as a value-laden concept suggests that the Japanese have for some time placed a value on that type of information. The level of literacy and the size of Japan's mass media are often cited by other Japanese as evidence of their society's progress. Although Wada (1986) and others point to the fact that Japan continues to be an importer of information and might wish to question the extent to which Japan has come to be a 'high-level information society', there seems in the literature concerning the 'informationalization' of Japanese society a clear shift from simply an interest in the hardware and in the increased capacity to store large quantities of data to a concern with the development of new organizational forms for analyzing and processing information, and with the significance of such developments for Japanese society as a social system (cf. Nihon Rōdō Kyōkai 1986).

Although 'information society' continues to be a vague term, Itō (1977: 14–15) argued some time ago that the term refers to three general phenomena occurring in Japanese society. One is

177

the increase in the volume of information in Japanese society, which he estimated in 1975 to be fifty times the level in 1965. Another is the accelerating rate at which Japanese are required to process various kinds of information. The third is the increasing importance of access to information as a criteria accounting for the stratification of society. For better or for worse, the move toward a more information-oriented society seems to be fully under way in Japan, with the government solidly supporting the 'informationalizing' programmes of the various ministries. Those programmes – all with *katakana*-studded labels – include the Teletopia Project (Ministry of Communications), the New Media Community Concept (MITI), Greentopia activities (the Ministry of Agriculture and Forestry), the design of Media Terminals (Ministry of Transport) and the building of Intelligent Cities (Ministry of Construction) (cf. *NKSC*, 16 Sept. 1986: 29). The books on 'ME-ka' (micro-electronization) and 'OA' (office automation) are making way on the shelves in the business management sections of the large city bookstores for volumes which deal explicitly with these broader and more abstract concepts of 'informationalization' (for example, cf. Hosokawa *et al.* 1984).

The awareness of the importance of education in national development is not new. Japan's modernization cannot be understood apart from the drive to acquire information, particularly technology, from abroad. The emphasis attached to formal education in Japan and its perceived role in promoting the nation's development was highly evaluated by those who formulated the Karachi Plan and has since been accepted as an important phenomenon in Japan (cf. Nakayama 1975; OECD 1971; Vogel 1979). Dore noted some time ago (1965) that the level of male literacy was quite high even in the Tokugawa period. Levine and Kawada (1980) among others have documented the emphasis on education following the Meiji Restoration, and the Imperial Rescript on Education is commonly cited (or even reprinted) in many of the textbooks on Japanese history and modernization (for example, cf. Passin 1965).

More concrete is the concern with 'examination hell' and with acquisition of facts in order to enter Japan's more prestigious educational institutions. On a per capita basis, newspaper circulation is among the highest in the world, and the range of periodicals and books is enormous. The large number of cultural centres and private classrooms which have appeared up and down the country over the last ten to fifteen years no doubt reflects the demand for various kinds of tuition in a wide range of individual pursuits. The 'Survey of Reading Habits' conducted annually by the *Mainichi Shinbun* indicates that the 'average Japanese' spends considerable time each day reading newspapers (35 minutes), perusing books, magazines and other material (45 minutes) or watching television (141 minutes) and listening to the radio (39 minutes) (*MSC*, 27 Oct. 1986: 10). The much larger and detailed NHK survey puts the figures for 1980 at 21 minutes (newspapers), 15 (other reading material), 177 (television) and 39 (radio), and reveals that the time spent in these activities has actually increased slightly over time (NHK Hōsō Yoron Chōsasho 1982: 91).

Finally, mention might be made of the Japanese infatuation with the concept of intelligence. A cross-national study of intelligence by a British group in 1982 showing the Japanese to have the highest IQs was widely publicized in Japan, and Tsunoda's volume (1978) on the Japanese brain was for some time a best-seller (also cf. his popular tape, Tsunoda 1984, and Higuchi 1972). Prime Minister Nakasone's remarks on lower levels of intelligence in America were also seen in many reports as being quite an accepted viewpoint in Japan.

The concern with information and intelligence can also be seen in the large number of proverbs which deal with intelligence, the plight of fools and idiots, and the prosperity and happiness which accompany intelligence.

(1) *heta no kangae yasumu ni nitari*
   (Much fails when fools think.)
(2) *baka mo yasumi yasumi ie*
   (Fools say little of interest.)
(3) *kanjō atte zeni tarazu*
   (A fool often finds himself short of his reckoning.)
(4) *oni mo shitta oni ga yoi*
   (The devil you know is better than devil you don't know.)
(5) *chie wa bandai no takara*
   (Wisdom is better than riches.)
(6) *shiranu koto wa hito ni toe*
   (Knowledge comes from asking.)

There are also a large number of proverbs concerning the essence of knowledge.

(1) *shirumono wa iwazu, iumono wa shirazu*
    (Talking is not knowing; and those who know don't talk.)
(2) *kannan naji o tama ni su*
    (Adversity makes men wise.)
(3) *nama byōhō wa ōkega no moto*
    (A little learning is a dangerous thing.)
(4) *haya gatten no hayawasure*
    (Soon learnt, soon forgotten.)

Here too, however, there is advice to avoid putting too much stock in knowledge alone, although it sometimes comes in a back-handed fashion:

(1) *shiranu ga hotoke*
    (Ignorance is bliss.)
(2) *baka ni kurō nashi*
    (A fool's life is without trouble.)

A   Types of information

In talking about information, it is useful to consider at least two subcategories, knowledge with a high instrumental value and knowledge which serves primarily to satisfy an inner curiosity and which can be said to have primarily an expressive value.

1 Instrumental information   Much of the information generated and processed in Japanese society is concerned with economic activity. Although few of the facts crammed into one's head for entrance examinations seldom have any direct relationship to the content of one's work, most students are aware that the ability to retain factual information and to pass examinations is directly linked with their employment prospects. The large manufacturers want to hire high-school graduates who will be able to utilize the techniques commonly associated with quality control activities. In this volume, Koike touches upon the broader notions of skill and the cluster of production-related knowledge which are necessary for QC circles to work. At a more basic level, however, there is a fair array of simple statistical and analytical skills which are necessary to initiate the exercise. These include bar graphs and histograms, Pareto (accumulative frequency) curves, fishbone diagrams, scatter plot diagrams, flow charts, checklist construction, survey techniques and sampling procedures (cf. Tsuruda 1986). If this seems to be an 'unbelievable' achievement for high-school graduates, one needs only to recall the extent to which the sports pages in Japan's national papers use fancy charts and diagrams to present interpolations of the likely performance of top athletes under several different assumptions.

At the 'higher levels', university graduates with an eye on top managerial posts in Japan's large firms are expected to have a basic understanding of company-wide information systems, interchangeable and multi-purpose data bases and information networking (cf. Shimada 1986: especially pp. 2–100). Managers at this level are also expected to absorb a good deal of 'cultured information' about leadership and human relations drawn both from Western scholarship and Eastern philosophy and from uniquely Japanese syntheses of the two, as the recent boom in Yasuoka Masahiro's 'Yōmeigaku' reveals. Little needs to be added about the obvious growth of the information supplying and servicing industries which have mushroomed over the past two decades.

In referring to information as a social resource, we are talking not only about technology, fairly confidential information obtained within an organizational setting or the processed data which comes out of the computer, but also about (1) various subjects from the basics of chemistry and biology to a basic appreciation of music, (2) news on current events and the 'word around town', and (3) a feeling for social customs and etiquette. Reference is made not only to various social skills and to a suitable awareness of which clothes to wear and how to introduce oneself, but also to having information concerning the labour market, whom to see about employment, the questions or format of particular school and company entrance examinations, the linkages among educational institutions at various levels, and the interconnections between the educational sector and the employment sector.

2 Information as a consumer good   In Japan there are a wide variety of venues for learning all kinds of hobbies or skills related to the enjoyment of one's leisure. A small sample of the pastimes taught in these courses would include *bonsai*, calligraphy, cooking, sewing, *shōgi*, gold inlay, flower arrangement, charcoal painting, tennis and photography. Sometimes, instruction in one or more of these activities is offered after working hours by the larger firms as an attractive fringe benefit for their employees. Many individuals make their own private arrangements and visit schools or a teacher's home to acquire this kind of knowledge. The growth of *kakushu gakkō* (miscellaneous schools) providing this kind of education has been remarkable, and advertisements for such tuition appear daily in the newspapers and with each issue of the weeklies and the monthly magazines.

In another direction the mass media supplies a steady diet of rumours, puzzles and generally 'light information' in which satisfaction is attained merely from being the first to pass it on. This would also be some of the value of sports news and the broadcasting of sports events. Information on fashion and crime would also fall into the same category. It is difficult to see how one benefits instrumentally by the knowledge that some movie actress does or does not wear panties of a certain colour. As Asano (1984 and 1985) notes, although few readers gain any lasting utility from knowing the real name of a criminal or from seeing his or her picture in the newspaper, many enjoy browsing through articles about such matters. The circulation of such ill-informed opinions often means that suspects are tried and found guilty in the mass media and by the public long before their case gets to the courtroom. One could say that much of the information circulated as *nihonjinron* also falls into this subcategory of stereotyped information. Finally, there are the comic books and weekly magazines at the local bookstore and the home dramas on television. If there is a utilitarian value in all this information, it is in the recipient's being able to converse with others, since most people have some knowledge of this genre. Its apparent irrelevance allows individuals from different backgrounds to develop a relationship on bases apart from the 'business at hand' which, as the only basis for dialogue, may actually be a serious source of conflict.

The sudden growth in the media's involvement in providing these kinds of information for mass consumption has sparked a considerable debate. In addition, the Prime Minister's concern with spies and the recent moves to implement anti-espionage legislation have run against the aims of civil groups to foster the development of legislation requiring the government to make more of its information available to the public. The trade-off between the right-to-know and the right-to-privacy was also at the centre of many of the pollution cases where firms even destroyed information and where employees (including union members) stonewalled when concerned members of the public wanted to know about the firm's production processes. The beating of Eugene

Smith is one symbol of the struggle for this kind of valued information.

One of the themes for Newspaper Week in 1986 was the need for more 'warmth' (*atatakasa*) in news reporting. Most newspapers had editorials which noted the slide toward sensationalism at any cost because (1) the public seemed to want to buy that kind of information, and (2) the competition among the 'photo weeklies' (such as *Focus* and *Friday*) for readers is so fierce that editors will stop at no lengths to produce the ultimate 'exposure' or the most shocking photograph (cf. *MSC*, 15 Oct. 86: 5; *JT*, 24 Oct. 86: 16). The 3-million-yen suit of the distinguished publishing firm, Kodansha, for a photograph (secretly taken of a woman cooking in her kitchen) in its weekly, *Friday*, is but one example (*JT*, 23 Oct. 86: 2; *JT*, 25 Oct. 86: 2).

Another issue is the release of the name of criminal suspects, those who might have civil cases pending in court, and others who have engaged in 'controversial behaviour'. The problem is not just that others will 'know'. By releasing names, the persons in question instantaneously become 'public figures' and are often subjected to threatening phone calls or to other forms of psychological and physical harassment. Possession of information has consequences for power relations in society.

Video copyrighting is yet another issue. For many years, copyrights to books have been only loosely protected as photo-copying became widespread, certainly in academia. Partially reflecting developments abroad, the debate on copyright in Japan has brought to the surface rather strong feelings about the 'ownership' of this type of 'information'.

B   The acquisition of knowledge

These various forms of knowledge are acquired in diverse ways: life at school, life at home, playing with interesting toys and games, socializing with others in various walks of life. In recent years the importance of networking has received much attention in the writings concerning the career prospects of Japanese women. Books for young employees seeking managerial positions repeatedly emphasize the importance of self-education, self-enlightenment and other forms of individually oriented approaches to acquiring a broadly based knowledge (of which only some are directly related to the running of a modern firm). In this volume

Koike discusses how broadly based technical knowledge is acquired through a career structured around job rotations in the factory. Although the recommendations of the Provisional Council on Educational Reform (Rinji Kyoiku Shingikai) are phrased in very abstract terms, they too underline the importance attached to 'lifetime education'.

Although knowledge can be acquired in a variety of ways, one cannot overlook the importance of how compulsory education is organized in Japan. Emphasis is placed on 'moral education' (for example, the proper way to conform), and various kinds of regulations and punishments are built into the system to ensure that the lessons are remembered. The proliferation of preparatory schools serve to channel knowledge to a select few from the wealthier families in society. For women bent on a career as a housewife and mother, there are courses to prepare them for marriage (*hanayome shugyō*) and to give them a 'finishing' (*reigi*) and manners (*sahō*) appropriate to their station in life.

The importance of acquiring information also comes out in the fact that some kinds of information are occasionally acquired illegally or in socially unapproved ways, just as is income. Although the number of students who get into universities and other schools through the 'back door' is not known, stories about such entrance at medical schools are legend in Japan, and 'entrance scandals' appear in the news each year. Japanese companies are known to use 'spies', to be extremely security conscious, and to investigate as discreetly as possible the personal activities of prospective employees.

5 Reward fungibility

The model of stratification presented here does not require that there be a correlation between the amount of power, income, information and status that individuals acquire. It even invites speculation that the variation in the level of correlation from one society to another might assist in explaining differences among societies in their levels of conflict and in the way in which social inequality is structured and perceived. However, it was posited above that there will be high positive correlations in most societies. This is because one type of reward can often be exchanged for another type in line with the dynamics of the social exchange model. The extent of such correlation and the processes of exchange in Japanese society require further study.

Both in the theoretical discussion above and in the citation of the proverbs with regard to the Japanese context, it was suggested that the various rewards were interchangeable, and also that there was likely to be a strong correlation among the amounts of each reward which each individual received. At the present there is no comprehensive set of survey data for Japanese society which would allow us to test carefully this proposition about fungibility with the individual as the unit of analysis. However, a number of illustrations can be presented which might give some idea of the grey or overlapping areas where one type of reward seems to function as another type.

The value of some information is relative to the existence of competing information. People can come to have relatively more information by displacing the information of others. Accordingly, the dissemination of information is partially a competition aimed at detracting attention from other information. As words like 'propaganda' and 'brain washing' readily suggest, much information created in modern society has an ideological dimension. It consists of value-laden theories about the status of people, social arrangements and commercial products.

The images created by advertising, for example, shape the view many Japanese have of themselves and of others. In the mid-1980s many firms were spending vast amounts to improve their corporate image. The reasons for this behaviour are compound. Some executives have found that they can introduce new ideas and even change corporate structure under the guise of improving 'corporate image'. Others have found it necessary to do so in order to launch new products or services with which their company has not previously been associated. For others, it fulfils a morale-boosting function (cf. Tanaka 1986; Orita 1986; Okada 1985). A further function, which might be raised out of the past when corporate management was under fire for pollution and hoarding, would be the legitimation of management. A good deal was written about business ethics in the late 1960s and early 1970s (cf. Narumo 1970 and Okamoto 1973). The current authors suspect that the recent concern with corporate image reflects a combined concern with all of these issues. The use of company logos, the wearing of company badges or pins – as well as the singing of company songs and the chanting of company slogans at morning gatherings (*chōreikai*) – are all commonly cited examples of efforts to keep corporate identity uppermost in the minds of ordinary employees in Japan's large firms. Clark's brief references (1979) to the 'society of industry' also point to the importance of this kind of image building among the Japanese who, he alleges, are more aware of the way companies are ranked in each industry than are perhaps the people in other societies. It is not an accident that the Japan Council of Organizations for Young Workers presents its awards on the third Saturday of July; in doing so there is an explicit reference to the idea of *yabuiri*, which might be translated as 'servants' day' or 'apprentices' day', the time of year when young persons were magnanimously given a day off and some spending money so they could visit their families in the rural areas for *obon* in July and for the commemoration of their coming of age in January.

Sports and entertainment are an area where status, income and political influence become intertwined. The overlapping has no doubt become more pronounced with the development of the mass media and commercial advertising. Takamiyama, Japan's first top-class *sumō* wrestler from abroad, recently commented that a wrestler's pay is poor, but that the commercials pay well (Ray 1986; 13). Many entertainers and some intellectuals have been able to convert their popularity in the media into votes at the polls on election day, the most recent example being the comedian Nishikawa Kiyoshi.

The proposition concerning fungibility becomes even more evident when attention is focused on the agents of stratification. For example, the wage/income differential between men and women is well established. Women's relative absence from managerial positions in the private sector and from the elected legislative bodies, their lack of access to higher education and their 'failure' to be honoured with the state's medals and other awards also require little elaboration. In terms of ethnicity, the Burakumin and Koreans have disproportionately small shares of all rewards. Education levels and 'functional literacy roles' are lower. Income is lower. Although through collective action they are able to bring political pressure to bear, individuals are much less able to acquire positions of authority. The low esteem in which they are held may be confirmed by reference to marriage patterns and to the more blatant forms of discrimination that members of these minorities experience in their everyday lives. Little needs to be said about the dualities associated with firm size. Employees in the large firms enjoy not only better economic remuneration; they also tend to have more opportunity to acquire information and to have the tenured security and the demeanour associated with a privileged status within society.

6 Stratification and the differentiation of behaviour in Japan

The 'agents of stratification' delineate not only the lines of inequality. They also point to significant variations in behaviour. In the remaining paragraphs, several examples of such variation are provided. Elsewhere the authors (1986: 342–56) have written about the variation which occurs in political attitudes, the size of the male–female wage differential, language and the crime rate. That discussion also touched upon the structure of the labour market, voting behaviour, family life, the uses of leisure, popular disturbances and religious affiliation. In this condensed presentation, still other examples are presented to illustrate the way in which variation is associated with the agents of stratification introduced above. The behaviours cited here are from the areas of health, consumer behaviour, interpersonal relationships, religious practices, and orientations toward music.

A Health

With a life expectancy over seventy-five years, the longevity of the Japanese in the late 1980s is among the highest in the world. However, the chances of living to a certain age are not the same for all Japanese. Longevity for men and women varies by more than five years, and this gap has widened over time (Kōseishō Daijin Kanbō 1980: 58). Longevity also varies by geographic area, being 73.8 for men in Akita and 75.8 for men in Tokyo (Jinkō Mondai Shingikai 1974: 366–7). Although we do not have data to substantiate the point, it is our belief that average life expectancy also varies directly with family income and one's socio-economic status.

It is not surprising, then, that the likelihood of contracting various illnesses also varies in these ways. It increases with age (*MSC*, 4 July 1986: 15) and is lower among women for many illnesses (newspaper article from women's file). Another survey (NHK, Hōsō Yoron Chōsa Kenkyūjo 1981: 36–7) reported that the percentage of Japanese experiencing pain in their hips and shoulders increased with age, but was consistently higher for women in all age groups (and especially high for working women in the child-rearing age groups). The same study further reveals that the extent to which persons worried about their health also varies by age, sex, industry and occupation, as does the extent to which people feel compelled to overwork themselves, to overdo things, and to submit themselves for physical examinations (pp. 16–26). Finally, the 'health map' prepared by the Ministry of Welfare (Kōseishō 1985) confirms that there is considerable variation in the incidence of various illnesses in Japan. While that survey does not report on the relationship of illness to family income, it does record the per capita average annual medical expenses for elderly persons as being Y508,000 (US$2,000–3,000) in 1985 – a figure which represents roughly 10 per cent of estimated average annual *household* income for all employee households in the same year.

In the area of industrial accidents, the figures reported from the Survey on Industrial Injuries (Rōdō Saigai Dōkō Chōsa) show that accident rates vary significantly by firm size, industry and sex (cf. Rōdōshō 1986: 74–7). Interestingly, the same variables seem to account for variation in the willingness of firms to invest in safety measures (in terms of administration, equipment and education) or to take special steps to protect older workers whose presence in the labour force is increasing over time (cf. the Survey on Industrial Safety and Health [Rōdō Anzen Eisei Kihon Chōsa] as presented in Rōdōshō Daijin Kanbō Jōhōbu 1981: 232–41). In terms of firm size and industry, the enterprises with longer hours of work tend to be the ones which have the higher accident rates, a finding which is again not surprising given the relationship between fatigue and accidents (cf. Hosokawa 1981: 58, 184–9 and 253–4). Finally, the Research Institute for the Science of Labour (Rōdō Kagaku Kenkyūjo 1959: 213) presents data showing that the incidence of tuberculosis in the 1950s varied inversely by income class and occupational status.

It might also be argued that the availability of medical services varies with income (Hino 1986: 12) and employment status (for example, in terms of the coverage provided by different insurance schemes). Access to medical facilities also varies from urban to rural areas (Kōseishō Daijin Kanbō 1980: 117). There is also a circular kind of causation, as persons with certain types of illnesses (infantile paralysis, the blind or the victims of the bombing in Hiroshima and Nagasaki) have been discriminated against in the past both at work and in the education system, and this has tended to disadvantage them further in terms of their access to societal rewards.

B   Consumer behaviour

In recent years, a good deal of attention has been paid to the segmented nature of consumer behaviour and of life styles in Japan, especially among the urban population. As the title of one book suggests (Hakuhōdō Seikatsu Sōgō Kenkyūjo 1985), there has been a shift away from the notion that Japanese society is a *'taishū'* (mass) society toward an image of Japanese society as a *'bunshū'* (segmented) society. The same theme has also been taken up by Yamazaki (1984) and Fujioka (1984). Ejiri (1985) has also noted the importance of targeting specific social strata, as opposed to the effort to sell to all Japanese, if department stores are to survive in the competition with other retailers.

Even the most recent survey of the Prime Minister's Office reveals a move away from the 'middle-class' consciousness which has so far been emphasized in most descriptions of Japanese society (cf. *NKSC*, 3 Nov. 86: 1; *MSC*, 5 Nov. 86: 5). While there is room to debate the methodology of the survey and the extent to which it has over time really grasped the subjective consciousness of the Japanese or really reflected in a meaningful way the social structure (and thereby room to contemplate the extent to which such a consciousness was ever more than an image created through the survey and its coverage in the media), the discussion here is limited to providing a few examples of how differentiation has occurred in the Japanese retail market.

The above report by Hakuhōdō (1985: 167) suggests that the simple rule of thumb which reads 'high price = high quality and cheap price = poor quality' is no longer an adequate guide to consumer behaviour. Consumers are, in addition, paying attention to the actual utility of goods in terms of their everyday lives. This means that two changes are occurring. One is further differentiation in consumer behaviour; the other is greater sensitivity to the importance of the variables (that is, the agents of stratification) which account for income inequality and shape decisions about life-style and targeted life-styles.

The examples of product differentiation are considerable. In the media, attention has been given to the emergence of magazines with information on living styles (*josei seikatsu jōhōshi*) at the expense of the more traditional women's magazines which sprang up in the 1960s (*fujinshi*). As a completely different genre, the former is seen as providing images of differentiated life styles pursued by different types of Japanese women, while the latter has been known for its promotion of mass products and a standardized image of what it means to be 'the typical Japanese woman' (cf. *MSC*, 15 Sept. 1986: 8).

C   Interpersonal relationships

Regional differences in the nature of interpersonal relations manifest themselves in several ways. One is in family style. Fukutake's classic study (1949) of *ie* structure in two areas suggested a clear distinction between (1) the hierarchically structured households in the Tōhoku and Chūbu regions, where the main household (*honke*) dominated the branch households (*bunke*) within the overall framework of the *dōzoku*, and (2) the more collectivistically organized self-help groups (*kō*) which existed in western Japan for the performance of various economic, religious and social functions. Fukutake referred to the first as representing the principle of '*dōzoku ketsugō*' and the latter as representing the principle of '*kōgumi ketsugō*'. In those terms, the north-eastern part of Japan would be relatively more vertical, while those in the western part would be relatively more horizontal.

A survey by NHK's Public Opinion Research Institute (1979) indicated other regional differences. In the Tōhoku, Shikoku and Kyūshū regions, which represent the poorer areas of Japan, it was found that interpersonal relationships were more restricted but much more intense when they did occur, whereas in the major urban areas such as Osaka and Tokyo, individuals seemed to have a larger number of acquaintances but with weaker bonds of trust on the average.

Another study by the Public Opinion Research Unit of the Sankei newspaper company (1976: 88–9) shows that the practice of gift giving varies with occupation. For example, nearly all persons (98 per cent) of management-track positions engage in *osebo* gift giving at the end of the year, whereas only 84 per cent of those in commercial and service occupations and 72 per cent of ordinary *sarariman* did so. Although these differences are not so pronounced when it comes to *chugen* gift-giving in the summer, among Japan's salaried employees those in personnel management were more likely to give gifts than those doing office work; those doing technical work were the least likely to give gifts. Sex and age also affected the outlook that the survey's respondents had concerning the practice of gift-giving. Overall it would seem likely that the decision to give gifts is determined by one's position in the various stratification subsystems. A single woman doing clerical work in a large office would behave very differently from a middle-aged man who is self-employed as a solicitor.

D   Religious practices

According to another survey by the NHK Public Opinion Research Institute (1984: 38–70) beliefs also vary in a similar way. Praying at a small Buddhist altar or Shinto shrine in one's home is correlated positively in a linear fashion with age. It is inversely correlated with population density: more rural residents pray than do city dwellers. Women engage in such praying much more frequently than men. The people who do pray are obviously more likely to believe that their prayers will be answered. When it comes to fortune telling, however, women more than men, but younger rather than older persons seek comfort from such diviners.

Basabe's survey (1968: 91–107) of Japanese men indicates that positive attitudes toward religion correlate with age, and that occupation influences religious orientations in a variety of ways. Dator's survey data (1969: 93) show that a disproportionately large number of Sōka Gakkai members (as well as Christians) are in upwardly mobile social groups, whereas believers in Shinto and Buddhism are more likely not to have experienced social mobility. Morioka (1975) and others have illustrated in some detail the ways in which the belief in folk religions remains strong in rural areas. On the other hand, only a limited number of people in large cities participate in religious festivals symbolizing seasonal changes and community solidarity.

E   Music appreciation

Likes and dislikes in music vary markedly in Japan. Yet another survey by the same NHK institute (1982: 68–90) reveals very clear differences by age, occupation, educational background and city size. Age was the most significant determinant, with the older generations preferring folk-songs; the immediate postwar generation, sentimental melodies; those growing up in the 1960s, the theme songs from well-known movies; and the most recent generation of adults, '*nyū myūjikku*'. Suzuki's interesting study (1981) of popular songs also indicates clear differences based on geographic region, age, gender, occupation and the industrial sector in which one is employed.

The proportion of households possessing a piano also differs by region, Nara having the highest proportion with 40 per cent, followed closely by such urban prefectures as Saitama, Chiba, Osaka, Tokyo and Kanazawa (Sōrifu 1979).

The popular Japanese leisure-time activity known as '*karaoke*' (which involves an individual singing a song in tune with a pre-recorded melody stored in a special play-back tape recorder) appears to be more popular in some regions than in others. According to a 'white paper' prepared by a *karaoke* equipment company in 1987, the proportion of households having a *karaoke* player is highest in Yamagata prefecture (26.1 per cent), followed by Aichi (19.1 per cent), Tochigi (19.0), Gumma (18.7) and Fukushima (18.7). All of these prefectures are in the north Kantō and Chūbu regions. *Karaoke* seems to be least popular among households in Kyōto (6.7 per cent) (*ASC*, 22 April 1987: 25).

7 Conclusion

This paper has argued that Japanese society can usefully be understood in terms of the multi-dimensional model of stratification. The model presents a vision of society which attaches importance to social differentiation. It posits that an individual's access to various social rewards (namely, income, power, information and status) is determined largely by reference to 'the agents of stratification': (1) occupation, (2) employment status, (3) various characteristics of one's employer and the industry in which one is working, (4) age, (5) gender, (6) educational background, (7) geographic location and (8) family ties. It also posits that there will be a loose but fairly strong positive correlation among the amounts of the four different types of rewards individuals receive, although the amount of status inconsistency is seen as varying from society to society, and from one time period to another even in the same society. Accordingly, changes in the nature of fungibility provide important clues for the study of social change. The study of the agents of stratification will assist in understanding the dynamics of change initiated by various social stratum. As strata are always in a process of becoming and dissolving as social classes, the criss-crossing will help to highlight the way an individual's sense of collective consciousness is pluralized or diffused.

That variation in many types of behaviour can be fairly accurately and consistently predicted by reference to the agents of stratification is commonly accepted by students of social stratification. Moreover, social scientists utilize the stratification or demographic variables mentioned above in all the disciplines concerned with the study of social and individual behaviour. The model is presented first as a corrective to the tendency to generalize about 'the Japanese' which seems to have characterized a good deal of the writing on Japanese society. Even conceding that there may be fewer and/or smaller sub-groups in Japan, and that religion is a less divisive element in Japanese society, there are still many other dimensions in which structured social inequality occurs. The importance of these other dimensions within the overall multi-dimensional framework counsels against overemphasizing the homogeneity of the Japanese people. Accordingly, the discussion concluded with examples of how the agents of stratification account for variation in the behaviour of Japanese. The initial findings presented here and elsewhere (for instance, Mouer and Sugimoto 1986: 242–356) suggest that the variation in much behaviour is patterned along the lines of the multi-dimensional stratification model. At this stage, however, caution is advised in extrapolating to say that all behaviour will vary in these ways. There will always be important occurrences of status inconsistency. Moreover, the research does not preclude there being across-the-board differences in behaviour among different societies and cultures.

Reference to the multi-dimensional model of stratification is seen as a useful first step in evaluating national differences which do appear in aggregate data. As Johnson (1983: 33–7) has argued, there has been a tendency, in explaining such national differences, to fall back too readily to citing differences in national culture. The search for explanation might better begin by looking at differences in demographic profiles, rather than by focusing on alleged differences in national cultures.

The model facilitates such an approach in several ways. First, it calls for more systematic examination of how national differences can be explained by cross-national similarities in the patterns of variation with different distributions of the population. It is argued by some, for example, that the international differences in the male–female wage differential which appear in aggregate data change considerably when the wages of the individuals surveyed are standardized to account for variation in age, education, occupation and years of continuous employment. This would be true of many other forms of behaviour.

By focusing attention on intra-societal variation and on differences in demographic profiles, the model provides a framework for more rigorous inter-societal comparisons, a framework which might further curb the tendency to fall back on national character or culture as the major explanatory variable. The model suggests that comparisons ought to be made at three levels. It is the third level of comparison, the 'comparison of comparisons', that reveals the similarities and differences among various societies in more sophisticated ways.

Humans are not perfectly programmed robots: miscalculations and imperfect information, differences in time perspective, social mobility, inequalities in the current allocation of resources and chance occurrences account for constant reassessments of the rewards one targets, one's relative positioning in the various cross-cutting dimensions in which inequality occurs, and the strategies one sees as being effective in achieving one's goals given one's location at a particular position in the stratification matrix.

The model presented above embodies an invitation to consider more carefully the notion of values in terms of the way self-interest is conceptualized and the perceptions of how societies are structured. Although human motivation is seen as complex and there may be many instances of 'altruistic behaviour', the model suggests that the behaviour of many individuals can be understood as being directed through some process of rational calculation toward attaining 'the better life' as defined in terms of acquiring a larger share of various social rewards or resources.

If the above arguments make sense, the multi-dimensional framework presented above will tend to yield a vision of Japanese society which allows for variation, eschews national character stereotypes (particularly when it comes to imputation of value orientations), and pays attention to inequality and the dynamics of hierarchy (including conflict and various types of control).

From this perspective, our attention is directed to the problem of delineating the 'true interests' of individuals. The theoretical difficulties which will confront those wishing to attack this problem are immense. Efforts to distinguish between true and false consciousness are likely to lead to a huge morass. However, while the difficulties are apparent, the heuristic value, indeed necessity, of progressing in this area is evident. A first step might be to consider more carefully the distinction between national interest, community interests, organizational and group interests and individual interests. In Japan today there continues to be a feeling among many persons that measures of GNP per capita do not reflect the well-being of the people, especially with the 'artificial' rise in comparative terms owing to the appreciation of the yen. Furthermore, the official interpretations of income equality and surveys revealing that 90 per cent of the population has middle-class consciousness are not very convincing. Although management in big business and union leaders in big enterprise unions have allowed their consultations and negotiations to highlight across-the-board improvements in monetary income, many ordinary Japanese continue to entertain understandings which point to there being a considerable discrepancy between the vocabulary of public discourse and the realities of life. Somewhere in the changing perceptions of this discrepancy will lie some of the answers to the dynamics of Japanese society.

References

Asano, Ken-ichi
    1984 *Hanzai Hōdō no Hanzai* (The Crime of Criminal Reporting) (Tokyo: Gakuyō Shobō).
    1985 *Hanzai Hōdō wa Kaerareru* (Criminal Reporting Can Change) (Tokyo: Nihon Hyoronsha).

Basabe, Fernando M.
1968   *Religious Attitudes of Japanese Men* (Tokyo: Charles E. Tuttle).
Befu, Harumi
1980   'The Group Model of Japanese Society and an Alternative',
Rice University Studies, vol. 66, no. 1 (Winter), 169–87.
1982   'A Critique of the Group Model of Japanese Society', in
Japanese Society: Reappraisals and New Directions, edited by Yoshio
Sugimoto and Ross Mouer as a special issue of *Social Analysis*, nos.
5/6 (Dec. 1980), 29–43.
Chūō Rōdō Saigai Bōshi Kyōkai (Central Association for the Prevention
of Labour Accidents)
1985   *Anzen Eisei Nenkan: Shōwa 60-nenban* (The Yearbook on
Industrial Safety and Hygiene: 1985) (Tokyo: Chūō Rōdō Saigai
Bōshi Kyōkai).
Clark, Rodney C.
1979   *The Japanese Company* (New Haven, Conn.: Yale University
Press).
Dahrendorf, Ralf
1969   'On the Origin of Inequality Among Men', in *Social Inequality:
Selected Readings*, edited by André Béteille (Baltimore, Mid.:
Penguin Books), 30–40.
Dator, James Allen
1969   *Soka Gakkai: Builders of the Third Civilization* (Seattle, Wash.:
University of Washington Press).
Dore, Donald P.
1965   *Education in Tokugawa Japan* (London: Routledge & Kegan
Paul).
Ejiri, Hiroshi
1986   'Itaku Hanbaisei no Mondaiten: Shisutemu no Sabetsuka to
Yūetsuka o Mezasu' (Problems in the Contracted Sales System;
Toward Customer Differentiation and Store Character), *Sankei
Shinbun* (15 May), 9.
Fujioka, Wakao
1984   *Sayonara, Taishū* (Farewell to the Masses) (Tokyo: PHP
Kenkyūjo).
Fukutake, Tadashi
1949   *Nihon Nōson no Shakaiteki Seikaku* (The Social Characteristics
of Japanese Villages) (Tokyo: Tokyo Daigaku Shuppankai).
Gordon, Milton
1958   *Social Class in American Sociology* (Durham, NC: Duke
University Press).
Hakuhōdō Seikatsu Sōgō Kenkyūjo (ed.)
1985   *'Bunshū' no Tanjō* (The Emergence of the 'Smaller Masses')
(Tokyo: Nihon Keizai Shinbunsha).

Hamaguchi, Eshun
  1977 *'Nihon-rashisa' no Saihakken* (Rediscovering 'Japaneseness').
    (Tokyo: Nihon Keizai Shinbunsha).
  1982 *Kanjin-shugi no Shakai Nippon* (Importance of Interpersonal
    Relationships in Japanese Society) (Tokyo: Tōyō Keizai Shinpōsha).
  1986 *Kōdo Jōhō Shakai to Nippon no Yukue* (High-level Information
    Society and the Direction of Japan) (Tokyo: Nippon Hōsō Shūppan
    Kyōkai).
Hane, Mikiso
  1982 *Peasants, Rebels and Outcastes* (New York: Pantheon Books).
Hara, Junsuke
  1980 'Kaisō Kōzōron' (Theories on Social Stratification) in *Shakai
    Kōzō* (Social Structure), edited by Yasuda Saburō as vol. IV in
    Kiso Shakaigaku (Fundamentals of Sociological Theory) (Tokyo:
    Tōyō Keizai Shinpōsha), 34–54.
Higuchi, Kiyoyuki
  1972 *Nihon no Chie no Kōzō* (The Structure of Japanese Intelligence)
    (Tokyo: Kōdansha).
Hino, Hideitsu (ed.)
  1986 *Nihon Iryō no Shōten* (Focal Point in Japanese Medical Services)
    (Tokyo: Akebi Shobō).
Hosokawa, Migiwa
  1981 *Shokugyōbyō to Rōdō Saigai – Rōdōsha no Seimei to Kenkō o
    Mamoru Tame ni* (Occupational Illness and Industrial Accidents –
    Steps to Protect the Life and Health of Workers) (Tokyo: Rōdō
    Keizaisha).
Hosokawa, Migiwa; *et al.*
  1984 *VDT Rōdō Nyūmon* (A Primer on Employing Video Display
    Terminal Operators) (Tokyo: Rōdō Kijun Chōsakai).
Itō, Shuntarō
  1985 *Hikaku Bunmei* (Comparative Civilizations) (Tokyo: Tokyo
    Daigaku Shuppankai).
Itō, Zen-ichi
  1977 'Jōhōka Shakai to Kokumin Seikatsu' (Information-Oriented
    Society and the National Life Style), in *Chishiki Sangyō e no Tenkai*
    (The Development Toward Knowledge-Intensive Industries), edited
    by Itō Zen-ichi *et al.* as vol. IX in *Kōza Jōhō Shakaikagaku* (The
    Lecture Series on the Social Science of Information) (Tokyo:
    Gakushū Kenkyūsha), 14–21.
Jinkō Mondai Shingikai (The Advisory Council on Population Problems)
    (ed.)
  1974 *Nihon Jinkō no Dōkō: Seishi Jinkō o Mezashite* (Trends in the
    Population of Japan: Toward a Stable Population) (Tokyo: Ōkurashō
    Insatsukyoku).

Johnson, Chalmers
   1983   'The Internationalization of the Japanese Economy', in *The Challenge of Japan's Internationalization*, edited by Hiroshi Mannari and Harumi Befu (Tokyo: Kodansha International), 31–58.
Kinokuniya Shoten
   n.d.   'Bungakushō Jushō Tosho Risuto' (A List of Books Receiving Literary Prizes) (Tokyo: Kinokuniya Shoten).
Koschmann, J. Victor
   1978   *Authority and the Individual in Japan* (Tokyo: University of Tokyo Press).
Kōseishō Daijin Kanbō Tōkei Jōhōbu (Division of Statistical Information, Minister's Office, Ministry of Welfare)
   1980   *Kōsei Tōkei Yōran Shōwa 50-nenban* (The Yearbook of Welfare Statistics: 1985) (Tokyo: Kōsei Tōkei Kyoku).
Krauss, Ellis S.; Rohlen, Thomas P.; and Steinhoff, Patricia G. (eds)
   1984   *Conflict in Japan* (Honolulu: University of Hawaii Press).
Larson, Margali Sarfatti
   1977   *The Rise of Professionalism: a Sociological Analysis* (Berkeley, Cal.: University of California Press).
Lenski, Gerhard
   1966   *Power and Privilege: a Theory of Social Stratification* (New York: McGraw-Hill).
Levine, Solomon B.; and Kawada, Hisashi
   1980   *Human Resources in Japanese Industrial Development* (Princeton, NJ: Princeton University Press).
Morioka, Kiyomi
   1975   *Religion in Changing Japanese Society* (Tokyo: University of Tokyo Press).
Mouer, Ross; and Sugimoto, Yoshio
   1986   *Images of Japanese Society: a Study in the Structure of Social Reality* (London: Kegan Paul International).
Najita, Tetsuo; and Koschmann, J. Victor
   1982   *Conflict in Modern Japanese History: the Neglected Tradition* (Princeton, NJ: Princeton University Press).
Naka, Kaoru
   1973   *Kunshō no Rekishi* (The History of Commendations), *Bunka Fūzoku Sensho* (Series on Cultural Customs), no. 8 (Tokyo: Yūzankaku).
Narumo, Shūichi
   1970   *Kigyō no Shakai Sekinin* (The Social Responsibility of the Business Firm) (Tokyo: Nihon Keizai Shinbunsha).
Neustupný, J. V.
   1982   'On Paradigms in the Study of Japan', in *Japanese Society: Reappraisals and New Directions*, edited by Yoshio Sugimoto and

Ross Mouer as a special issue of *Social Analysis*, nos. 5/6 (Dec. 1980), 20–8.

NHK Hōsō Yoron Chōsa Kenkyūjo (The NHK Public Opinion Research Centre)
1979   *Nihonjin no Kenmin-sei* (Prefectural Characteristics of the Japanese) (Tokyo: Nihon Hōsō Shuppankai).
1981   *Nihonjin no Kenkōkan* (How Japanese View Their Health) (Tokyo: Nihon Hōsō Shuppankai).
1982a   *Nihonjin no Seikatsu Jikan 1980* (The Way Japanese Use Time: Report on the 1980 National Survey) (Tokyo: Nihon Hōsō Shuppankai).
1982b   *Gendaijin to Ongaku* (Music in Contemporary Japanese Society) (Tokyo: Nihon Hōsō Shuppankai).
1982c   *Nihonjin no Seikatsu Jikan: 1980* (Japanese Uses of Time: 1980) (Tokyo: NHK Hōsō Shuppankai).
1983   *Terebi Shichō no 30-nen* (Thirty Years of Television Viewing) (Tokyo: Nihon Hōsō Shuppankai).
1984   *Nihonjin no Shūkyō Ishiki* (Japanese Views of Religion) (Tokyo: Nihon Hōsō Shuppankai).
Nihon Kinrō Seishōnen Dantai Kyōgikai (Nikkinkyō) (Japan Council of Organizations for Young Workers)
1986   *Seiun* (The Blue Sky) [an in-house publication explaining the Structure and Activities of Nikkinkyō] (Tokyo: Nikkinkyō).
Nihon Rōdō Kyōkai (The Japan Institute of Labour) (ed.)
1986   *ME kara IT e* (From Micro-Electronics to Information Technology) (Tokyo: Nihon Rōdō Kyōkai).
Nihon Sangyō Anzen Rengōkai (Japan Federation for Industrial Safety)
1963   *Anzen Undō no Ayumi* (A History of the Safety Movement) (Tokyo: Nihon Sangyō Anzen Rengōtai).
Okada, Gō
1986   *Nihongata 'CI' Senryaku* (Japanese Strategies for Developing Corporate Identity) (Tokyo: Dōbunkan).
Okamoto, Hideaki
1973   'The Social Responsibility of the Enterprise: Some Proposals by Keizai Doyukai', *Japan Labor Bulletin*, vol. 12, no. 11 (Nov.), 4–10; vol. 12, no. 12 (Dec.), 6–12.
Organization for Economic Cooperation and Development
1971   *Reviews of National Policies for Education: Japan* (Paris: OECD).
Orita, Yoshirō
1986   *Shin CI Kakushin* (The New Revolution in Corporate Identity) (Tokyo: Nikkan Kōgyō Shinbunsha).
Parsons, Talcott
1954   'Social Classes and Social Conflict in the Light of Recent

Sociological Theory', in *Essays in Sociological Theory*, edited by Talcott Parsons, rev. edn (New York: Free Press), 418–27.

Passin, Herbert
1965 *Society and Education in Japan* (New York: Bureau of Publications, Teachers' College, Columbia University).

Ray, Stephen E.
1986 'Jesse: Sumo Life Not for Everyone', *Japan Times* (31 Oct. 1986), 13.

Rodō Daijin Kanbō Seisaku Chōsabu (Policy Planning and Research Department, Minister's Secretariat, Ministry of Labour)
1981 *Rōdō Tōkei Nenpō 1980* (Yearbook of Labour Statistics: 1980) (Tokyo: Rōdō Hōrei Kyōkai).

Rōdō Kagaku Kenkyūjo (The Institute for the Scientific Study of Labour) (ed.)
1959 *Nihon no Shokugyōbyō Hassei Yōin to Yobō Igaku Taisaku* (The Cause of Occupational Illness in Japan and Preventive Medical Measures) (Tokyo: Tōyō Keizai Shinpōsha).

Rōdōshō (Ministry of Labour) (ed.)
1986 *Rōdō Hakusho* (Labour White Paper) (Tokyo: Nihon Rōdō Kyōkai).

Sankei Shinbunsha Yoronchōsa-shitsu (The Public Opinion Survey Division of the Sankei Newspapers) (ed.)
1976 *'76 Iken to Ishiki no Hyakka Jiten* (The Encyclopaedia of Japanese Opinions and Attitudes, 1976 edition) (Tokyo: Sankei Marketing).

Shimada, Sei-ichi
1986 *Kaisha Jōhō Kanribu* (The Information Control Division in the Business Firm) (Tokyo: Hōrei Sōgō Shuppan).

Sōrifu (Prime Minister's Office)
1979 *Zenkoku Shōhi Jittai Chōsa* (National Survey of Consumption Patterns) (Tokyo: Ōkurashō Insatsukyoku).

Sōrifu Shōkunkyoku (The Prime Minister's Office, Bureau of Commendations) (ed.)
1986 *Eiten Jimu no Tebiki* (An Administrative Handbook on Public Honours) (Tokyo: Gyōsei).

Sugimoto, Yoshio
1981 *Popular Disturbance in Postwar Japan* (Hong Kong: Asian Research Service).

Sugimoto, Yoshio; and Mouer, Ross
1982 *Nihonjin wa 'Nihonteki' ka* (How Japanese Are the Japanese?) (Tokyo: Tōyō Keizai Shinpōsha).

Suzuki, Akira
1981 *Kayōkyoku Besuto Sen no Kenkyū* (A Study of the Best 1,000 Hit Songs) (Tokyo: TBS Buritanika).

Tanaka, Sōji
1986   *Za CI Bijinesu* (The Corporate Image Business) (Tokyo: Saimaru Shuppankai).

Tanaka, Yasuo
1981   *Nantonaku Kurisutaru* (Crystal Always) (Tokyo: Kawade Shobō Shinsha).

Tsunoda, Tadanobu
1978   *Nihonjin no Nō: Nō no Hataraki to Tōzai no Bunka* (The Brain Structure of the Japanese: Functions of the Brain and Eastern and Western Culture) (Tokyo: Taishūkan).

1984   *Nō no naka no Shōuchū* – '*Nihonjin no Nō' Kenkyū no Shintenkai* (The Small Universe in the Brain – New Developments in the Study of the Japanese Brain) (Tokyo: Bisunesu Kasetto).

Tsuruda, Naofumi
1986   *Kigyō Taishitsu o Yoku suru TQC no Kangaekata-Susumekata* (The Idea and Approach of Total Quality Control for a Better Enterprise) (Tokyo: Nittō Shoin).

Vogel, Ezra
1979   *Japan as Number One* (Cambridge, Mass.: Harvard University Press).

Wada, Ryūko
1986   'Sofutoka Shakai no Keizaigaku' (The Soft Side of Economics), *Nihon Keizai Shinbun* (chōkan) (13–15 Oct. 1986), 13 and 23.

Wessolowski, W.
1969   'The Notions of Strata and Class in Socialist Society', translated from Polish by André Béteille, in *Social Inequality: Selected Readings*, edited by André Béteille (Baltimore, Md.: Penguin Books), 125–33.

Yamazaki, Masakazu
1984   *Yawarakai Kojinshugi no Tanjō* (The Advent of Soft Individualism) (Tokyo: Chūō Kōronsha).

Chapter Six
The Transition of the Household System in Japan's Modernization

Kawamura Nozomu

1 Introduction

'Modernization' has become an important part of our social science jargon. It is also a word commonly used in the mass media and in our everyday lives. Although the concept has not been very precisely defined, in using the term there is often the presupposition that societies develop from a pre-modern state of affairs. Moreover, in whatever way the term is used, the implication seems to be that 'modern society' is a universally applicable abstract concept. In some schemes 'modern society' is equated with 'capitalistic society', whereby 'capitalistic society' also becomes a universal concept. Nevertheless, although capitalistic societies may share certain features, each has its own national character and indigenous elements. These peculiar characteristics are neglected when we talk about capitalistic society in general. As a historical fact, 'modern capitalistic society' first appeared in England; it then soon afterwards appeared in other Western countries. The fact that these countries shared common Mediterranean cultural traditions meant that the initial formulation of a theory of modernization tended to ignore the experiences of non-Western societies. One result is that people have tended to confuse 'modernization' and 'Westernization'. In Japan, for example, indigenous elements have often been regarded as deviations or aberrations not in keeping with the main course of modernization.

In this chapter I would like to trace the process of modernization in Japan with special reference to the household system. Japan changed greatly after the Meiji Restoration in 1868. Within a short period of less than fifty years, Japan became the first non-Western nation to develop a full-blown capitalistic system. However, the process of modernization was somewhat different from that experienced in the other Western societies, because many traditionally Japanese elements remained.

The Meiji government overthrew the Tokugawa feudal regime and established a new order. However, unlike many of the Western examples, and especially those of Britain and France, in Japan there existed no third estate to assist in promoting the bourgeois revolution. Change was supported rather by those who felt that Japan faced a national crisis which threatened the nation's independence. To maintain its independence, the newly established national government felt inclined to adopt capitalistic modes of production. However, there were no inner prerequisite conditions for capitalistic development. While state policies called for capitalistic development, large numbers of people still lived in rural areas where society was still organized around the traditional ties of the household and village community. In other words, capitalistic society did not emerge spontaneously in Japan as it had in many Western societies. From the beginning the Meiji government formulated policies to bring about industrialization and concomitant increases in production, national wealth and military strength. Although Japan's capitalist economy began to grow at a remarkable rate, growth was promoted by the national government from the very beginning.

At the time of the Meiji Restoration conditions had not yet reached a stage where feudalism would spontaneously dissolve itself or where a capitalist economy would simply just appear. The leaders of the Meiji government took it upon themselves to introduce modern techniques of production from the West along with social technologies related to the legal and educational systems and to the role of modern communications. The leaders also used public funds to establish public enterprises which were later transferred to the control of privileged merchants at bargain prices and then given special protection as private enterprises. For this reason many of the privileged merchants remained loyal to the government and supported its national policies. It was in this fashion that Japan's budding entrepreneurs became fascist monopoly capitalists rather than bourgeois monopoly capitalists.

This kind of modernization was not imposed from above without great difficulty. Public enterprises were not efficient, because neither managers nor workers were placed in a truly competitive situation. Managers were governmental officials who were formerly in the warrior class. They had no idea about how to run a modern factory, apart from controlling people and keeping bureaucratic records. These were not insignificant skills. However, workers who came from rural areas were not properly trained and were forced to do heavy labour under very poor, even inhuman, working conditions. Neither managers nor workers required an inner spirit like the Protestant Ethic for this system to work. There needed only to be a firm sense of purpose among the elite and a clearly defined system of authority.

The selling of the state enterprises to the privileged merchants did not particularly change things. The new 'capitalists' managed the factories as household businesses. The ownership of factories belonged not to individuals but to households. In other words, whole families were made responsible for each business purchased. The households formed giant family trusts in which each of the main-stem families controlled a number of branch families. Poor peasants were recruited to become members of these big households or their branches. The idea of the enterprise as one big household was maintained as various technologies were introduced and new industries developed.

The policy of acquiring Western techniques while fostering the traditional 'Japanese spirit' (*wakon yōsai*) naturally produced contradictions. For example, traditional values were seen by the workers as being irrelevant once profit making became the major goal of the new capitalists. Workers became aware of their own human rights and began to resist patriarchal domination. However, the 'Japanese spirit' still served as a powerful ideology which could bridge many of the antagonisms which arose between the new capitalists and the labour they utilized as Japan's industrialization progressed.

2 The pre-Meiji family

Three types of family structure are often identified in the literature on the family: (1) the compound family, (2) stem families and (3) conjugal families. In pre-Tokugawa Japan the most important unit was the extended compound family. The Japanese word '*ie*' originally referred to a residence or to the premises. The relationship between *oya* (parents) and *ko* (children) was not necessarily a biological one. Members of the family lived in the same house or on the same land. The '*oya*' was the leader of the household. He lived together with the other members who were his *ko* or followers. The head of an *ie* was a man who played the role of the fictive parent for all the members. As the head of the family, the *oya* needed to possess some leadership qualities and some charisma if he was to control the other members of the family.

Figure 6.1 shows a compound family where all males have remained in the family and brought their brides into the family. This type of family grows in size generation by generation, and becomes an extended family. When it reaches a certain size, it will divide. Until division occurs, the distinction between lineal and collateral descendants is not significant. The head of the family is not necessarily a lineal descendant. It is possible for others with charisma and other leadership qualities to become the leader of the *ie* (that is, the working group) regardless of their genealogical status.

The extended compound family lost its importance during the Tokugawa period. Land taxes were normally paid to the feudal lords by the small stem family. However, families in a village were given collective responsibility for the land tax. Teams of peasant families were formed; each team was called a '*gonin-gumi*'. When one family failed to pay its land tax, the other four families were made to pay the difference. If a '*gonin-gumi*' failed to pay its share, the village as a whole was made to pay. These semi-legal regional relationships between peasants thus came to be more important than blood ties. Nevertheless, the continued emphasis on primogeniture meant that blood relationships would retain some importance when defining interpersonal relationships within the village community.

Under these new arrangements, the stem family emerged as the major family unit. In the stem family, the first-born son succeeds

Figure 6.1   *Three Types of Family Structure*

(1) The compound family

(2) The stem family

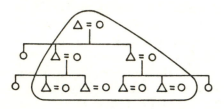

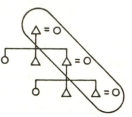

(3) The conjugal family

as head of the family; other sons set up branch families or marry out if at all possible. Otherwise they remain unmarried. Daughters marry and enter other households, except when all the children are girls. The continuity of the household is a central concern for the head of the family. The eldest son has special privileges and obligations.

Depending on the life cycle of the family, a stem family might be a conjugal family consisting of parents and their unmarried children. However, the conjugal family has completely different principles from the stem family. First of all, a stem family exists as a collectivity and the marriage means initiation of a bride into the husband's family. She must assimilate to a family which already exists. In the case of the conjugal family associated with the modern nuclear family, marriage means establishment of a new family. When the new couple has children, the family increases in size and the notion of the family changes. When the children marry and become independent, the husband and wife are again the only members of the family. If either dies, the family is dissolved.

In Japan these stem families tended to form a lineage group called '*dōzoku*'. This type of lineage group can best be seen in the rural areas where agriculture has been practised on a small scale by owner peasants. The small size of the land holdings makes it difficult for tenant farming to develop. The division of arable farm land becomes difficult despite the new civil law. The land is the property of the household and should be managed by the next head. Under these conditions, the *ie* and the *dōzoku* in the village community still function in some way.

If there are ten farm households which have the same family name in a village and each household recognizes the other as belonging to the same lineage relationship, the ten households are referred to as a '*dōzoku*'. One possible constitution of a *dōzoku* in a village is shown in Figure 6.2. Household A is the original lineage group. As the main family, A has over time produced a number of branch families (B, C, D and E). As they in turn grow and prosper, the branch families – B, C and D – come to consider themselves as main families and they set up their own branch families (F, G, H and I). In the case of B, its branch family (F) sets up its own branch (J), thereby giving B a sub-branch family (J). From the point of view of A being the family of origin, B, C, D and E are branch families; F, G, H and I are 'sub-branch families'; and J is a 'sub-sub-branch family'.

Figure 6.2 *A Dōzoku Consisting of Ten Households*

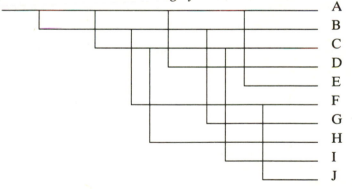

Dōzoku is the local group which functions within the village community. The establishment of new branch families within a village is a prerequisite if *dōzoku* are to exist. When the second or third son goes to another village or town and starts a new family without receiving any family property, the new family is not recognized as a member of the *dōzoku*. When males other than the successors were allowed to establish branch families in the same village, the number of families in the *dōzoku* increased. However, it was very difficult to establish a new branch family in the same village because the size of each lot of land owned was often too small to divide any further. Therefore, the development of *dōzoku* could occur only among the wealthy farmers. The idea of the *dōzoku* in the broadest sense can also be understood by examining the diagram in Figure 6.3.

Figure 6.3   *The Idea of* Dōzoku *Relationships: the Branch Families of the Main Family (*Honke*) after Fourteen Generations*

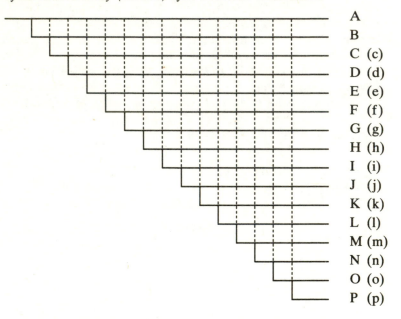

If every head of a family has two sons and the elder succeeds his father, while the younger establishes his own branch family, the solid lines show how A's branch family (B), sub-branch family (C), sub-sub-branch family (D) and so on are established with each succeeding generation. If in each generation the main family A continues to produce its own branches (c, d, . . . , p) and B, C and so on, each in turn do the same thing, it is easy to see how the original family comes to stand at the top of a huge genealogical hierarchy of *dōzoku*, all derived from A and all able to trace their origins back to an original main family (that is, A).

3   The prewar family

In Japan's rural areas, the large landlords became members of the new ruling class. By controlling the village communities, they could mobilize not only their own tenants but also other peasants with less power. They could manipulate the regulations of the village community to their own advantage and worked to construct a power hierarchy based on the household being the unit of land ownership. Before the Meiji Restoration, the village had been the unit for collecting land taxes (namely, rice). With the Meiji Restoration, this function was shifted to local administrative bodies. However, the use of common land and irrigation arrangements continued to be matters which the local community decided. The units of village community were not individuals, but households which had their own land. Under this system, tenants were not full members of the village community. Land was owned by a household as a whole and not by individual members of the household.

The legal system of the household as laid down in the Japanese civil law before World War II defined the legal rights of members of a household, and those of the head of the household (who was usually male and aged over twenty-five). The family was defined as 'kin of the household who live in the head's house and their wives'. The prewar civil law also provided that 'all children should belong to the household of their father'. The head of a family was to control and manage his household's property which would then be inherited by his eldest son. Other sons and all daughters were distinguished from the eldest son. Other sons could establish new branch families, and daughters could become members of other families upon marriage. During the war, this kind of family system was praised as being uniquely Japanese.

Under the landlord system in prewar Japan, there were two types of landlords. One did not cultivate any land at all, but lived on the rent from the land he owned. The other cultivated some of his land and rented some. The latter tended to develop his own *dōzoku* group and tried to control his branch and sub-branch families through the manipulation of land agreements. However, the relationship between landlord and tenant did not always coincide with the relationship between main and branch families. In other words, genealogical status was quite different from status based on land ownership and landlords were not always the main families. In Figure 6.2 household A enjoyed the highest status in the *dōzoku* groups regardless of its economic power. Also, the age of a household did not automatically decide its rank within the *dōzoku* group. Only among the same branch families, did the date of establishment determine status within the group. For example, among the branch families of A, B enjoys the highest status and E the lowest. But households established before E (for example, F, H, G and I) have less status than E because they are sub-branch families of A.

In maintaining the lineage group, the important issue has not been the biological relationship but the sociological one. Nor are the 'real' historical facts about the relationships between the main and branch households particularly important as long as lineage relationships are mutually recognized. In the end, we are talking about subjective judgements. In many cases, no one knows the actual lineage relationships. In the prewar period, landlords which were branch families often manipulated the records on lineage and called themselves the main families when the evidence concerning the family status as a branch family was not clear. Of course, the longer a family's position as the main family had been established the better; however, this was not a necessary condition. Even without the status of being a main family, the rule of a landlord family was based on its ownership of the land. Lineage relationships were simply an important means of legitimating his power and of evoking a spontaneous willingness among members of the village to follow the dictates of the main household under the landlord system. As an ideology, the consciousness of household and lineage group worked to suppress individual rights and freedom.

4 The family during the war

During the war, people who stood against the war were condemned as being 'non-Japanese' because they would not admit they were sons of the Emperor. Such people were treated roughly by the police and the various military agencies, and such treatment was legitimized by the very fact that they were not considered 'real Japanese', regardless of whether they were Christian or Buddhist, democrat or socialist.

210

The main family continued to be the imperial household headed by the Emperor. Figure 6.3 provides a framework or world view in which all Japanese families are, at least theoretically, derived from the imperial family. Thus, for many Japanese, the Japanese state can be understood through the analogy with the large extended family or *dōzoku*. In those terms, the Emperor, as the head of the original main family, can thus be said to head the whole nation, and all the Japanese people can be seen as being offspring of the Emperor. This is the origin of the ideology of the Emperor system (*tennōsei*) or 'state familism' (*kazoku-kokka*).

The governing elements pushed the idea that each Japanese person was an ancestor and, therefore, an heir in the lineage of the Emperor. The Emperor's power and authority was legitimated by his genealogical prestige. The jurisdiction of each family head was enlarged with the passage of time. The extension of the family over time was seen as a process which was accompanied by an enlargement of the family's special territory. As Maruyama (1962) points out, 'the endless flow of value from the centre towards the circumference is assured by the fact that the axis is infinite, as expressed in the familiar phrase, "the prosperity of the Imperial Throne coexists with heaven and earth"'. The connection of the Emperor system and the family system was discussed in detail by Tsuda Kōzō in his 'The Present State of Japanese Fascism', which was written during the war.

> According to the family-system principle of Japan the keynote of society is not the demand for individual rights, as in the modern countries of the West, but service to the family as a whole. Socially each family is an independent animate body, a complete cell in itself. The individual is no more than a part or an element of this complete cell. Our nationalism should be the extension and enlargement of this family-system principle. This is perhaps because our nationalism is nothing but the union of these families at the national level. The Emperor is the sovereign, the family head, the centre; and general representative of the State as a united body. (Cited from Maruyama, 1962: 32)

The Japanese people were expected to serve the Emperor even in their private lives. They were joined to the Emperor just as members of a family were responsible to the head and his ancestors.

Thus, under the rule of the Emperor, the private sphere could not exist independently from the public sphere. Theoretically, the state could, in the Emperor's hands, control the inner life of the people and circumscribe their 'civil freedoms'. Such was the myth of the Emperor system. This ideology was given special attention by military officers, right-wing groups and the monopoly capitalists. Traditional and revered symbols were manipulated to mobilize the people for 'Japan's great war'. Big business took the initiative in building up the myth of the divine Emperor and used the myth to enhance its own profits.

It should be noted that the Emperor system functioned to enhance the political power of big business. One popular slogan during the war was 'self-annihilation for the sake of the country', a phrase which glorified selfless devotion to the company through one's job. It seems incredibly naïve to suppose that Japan rushed headlong into the war only because of the lack of individuality, civilian control or civil social order. Japan engaged in aggression just like other modernized Western countries where individualism was held to be a virtue. Many scholars who have pointed out that Japanese society is a 'family-type society' often see this characteristic as being a pre-modern feature. They fail to see how it was deliberately created in order to maintain big business. According to the ideology which resulted, a subject's absolute loyalty to the Emperor could be demonstrated by giving absolute loyalty to the capitalist enterprise.

5 Postwar continuities in the family

After the war the situation changed. Under the occupation, a new constitution was proclaimed and the old civil code was dismantled. Under the new constitution the sovereignty which had resided in the Emperor was officially shifted to the Japanese people. Land reforms were initiated, and the landlord–tenant system was dissolved. However, several traditional concepts of the household still remained. The idea of genealogical relationships within the *dōzoku* will continue to provide a basis for analyzing the important aspects of the Japanese family as long as the Emperor continues to be an important symbol.

A The Emperor

One aspect was the idea of there being something special about Japan's unbroken line of emperors. The new constitution defines the Emperor as the symbol of the Japanese nation and of national integration, and provides for the imperial throne to be dynastic in line with the imperial household code. According to the code, 'the throne should be succeeded by the oldest male in the imperial line', and the order of succession is as follows: (1) the Emperor's eldest son, (2) the Emperor's eldest grandson, (3) other male descendants of the Emperor's eldest son, (4) the Emperor's second son and his male descendants, (5) other male descendants of the Emperor, (6) the Emperor's brothers and their male descendants, (7) the Emperor's uncles and their male descendants. This order is shown in Figure 6.4.

Figure 6.4   *Order of Succession to the Japanese Throne*

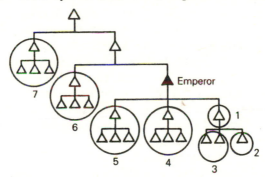

The concept shown in Figure 6.4 is based not only on notions of the stem family and on the principle of primogeniture, but also on the notion of the compound family as well. The rules of succession to the throne, it should be noted, are slightly different from those which govern the stem family. In the case of the stem family, a head without a son must take a son-in-law into the family. Usually this is done by having the eldest daughter's husband adopted into the family. If there are no children in the family the head adopts a child as his son. However, the principle of imperial succession rests on the old idea of there being a compound family; accordingly, the principle of adoption is not recognized in the case of the imperial household. Also, the imperial throne should be occupied by a male; females should not succeed to the throne. Accordingly, there is no empress regent.

B   Patrilineal descent

The idea of the patrilineal family has also remained important in postwar Japan, and is supported by the ideology of the Emperor system. However, the blood ties of the family are often social rather than biological. Nevertheless, members of the family are conscious of having a common ancestor, that is, the common ancestral 'father'. Ideally, the lineage is based on some blood tie through either the male or the female. The idea calls for biological or blood ties. Each individual should have two parents, two grandfathers and two grandmothers. In the case of the patrilineal family, one male ancestor may have many descendants.

Ideally, the father of a given family can trace his lineage up to the father of the local clan, and then to the father of the community. Thus the idea that the Emperor is the 'Father' of a collection of families living in Japan has a fairly firm ideological basis.

The system of the stem family has continued to exist in postwar Japan although the New Civil Code of 1947 does not provide for the family head to have any legal rights, and stipulates that inheritance should be equally divided among the children regardless of age and sex. A visit to any Japanese graveyard will reveal that many people continue to think in terms of the stem family, not the nuclear family. Graves are not for individuals; they are for stem families. Only the members of a stem family (the head of a family and his wife, his successors and their wives and children dying before they have reached adulthood) are buried in the same grave. Males other than the successors have to build their own graves (that is, graves for branch families). The landlord system was abolished through the postwar land reforms. Tenants at that time were liberated and were given land from their landlords at a nominal price. However, the land reform did not alter the very small size of the agricultural enterprises which were carried by the peasant households. Therefore, even after the land reforms, the household and its lineage groups have continued to be a main concern among rural people. Even in urban Japan, the ideas of the *ie* and the *dōzoku* still remain in the people's consciousness, and such concepts have not disappeared even after the rapid economic growth of the 1960s.

6   Structural continuities in the postwar family

Economic development has resulted in many persons in agriculture leaving the industry and moving into other industries since the end of the 1950s. The agricultural population declined from 37.9 per cent in 1955 to 12.6 per cent in 1975. But the total number of farm households declined only 10 per cent from a fairly constant 5.5 million before the war to 5 million in 1975. One reason is that even after young males moved into the cities, the old people and women continued to work the family farm. Therefore, although the number of households dropped only slightly, the number of farmers who worked full-time as farmers decreased from 50.0 per cent in 1950 to 12.4 per cent in 1975.

One result has been that many of the young people who went to the cities and worked in other industries remained as part of their original family and consciously think of themselves as being members of 'their rural family'. Many second and third sons who left their villages and built new families in the cities – families which they regarded as branches of their main family back in the village – have established their own graves according to the principles of primogeniture.

Dōzoku groups in the rural areas continue to be functional groups. Each household in the *dōzoku* continues to cooperate with others. Through various forms of mutual aid – including assistance with various agricultural tasks – the sense of solidarity among members of the *dōzoku* is maintained and strengthened. In some cases, the main original family may receive a disproportionately large amount of mutual aid. However, this depends mainly upon situations, because lineage status does not always correspond to economic status. Moreover, mutual aid does not have to be exchanged everyday for the *dōzoku*'s consciousness to be maintained.

Even in cities where cooperation among households within the *dōzoku* grouping is weak or almost non-existent, the consciousness of the *ie* and the *dōzoku* continues to be especially strong in religious events. For example, the funeral ceremony in Japan is still a family event, and the main family still has a special role to play at such times. The idea of ancestor worship, which can still be seen in many annual events, is linked to the notion that there is an eternal continuity to the family. In the summer, for example,

Japanese have a special event to celebrate their ancestors. Family heads – especially the heads of main families – play an important role in those celebrations. Also, marriage ceremonies continue to be not for the bride and the bridegroom, but for their two families. Marriage symbolizes a new relationship between two families and their kin. A bridegroom's family is seen as obtaining a new family member, while the bride's family is seen as losing a member. A bride is still seen as leaving her own family and entering the family of her husband.

7 The family as a continuing ideology

Therefore, regardless of the actual cooperation within a lineage group, several practices underline the continuing importance of the *ie* and the *dōzoku* in the everyday lives of most Japanese. For example, the concept of the family is still used by Japan's monopoly capitalists to manipulate employees ideologically. Even now many capitalists and top managers are enthusiastic about the idea of reviving the myth of the Emperor system. For example, in 1964 a director of the Japanese Federation of Employers' Associations, Maeda Hajime, argued that

> the national character of the Japanese people lies in their
> respect for the emperor as the symbol of national integration
> and as the authentic locus for national sentiment. This is the
> unique feature of the Japanese nation. Under such
> circumstances, economic growth and the development of
> economic enterprises are possible. If this were only
> admitted, then the Japanese way of managing enterprises
> could be automatically understood by all.

In order to couple loyalty to the enterprise with loyalty to the Emperor, the idea of the family is utilized. Enterprises are portrayed as families, and the state continues to be portrayed as a family of families, although the vocabulary has changed. In Japan, the policies to promote 'cooperation' between labour and management were developed as part of the enterprise-as-family ideology.

The capitalists in Japan have used this ideology to persuade workers to accept lower wages and longer hours of work than they would otherwise accept. The enterprise-as-family ideology calls for the absolute submission of the employee to management, and in return for management to somehow look after the employee. Even labour unions are seen as part of the company system, and workers who act against management are often suppressed by both management and by union officials.

One example is provided by Sony, a famous electric company. In its company newspaper for January 1972, employees are told that they and management are the crew of the same boat with similar interests regardless of position. Employees are warned that 'there might be some workers amongst you who will try to drill a hole in the bilge although they are the crew of our own boat'. Such workers are dismissed as 'naïve persons who cannot understand the fact that we happen to ride in the same boat and share the same fate'.

Labourers who insist on their own rights and a fair wage are labelled 'criminals' for 'drilling a hole in the company's boat', which is one among many in the nation's imperial flotilla. If the enterprise is a family, those who rebel against management are made to look like spoilt children disobeying their parents and disturbing the peace and harmony of the family. When employees of the same company are seen as the crew of the same boat, labourers with class consciousness come to be subversive elements. Those who row hard and try to push their boat to the head of the fleet are given special privileges by the coxswain. For employees of one company, the crews of the other boats are portrayed as being rivals. From this point of view company unions are seen as being an informal device for motivating the workers to row harder for the sake of their crew and thereby for the entire imperial flotilla.

8 Vertical relationships and social class

Despite this one-for-all and all-for-one ideology, class consciousness does exist in Japanese society. Nevertheless, it is the ideology which is often given exclusive attention by the scholars emphasizing the uniqueness of Japanese society. For example, Nakane (1970: 87) characterizes Japanese society as follows:

> The overall picture of (Japanese) society . . . is not that of horizontal stratification by class or caste but of vertical stratification by institution or group of institutions. . . . Even if social classes like those in Europe can be detected in Japan, and even if something vaguely resembling those classes that are illustrated in the textbooks of Western sociology can also be found in Japan, the point is that in actual society this stratification is unlikely to function and that it does not really reflect Japan's social structure. In Japanese society it is really not a matter of workers struggling against capitalists or managers but of company A ranked against company B.

In arguing that vertical relationships predominate in Japanese society, Nakane argues that basic social cleavages occur on a horizontal plane between vertical groups.

However, she does not describe how vertical relationships themselves are maintained by the power of the ruling class. She ignores the power of the big business corporations and others who have enough concentrated power to control or to co-opt other members in society. Nakane stresses vertical relationships as cultural phenomena rather than as political phenomena, overlooking the fact that Japan is one of the most politically centralized nations in the world. One of the most conspicuous features of Japanese society is the extent to which political power is centralized. Power is more centralized in Japan than in other industrial countries, and Japanese managers seem to enjoy more rights *vis-à-vis* the worker than do managers in other countries.

The concept of vertical relationships yields two ideal types for analyzing societies. One type is horizontally stratified by class; and the other is vertically stratified by organization. According to Nakane, in Japan social cleavages occur among vertically defined groups, and horizontal struggles between workers and capitalists do not exist. Competitive relationships develop between company A and company B.

If we consider carefully the two principles of stratification shown in Figure 6.5, it becomes clear that the possible types are at least four, not two. For example, in society III in Figure 6.6, both vertical and horizontal relationships are predominant; in society IV neither type is predominant. In the first instance, Nakane associates Type I with Japanese society and Type II with Western societies.

Figure 6.5 *Nakane's Two Principles of Stratification*

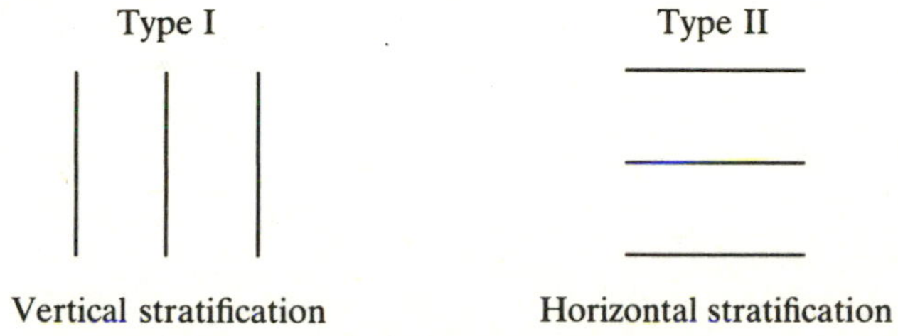

Type I   Type II

Vertical stratification   Horizontal stratification

At the same time Nakane also contrasts Western individualism (for example, values consistent with Type III) with Japanese groupism or consensus (for instance, values consistent with Type IV). Accordingly, types I and III are both models of Japanese society, and types II and IV are seen as being models for understanding Western societies. She does not mention the possibility of change, but rather insists that the vertical structuring of Japanese society will remain unchanged. At the same time, the implicit assumption that Japanese groupism might be a trait of pre-modern societies is accepted. In other words, the idea that Western individualism is a more advanced form of social relationship is implicitly expressed.

As for developmental directions in general, the most familiar assumption is that values will shift from being pre-modern to being modern or from being status-based to being contract-based. Using Parsonian concepts, this is a process of moving from collectivistic orientations to individualistic orientations, from affection to affection-neutrality, and from status criteria to performance criteria. These kinds of changes are part of the process of changing from groupism to individualism. But as a typology, any of several types of change are possible. Returning to Figure 6.6 we can imagine a change from the Type IV to Type I to II or even to Type III. However, a close examination of Nakane's volume suggests that she is concerned only with types I and II. Her diagrams also suggest that the horizontal type of social relationship is more desirable than the vertical type. The diagrams are redrawn in Figure 6.7.

Nakane uses her diagrams to illustrate how the fundamental relationships in 'horizontal societies' form triangles (Example I in

Figure 6.6 *Four Types of Society*

Type I

Type III

Type II

Type IV

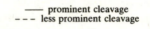
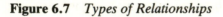
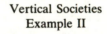

——— prominent cleavage
- - - less prominent cleavage

Figure 6.7 *Types of Relationships*

Horizontal Societies
Example I

Vertical Societies
Example II

Example III

Example IV

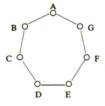

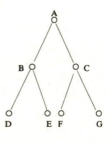

Figure 6.7), whereas the fundamental relationships in 'vertical societies' form only the inverted V (Example II). In the horizontal type of societies, the basic triangle can develop into a square, a pentagon, a hexagon and so on (Example III). In the vertical societies, however, organizational growth simply results in bigger pyramids, with only one person at the apexes (Example IV). If the diagrams correctly reflect relationships the society with 'vertical structures' would not have vertical cleavage along the parallel vertical lines shown in Figure 6.5. Nor would the 'horizontal structure' result in horizontal cleavages along the parallel horizontal lines shown in Figure 6.5.

According to Nakane's model, the predominance of vertical relationships in Japanese society precludes the existence of institutions in their own right. The society described by Nakane is integrated only by a series of one-to-one personal relationships. The idea of the pyramid alone is too simple to explain any unique trait of Japanese society. This pyramid model is equally applicable as a means of describing the general bureaucratic organizations of any society: offices, factories, military bodies and political parties.

This is not to suggest that vertical relationships do not exist in Japan. The basic social relationship in Japan is not only vertical; it is also genealogical. It is characterized by a fundamental paternalism. However, it should be emphasized that the idea of genealogical relationships has been maintained and given meaning as an ideology by big business corporations. So we can say that vertical relationships in reality reflect how power is centralized in the hands of the central government and big business corporations. The idea of genealogical relationships centred on the Emperor is but one ideological expression used to maintain such political domination.

As for the choice between egalitarian societies and hierarchical societies, there would be little question even for most Japanese. Nakane's argument that the pyramidal type of social relationships in Japan will not change is simply based on unilinear extrapolation. Nakane does not mention the actual power of big business corporations; she tends to assume that Japanese people are by their very nature docile and submissive to authority.

9 *Ie shakai*

In 1979 an important book was published by Murakami, Kumon and Satō. Treating the notion of the *ie* as the basis of Japanese civilization, the volume argues that the uniqueness of Japanese society rests on a special orientation to interpersonal relations (*aidagarashugi*), and on the awareness which Japanese have of their relationships with others. Emphasis is also placed on the extent to which the *ie* consciousness (as opposed to Western individualism) has facilitated Japan's modernization and industrialization. The three authors argue (pp. 43–4) that Western individualism produces a kind of natural (*shizenteki*) though qualified (*genteiteki*) kind of group phenomena, but not the purposefully structured (*jin-iteki*) and unqualified (*mugentei*) sense of the group which is found in Japan. However, they do not explain what a natural and/or qualified group might be, although they seem to be assuming it is some form of nuclear family. Moreover, as in other *nihonjinron*, they do not define key terms such as individualism (*kojinshugi*), groupism (*shūdanshugi*) or the special relational orientation (*aidagarashugi*) in a way that allows for the concepts to be clearly differentiated.

Although the authors seem to draw upon Watsuji (1934) in order to contrast the etymological origins of the Japanese word *ningen* (meaning 'between people') and the meaning of *homo* or *anthro* in English, claiming that the Japanese word implants an interrelational orientation in the minds of the Japanese when they think about mankind, they fail to note Watsuji's emphasis on the way in which humans in any society are, first of all, individuals and overlook the way in which their interrelatedness emerges out of the groups or communities they form (cf. Watsuji 1935: 166–70).

I believe that the picture of how any new type of society is formed would be similar in this regard. Individuals do not just drift together to form societies naturally. Societies are consciously formed. Social groups are simultaneously a means and an end for individuals; their sway over the individual is both qualified and unqualified; and their formation is at the same time spontaneous and contrived. For this reason, the description which pits Western notions of modern society based on individualism (*kojinshugi*) against *ie* society based on interpersonalism (*aidagarashugi*) is clearly tied to the vocabulary of a particular historical context. Accordingly, '*aidagara*' is not used to refer to the actual structure of the family (*kazoku*) or to the *ie*, but to a kind of organizational principle. Little attention is paid to the disintegration of the family in postwar Japan, a phenomenon occurring especially in the 'new middle stratum'. Moreover, the extent to which the *ie* form of organization fits the organizational ideal found in many business firms and other bureaucratically rational organizations is played down, as is the extent to which it is used as an ideology to justify such practices as enterprise unionism, life-time employment and seniority wages for a small elite in the labour force.

In other words, it serves more as an ideological prescription rather than as a concept for describing social reality. In differentiating (1) vertical orientations in the parent–child relationship, and the sense of continuity and genealogy of the Japanese family from (2) the more individually oriented or balanced husband–wife relationship and the limited time span of the Western nuclear family, the proponents of the *ie* society theory draw from the ideology currently used in middle-range organizations such as the business firm. The work by Murakami *et al.* serves to verify the general argument advanced in this paper that the concept of *ie* continues to be used as ideology to legitimate a certain cultural form. By presenting the *ie* as basic to Japanese culture and way of thinking, and then saying that such a way of thinking is inherent in the Japanese mental make-up, Murakami *et al.* present the *ie* as a kind of cultural given. The logic seems to be that what already exists should continue to exist, and that by proving its existence in the past one also justifies its existence in the future. This reasoning can be seen in the preamble to various public planning documents such as *Bunka no Jidai* (The Age of Culture) which was one of the reports prepared by the study group of former Prime Minister Ohira. (It may also be interesting to note, in this regard, that one of the authors of the above-mentioned book was a member of the study group.)

The ideological emphasis described above is consistent with the authors' emphasis on genealogical continuity (*keifusei*) in the *ie* thought pattern itself and in the tendency both to play down prewar and postwar differences and to highlight the continuing importance of the *ie* in family organization despite the obvious changes brought about by the war and its aftermath. The emphasis on continuity leads to a basic confusion between what is historical fact (a problem of describing a culture in a particular historical context) and the choices that need to be made with regard to democratic forms of government (a problem of selecting a desirable direction to pursue in terms of social organization).

In emphasizing a vision of social reality in Japan which can be used as a suitable ideology in maintaining a certain social order in the running of Japan's large enterprises, the three authors have tended to highlight the functional aspects by focusing on the importance of abstract roles and fictional kinship relations. This has meant that blood ties are played down in explaining the ideology that binds the family together and in explaining the conceptual framework which put the Emperor at the head of the Japanese nation. Like Nakane, they write about a kind of truncated genealogy which may be found in firms A, B and C, but do not discuss the fictional blood ties which connect the imperial family with the general populace. It is a view which allows for technological modernization to be introduced from above while justifying in the name of the 'Japanese way' policies which threaten individual freedoms, democratic forms of interaction and human rights in general. By concentrating attention on the middle levels of organization in Japanese society (as shown in Figure 6.8) the ideological superstructure is overlooked along with the actual realities of the social and family structure in contemporary Japan.

By legitimating the hierarchical ordering of society, the *ie* serves as an ideology which ties the community (*mura*) to the nation (*kuni*). The work by Murakami *et al.* is distinguished by the normative emphasis it places on the validity of the *ie* as the key cultural concept by which economic and civic groups can most logically be formed in Japan. One could say that by limiting the vertical ideology to legitimating the hierarchical structure of middle-range organizations in society, the possibility of rather horizontal ties at both the level of the state and the level of the local community is left open. This would mean, in essence, that the Emperor system could be dismantled. In other words, the notion of *ie shakai* as an ideology seems to allow for a more flexible notion of society, and for this reason can be said to be considerably more sophisticated than earlier formulations of the Japanese family as an ideology.

Figure 6.8   *Focus of Attention in* Ie Shakai *Theories*

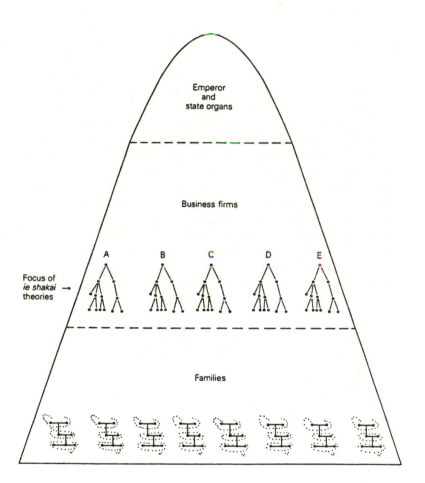

10   Conclusion

No matter how much Japanese society is Westernized, the 'household consciousness' will remain in many aspects of Japanese culture. However, this is somewhat different from having it deliberately forced upon people as ideology in order to suppress individual rights and freedoms. Traditional values which put emphasis on communal interests are preserved in the everyday life of the common Japanese. This cultural tradition originates from centuries of communal life in Japanese families and communities. The emphasis on vertical relationships, as opposed to horizontal relationships, however, provides a good example of how traditional values are manipulated for ideological purposes. Under certain circumstances, however, a move to establish new communities or new communal ways of life will emerge. It is unlikely that in Japan complete independence of each person will occur first, with some kind of solidarity between independent persons then emerging. Such mechanical distinctions between two stages of development do not seem relevant to the Japanese experience.

In 1908, an editor of a socialist journal for women's liberation in Japan wrote as follows in an editorial entitled 'Japanese families in the future':

> affection between the husband and wife or between parents and their children, which are natural and strong sentiments, will become the central forces in the family. . . . In our present society love for one's sons, parents, wife and oneself is made to contradict one's love for others and for society. . . . If one can love himself, his family members and relatives without contradicting his love for others and for society, then all these different loves can develop as the admirable, beautiful and true sentiments of each human being.

These observations about the family ring true in Japan even today. The revitalization of the horizontal relationships and solidarity among common people in traditional groups is still seen by many people as being a valid choice and as being the desirable path to be taken.

References

Befu, Harumi
   1971   *Japan: an Anthropological Introduction* (San Francisco, Cal.: Chandler).
Dore, Ronald P.
   1958   *City Life in Japan: a Study of a Tokyo Ward* (London: Routledge & Kegan Paul).
   1973   *British Factory–Japanese Factory: the Origins of National Diversity in Industrial Society* (London: Oxford University Press).
Fukutake, Tadashi
   1967   *Japanese Rural Society* (London: Oxford University Press).
   1974   *Japanese Society Today* (Tokyo: University of Tokyo Press).
Kawamura, Nozomu
   1980a   *Sociology and Society in Early Modern Japan* (Melbourne: La Trobe University).
   1980b   'The Historical Background of Arguments Emphasizing the Uniqueness of Japanese Society', *Social Analysis*, nos. 5/6 (Dec.) 44–62).
   1982   *Nihon Bunkaron no Shuhen* (Some Aspects of Theories Concerning Japanese Culture) (Tokyo: Ningen no Kagakusha).
Maruyama, Masao
   1962   *Thought and Behaviour in Modern Japanese Politics* (London: Oxford University Press).
Murakami, Yasusuke; Kumon, Shunpei; and Satō, Seizaburō
   1979   *Bunmei toshite no Ie Shakai* (The *Ie* Society as Civilization) (Tokyo: Chūō Kōronsha).
Nakane, Chie
   1970   *Japanese Society* (London: Weidenfeld and Nicolson).
Parsons, Talcott; and Smelser, Neil J.
   1956   *Economy and Society* (London: Routledge & Kegan Paul).
Plath, David
   1980   *Long Engagement: Maturity in Modern Japan* (Stanford, Cal.: Stanford University Press).
Smith, Thomas C.
   1959   *The Agrarian Origins of Modern Japan* (Stanford, Cal.: Stanford University Press).
Vogel, Ezra F.
   1979   *Japan as Number One: Lessons for America* (Cambridge, Mass.: Harvard University Press).
Watsuji, Tetsurō
   1934   *Ningen no Gaku toshite no Ronrigaku* (Ethics as a Human Science) (Tokyo: Iwanami Shoten).
   1935   *Fūdo – Ningengakuteki Kōsatsu* (The Environment: Some Thoughts From Human Science) (Tokyo: Iwanami Shoten).

Chapter Seven
Resolving Social Conflicts: a Comparative View of Interpersonal and Inter-group Relations in Japan

Susan J. Pharr

1 Introduction

Conflict is endemic to social life. All who live in social groups
exhibit differences in wealth, in power, in beliefs, in commitments
to the way things are and to how they might be, in personality, in
ability and in interests. As members of one or more groups,
individuals interact with persons in their own group, but also with
persons belonging to other groups. In the normal course of events,
most individuals are constantly dealing with persons who have
different sets of interests; this means that conflicts of interest are
a major feature of everyday life in most complex societies. Often
the result is social conflict.

Studying conflicts reveals how disorder and dissensus are dealt
with in day-to-day relations between groups, and at the same time
provides an interior view of the social organization of a society,
of how power is distributed within it, and of how the latter may
be changing. The study of conflict within any given society raises

questions relevant to our understanding both of stability and instability, power and powerlessness, consensus and dissensus, and continuity and change. Since conflict is basic to all societies, the analysis of conflict provides a methodology for comparing societies cross-nationally both at the macro-level (for example, as to how whole societies compare in their patterns of conflict resolution and in the degree to which there is agreement over the terms of social relations) and at the micro-level (for example, in how patterns of resolving conflicts at the personal, the group and the inter-group level compare). For all these reasons, the study of conflict provides an inviting avenue for approaching the comparative study of Japanese society.

Since conflicts arise constantly, and often emerge out of a vast array of differences in the allocation of resources among individuals and groups in a given society, any analysis that lends itself, implicitly or explicitly, to cross-national comparison must begin with a decision about the unit of analysis that isolates the key variables. This chapter follows the procedures adopted by Gusfield (1966), Tsuratani (1977) and Pharr (forthcoming) in defining the unit as a status-based conflict – a conflict arising out of the effort of an individual or a group to adjust their status position upward in relation to other individuals or groups.

Status-based conflicts are numerous. The focus here is on status-based conflicts in which the statuses of the two parties are ascribed or dictated by age, sex, caste background, or other attributes that are assigned at birth and normally beyond the powers of the individual to change. The methodology has been to assemble data on several cases of status-based conflict that have surfaced in Japan over the past two decades, each case involving inequalities produced by different attributes. The first case study involves conflict between women and men at work; the second, between generations in a political party; and the third, between a group of *burakumin* and the majority (namely, those who are not *burakumin*).

A   The importance of status-based conflict in terms of democratic ideologies

In terms of developing a comparative perspective, status-based conflicts involving ascribed attributes are important for two reasons. First, in arguing that status inequalities based on age, sex and other ascriptive attributes are a crucial source of conflict in contemporary Japan, it is argued that the nature of social structural characteristics is such that they themselves may be viewed cross-culturally. A hierarchically ordered feudal system ended so recently in Japan that ascribed rank and status continue to be key ordering principles in social relations despite the remarkable changes that have occurred over the past century. The continuing importance of ascribed status in shaping relations between groups has been one of the most agreed-upon features of the Japanese social order. This was true in the work of Benedict (1946) and in the work of Abegglen (1958), Cole (1971) and Austin (1975) on the productivity of Japanese workers – studies which emphasize the nature of junior–senior relations in the workplace as a partial explanation for Japan's success. Though the work of Nakane (1970) and others who have attempted to construct an entire model of Japanese society based on the persistence of status inequalities has been criticized as taking the argument too far, few analysts of Japanese society would be prepared to discount the importance of the basic social structural characteristics that are the building blocks of such a model.

Numerous writers – including students of worker–employer relations, the family, group behaviour, and other arenas of Japanese social life – have argued that orderly junior–senior relations and the hierarchical ordering principle more generally have contributed to social integration and consensus in Japan (Abegglen 1958; Cole 1971; Austin 1975; Rohlen 1976; and Vogel 1975). As the opening remarks in this chapter suggest, however, inequalities which provide a key basis for social integration under certain circumstances will, under other conditions, be a significant locus of conflict, for the very reason that status represents such a fundamental adjustive mechanism in Japanese society.

The research reported here supports the observations of Tsuru-tani (1977) who sees status inequalities as an increasing source of conflict, primarily because of the ideological changes which are occurring in Japanese society. These changes, it is argued in this chapter, have had a major impact on the nature of interpersonal and intra-group and inter-group relations. In the past, hierarchically ordered status relations in Japan were supported by an ideology that affirmed the legitimacy of the authority exercised by status superiors in junior–senior relations. Since World War II, however, as a result of social and political changes set in motion by the

Allied occupation, democratic values challenging that authority received the sanction of official ideology. Democratic values (which, of course, had had considerable influence in Japan well before 1945) gained even further ideological authority with Japan's postwar internationalization and its increasing identification with the liberal democracies.

Democratic ideology thus is available in Japan today to those who – in the context of the interpersonal, intra-group or inter-group relations in which they find themselves – suffer from status-based discrimination and are prepared to engage in conflict to try to improve their lot. Holding aloft the ideology of democracy, status inferiors can challenge the legitimacy of the authority being exercised over them by their status superiors. When status-based conflicts are viewed in this way, it is possible to see the dynamics involved in the breakdown of Japan as a harmonious, consensual society. For, as Weber notes, consensus in social relations is possible only to the extent that existing power arrangements are affirmed and those exercising authority are accorded legitimacy. To the extent that a counter-ideology is available to challenge that authority and to undermine the claim to legitimacy of those in positions of power in social relationships, the basis for consensus breaks down. Focusing on status-based conflicts, then, is in recognition of the particular importance of such conflicts in contemporary Japan, given certain social structural characteristics and changes in the values supporting them.

B The importance of status-based conflict and the growing significance of non-economic issues

A second reason for singling out such conflicts is that status issues appear to be gaining salience in advanced industrial nations more generally. Western conflict theorists have been concerned primarily with conflicts over ownership, use and distribution of economic goods rather than over social inequalities resulting from ascribed status. Numerous observers (for instance, Inglehart 1971; Ike 1973; Flanagan 1982) argue that a shift may be occurring today away from struggles over economic interests to struggles over issues of value and meaning. Although the economic retrenchments occurring in most of the advanced industrial countries today are reminders that economic issues have hardly lost their salience, it can be argued that issues of meaning and value clamour for equal attention. In fact, it may be argued that many issues classified as conflicts over economic interests are as well – or better – understood as issues of value and meaning. One can point to the increased importance of non-economic issues in collective bargaining, the struggles of middle-class women to renegotiate their roles and status, and the concern with non-economic issues that has marked many protest activities in advanced industrial societies (over, for example, the problems of the handicapped and of old people) in recent years as striking examples.

If these trends are general ones affecting all the advanced industrial nations, then Japan is a particularly good example of a country in which such a shift is taking place. It is often reported that 90 per cent of the Japanese today regard themselves as middle class, and there has been much discussion in Japan of the meaning of the rise of the vast 'new middle class' that, according to one view, is unmatched in size compared to any other society in the world today (Murakami 1982). The shift from struggles over economic interests to struggles over meaning may be observed, not only in the types of status-related issues dealt with in this chapter, but in the nature of numerous other conflicts that arose in Japan in the 1970s and early to mid-1980s. These include conflicts over peace-related issues, over nuclear energy and environmental policy, over the practices of big business in Japan (for example, truth-in-packaging issues), over moral and ethical issues (such as the Lockheed scandal and other, more recent, cases of political corruption), over various symbolic and cultural issues (like the Narita airport protest and the controversy over what type of calendar Japan should adopt), and over the social and psychological (as well as economic) problems of ageing.

For both reasons, then, status-based conflicts provide a window on Japanese society today in comparative perspective, and allow for a closely-focused investigation of the nature of interpersonal, intra-group and inter-group relations. At the macro-level, the research has been concerned with how conflicts over the issue of status inequality affect the nature of Japanese society and politics. At the micro-level, it explores how individuals and groups respond to changing values concerning the importance of status, and how social conflicts between and among individuals and groups is resolved in Japan.

2 Methodology

Extensive material gathered on three specific cases of status-based conflicts during field work in Japan in 1978 has been supplemented by the analysis of secondary materials acquired since that time. Each case is briefly introduced here.

A Gender-based conflict

The first case involves the ascriptive attribute of sex. It focuses on a small group of female civil servants in one division of a public bureaucracy who formed a movement to protest against a specific duty assigned to them on the basis of sex: the making and the pouring of tea several times a day for the men in their particular division of the Kyōto City Office. Inter-sex conflict is central to any study of status-based conflict in Japan because women, in sheer numbers, make up a vast proportion of the population who continue to be assigned positions of status inferiority in numerous social contexts. The case selected for this study holds particular interest because it involves conflict over an activity (the serving of tea) that is a significant symbolic act tied to women's traditional status. It thus provides a close look at the subtle psychological and symbolic issues that appear to characterize status-based conflicts.

The conflict is also of special significance because the larger issue it raises is whether the state, speaking through the rules, regulations and employment practices of the public bureaucracy, can continue to sanction and perpetuate status inequalities based on sex while officially upholding an ideology of meritocracy and egalitarianism. How this larger issue, which arises in the values and practices of public bureaucracies in most societies today is resolved worldwide, has profound consequences for contemporary social arrangements (cf. Szalai 1973). In this sense, the case has particular comparative relevance.

B Age-based conflict

The second case involves the ascriptive attribute of age. It examines the conflict that arose within the Liberal Democratic Party, resulting, in 1976, in the formation of a splinter party, the New Liberal Club, by a group of younger LDP members. Although several LDP members involved in the breakaway, and a number (though still a minority) of persons who ran on the NLC ticket were not young, even by Japanese standards, the leaders of the NLC and the preponderance of those who joined the party were men in their thirties and forties, and left the LDP at the culmination of a conflict that involved numerous grievances associated with their status as juniors in an age-graded party hierarchy.

As is the case with most complex conflicts, numerous causative factors apart from age-related issues were involved, but the intergenerational component loomed large. The New Liberal Club has remained small, and can hardly be considered a major player in Japanese politics today, but the case commands attention as a window on a type of conflict, involving inequalities in authority based on age, that continues to surface in the political parties and in Japanese organizational life more generally (cf. Mainichi Shinbunsha Seijibu 1975).

C   Caste-based conflict

The third case involves the ascriptive attribute of caste. The legacy of caste affects some two to three million people in Japan who are known as '*burakumin*' (the term literally means 'people of the hamlet' and referred to the fact that they were required by law to live in segregated villages prior to their official emancipation in 1871). The *burakumin*, like the untouchables of India, were originally assigned their outcaste status because they handled the killing and butchering of animals, the tanning of hides, leather-work, and other tasks regarded as filthy and despicable under the tenets of Buddhism.

In the 1980s, however, long after the legal basis for their outcaste status has been removed, the *burakumin* continue to be exposed to numerous forms of status-based discrimination. However, after many centuries of quiescence to their position of status inferiority *vis-à-vis* all other social groups, they began to protest against that position in this century. *Burakumin* movements now shake the foundations of local and prefectural politics in Japan and, because both the Japanese Communist Party and the Japanese Socialist Party vie for their support, conflicts arising from *burakumin* activism threaten the prospects for coalition at the national level (Rohlen 1976).

The particular conflict referred to here arose in 1974, and involved the demands of a local branch of the Buraku Liberation

League (BLL), a leading group with links to the Japanese Socialist Party, to organize a study group on *burakumin* problems in a local high school in the prefecture of Hyōgo near Osaka.[1] This conflict culminated in a violent confrontation between teachers and members of the League in which there were numerous physical injuries. Fourteen League members were put on trial on charges relating to the dispute, and the political consequences of the incident, locally and nationally, have been far-reaching.

3 Stages of conflict

This chapter explores the dynamics and characteristics of social conflicts. The analysis employs a comparative framework developed from the work of Western conflict theorists. It draws together, in a preliminary way, some thoughts about the nature of interpersonal, intra-group and inter-group relations in Japan as it is revealed in the context of conflict situations.

Social conflicts unfold in a series of stages that have been well analyzed by Western conflict theorists such as Coleman (1957), Kriesberg (1973) and Coser (1967). Their point of origin is an objective situation involving an incompatibility of goals pursued by the two or more parties. At this *first stage* the conflict latent in the objective situation may or may not become manifest at the level of individual consciousness (cf. Coleman 1957: 4; Di Palma 1973: 3; Kriesberg 1973: 24). The focus of the analyst at this stage is on identifying the conditions that have the potential for giving rise to a conflict.

In the *second stage*, the conflict becomes manifest, although to say this belies the complexity of the process by which it occurs (cf. Kriesberg 1973: 6). Obviously, the beginning point of the process is in the changing consciousness of one or more individuals out of the pool of those potentially affected by the objective conflict situation. An individual could, of course, proceed directly into conflict when the goals of another individual or the direction of a group becomes incompatible with his or her own interests. In the

1 This information comes from interviews with officials at the *Buraku* Liberation League headquarters and with persons in various study groups in Kyōto, Osaka and Tajima (June–August 1974).

conflicts selected for this study, however, a change in consciousness of one or more individuals gradually spread among those potentially affected so that, at last, a critical mass resulted in a collectivity forming to engage in the conflict. Bearing in mind the concerns of this volume with distinguishing various levels of Japanese society, the developments at this stage are of particular interest, because they reveal the linkages between the individual, the interpersonal and the group levels. One of the crucial questions to ask about this stage is how the various levels interact on the way towards group formation.

In the *third stage*, the parties initiate conflict behaviour. The relevant questions to ask at this stage concern the modes of conflict (for example, persuasion, coercion, reward), adopted by the parties in pursuit of their conflicting goals and the degree to which third parties play a role (cf. Kriesberg 1973: 110; Coleman 1957: 11–15). These questions are useful to ask about conflicts in Japan because they highlight in a comparative context some of the key interpersonal relationships alleged to be unique to Japan in much of the literature on Japanese society and culture.

Thus, for example, we can ask about the role of third parties in an inter-group conflict in Japan without getting locked into a discussion of go-betweens that presumes their existence and/or treats the phenomenon as unique to Japanese culture.

In the *fourth stage*, the conflict escalates and de-escalates in response to changes in intensity and scope. In the *fifth* and *final stage*, the conflict terminates. Although one conflict may well begin a new one, any specific conflict has some kind of outcome (cf. Coser 1967: 37–9; Schelling 1966: chs II and III; Kriesberg 1973: 205). In addition to these stages in the life of a given conflict, there is a further stage in which the effects of the conflict feed back into the objective conditions that potentially will give rise to further conflicts. This feedback process by which social structures and values undergo adjustments provides the central dynamic of social change (Coser 1967: 19–35). How this model applies to empirical data on conflict in Japan and what implications may be drawn for the individual and for interpersonal, intra-group and inter-group relations will now be explored.

Stage one: the objective basis for conflict
The objective basis for status-based conflicts arising out of ascrip-

tive attributes is in the nature of status inequality itself. In the status-based conflict involving the tea-pourers, the conflict began in the objective conditions that define the status of women in the workplace in Japan and, more specifically, that defined the status of women in a particular public bureaucracy in the early 1960s. The objective basis for conflict was in the tension between (1) the official ideology of the workplace, which forbids discrimination on the basis of sex and upholds the principle of equality, and (2) the informal ideology, derived from traditional values, which structures women's roles and opportunities in the labour market on the basis of their ascribed status as women.

The same may be said of the case involving younger generation LDP members who in 1976 broke with the LDP to form the New Liberal Club. The objective condition for such a conflict was located in the terms of age-based status relations within the LDP and within Japanese organizations more generally. In the typical pattern of Japanese organizational life, the distribution of authority is weighed heavily in favour of senior generations of leaders in Japan who monopolize political resources – money, power and position – and allocate them to their subordinates on the basis of the age-graded hierarchy. Subordinates ideally are expected to acknowledge the authority of their superiors through various types of deference behaviour and to demonstrate their loyalty to their seniors.

Finally, the third case study at Yōka High School illustrates the same pattern. The objective conditions defining the status of *burakumin* are a constant in Japanese life today, and arise out of the status relations which have persisted between majority Japanese and *burakumin* on the basis of the latter's former outcaste status. Although discrimination against *burakumin* was legal up until 1871, *burakumin* are in 1980 still exposed individually and collectively to numerous forms of discrimination ranging from their treatment at work to extraordinarily subtle forms of behaviour (for example, avoidance behaviour, and lack of warmth and/or of eye contact in interpersonal communications). The *burakumin* continue to feel that they are receiving signals which indicate to them that they are regarded as inferiors by the majority of Japanese.

In each of the three cases, then, the conditions that have the potential for giving rise to conflict are inherent in status relations which have existed in Japan since the early Meiji period (and before). To the extent that traditional values upheld the legitimacy of the power exercised by status superiors in status relations in Japan, it was unlikely that objective conditions of inequality would give rise to conflict. However, as democratic ideology from abroad has spread over the past one hundred years (intertwining in the process with indigenous forms of democracy that have traditionally coexisted with hierarchy in Japanese culture) and has gained legitimacy in postwar Japan, the power exercised by status superiors *vis-à-vis* those below them is implicitly challenged, thus increasing the possibility that specific conditions of inequality may give rise to conflict.

Stage two: the conflict becomes manifest

The gradual changes in ideology governing status relationships in Japan provide the larger backdrop to occasions in which any objective situation gives rise to conflict. But these larger ideological changes alone hardly explain a specific outbreak of conflict. For there are obviously a myriad of occasions in which conditions of status inequality – as experienced by women, younger people, and *burakumin* – do *not* lead to conflict, even in Japan of the 1980s. We may assume that many years in an educational system that has promoted the principles of democracy and egalitarianism has exposed most status inferiors to the ideology that would justify a challenge to the terms of such status relations. And yet relatively few status inferiors are prepared to act. Therefore, the next task is to identify the particular conditions under which a given episode of status-based conflict will arise.

If we argue that ideological change of the type just discussed constitutes a necessary, but not sufficient, condition for conflict to arise, one key question we must first take up is whether most Japanese are conscious of such change to the point that they perceive and are disturbed by the inequality inherent in status relations in which they find themselves. If not, and if most Japanese continue to accept the terms of those relations without feeling that there is a contradiction between the democratic ideology heralded in the laws and taught in the schools, on the one hand, and the traditional terms of status relations, on the other, then outbreaks of status-based conflicts in Japan today are isolated incidents that are not indicative of broader social change.

The question of whether Japanese are conscious of status

inequality is particularly important from the standpoint of proceeding with a comparative analysis of social conflict. An *etic* mode of analysis, as discussed elsewhere in this volume, would treat status inequality as a concept applicable cross-culturally without asking whether inequalities inherent in social structural characteristics are perceived as such within a particular cultural context. An *emic* mode of investigation requires us to look at Japanese perceptions of such characteristics to discover their meaning in that particular society. In my own work, based on the analysis of case material, I argue that status inequalities are perceived as such by most Japanese, particularly by postwar educated people who have been exposed to democratic ideology throughout their schooling.

As one example of the type of evidence that supports that view, we may point to the public reaction to the breakaway of the New Liberal Club from the LDP in 1976. When the original six members of the New Liberal Club broke with the LDP, the move was immediately hailed in the press and among the public as a challenge of the old by the young. The younger generation within the LDP, the media said, had tired of party gerontocracy. The LDP's leadership, said the respected journal *Ekonomisuto* (5 July 1977: 34), was a 'group of grandfathers' whose views were no longer those of the nation. Younger LDP members, noted one writer, applauded the departure of Kōno Yōhei and his colleagues from the LDP, as did younger people in business circles and among the public. Surveys designed to assess the new group's following confirmed that the group had a strong base of support among younger voters (Hosojima 1976).

This response to the breakaway supports the view that the conflict inherent in junior–senior, or inferior–superior, relations is widely perceived in today's Japan. The media readily interpreted the move as involving intergenerational conflict and a challenge to the structure of authority in the party. The public, especially younger voters, could understand the rationale for the break well enough to support Kōno and the other junior men who left. It appears, then, that the 'awareness process' by which inherent tensions over status inequalities become manifest is well advanced in society at large. All three case studies presented an abundance of evidence that status-related grievances are well understood in today's Japan, even by people who might not be prepared to challenge the terms of status relations in their own lives, and even by people who do not view the grievances of status sympathetically.

We may now investigate the conditions under which a specific episode of status-based conflict is likely to arise – the conditions under which individuals in Japan who are locked into interpersonal relations with persons of superior status become conscious of the inequality and bothered by it to the point they are prepared to engage in conflict behaviour to protest in order to try to improve their lot. Based on the writings of Goffman (1967), Douglas (1973) and others who have analyzed the types of deference behaviour and status rituals that are called for in relations between persons of unequal status, I hypothesized that status rituals give the performer greatest satisfaction when at least five conditions are met: (1) when the deference behaviour is warmly rewarded by reciprocal behaviour; (2) when the deference behaviour is felt by the one engaging in it to be well deserved (for example, in the case of a military salute, the salute has more meaning and comes more easily when the saluted is a hero and general rather than a little-respected lesser officer); (3) when the behaviour called for is congruent with expected behaviours in other roles; (4) when the status differential due to the ascribed attribute is reinforced by other status differences (such as in socio-economic background, educational level, period of employment, bureaucratic rank and so on); and (5) when the reward structure associated with deference behaviour offers maximum benefits. To the extent that these conditions are not met, the possibility of conflict arising out of inequalities in status relations is increased.

Each of the case studies presents detailed empirical evidence to bear out this hypothesis, but the case of the tea-pourers' rebellion illustrates the various points especially well. The tea-pourers' rebellion occurred in only one division (the Housing Division) of the huge Kyōto City Office. When the situation of women employees in that particular division was examined, it was apparent that none of the five conditions just described was being adequately met. The Housing Division was one of the new divisions in the bureaucracy, and its office routines were reported by the workers interviewed for the case study to have an unsettled quality. Everyone seemed rushed and on different schedules, with builders, architects and planners hurrying in and out of the office. A number of higher-status males, particularly the architects, appeared, by all accounts, to take personal services of all kinds for granted. Meanwhile, the volume of work in Japan's construction boom period of the 1960s was rising. Successive waves of 'rationalization'

in office tasks had increased women's share of the workload
without a corresponding decrease in the number of unofficial
chores the women were expected to perform, including tea-
pouring. Little thought had been given to how the latter duties
might conflict with the women's regular work assignments and
deadlines.

Referring back to the five conditions, it can be said that in the
hurried atmosphere of a newly established division, there was little
warmth in face-to-face relations, draining deference behaviour of
its emotional rewards. Meanwhile, the attitude of the older male
professionals, especially the architects – their lack of basic courtesy
and generosity and their failure to acknowledge favours – made it
onerous to perform the tea-pouring rituals. Due to changes in the
nature of the workload in the division, there was an increasing
lack of congruence between the content of the tasks expected of
the women in their roles as workers and the tasks expected of
them due to the ascriptive attribute of sex. Meanwhile, college-
educated women had begun to enter the Housing Division, leading
to status incongruity. High school graduates without special skills
were less likely to see tea-pouring as demeaning, whereas college-
educated women were more likely to see such tasks as 'beneath
them' and as inappropriate to their level of training, experience
and skills. For all these reasons, then, the status rituals expected
of the women were losing their meaning and becoming onerous,
and the conditions that might have constrained conflict behaviour
were not in place.

The fifth condition hypothesis concerning constrained conflict
behaviour involved the reward structure. Such behaviour is less
likely to occur when the rewards associated with deference are
maximized. In the case of the tea-pourers, the emotional rewards
of tea-pouring had diminished, as indicated. The case of the New
Liberal Club breakaway from the LDP illustrates even more vividly
how a reward structure can fail to operate for a specific group of
individuals locked in relationships of status inequality. The case
study revealed that the key group of younger men (Kōno Yōhei,
Yamaguchi Toshio, and Nishioka Takeo) who broke with the
party were younger LDP members who had the least to gain from
the party's reward structure (that is, from the financial, political and
psychological rewards normally associated with being a member of
a faction). All three were *nisei* (second-generation politicians); as
sons of famous political fathers, they had inherited not only safe

seats, but the personal financial connections that went along with them. Compared to other junior men in the LDP, these men had least to lose from challenging the terms of status relations in the party.

Although the five conditions mentioned above frame the circumstances under which status-based conflict is more likely to arise, they cannot explain the complex process by which individuals who are experiencing status inequality prepare to move forward to seek remedies. To understand that process, the focus quickly falls on the one or more individuals in a given situation who initially experience a transformation of consciousness that brings them to the point of contemplating action. These are the persons who assume the crucial leadership or organizational role in drawing others to the cause. In each of the case studies, key individuals set the conflict in motion – a finding that in and of itself provides a basis for questioning the group model as it has been seen to apply to Japan. In the case of the NLC breakaway, Kōno Yōhei played a highly visible role as such a leader. In the tea-pourers' rebellion, a woman bureaucrat was persuaded by a male union activist in the Kyōto City Office to take the reins of leadership in organizing to protest against the women's situation in the Housing Division. In the Yōka High School incident, a *burakumin* who had emerged as a local leader of the Buraku Liberation League (BLL) played the key leadership role. Prior to the incident, he had embarked on a campaign throughout the area to recruit young *burakumin*, including those who ultimately staged the protest at Yōka High School, to the BLL movement and to raise their consciousness about the problems of *burakumin*.

In each case, the conflict gained momentum as these key leaders, often surrounded by several lieutenants, became agents of change in a consciousness-raising process through which other status inferiors were drawn to the cause. It is through this process that a group is welded together and becomes prepared to take action on behalf of agreed upon objectives. The steps along the way are manifold: the transformation of consciousness of the leader; the recognition by a small group of supporters of his or her leadership and the spread of the new consciousness from the leader to this inner circle; conversion of other followers to the leader's analysis and interpretation of the objective situation; the growth of the collective consciousness of the group and the accompanying growth of group solidarity; objectification and distancing from 'the enemy' (that is, status superiors) to the point that action-taking becomes psychologically possible; the development of concrete goals to be pursued by the group to improve their lot and to challenge the authority of the status superiors; and coming to agreement over the priorities among the goals and over modes of conflict to be adopted. All of these steps are part of the overall process by which the conflict inherent in an objective conflict situation becomes manifest prior to the initiation of actual conflict behaviour by a status-deprived group *vis-à-vis* a group of status superiors.

In reviewing the case studies to see how this process unfolds in real life, several features stand out that deserve analysis for what they tell us about status-based conflicts in Japan and about the way in which they become manifest. The first characteristic is the importance of the status of the leaders in establishing a role in the conflict. In general, within a pool of status inferiors who are affected by a given objective situation, the leadership reins appear to be taken by individuals whose status, by various measures, sets them above the others. In the case of the tea-pourers' rebellion, for example, the woman bureaucrat who emerged as the leader of the protest and one of her closest lieutenants were the only two college-educated women in the Housing Division. The male union activist who early on had persuaded her to take the reins saw her as the group's natural leader on the basis of her education. It can be argued, of course, that her selection on the basis of such a criterion was justified substantively. Survey data in Japan typically verifies that dissatisfaction over women's roles and status is highest among college-educated (as opposed to less-educated) women and thus the probability that college-educated women would be concerned over women's treatment in the office was high (Ministry of Foreign Affairs 1975; Iwao 1977). But the ease with which she took on the role and the readiness with which the other, less-educated women accepted her leadership indicates the importance of status considerations in all areas of Japanese life, including status-based conflicts.

Another manifestation of the importance of status considerations in the growth of a group protest effort was the key role played by higher-status individuals outside the group in legitimizing conflict behaviour. The role played by the male union organizer in singling out a leader for what became the tea-pourers' movement is an illustration. Another example is the role played by the Japan Socialist Party in relation to the Yōka High School incident, in which the party (speaking through non-*burakumin* officials in the community and in the high school) actively supported the efforts of *burakumin* students in the high school to get approval for the study group they sought. In both cases the outside agent can be seen as having functioned to legitimize the protest. In essence, these outsiders from the superior status group did what they normally do in the overall pattern of interaction with status inferiors: used their authority, but this time to legitimize the substitution of a new ideology of inter-status relations based on democratic values for an old one based on traditional values.

From the standpoint of the status inferiors, these acts of legitimation not only lent authority to their own emerging view of the objective conflict situation, they also helped relieve the anxiety attendant upon contemplating hostile actions against status superiors. The intercession or show of support by a third party from the ranks of the status superiors also served to reassure status inferiors that their new view of reality was comprehensible to at least some status superiors. The argument is not advanced here that the phenomenon just described is unique to Japan. The role played by white liberals in the civil rights movement in the USA and the role played by men in women's suffrage and in feminist movements in the USA, Britain (and, indeed, Japan, recalling the role played by Mori Arinori and Fukuzawa Yukichi) suggest that the role of high-status third parties may be a cross-culturally significant feature of status-based conflicts.

A second characteristic of the process by which the conflict becomes manifest was the degree to which the problems of the status inferiors were not spelled out in the process of consciousness-raising. For example, both the male union activist and the woman bureaucrat who played key roles in the tea-pourers' rebellion reported no discussion of specific problems that women faced in the Housing Division. From the beginning, there was a tacit understanding between them that women in the division had numerous legitimate grievances. Similarly, in the Yōka High School incident, the *burakumin* students who launched the protest appeared to agree from the outset that *burakumin* students at Yōka had justifiable grievance; spelling them out in detail was not required. The reason for leaving such grievances unstated, it may be argued, goes back to a point made earlier: the objective conflict situation inherent in status relations in Japan is near the surface of consciousness for many people. Relatively little discussion is needed for individuals – and especially the status-deprived – to 'see' the lines of conflict. Discussion and consciousness-raising thus focuses more on building solidarity within the group to do something about 'the problem' and developing conviction through mutual reinforcement that action-taking is justified, than on analyzing exactly what 'the problem' is.

Both of these aspects of status-based conflict in Japan, which came to light in case studies, deserve further study. On the question of how status operates as an ordering principle in the organization of status-based conflicts, cross-cultural research is most certainly needed. Clearly the phenomenon is not unique to Japan; however, given the importance of the vertical ordering principle in Japan historically and today, we can hypothesize that the role of high-status individuals in legitimizing conflict on the part of status inferiors would be especially important in Japan, as compared to other societies with longer egalitarian traditions. This hypothesis invites testing.

Similarly, the tendency in Japan not to spell out status grievances in the process of preparing for action-taking deserves cross-cultural study. Freeman's research (1975) on the women's movement in the USA has stressed the need for specifying and discussing specific grievances as a crucial part of consciousness-raising. What goes on in a status-deprived group in Japan prior to action-taking needs further study in a comparative context. Looking at much that has been written about the nature of Japanese communication styles, it is reasonable to think that the Western deductive analytic approach to problems, in which the individual dissects the problem and studies all its parts, is fundamentally at variance with Japanese communication and problem-solving styles, but exactly what *does* occur in Japan needs further study. Given the continuing legitimacy with which the authority exercised of status superiors is exercised in inferior–superior relations, it may be that consciousness-raising necessarily focuses on the legitimacy of action-taking, rather than on the costs of status inferiority, which are well understood.

Stage three: the initiation of conflict behaviour

Once there is an awareness of an inherent conflict and a consensus is arrived at within the group of status inferiors that action-taking of some type is called for, the conflict is set in motion. If redress (for example, concessions on the part of status superiors) comes quickly, then a given conflict episode might well be laid quickly to rest. If the band of status inferiors meets resistance, however, the conflict is likely to become a drawn-out affair, and to proceed through many stages of escalation before it begins to de-escalate.

The case studies I have developed suggest that the action-taking phase of a status-based conflict typically begins with an effort on the part of status inferiors to get a resolution for their grievances through existing institutions for conflict resolution. Only when this effort fails do they 'take matters into their own hands'. In the case of the tea-pourers' rebellion, the women bureaucrats first attempted to get the union for the Kyōto City Office to take up their grievances. The women, early on, had constituted themselves as a 'Women's Section' of that union and had gained official union approval for their group. However, the union, which has the obvious channel for resolving a conflict involving worker grievances, refused to take up the types of issues that were of concern to the women. Similarly, in the Yōka High School incident, the group of *burakumin* students had a series of meetings with school officials to gain approval for the study group they wanted to establish in the high school; they attempted, in other words, to 'go through channels' before they resorted to protest tactics.

Finally, in the case of the New Liberal Club breakaway, the group who ultimately left the LDP first attempted to get the party to hold an official party election within the LDP as a way of gaining a forum for the airing of their grievances. One of their foremost complaints as party juniors was their exclusion from key party decisions, such as the selection of the party president (who automatically, given the LDP's majority, becomes the prime minister). At that time, the selection was decided informally by party elders, consonant with the far-reaching authority they exercised as status superiors. Had Kōno and his followers been able to force an election, they would have opened a channel for the renegotiation of authority relations in the party by legitimizing the participation of juniors in party decisions. In each case, then, status inferiors can be seen as having attempted either to use an existing channel for airing their grievances or to gain official approval for a new one. Only after those efforts failed did they adopt other strategies of conflict resolution that had more dubious standing in the eyes of their status superiors.

Another question to ask about a conflict concerns the modes of conflict behaviour adopted by the parties to the dispute. The most striking overall finding was that the range of acceptable alternative

modes of conflict resolution available to status inferiors appeared
to be severely limited, leading them to resort to extreme measures
with the effect that the conflict escalated. Coercion, persuasion
and reward are the usual strategies available to parties in a conflict.
Both persuasion and reward – the non-coercive alternatives – are
hard for status inferiors to use, given the terms of inferior–superior
relations in Japan, for it is status superiors who normally do the
persuading and the reward-giving in such relationships. Thus, for
example, in the case of the New Liberal Club breakaway, persuasion in the form of 'politicking' would have been a reasonable
method for one politician to adopt in any effort to change the
views or behaviour of a fellow party member, but 'politicking' by
party juniors in direct fashion with the aim of persuading their
seniors is not acceptable behaviour in the context of Japanese
factional arrangements. Similarly, since party seniors monopolize
the reward structure, it would run counter to the norms of inter-
status relations for the juniors to offer rewards to seniors, even if
the former had such rewards at their disposal. The same may be
said in the case of the Yōka High School incident. The *burakumin*
involved in the protest, whose position of inferiority due to their
caste origins was reinforced by an inferiority due to their age and
student status in a conflict *vis-à-vis* their teachers, were not in a
position to use the method of persuasion, and, practically speaking,
they had few resources to offer as rewards.

Given a lack of alternatives, status inferiors appear to have two
major strategies available to them. One is to turn to a third party
from a higher status group to improve their chances of resolving
the conflict, and thereby to try to engage in 'alliance politics'. The
tea-pourers adopted this strategy by enlisting the support of the
younger male bureaucrats in the office before they put coercive
modes of protest into operation by refusing, on a given day, to
pour tea for the men in the division. The actual function of such
an alliance is the same alluded to earlier in the discussion of the
use of third parties: the younger men, in effect, were asked by the
women to use their authority as members of the superior status
group (that is, men) to legitimize the women's defiant action. The
events leading up to the New Liberal Club breakaway similarly
reveal an attempt to use alliance politics. The group led by Kōno
ultimately decided to promote one of their own (a junior man,
Kōno himself) for LDP party president as a way of forcing open
the process of selecting that official. But before they did so, they

looked for a candidate to back from among several men in the party with higher status (in terms of age) than their own. They went to three members of a middle generation of leadership within the LDP and tried to persuade them to run for the post with a guarantee of the junior men's support. Although each of the potential candidates refused to be nominated, exploring the route of using a third party represented search for a workable conflict strategy. It may be noted that in each case, the persons approached were in a 'middle' group in status terms – one that had the potential of serving as a buffer between two widely separated status groups.

When other modes of conflict behaviour are insufficient, then status inferiors are pressed to use coercive measures. In the case of the Kōno group, the break with the Liberal Democratic Party represented the ultimate coercive strategy. Like the act of a spouse who finally sues for divorce, the break formally signalled the end of a long effort to resolve the conflict by less drastic means. When the efforts at alliance politics bore no fruit for the tea-pourers, they decided to terminate suddenly the tea-pouring rituals. In the case of the Yōka High School incident, the conflict escalated rapidly as the *burakumin* turned to a variety of coercive measures, from a sit-in demonstration, to a hunger strike, to physical confrontation.

The problems for status inferiors of finding an existing institutionalized channel for the resolution of their grievances and of finding legitimate models for pursuing their goals are acute ones. How acute is well illustrated by one type of strategy that *burakumin* have adopted. Since the early 1920s, the *burakumin* liberation movement has often used a mode of conflict behaviour known as *kyūdan*. In a typical denunciation session, a group of *burakumin* (the number varies from four or so to a group in the hundreds or even thousands) confront a person who is accused of discriminatory behaviour and charge him or her with having behaved unacceptably. The session has multiple aims: to educate the accused about the nature of discrimination; to exact contrition; to secure a written confession and promise to redress the situation. In the sessions, *burakumin* may shout, stamp the floor, make angry gestures, use insulting language or chant. The attempt is to cause a transformation of consciousness – a conversion experience in which the accused suddenly sees, in horror, the error of his or her ways. Another aim obviously is to deter future discrimination by making clear to others what happens to those who discriminate. The BLL has been quite successful in achieving this latter aim. Fear of being the target of *kyūdan* is widespread in Japan among those whose work brings them in contact with issues relating to *burakumin*.

As a coercive tactic used in status-based conflicts, denunciation sessions represent a radical attempt to bring status superiors and status inferiors together in a setting in which the terms of exchange – unlike those in inter-status relations normally found in Japan – favour the inferiors. The tactic creates a forum in which the other modes of conflict behaviour such as persuasion and reward (the release of the accused following the confession) can be used. Without the use of such tactics, these modes are precluded under the traditional terms of inferior–superior relations. That *burakumin* have felt compelled to resort to the use of *kyūdan* dramatically illustrates the formidability of the barriers that status inferiors face in Japan, and the extent to which the means of resolution are limited.

Stage four: escalation and de-escalation

The previous sections have traced some of the steps that mark the path of escalation. Typically, more moderate modes of conflict resolution are tried and found wanting. Successively, more militant methods are tried and the conflict escalates. At Yōka High School the *burakumin* first used the normal channels for airing their grievances; they then turned to the sit-in, before resorting to a hunger strike. Only after that did they engage in physical confrontation with their status superiors and hold denunciation sessions with each of them. The conflict escalates for a number of reasons. The normal channels of conflict resolution will not take up the grievances of status inferiors. The volatile nature of status-based conflicts in Japanese society today points to the fact that there are few legitimate modes of conflict behaviour available to the status-deprived.

In addition to these factors there was the retaliatory behaviour of the status superiors who are the targets of the protest. In the three case studies, status superiors made few concessions, even when the conflict was escalating rapidly. At Yōka High School, for example, the teachers refused to meet with the students to discuss the issue of authorizing the study group on *burakumin* problems, even when the normal routines of the high school had been disrupted by a sit-in, followed by a hunger strike, of students in the hallways. In short, the teachers stonewalled, ostensibly because, as several stated later in interviews, they were sure that such a meeting would not lead to a resolution of the conflict.

Not only did status superiors not pursue strategies aimed at containing or de-escalating the conflict, but they met the inferiors' initiatives with responses that could only add fuel to the fire. For example, prior to the physical confrontation that occurred in front of Yōka High School in November 1974 between the members of BLL and the teachers, the teachers had gone *en masse* to a hot springs resort where they stayed overnight, undoubtedly to rest and discuss strategy. They showed up for work the next day in one bus. By that time, members of the BLL had parked sound trucks next to the school compound and mounted lights trained on the campus preparatory to conducting a *kyūdan* session. The teachers, in other words, appeared to be preparing for, and rushing *en masse* towards, a confrontation. The news that they had retired in a group to a hot springs resort to rest up and prepare for what was ahead only served to inflame their opponents.

It is striking, given the sensitivity of status grievances, that superiors in a number of incidences responded to the conflict behaviour of status inferiors with language that demeaned their opponents and dismissed or belittled the seriousness of their grievances. As a shocking example in the aftermath of the Yōka High School incident, an official publication of the Japan Communist Party which had backed the teachers in the dispute compared the BLL members who had been involved in the dispute to 'blood-thirsty wild beasts', a charge that echoes the deepest type of prejudice toward *burakumin* arising out of their traditional associations with blood and bestiality (NHK 1974). It is hard to imagine a label that could be more offensive to *burakumin* sensitivities. In the case of the New Liberal Club breakaway, the terms used by Liberal Democratic Party members to the press, to members of the Kōno group (by the latter's account) and to me in interviews subsequent to the breakaway to describe Kōno and his followers were belittling, such as 'spoiled brats', 'incubator babies' and 'runaway girls'.

The use of such labels by status superiors in status-based conflicts may be seen as their attempt to reassert authority over their subordinates and to dismiss the inferiors' claim to a right to protest the terms of status relations. The deprecatory terms reassert the superiority of the superiors and the inferiority of the inferiors. By calling a group of juniors 'spoiled brats', the seniors dismiss their ability to act independently; by labelling *burakumin* 'wild beasts', the majority reminds readers why *burakumin* were assigned a position of status inferiority in the first place. Needless to say, the use of deprecatory labelling by status superiors escalates a conflict and decreases the possibility that a resolution can be found.

Stage five: termination of the conflict

In none of the three conflicts were status inferiors and status superiors able to reach a reconciliation in which the superiors yielded and granted, in a clear and unambiguous way, what the inferiors sought. Having failed to gain accommodation within the LDP, the Kōno group saw themselves forced to leave the party, in effect renouncing the junior–senior relationship entirely. The *burakumin* dissidents in the Yōka High School incident not only failed to gain a permanent foothold for the BLL within the high school; by the admission of many leaders associated with the movement in the Kyōto-Osaka-Kobe area, the escalation of the conflict set back the *burakumin* liberation movement throughout the entire region in Japan. The tea-pourers' rebellion lasted so long as the principal leaders stayed in the Housing Division, and during that period the tea rituals were disrupted, with tea available mainly on a serve-yourself basis. But four years after the rebellion, all the key women had either left the office to get married or had been transferred. Thereafter, the tea routines were gradually resumed in the division. Even more significant, the rebellion never at any point spread to other divisions in the Kyōto City Office. Thus, in none of the three cases were the status-deprived successful in gaining redress for their specific grievances.

At the same time, however, none of the conflicts resulted in an unambiguous victory for the status superiors involved. In the case of the New Liberal Club breakaway, the immediate effect on the Liberal Democratic Party was that it lost seats to the new conservative group and had its internal problems publicly aired. Although the defection in no way set back the LDP permanently, it hardly helped the party. In the Yōka High School incident, the teachers who were injured in the physical struggle were heralded by some as martyrs in the immediate aftermath of the incident, but a number reported in interviews in 1978 that there had been much public criticism of the teachers for their part in the conflict, and that the transfer of several teachers from the high school represented an effort on the part of school authorities to break their solidarity and to punish the teachers collectively. In the case of the tea-pourers' rebellion, it was not possible to find out how the men in the division felt once the tea routines were restored, but there was little indication that male employees in the City Office saw the dispute as permanently laid to rest. Perhaps the best evidence of the climate of feeling in response to the rebellion was the reception that my questions gained *nine years later* when I interviewed high-ranking male officials in the City Office about the struggle. Their faces visibly darkened, and they spoke of the rebellion in a tone that could only be described as outraged. In none of the case studies had victory brought satisfaction to the status superiors, even to the extent that it had been achieved.

When we examine why none of these conflicts resulted in more of a victory for status inferiors, three explanations invite further study. First, in each of the cases, some of the most important goals of the status inferiors were symbolic, and thus seemingly difficult for the superiors to cede. Although certain instrumental goals were sought (for example, approval for the study group in the case of *burakumin* protest), the status inferiors were also asking for a different and better way of being treated by those above them – a general, diffuse goal that required a renegotiation of the traditional terms of status relations. Theorists such as Edelman (1964) led us to expect the powerful to yield on symbolic issues or, at any rate, to manipulate symbols themselves as a way of avoiding concrete concessions, but the behaviour of status superiors in cases of status-based conflicts appears to be precisely the opposite. For example, in the tea-pourers' rebellion, the women had a number of concrete demands, such as one for new tea-making equipment, in addition to their demand for a change in the tea routines of the office. The concrete demands were met readily; it was the symbolic concession sought in a renegotiation of the tea-pouring rituals that was difficult for the women to exact from the men. In cases involving status-based conflict, yielding on symbolic issues requires a fundamental recognition on the part of status superiors that something is amiss in the nature of superior–inferior relations, a concession that threatens the very basis of social relations in Japan.

A second reason why victory proved so difficult to achieve is because the ideological debate in Japan over what norms should guide interpersonal relations is not resolved. As noted at the outset, democratic norms have gained ground in the postwar period and are available as ideology to status inferiors who want to improve their lot. But the traditional ideology of inter-status relations in which inequality is thought to be natural and proper still has much support in the culture, particularly among the prewar-educated generations who occupy positions of power (and who predominated among the status superiors in each of the three case studies). In status-based conflicts in Japan, status superiors thus operate from a position of strength. This is in contrast to the situation in countries with longer egalitarian traditions, such as the United States or Australia, where the ideological question has been settled, and where there is widespread agreement in the culture that the appropriate norms governing interpersonal relations are democracy and egalitarianism, even if there is disagreement about how to implement them.

A final obstacle to success was the lack of institutionalized channels for the resolution of status-based conflicts. In most cases, the real issues in conflicts involving status inequalities cannot be taken to the unions, the courts or other mediating agencies because these channels are not yet ready to entertain challenges to the legitimacy of the authority exercised by status superiors. It may be noted that established channels for the resolution of social conflicts are maintained by those who themselves enjoy the prerogatives of status superiors as a result of the inequalities being questioned. To challenge the terms of inferior–superior relations in Japan is to raise questions about the legitimacy of patterns of interpersonal interaction that are ubiquitous in Japanese social life and thus to raise questions about the system itself.

For all these reasons, status-based conflicts face formidable barriers on their way to satisfactory or decisive resolution. The fact that conflicts stay outside the normal channels for resolving social problems means that the resolution of a given episode does not carry authority in relation to later episodes. The failure of structures to respond to pressures from status inferiors paves the way for a repetition of similar incidents. Tea-pourers' rebellions and conflicts over related issues continue to surface, not only in the Kyōto City Office, but in Japanese organizations and bureaucracies more generally. *Burakumin* protests similarly recur, as do struggles within organizations in which intergenerational issues are at stake. Fuelled by value change, separate episodes bubbling to the surface represent a steady pressure from below for adjustments in status relations, and at the same time contribute to a rise in the overall level of social conflict in Japan.

4 Conclusions

The preceding analysis has numerous implications for the study of intra-group and inter-group relations in Japan.

All three cases offer insights into the role of the individual in collective undertakings in Japan. The case studies provide ample evidence to challenge the collectivity model and to affirm the importance of individual leaders in a group context. Although each case involved conflicts initated by groups, there were individual leaders in each who played critical roles in group formation, in solidarity building, and in maintaining the group's resolve in the face of pressure once a social conflict was under way. These leaders were readily identifiable and did, in each case, take responsibility for the outcome of the group's struggle. Thus the collectivity principle as it has been assumed to operate in Japanese groups at the expense of individual leadership, and the parallel notion of collective responsibility over individual responsibility, are not borne out in these cases of status-based conflicts.

The case studies also provide abundant illustrations of the problems of resolving interpersonal conflicts across status lines in Japan. As a result of value changes that have occurred in Japanese society, the conflict inherent in such relations appears to be close to the surface of consciousness for most people in Japan today. But they may not be prepared to attempt renegotiation of those relations in their own lives when conflicts arise and they may be unsympathetic to the grievances of status inferiors.

Interpersonal relations across status lines at a minimum are marked by major difficulties in communication. How else can we explain why all three of these conflicts escalated so precipitously? The non-coercive modes (reward and persuasion) of conflict behaviour normally at the disposal of persons engaged in social conflict were precluded by the terms of the existing status relations, in which status superiors monopolized the rewards and were thought to be the ones who should do the persuading. Accordingly status inferiors had to choose between total capitulation and the use of coercive measures, with the effect of further breakdown in their interpersonal relations with status superiors and escalation of the conflict.

Apart from how interpersonal relations operate across status lines, the case studies revealed much about interpersonal relations with the group. What stood out in particular was the role of status in mediating interpersonal relations in a group context, even in groups out to improve their overall situation of status inferiority. Thus, it will be recalled, the leaders who emerged from within the ranks of a group of status inferiors typically were persons of higher status relative to their fellow members.

If the case studies reveal the difficulties of interpersonal relations across status lines, they also affirm that the interaction of two groups of unequal status mirrors the same problem. All case studies showed that groups of status inferiors felt compelled to resort to coercive means to pursue their grievances because other methods of conflict behaviour were inadequate or were precluded by the terms of inter-status relations. The use of *kyūdan* by *burakumin* highlights the tremendous difficulty that the status-deprived have in pursuing their grievances against individuals and groups of higher status. Whatever the critic may think of the *kyūdan* method, its use is a clear indication of the remarkable barriers to inter-status communications that exist in Japan.

The case studies also shed light on the problems of resolving conflicts between groups in Japan. Nakane (1970) and others have argued that conflicts across the lines that separate vertical groups are hard to resolve in Japan, and the cases support this view. Conflicts over the issue of status may constitute a 'worst' case in this regard, for reasons discussed elsewhere (Pharr forthcoming). There are few institutionalized channels for the resolution of social conflict that are open to the grievances of status inferiors, making the resolution of conflicts involving them exceptionally difficult.

At the same time, however, the cases affirm that bridges between groups can be built. Third parties of higher status offer the status-deprived a chance to gain legitimacy for their cause. *Kyūdan* itself represents a radical attempt to create a new channel of communication across a deep abyss. Through alliance politics and other methods, then, status inferiors use building blocks provided by the culture to construct bridges across status lines.

References

Abegglen, James C.
1958   *The Japanese Factory* (Glencoe, Ill.: The Free Press).
Austin, Lewis
1975   *Saints and Samurai* (New Haven, Conn.: Yale University Press).
Benedict, Ruth
1946   *The Chrysanthemum and the Sword* (Boston, Mass.: Houghton Mifflin).
Cole, Robert E.
1971   *Japanese Blue Collar* (Berkeley and Los Angeles, Cal.: University of California Press).
Coleman, James S.
1957   *Community Conflict* (New York: The Free Press).
Coser, Lewis A.
1967   *Continuities in the Study of Social Conflict* (New York: The Free Press).
Di Palma, Guiseppe
1973   *The Study of Conflict in Western Society* (Morristown, NJ: General Learning Press).
Douglas, Mary
1973   *Natural Symbols* (New York: Vintage Press).
Economic Planning Agency (Government of Japan)
1971   *Kokumin seikatsu hakusho* (White Paper on National Life), (Tokyo: Economic Planning Agency).
Edelman, Murray
1964   *The Symbolic Use of Politics* (Urbana, Ill.: University of Illinois Press).
Flanagan, Scott C.
1982   'Changing Values in Advanced Industrial Societies: Inglehart's Silent Revolution from the Perspective of Japanese Findings', *Comparative Political Studies*, vol. 14, no. 4 (Jan.), 403–44.
Freeman, Jo
1975   *The Politics of Women's Liberation* (New York: McKay).
Goffman, Erving
1967   *Interaction Ritual: Essays on Face to Face Behavior* (New York: Anchor Books).
Gusfield, Joseph R.
1966   *Symbolic Crusade: Status Politics and the American Temperance Movement* (Urbana, Ill. and London: University of Illinois Press).
Hosojima, Izumi
1976   'Hoshu yurugasu Kōno shintō' (The new Kōno Party that shook the conservatives), *Ekonomisuto*, vol. 54, no. 29 (29 June), 10–14.

Ike, Nobutaka
   1973   'Economic Growth and Intergenerational Change in Japan',
   American Political Science Review, vol. 67, no. 4 (Dec.), 1194–
   1203.
Inglehart, Ronald
   1971   'The Silent Revolution in Europe: Intergenerational Change in
   Post-Industrial Societies', *American Political Science Review*, vol.
   65, no. 4 (Dec.), 991–1017.
Iwao, Sumiko
   1977   'A Full Life for Modern Japanese Women', in *Text of Seminar
   on Changing Values in Modern Japan*, edited by Nihonjin Kenkyūkai
   (Tokyo: Nihonjin Kenkyūkai).
Kreisberg, Louis
   1973   *The Sociology of Social Conflicts* (Englewood Cliffs, NJ:
   Prentice-Hall).
Mainichi Shinbunsha Seijibu
   1975   *Seihen* (Political Change) (Tokyo: Mainichi Shinbunsha).
Ministry of Foreign Affairs
   1975   *Status of Women in Modern Japan* (Tokyo: Foreign Ministry).
Murakami, Yasusuke
   1982   'The Age of New Middle Mass Politics: the Case of Japan',
   Journal of Japanese Studies, vol. 8, no. 1 (Winter), 29–72.
Nakane, Chie
   1970   *Japanese Society* (Berkeley and Los Angeles, Cal.: University
   of California Press).
Nihon Kyōsantō Hyōgoiinkai (Japan Communist Party Hyōgo Branch
   Office)
   1974   'Ima . . . Tajima de okotte irukoto: bōryoku shūdan Asada
   ippa no kyōiku hakai' (Now . . . what's been happening in Tajima:
   the destruction of education by the violent Asada group) (Kōbe:
   Nihon Kyōsanto Hyōgiinkai).
Pharr, Susan J.
   1982   'Liberal Democrats in Disarray: Intergenerational Conflict in
   the Conservative Camp in Japan', in *Political Leadership in Modern
   Japan*, edited by Terry E. McDougall (Ann Arbor, Mich.: University
   of Michigan Press), 29–50.
   Forthcoming   *Status Politics in Japan: Social Conflict, Authority, and
   the State* (Berkeley, Cal.: University of California Press).
Rohlen, Thomas P.
   1976   'Violence at Yōka High School: the Implications for Japanese
   Coalition Politics of the Confrontation Between the Communist
   Party and the Buraku Liberation League', *Asian Survey*, vol. 16,
   no. 7 (July), 682–99.

Schelling, Thomas
  1966   *The Strategy of Conflict* (Cambridge, Mass.: Harvard University Press).
Szalai, Alexander
  1973   *The Situation of Women in the United Nations*, Research Report no. 18 (New York: UNITAR).
Tsurutani, Taketsugu
  1977   *Political Change in Japan* (New York: McKay).
Vogel, Ezra F. (ed.)
  1975   *Modern Japanese Organization and Decision-Making* (Berkeley, Cal.: University of California Press).

Chapter Eight
Interest Groups and the Process of Political Decision-making in Japan

Sone Yasunori

1 Introduction

Any account of a society's political structure relies upon some methodological assumptions. Different assumptions lead to different interpretations or explanations of the political structure. There is, therefore, room to debate the nature of Japan's political structure. Even if the Japanese system is viewed as being a democracy, disagreements will arise as to who really has influence, as to the groups which have power, and as to the exact nature of the relationships between the various actors (Sone 1982).

In addition to different assumptions, inadequate analysis also accounts for differing viewpoints. Until recently, there was a tendency to focus on the elites. Although Japan's mainstream political scientists now take a more-or-less pluralist view of politics in Japan, in the early 1980s there were only a handful of pluralists in Japan. This contrasts sharply with the situation in the United States where pluralist interpretations seem to have an institutionalized place in political analysis, even though their position has come under heavy criticism during the last ten years. The idea of there being a triangular alliance among big business, the Liberal Democratic Party and the bureaucracy continues to be used as a convenient method of interpretation. This is despite the criticism of most researchers (for example, Fukui 1977). Similarly, journalists tend to focus their analyses of the Liberal Democratic Party almost entirely on factionalism. However, while it is certainly important to consider factional competition in studying intra-party politics which occur, for example, in the presidential elections within the LDP, inter-party politics must also be considered, and here the impact of factional politics is relatively weak. Simplistic interpretations of the role of the Ministry of International Trade and Industry also abound. The views vary from those which portray it as being the General Staff Office of 'Japan Incorporated' to those which dismiss it merely as an 'information centre' offering trips to Japanese firms. In each of these examples, the failure to consider substitute models is often aggravated by deficiencies in the analysis itself. In considering earlier attempts to assess Japanese political structures, several points need noting. First, many interpretations which emphasize the role played by the Japanese government (or bureaucracy) as being peculiarly Japanese have taken the United States as the comparative standard. It would be useful to have comparisons with other advanced countries which also have parliamentary systems of government. When studying the policy-making process in general, and interest-group politics in particular, the US–Japan comparison alone is not sufficient. When examining Japanese consultative councils, the experiences of Sweden, Denmark and Norway seem more relevant than the situation in America.

Second, most analyses of Japan's interest groups, including those of Ishida (1960) and Taguchi (1969), have focused on specific aspects such as the organization or the leadership. Less attention has been paid to the positioning of interest groups, including all the ministries and their agencies, *vis-à-vis* themselves and within the broader political processes which are part of everday life in Japan. Micro-political analysis needs to be complemented with a macro-political analysis.

Third, although it has commonly been accepted that there is a direct link between interest groups and the interests they represent, closer examination is required. What kinds of interests do these interest groups actually pursue? Which framework or methodological approach is most suited for the analysis? In the analysis of decision-making, more attention needs to be paid to how these interests find some expression in the decision-making process, if they do so at all.

With these three issues in mind, an attempt was made to discover the way in which interest-group politics are structured in Japan. Given the two problems mentioned above in the preceding paragraph – (1) the problem of assumptions and the failure to be more imaginative in thinking of substitute models, and (2) deficiencies in the analysis, meaning the absence of solid empirical field work or data collecting and the careful analysis of these findings – this chapter focuses on the political dynamics of groups, on the role they play within the political system and on their mutual interaction.

An initial reading of the literature suggests there are several completely different interpretations. In addition to the contrast between elitism and pluralism (cf. Fukui 1977: 22–48), a distinction can be drawn between those who write about the US type of 'interest-group liberalism' (Lowi 1979) in Japan and those who see in Japan's interest groups certain corporatist tendencies (Yamaguchi 1982). In order to avoid confusing these various interpretations, this chapter will develop from three general orientations, which may be explained as follows.

First, in pursuing their own interests, interest groups will seek to use means which are within the political process. The national constituencies for Japan's House of Councillors provide one arena where some of Japan's mass organization can demonstrate their influence. At the same time, they also provide a means of seeing the kinds of groups which use the ballot to place their own representatives upon the political stage.

Second, if interest groups are assumed to have political goals, then naturally we ought to pay attention to the way in which they affect the distribution of social resources. Some idea of their values – or at least the values of the more influential interest groups – can be obtained by considering the distribution of resources which occurs in the budget and in the financial expenditures of government at its various levels.

Third, even though interest groups might not manifest themselves conspicuously in the above two ways (that is, by electing their representatives and by receiving social resources), they can still be influential. While their influence ought to be discerned somewhere in the political decision-making process, an analysis of all the political decision-making is impossible. However, we might be able to consider as one indicator the extent to which they have a presence on the various advisory councils (*shingikai*) which are associated with the ministries and their agencies. The assumption is that, as a matter of policy, each ministry seeks to guarantee (1) that interested parties take part in these councils, and (2) that men of learning and experience are chosen to be members of these councils. While the importance of 'non-decisions' in the processes of decision-making and agenda-setting obviously needs to be recognized, the hypothesis that corporatism has emerged without reference to labour's representatives (Pempel and Tsunekawa 1979) has some serious defects which are readily apparent if we make a more comprehensive study of the membership of advisory councils in Japan (cf. Sone 1985 and Appendices A and B). The results of such a study will show that the membership of the councils is much more inclusive than Pempel and Tsunekawa indicate, although, to be sure, all interests are not equally represented.

The argument here is not that all the activities of all the interest groups in Japanese politics can be explained by means of the three propositions just set forth. However, I think an initial exploration along those lines will provide a sufficient basis for carrying out future studies of these groups. Obviously, the influence of interest groups may be examined from several angles. Three related phenomena which come immediately to mind are (1) decision-making at national conventions, (2) the relations between party leaders and the interest groups, and (3) the recruitment of business leaders and other private citizens to serve in government at the ministerial level (a fairly uncommon phenomenon in Japan).

In considering these hypotheses, we must be aware of several changes in the 1980s. First, the electoral law concerning the House of Councillors was revised in 1982. The change from the relative plurality rule to proportional representation at the level of the national constituency has affected the behaviour of interest groups in many ways. It is now more difficult to infer a relationship between the relative influence of an interest group and the number of representatives in the House of Councillors.

Second, the hypothesis concerning distributive effects of politics continues to hold, but needs to be modified. The large fiscal deficits and the administrative reforms in the early 1980s have shifted the focal point in political processes from output in the form of government appropriations to input in the form of government revenue, particularly in taxation and the question of tax reform. With a clamp being put on expenditure, interest groups have redefined their aims. Although those sectors of the economy most adversely affected by the two oil shocks have pleaded for help from the government, the prevailing concept in Japan in the 1980s is that of the 'zero-sum society'. This means that the situation today is quite different from that which characterized the period of rapid economic growth.

Third, the role of the Advisory Councils has changed following the reforms introduced by the Rinji Gyosei Chosakai (the *Ad Hoc* Council on Administrative Reform). There has been an increase in the number and the influence of these *ad hoc* councils established directly under the Prime Minister. Other notable examples of such councils include the Rinji Gyosei Kaikaku Suishin Shingikai (the *Ad Hoc* Council to Provide Administrative Reform), the Rinji Kyōiku Shingikai (the *Ad Hoc* Council on Education) and the Nihon Kokuyū Tetsudō Saiken Kanri Iinkai (the Administrative Committee to Restructure the National Railways).

Fourth, in recent years the attention of Japanese political scientists has come to focus sharply on the Liberal Democratic Party, on the bureaucracy, on the *zoku-giin* (policy experts in the LDP) and on similar topics which seem to bring out the more pluralistic aspects in Japanese politics. However, while these facets of the political process seem to fit well with pluralist interpretations, there are those who have sought to explain Japanese politics more in corporatist terms. Many observers have commented that the LDP has become somewhat more influential than the bureaucracy in the area of policy-making. At the same time, the successful role played by the *ad hoc* councils has weakened the traditional influence of the party *vis-à-vis* the bureaucracy; the councils have helped party leaders break away from a certain 'immobilization' in the bureaucratic-parliamentary process by skirting around the *zoku-giin*. The result has been that many of the vested interests in the party and in the bureaucracy (which interest groups have supported) have been challenged.

These changes mean that the reader will observe some contrasts between the political situation in the mid-1980s and the situation in the early 1980s when the ideas in this paper were first formulated. However, the major conclusions continue to hold and the arguments are presented here in their original form. On a few points some additional comments have been added to the concluding section.

2   Interest groups and the House of Councillors' national constituency

The system of having a national constituency for Japan's House of Councillors (HOC) can be described as being peculiarly Japanese. This would also be true of the medium constituency system used in elections for the House of Representatives (Lijphart, Pintor and Sone 1986). Although similar constituency systems can be found in Holland and in Israel, the successful candidates are not elected by a relative plurality as in Japan. The goal in founding this system was to have from all over the nation notable intellectuals and accomplished persons from various vocations represented in Japan's legislature. However, the system does not seem to function in that way at the present time. Today 'talent stars' – people whose faces have become familiar to the electorate through the mass media, particularly television – are more likely to be elected than learned persons. As for accomplished persons, their chances to be elected have come to depend largely on the organization that puts them up for election.

Reform of the national constituency for the HOC has been debated politically for several reasons. One is the enormous cost of the system. It is also argued that it is impossible for candidates to cover the entire country in their election campaigns.

The analysis here is not concerned with the objectives of the HOC or with reform of the electoral system. Given the present system, it is aimed at identifying the political organizations or interest groups that participate in it. In the elections for the Upper House in 1980, the minimal number of votes needed to be elected was 620,000. In order to win, a candidate needed to assemble a truly large number of supporters, and it was the various interest groups that functioned most effectively in pursuit of that number of votes. Accordingly, the analysis has two aims. One is to identify the interest groups which are important from the viewpoint of analyzing electoral behaviour. The other is to identify those interest groups which can be said to represent Japan.

Seats in the HOC national constituency number 100. The term is six years, and half are elected every three years. The successful candidates in the June 1980 elections for the HOC national constituency came largely from the following categories:

(1) the 'media talent' – people known throughout the nation because they appear often in the national media (e.g., movie actresses or television personalities);
(2) representatives of large-scale organizations (e.g., religious bodies, labour unions, etc.);
(3) people who succeed in being elected because they have received the recommendation of a large-scale organization (e.g., former bureaucrats); and
(4) candidates who were elected by the bloc vote given them by a particular political party.

The first category would include persons such as Aoshima Yukio, Miyata Teru, Nakayama Chinatsu, Santō Akiko, Yamaguchi Yoshiko and Hata Yutaka; we might also include as a kind of sub-group such people as Ichikawa Fusae, Hatoyama Iichirō, Minobe Ryōkichi and Saitō Eizaburō. One should not assume, however, that these candidates are elected solely on the basis of their popularity; to some extent they too received the support of various enterprises and groups. However, this group is excluded from this study. Also excluded from the analysis is the 'organized vote' held by Kōmeitō and the Communist Party. Their candidates can be said to fall within the fourth category. Historical changes in the relative importance of each of the categories has also been left for a future study.

Although the distinction between the second and third categories is not perfectly clear, the candidates in these two categories hold the most interest for us. To some extent, we can distinguish between candidates who are affiliated with certain organizations or groups and those who are not. There are, however, cases in which this distinction does not have much meaning. Nevertheless, if we begin by looking at persons in the second category, we can further subdivide them, as is done in Table 8.1.

In doing so, there are several points which should be noted. First, because these candidates have mustered the support and recommendation of various groups other than their principal support organization, it is difficult to describe them in a strict

Table 8.1 *The Support Groups of HOC MPs who Represent Large-Scale Organization by Political Party*

I Liberal Democratic Party	
religious groups:	Tazawa Tomoharu (Risshō Kōseikai)
	Murakami Masakuni (Seichō no Ie)
medical practitioners:	Marumo Shigesada (Japan Medical Association)
dental practitioners:	Sekiguchi Keizō (Japan Dental Association)
former army:	Okada Hiroshi (Military Pensioners)
war bereavement associations:	Itagaki Tadashi (Japan War Bereavement Association)
II Japan Socialist Party	
labour unions:	Fukuma Tomoyuki (Denki Rōren)
	Meguro Kesajirō (Dōrō)
	Noda Tetsu (Jichirō)
	Katayama Jin-ichi (Zen-dentsu)
	Suzuki Kazumi (Zen-senbai)
	Agune Noboru (Tanrō)
	Kasuya Terumi (Nikkyōso)
	Wada Shizuo (Jichirō)
burakumin:	Matsumoto Eiichi (Buraku Kaihō Dōmei)
III Democratic Socialist Party	
labour unions:	Tabuchi Tetsuya (Jidōsha Rōren)
	Mukai Nagatoshi (Denryoku Rōren)
	Karatani Michikazu (Zensen Dōmei)
	Itō Ikuo (Zōsen Jūki recommendation)

sense as being representatives of only a single interest group or organization. In the case of the candidates from labour unions, some had additional support from the private enterprises which employed them. Also, some organizations without their own candidate backed 'talent' candidates. For example, the Hitachi Group recommended Santō Akiko. The National Railways also sometimes gives its organizational backing with the combined support of both labour and management to a particular candidate.

Examples of this kind of organizational support base can also be found in the Democratic Socialist Party. It regularly gets four candidates elected in each election, one each from Jidōsha Rōren, Denryoku Rōren, Zensen Dōmei and Zōsen Jūki. Socialist party candidates often came from Nikkyōso and Kokurō. These unions were once able to get three or four of their candidates elected, but the number has decreased over time and is now one or none.

It is not easy to identify with certainty the political intentions of these interest groups. Nevertheless, religious groups such as Risshō Kōseikai and Seichō no Ie clearly seek to oppose Sōka Gakkai, their rival group which is the main supporter of Komeitō. A secondary aim is to solidify their own organization whenever there is an election. This second aim is a more general one which is shared with labour unions and other groups. Although Komeitō is itself a political party, it can trace its beginnings back to the Kōmei Seiji Remmei, which was centred on getting candidates elected to the HOC national constituency. Although they may not have much general political clout, organizations such as Nihon Izoku Kai (Japan War Bereavement Association), Gun-on-ren (Military Pensioners Federation) or even Kaihō Dōmei (*Buraku* Liberation League) spend a good deal of their funds to support successful candidates.

The Japan Medical Association, the Japan Dental Association and the various labour unions can be viewed as the classical type of interest group or pressure group. These groups also belong to the second category presented above. In general the groups in this category aim to elect Diet men who will look after their interests. It is still possible, therefore, to conceive of these as interest groups in the traditional sense. However, it is still necessary for their candidates to obtain over 600,000 votes to be elected. To succeed, these organizations must have connections with various related organizations. Although their own interests are often quite focused, these groups often affiliate with larger umbrella-type organizations.

Candidates in the third category have roughly the same type of interest groups supporting them as candidates in the second category. However, they are not directly affiliated to the organizations which support them (although there are also a few like this in the second category). LDP candidates who were formerly members of the bureaucracy are the classic example. Table 8.2 shows that most candidates of this type were those who had reached the highest posts in the bureacracy as permanent vice-ministers or directors of bureaux. One exception is Okabe Saburō. From the land improvement enterprises of the Ministry of Agriculture, Forestry, and Fisheries, he was an assistant director of the Agriculture Structural Improvement Bureau. Another was Kobayashi Kuniji. Elected in 1968 and 1974, he had been head of the Hokuriku Agricultural Administration Bureau. Kajiki Matazō was head of the Construction Department of the Agricultural

Structural Improvement Bureau before becoming a member of the HOC. Their political connections no doubt came partially through land improvement activities which put them in touch with a wide range of persons.

Table 8.2 clearly shows that the organizations from which these persons received support are closely linked with Japan's public enterprises, or are in spheres in which there is plenty of contact with such enterprises. Although it might at first appear like 'Japan Incorporated' or some similar monolith, it is difficult to say that the groups related to MITI and the Ministry of Foreign Affairs are by themselves large enough to ensure a candidate's election. Furthermore, even Hatoyama Ichiro from the Ministry of Finance has a 'talent' aspect. His central support constituency is an organization built around the Monopoly Corporation (which produces and sells tobacco), an association which contrasts with the generally more visible glamour of those involved in compiling the budget in the Budget Bureau.

What can we conclude from these data? First, various ministries have their own separate support constituencies, and these are used at the time of an election. For the various groups which form these support constituencies to pursue their own interests, principally by acquiring their own share of the national government's budget, they strengthen their links with the various ministries. Although the exact influence any one group can exert on any of the various ministries in the compilation of the budget is not measurable and it is certainly not uniform, the ability to field their own candidate(s) or to give needed support to a candidate from other ministries or agencies would serve to enhance their influence. Furthermore, the interests pursued here can be achieved for the most part by favourable decisions within the ministries or public enterprises, even though there is a strong tinge of individual interest as well. For example, the relation between the number of votes won by Okabe Saburō and the land improvement enterprises is shown by Table 8.3. The link appears, at least on the surface, to be quite strong.

Also, the various groups and organizations shown in Table 8.2 also relate to the destination of retired bureaucrats who engage in *amakudari*. The most important destinations will be found in the public corporations and public finance corporations. However, in order to win in an election, considerable money is required, and even then election cannot always be guaranteed. Still, the chances

Table 8.2 *Successful Candidates from the Various Ministries and Sources of Support*

Ministry of origin	Candidate	Sources of support
Ministry of Agriculture, Forestry and Fisheries	Ogawara Taichirō (10th) (Permanent Vice-Minister)	*Ministry-supported industries other than land improvement industries, food control operations.* Nokyō Chūō Kai, Nihon Ringyō Kyōkai, Chūō Chikū-san Kai, Shokuryō Jigyō Kyōdō Kumiai Rengōkai.
	Okabe Saburō (8th) (Asst. Director of Agricultural Structure Improvement Bureau)	*Land improvement industries.* Zenkoku Tochi Kairyō Jigyō Dantai Rengōkai, Zen-Nihon Kaitakusha Remmei, Tochi Kairyō Kensetsu Kyōkai, Nōgyō Doboku Jigyō Kyōkai.
Ministry of Construction	Itano Shigenobu (31st) (Permanent Vice-Minister)	*Public utility enterprises of roads, dams, sewerage, parks, etc.* Nihon Doboku Kōgyō Kyōkai, Zenkoku Kensetsugyō Kyōkai, Nihon Zōen Kensetsu Kyōkai (for Kantō, Tōkai, Chūgoku, Hokuriku, Kyūshu; excludes Niigata).
	Inoue Takashi (17th) (Permanent Vice-Minister)	*Public utility enterprises of roads, dams, sewerage, bridge-building, etc.* Nihon Doboku Kōgyō Kyōkai, Nihon Kensetsugyō Dantai Rengōkai, Nihon Dōro Kensetsugyō Kyōkai, Nihon Kyōryōgyō Kensetsu Kyōkai (Kinki, Shikoku, Tōhoku, Niigata).
Ministry of Transport	Kajiwara Kiyoshi (25th) (Bureau Director)	*Truck and bus licensing and approvals, marine transport, harbour construction.* Nihon Basu Kyōkai, Zen-Nihon Torakku Kyōkai, Nihon Sōko Kyokai, Naikō Kaiun Kyōkai.
Ministry of Finance	Hatoyama Iichirō (3rd) (Permanent Vice-Minister)	*Tobacco, salt, liquor tax and finance operations.* Zenkoku Tabako Kosaku Kumiai, Shiogyō Seiji Remmei, Zenkoku Kouri Sake-hanbai Dantai, Kakushu Kin-yū Kikan Dantai
Ministry of Posts and Tele-communications	Osada Yūji (15th) (Permanent Vice-Minister)	*Privately-owned post office operations, Nippon Telegraph & Telephone Public Corporation supervision.* Zenkoku Tokutei Yūbinkyokuchō Kai, Zenkoku Kan-i Yūbinkyoku Rengōkai, Denden Taishokusha Dantai Rengōkai.
Ministry of Home Affairs	Matsuura Isao (28th) (Permanent Vice-Minister)	*Approval of fund-raising of regional self-government bodies, distribution of tax allocated to local governments, fire-fighting operations.* Zenkoku Chōson Kai, Shichō Renraku Kyogikai, Nihon Shōbō Kyōkai.
Japanese National Railways	Etō Akira (25th)	*New lines planning, train services planning. Hotels, inns and related industries.*
Self Defence Force	Genda Minoru (20th)	*Self Defence Force related groups, pilot trainee related groups*, Shōkyō Rengō, etc.

Note: The figures in parentheses after each name indicates their rank in terms of the number of votes received.
Source: Hirose (1981), p. 31.

Table 8.3 *Okabe's Votes and Expenditures of Land Improvement Enterprises by Prefectures*

Prefecture	votes (%)	expenditure (%)	Prefecture	votes (%)	expenditure (%)
Hokkaidō	6.8	13.9	Shiga	1.7	2.3
Aomori	2.5	3.0	Kyōto	0.5	0.4
Iwate	2.0	2.3	Ōsaka	0.6	0.6
Akita	2.2	2.4	Hyōgo	1.9	2.5
Yamagata	2.7	2.7	Nara	0.7	0.7
Miyagi	2.5	2.7	Wakayama	1.4	1.1
Fukushima	3.0	3.4	Kagawa	1.2	0.8
Ibaraki	2.9	3.0	Tokushima	1.3	1.1
Tochigi	1.7	1.8	Ehime	1.7	1.6
Gumma	1.5	1.7	Kōchi	0.6	0.6
Saitama	1.0	1.1	Okayama	2.2	2.5
Chiba	1.8	2.1	Hiroshima	2.4	1.7
Tokyo	0.6	0.1	Tottori	0.8	1.4
Kanagawa	1.1	0.3	Shimane	1.8	1.9
Niigata	5.2	4.4	Yamaguchi	1.3	1.0
Nagano	2.0	2.5	Fukuoka	1.6	1.7
Yamanashi	0.7	1.1	Saga	2.0	2.0
Shizuoka	3.4	3.1	Nagasaki	1.4	1.0
Aichi	7.0	3.4	Kumamoto	2.9	2.6
Gifu	2.9	2.3	Ōita	2.5	1.7
Mie	1.9	2.0	Miyazaki	2.2	1.8
Toyama	1.7	2.2	Kagoshima	4.0	3.0
Ishikawa	1.9	1.8	Okinawa	0.8	1.1
Fukui	1.2	1.4	All of Japan	100.0	100.0

Note: Pearson's r = .7839, p<.01
Source: Hirose (1981), p. 21.

of someone with experience as a vice-minister or as head of an agency must be rated as fairly high. In this way a relationship between Japan's interest groups and the various ministries and agencies can to some extent be inferred.

Theories emphasizing the linkage between the LDP, big business, and the bureacracy do not explain well the above phenomena. It is more useful to examine how big business musters its own support from a variety of small interest groups. The fact that every ministry has its own network of contacts reflects the situation in which each ministry presents its budgetary requests separately to the Ministry of Finance. Mediating this connection are the various divisions (*bukai*) of the LDP's Seimu Chosaikai (Policy Affairs Research Council). In other words, if one is to speak of interest groups and the political process in Japan, one must consider the linkages between (1) interest groups, (2) the various subdivisions (*bukai*) of the LDP's Policy Affairs Research Council, (3) the standing committees of the Diet, and (4) the various ministries and agencies. Such an account must incorporate the confrontations between the various ministries and agencies, and between various interest groups. Such confrontations revolve around budgetary acquisitions and budgetary authority. A recent confrontation has occurred over the Post Office savings accounts. It has been a confrontation in which the Ministry of Finance has fought the Ministry of Posts and Telecommunications. In turn, the banks have campaigned against post offices. This battle surfaces at election time as a contest between bank-supported Liberal Democratic MPs and MPs favourable to the Post Office.

The various interest groups which carry out the 'front-line' activities are highly organized. Their own interests are defined as being an optimal share of the budgetary cake. The support given to candidates of one ministry or another (that is, to a particular LDP MP) is seen as a primary means of protecting and enhancing their share. That support provides the group with its link to the candidate's ministry.

To put it in other terms, the bureacracy in Japan 'is not the end of the line for all bureaucrats; for some it is the stepping-off point for a second career' (Hashiguchi 1977: 192). Besides, of those who plan to 'descend from heaven' to public corporations and public financial institutions through *amakudari*, not a few move into the political world. The HOC national constituency is considered to be a better stepping-off point to a political career than one of the constituencies for the House of Representatives. It is comparatively stable and is more suited to candidates who have a broad organizational base.

3 Economic expenditures and the distribution of monetary resources

The interest groups considered above concentrate their political activities on the budget allocations, with their advantages and disadvantages. Of course, the groups are also concerned with the legislative side as well. However, their major interest is in the country's fiscal management (namely, the budget). Although the budget is determined each year according to a rather pre-established formula, budget negotiations are the focus of their attention. For this reason, their activities do not accord with the classical theory of interest groups. Rather than pressuring the legislative branch, they direct their efforts at the administrative branch. While the preceding discussion focused on the way bureaucrats become politicians to mediate for their administrative branch, this section considers how Japan's financial affairs are constituted and the areas which receive financial support.

Here, too, the realities do not well match the popular image of 'Japan Incorporated'. First, the government does not simply supply funds to big businesses nor does it freely use its funds to orchestrate economic growth by 'subsidizing' large public-works projects. In this regard, Noguchi (1980: 46) argues that 'fiscal policy during the period of high economic growth after 1955 can be thought of as piecemeal attempts to shift resources to the country's "backward" regions and to indemnify those industries which were losing out in the process of economic growth'.

Japan's economic growth can be said to have been possible primarily because householders voluntarily saved their money in financial institutions. That was the source of funds for enterprises. But it was also because private enterprises (particularly those in heavy chemical industries and export-oriented industries) actively borrowed to expand their capital assets, the economy expanded rapidly. The government provided many incentives to private firms. These included special tax concessions. Even so, their overall importance was not great. It was right after the war that the government supplied funds to key industries in an aggressive manner. But that was *before* the period of economic growth.

Though the tax burden as a proportion of GNP has been low compared to other advanced countries, administrative reform and the restructuring of the economy are current topics of concern. In addition to the problem of annual revenue in relation to national debt, there is the problem of 'vested interests' being built into the annual process of budgeting, a problem which tended to emerge during the period of high growth. Reform is not easy precisely because any small change will have fundamental political and administrative repercussions.

Table 8.4 shows changes in the composition of the general accounts budget between 1955 and 1978. To a certain extent, it is possible to deduce which groups in society benefited from the national bursary.

Table 8.4 *Percentage Composition of the General Accounts Budget: 1955–78*

Expenditure	1955	1965	1970	1975	1978
Local finance	15.8	19.3	21.6	16.3	17.2
Defence-related	13.3	8.2	7.2	6.6	5.6
Public works	14.4	18.7	16.2	14.3	13.9
Industrial economy	6.0	8.5	11.8	11.6	9.3
(food control)		(3.5)	(5.0)	(4.4)	
Social security	13.6	17.0	15.8	21.7	22.2
Pension-related	8.5	4.2	3.6	3.6	3.9
Education-related	12.5	12.8	11.4	12.6	11.3

Notes: 1 The figures were compiled by Noguchi Yukio from 'General Accounts Classified by Purposes' in the *Zaisei Tōkei* (Finance Statistics) which is published by Ōkurashō (Ministry of Finance).
2 Up to 1975 inclusive the figures are for the revised budgets; for 1978 the figures are from the original budget.
Source: Noguchi (1980), p. 160.

'Local finance' refers to local tax grants and subsidies which form part of a system of indirect subsidies for regions with inadequate financial resources. The aim is to narrow regional differences. This system is important when considering local government in Japan. As the catch-phrase '30 per cent self-government' suggests, the inadequacy of local public bodies is legendary. Thought to be a political measure aimed at correcting income differences between the regions, the local tax grants allow for lobbying by various local public bodies. Although this kind of politicking did not fall within the scope of the interest groups mentioned in the preceding section, it is possible to consider various local public bodies as interest groups.

Although the public works expenditures are not aimed directly at correcting regional differentials, in practice they represent a redistribution of income towards the non-urban regions. Although the income per inhabitant of Japan's rural regions is 60 to 70 per cent that of the urban dwellers, the amount of public works expenditures per individual in rural areas is roughly the same level as that for city dwellers; and between 1970 and 1974, it even exceeded that for city dwellers.

Although defence-related expenditures have accounted for a decreasing portion of the budget over time, this has no direct relevance to the object of this chapter. Pension-related expenditures for military personnel, however, probably ought to be considered as a part of social security expenditures. The combined weight of the pensions and social security expenditures has remained fairly stable over time.

However, the conspicuous increase in social security expenditures by themselves is noteworthy. Obviously the increases in this area are due in part to Japan's having lagged behind in the development of its social security benefits. However, the discussion of Japan's social security needs has not always been systematic or rational. The budget allocations for social security have been increased without considering carefully the extent to which the various programmes fit together to form an integrated whole.

The accepted theory of interest groups does not explain well the improved budget allocations for the unrepresented and disadvantaged elements in society. Several explanations present themselves. First, it is possible to see this allocation reflecting strong pressures from the Medical Association and the pharmaceutical industry. About 40 per cent of the expenditures for social security goes for doctor's treatments, of which about one-half is for medicine (much of which is said to be for excessive medication). A second explanation is that the bureaucracy itself has come to act as a spokesman for the weak. A third view is that social security only happened to be the first area to benefit from the abundant financial resources available in a period of high growth. From this point of view free health care for the aged and child allowances were not created as the result of systematic policies. A fourth explanation, however, is that social security was the first area to benefit from Japan's economic growth because it had the strong support of public opinion. In the early 1970s newspapers and other mass media, as well as the parties in opposition, were all advocating the need for more social security and welfare (cf. Campbell 1979).

Much of the expenditure under 'industrial economy' in Table 8.4 is for agriculture and for medium-sized and small businesses. It may be termed 'assistance for retarded industries'. Agriculture receives preferential treatment through subsidies, various incentive schemes, tax concessions and various other financial measures. The price support for rice (making up of a deficit by means of food control accounts) is the best known of these. These allocations and policies are closely linked with the various interest groups mentioned above in the preceding section.

Looked at in this way, the relationship between politics and economics, or between the government and the marketplace, becomes clearer. Big business contributes the largest amounts of money to the Liberal Democratic Party, but it has not sent its own representatives to the HOC national constituency. The discussion in this section also counters the idea that the government's budget is structured to provide resources directly to big business. Rather, compared with other countries, Japan's direct tax (in particular, corporation tax) is relatively heavy. Of general revenue, income tax accounts for 40 per cent and corporate tax for 34 per cent, with the total being 76 per cent. In West Germany, the total is about 50 per cent, of which corporate tax is only 5 per cent. In France, the figures are 40 per cent and 10 per cent; in Britain and the United States corporate tax accounts for 8 and 25 per cent respectively. One might wish to argue that political contributions and the extent to which the interests of big business are articulated are two separate and independent phenomena. This would perhaps seem true if its representation was measured in terms of its tax burdens and government's fiscal policies.

Before reaching a conclusion in this regard, it may first be useful to consider the debate on financial construction and administrative reform. If big business were to lose as a result of administrative reform, we would expect some form of opposition from business circles. Although the loss may not show up in the budget figures themselves, we would expect to see some form of resistance to an infringement of even their latent vested interests.

According to Noguchi (1980), a well-known Japanese economist with expertise in the area of financial policy, the annual expenditure items which require re-examination are as shown in Table 8.5. The cost of the items in the table is about 7 trillion yen, equivalent to 18 per cent of the total budget. A saving of that amount would just about cover the public deficit of approximately 8 trillion yen. From another angle, it might be observed that grants-in-aid totalled 14.5 trillion yen, up 4.8 per cent over the previous year. Looking at the absolute amounts, the items that increased by 10 billion yen or more were (a) care for the aged, (b) child care, (c) medical care for the aged, (d) livelihood protection, (e) the liability for the non-votable expenditures on national health insurance, (f) national support for compulsory education, (g) private-school

Table 8.5 *Annual Expenditures which Require Re-examination (unit = 100 million yen)*

Items	1979 Budget
Government health insurance subsidies	4,305
Health Union insurance special subsidies	15
National health insurance medical care benefits subsidies	15,552
National health insurance unions special adjustment subsidies	71
National health insurance financial adjustment grants	1,859
National health insurance special financial adjustments	1,312
Public-expense medical care	2,140
Medical care of the aged	2,691
Livelihood-protection medical care relief	5,313
(sub-total for medical care expenses)	(33,258)
Food control expenses	8,959
Comprehensive agricultural administration expenses	2,010
Forestry promotion expenses	479
Fisheries promotion expenses	561
(sub-total for agricultural, forestry, fisheries subsidies)	(12,009)
Child allowances	768
National Railways subvention	6,181
Measures for small and medium-sized businesses	2,435
Private schools subsidies	3,104
Non-personnel expenses	11,196
Total	68,951

Source: Noguchi (1980), p. 58.

assistance, (h) sewerage systems, (i) housing finance corporations' interest supplementation, (j) paddy-field reorganization, (k) the National Railways, and (l) the Public Railway Construction Corporation. These items account for 99 per cent of the increase between the two years. In other words, according to Table 8.5, the areas which have received more allocations are precisely those which were listed as questionable to begin with.

What sectors of the community might resist any reforms in administration and government finance by opposing any cuts to these items which are based on 'individual budget recommendations'? Hashimoto (1981: 18) answers as follows:

The Japan Chamber of Commerce and Industry has already voiced [its objection to the cuts and its support for those allocations]. . . . Its views reflect the difference in the size of the enterprises it represents and the size of those affiliated with Keidanren.

That is to say, the ones benefiting from the present financial allocations are the small and medium-sized business firms affiliated with the Japan Chamber of Commerce and Industry rather than the big businesses.

This means that there is an extremely large disparity between the role played by big business in the economy and the distribution of resources in the political arena. That is to say that big business has extremely great economic influence and has benefited immensely in terms of profits as a result of Japan's rapid economic growth. However, although they may divert some of these profits to political contributions, they have not been able to affect the way the government's resources are distributed so as to benefit themselves directly.[1] In other words, they have become internationally competitive primarily as a result of their own initiatives. Is not this interpretation also possible?

A conclusion such as this, however, is not in accord with the views of Lindbolm (1980), who argues that large enterprises have a 'privileged position'. Certainly in human resources, organizational strength, funds and information, the large enterprises are second to none. In Japan they are at the very forefront. Even in international terms they are comparatively strong – first and foremost, of course, in terms of 'productivity'. Should we suppose that they do not at all use this great influence politically? Or should we suppose that they are interested only in such long-term interests as simply maintaining Japan's capitalist system, and that they would 'swing into action' only if developments suggested they would be seriously disadvantaged in the financial world? To consider this matter, a different type of analysis is required.

4 'Council politics' and the role of the *shingikai*

Here it is useful to look more carefully at the decision-making

1 One report claimed that an amount of approximately 1 billion yen in political contributions from financial institutions such as the city banks to the LDP's major fund-raising organization (Kokumin Kyōkai) was frozen because of the plans to distribute the funds in a manner that would leave out Post Office backers. *Asahi Shinbun* (29 Oct. 1981), p. 1.

process. If we assume that the interests of big business are real, but that they do not appear on the surface in a manner that could be grasped in the analysis of the preceding two sections, we might look for an expression of those interests 'behind the scenes'. One approach is to consider the structure and operation of *shingikai* (consultative councils). In 1979, 212 such councils had been set up by law (Gyōsei Kanrichō 1979). The councils are representative administrative organs attached to administrative agencies (such as *shō*, *fu* and *chō*). Unlike administrative committees, however, they have no right to make executive decisions. One scheme for classifying the various *shingikai* in 1985 is given in Table 8A(1) in the Appendix. A breakdown of their membership by the Ministry of Affiliation is given in Table 8A(2) in the Appendix.

One might suppose that an extremely wide range of interests would be reflected in this large number of councils which have been established to consider a broad range of policies. However, because the choice of personnel is made by the government, there is some doubt about whether the councils accurately reflect the vast array of interests which exists.

The aims of the council system are several. One is to provide specialized knowledge to the administrative process. A second is to assure a measure of fairness and neutrality in the development of administrative policies. The third is to regulate and coordinate the conflicting interests of various parties. There is also an element of adding 'authority' to the government's decisions by covering bureaucratic decisions with a 'cloak of respectability'.

Muramatsu's interviews (1981b: 125) with bureaucrats revealed that they gave various appraisals of the councils. Asked about the most significant effect of the system of councils on decision-making some answered that the 'policies and administrative decisions became fairer' as a result of the council system (30 per cent). Others replied that 'conflicts of interests were regulated' (30 per cent); yet others claimed that 'the councils were useful in providing specialist knowledge and new ideas' (25 per cent). A smaller number mentioned the role of the councils in 'giving authority to the decisions of the administration' (16 per cent). Middle-level bureaucrats were particularly of the opinion that councils are more or less for 'the regulation of interests'. A comparatively large number of LDP members of the Diet saw the councils as serving to 'add authority'. A number of opposition dietmen and top-ranking bureaucrats seemed to view the councils as a means of raising the level of 'policy-making' and of obtaining 'fairer policies'. Overall, there is no clear-cut agreement as to how the councils function. Kaneko (1979: 193) viewed the council as a cloak over Japan's bureaucratic administration. However, he also claimed that Japan is a leading country in terms of its use of council administration. In contrast to the political model based on hearings, public hearings and court-of-law legal procedures, Japan's 'consultative model' is based on the use of councils as an administrative procedure of the 'assembly type' which take account of interests at every level. Kaneko perceives the Japanese system as being similar to the French system of 'interest-representation councils'. In comparison with the way the French system functions, he argues that Japan's present system of councils is unsatisfactory in terms of the extent to which citizens can participate.

Political scientists are not agreed about the role played by the councils. It is one of the areas of Japanese life which is insufficiently researched. Their reputation for being used as 'cloaks' comes from the fact that the questions which are referred to them are *important problems*. In other words, the bureaucracy consults with the councils precisely because they are not dealing with a problem that falls within the ordinary or traditional scope of their concerns. New problems with wide policy implications and issues which will invite considerable public debate are given to the councils by the bureaucrats.

One view is that the councils in such cases are fulfilling the function of representing interest-groups. The opposite view is that they are not. The former view is represented by the opinions of the middle-level bureaucrats mentioned above. The latter view is represented by the Opposition members of the Diet and by Kaneko. Hence, Kaneko recommends a strengthening of their representative function and calls for more professionals and neutral experts to serve on the councils, which would be more in line with the French model. His argument is for a strengthening of the 'corporatist' aspects of the system.

At this point it is necessary to consider the arbitrariness of the selection of members to these councils. The selection process is in a way an exercise in ranking the interested parties as acknowledged by the various governmental agencies. Obviously there are interest groups not recognized by any agency (even if we leave aside for the moment the question of latent groups whose existence is too nebulous to deal with satisfactorily in the eyes of many contemporary political scientists). The more meaningful questions, however, concern the extent to which the influential groups, whose interests are manifest and known, are represented on the councils. It is not often that the make-up of a council is clearly put down in writing (the way it is for the Central Social Insurance and Medical Care Council, for which it is stipulated that eight members represent those who pay, that eight represent those who provide the medical treatment, and that four represent the public interest).

Another problem in this connection is the distinction between 'men of learning and experience' and 'representatives of the public interest'. Many councils include as 'men of learning and experience' specialists, university professors, influential people in the financial world, representatives of labour unions, and representatives of women's groups or consumer groups. While connected with the three functions of councils outlined above, the broad cross-section of participants makes it impossible to draw a simple conclusion concerning the representativeness of these councils.

With this note on the councils in the background, we can now consider one of the questions posed above in the third section: what is the political influence of Japan's economic circles and of big business? Many councils have representatives from the financial world, as well as members who are on the management of Japan's large corporations. Still, as we have seen, until now 'men of learning and experience' have formed the core, and few are selected simply to represent a particular interest. This is also true of other representatives, including those who come from the labour unions. It is not true that representatives of the financial world, acting as 'men of learning and experience', are a privileged majority in these councils. However, the make-up of participants differs greatly, depending on the character of the items to be deliberated upon. In huge councils, such as the Industrial Structure Council of MITI, there are up to 130 members and twenty subcommittees (*bukai*). There are a large number of parties from industry and representatives of the financial world, and the chairman of this council in 1979 was the chairman of Keidanren (Dokō Toshio). The consultative matters passing through it are of a diverse nature, and this is reflected in the extremely wide-ranging content to be found in its annual publication, *A Long-term Vision of the Industrial Structure* (Sangyō Kōzō no Chōki Bijon). If we classify the matters handled by the councils as macro or micro, it can be said that representatives of the financial world are, comparatively speaking, more likely to participate on councils which deal more with the macro-economic issues. For example, in such a council as the Rice Price Council within the Ministry of Agriculture, Forestry and Fisheries, its 'men of learning and experience' include producers, consumers, university professors and newspaper reporters. On the same ministry's Council on the Pearl Industry, however, the views of individual interests are strongly represented. The seven members of the Council on the Pearl Industry include (1) the director of the National Federation of Fishermen (Zengyoren); (2) the assistant director of Japan Pearl Exporting Union (Nihon Shinju Yushutsu Kumiai); (3) the chairman of the All-Japan Pearl Culture Fishing Industry Cooperative Federation (Zen-Nihon Shinju Yōshoku Gyogyō Kyōdō Kumiai Rengōkai); (4) the director of the Japan External Trade Organization [JETRO] (Nihon Bōeki Shinkōkai); (5) the director of the Central Bank for Commercial and Industrial Associations (Shōkō-kumiai Chūōkinko); (6) the director of the Central Bank for Agriculture and Forestry (Nōrin-chūō-kinko); and (7) the director of the Association for the Advancement of Japanese Pearls (Nihon Shinju Shinkōkai). There is a big difference in the make-up of membership of the councils, depending on whether they deal with macro-economic or macro-societal issues or they deal with micro-level problems of specific interest to limited sections of society.

Muramatsu (1981) also interviewed representatives from Japan's various interest groups. He examined the self-appraisals of each interest group and the extent of its own influence, and found that education groups, administration groups (*gyōsei kankei dantai* such as the League of Governors or the League of Mayors), and specialists' groups were more likely to believe they had a strong influence. Those in agricultural groups, economic groups and labour groups did not feel that their groups had much influence at all. Muramatsu's interpretation is that these economic groups are, for the most part (with exceptions such as Keidanren and Nikkeiren) enterprise groups. The reason they do not feel they have a large influence is that they each are in a competitive relationship with other groups and related administrative organs in dealing with broadly defined economic issues. For this reason, it is difficult for them to see the influence of their own representatives in concrete terms. The suggestion is that perceptions may depend on the 'monopolistic' position each group has within its own areas of interest.

If Muramatsu's findings are an accurate representation of how things are, the representatives of the various interest groups who appear on the councils may well be said to be participating as 'men of learning and experience'. On the surface, then, the councils would seem to offer a far wider range for diverse participation than the HOC elections discussed above in section 2 of this paper. Although this may on the surface seem to reflect the wide-ranging nature of contemporary administration, there are still many aspects of the councils that are as yet unknown. Because the deliberative process is almost never open to the public, one can only make deductions from draft reports. However, only the faintest idea of what goes on can be derived with these limitations on access to data and to the phenomena themselves.

Although the measurement of the influence that councils have on administration and legislation is an important issue, it is also one which exceeds the scope of this essay. However, the policies on which the various interest groups and the men of learning and experience consult are significant. They often form the basis for legislation or for administrative measures. Moreover, the many policy areas that require expertise are expanding over time. Nevertheless, if we look at the level of influence exercised by the government's Taxation System Investigation Committee and that of the LDP's Taxation System Investigation Committee, it may be said that in recent years the LDP's committee has had the greater influence. At the same time, without analyzing further the areas of contention handled by councils and their influence, it is still possible to see ways in which Japan's various interest groups are able to use the councils as a means of expressing their interests.

5 Interest-group liberalism and corporatism

Although theories of interest-group liberalism and themes of corporatism have aspects that run counter to the established theory of interest groups, the viewpoints also share some common ground. When he adopted the label 'interest-group liberalism', Theodore Lowi (1979) claims that he also considered using 'corporatism' or even 'syndicalism'. In the end, however, he concluded that there were clear differences between these two ideas. One difference is that the origin of interest-group liberalism is American, while that of corporatism is European. Also the emphasis on government administration comes more to the fore in the latter than in the former. Lowi (1979: 51) describes interest-group liberalism in the following manner:

(1) Organized interests are homogeneous and easy to define. Any duly elected representative of any interest is taken as an accurate representative of each and every member. (2) Organized interests emerge in every sector of our lives and adequately represent most of those sectors, so that one organized group can be found effectively answering and checking some other organized group as it seeks to prosecute its claims against society. And (3) the role of government is one of insuring access to the most effectively organized, and of ratifying the agreements and adjustments worked out among the competing leaders.

Of course, there are other definitions of the situation. Schmitter (1974: 93–4) uses the term 'corporatism'. He defines 'corporatism' as

a system of interest representation in which the constituent units are organized into a limited number of singular, compulsory, noncompetitive, hierarchically ordered and functionally differentiated categories, recognized or licensed (if not created) by the state and granted a deliberate representational monopoly within their respective categories in exchange for observing certain controls on their election of leaders and articulation of demands and supports.

Each definition places weight on the analytical framework. The differences between the two are few – a fact recognized by each of them. Schmitter's 'corporatism' gives the strong impression that it was 'artificially' created in the spirit of rivalry to counter the notion of 'pluralism'. It may be, however, that further research will reveal a need to redefine the terms after considering how interest groups in Japan fit (or do not fit) the two concepts just discussed.

It is quite clear that there are pluralistic groups in Japan. The

Table 8.6   *Membership in Various Types of Organizations in Six Countries (percentages)*

Type of organization	Country					
	Japan (1975)	USA (1963)	Britain (1963)	Germany (1963)	Italy (1963)	Mexico (1963)
Labour unions	16	14	22	15	6	11
Business	7	4	4	2	5	2
Professional	2	4	3	6	3	5
Farm	0	3	0	4	2	0
Social	12	13	14	10	4	4
Charitable	1	3	3	2	9	6
Religious	4	19	4	3	6	5
Civic-political	5	11	3	3	8	3
Cooperative	12	6	3	2	2	0
Veterans	0	6	5	1	4	0
Fraternal	17	13			n.u.	n.u.
Alumni associations	17	n.u.	n.u.	n.u.	n.u.	n.u.
Other	4	6	3	9	6	0
Total membership	59	57	47	44	30	24

Note: For Japan, women's groups and youth groups have been assigned to social groups; political groups are assigned to the civic-political category; hobby groups and sports clubs are classified as fraternal; and a separate group has been made for alumni associations, classmate associations and prefectural associations. The abbreviation 'n.u.' for 'not used' indicates categories which were not used in the compilation of the data in specific countries.

Source: For Japan, the figures were taken from Nakamura (1975), p. 200. For the other countries, figures were taken from Almond and Verba (1963), p. 302.

data in Table 8.6 suggest that there may not be a big difference compared with other 'civic cultures'. However, as Table 8.7 suggests, most groups in Japan have been formed since the war. Opinion is divided as to the political significance of these groups. For example, the competition in Japan between private enterprises is probably more intense than in most other advanced countries. Yet, when foreign trade or Japan's public enterprises are involved, one often gets the impression that everyone's interests are extremely well coordinated, thus inviting the 'Japan Incorporated' label. Is it really possible for pluralistic performers in the marketplace to come together suddenly in the face of outside pressure or to be unified quickly owing to their relationship with the government? It would at least seem that trading companies

Table 8.7 *Year in which Japanese Groups and Organizations were Founded*

	Before 1945	1946–55	1956–65	After 1966	Total (%)	No.
Agricultural	8.6	73.9	13.04	4.3	100.0	23
Welfare	3.3	40.0	33.3	23.3	100.0	30
Economic	7.9	44.3	34.1	13.6	100.0	88
Labour	3.8	51.9	28.8	15.9	100.0	52
Administrative	40.1	40.0	13.3	6.7	100.0	15
Educational	8.3	83.3	8.3	—	100.0	12
Professional	22.2	55.6	22.2	—	100.0	9
Civic-political	5.3	26.3	36.8	31.6	100.0	19
Other	25.0	50.0	25.0	—	100.0	4
All groups	9.2	48.8	28.2	13.9	100.0	252

Source: Muramatsu (1981b), p. 76.

Figure 8.1 *Expansion of Groups and Organizations since 1900*

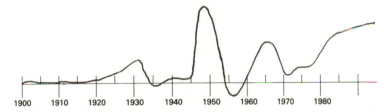

1900 1910 1920 1930 1940 1950 1960 1970 1980

Note: Figure 8.1 shows the growth rate at which the number of groups and organizations expanded in Japan from the beginning of this century.
Source: Muramatsu, Itō and Tsujinaka (1986), p. 44.

and other Japanese enterprises are making inroads overseas by extending their competition beyond the shores of Japan. Limiting the analysis to the domestic scene on the basis of the present situation without looking at patterns in trade and industrial policy over the postwar years, it would seem that the MITI has not served as a kind of 'General Staff Office' regulating economic interests within Japan. For example, it can be said that relations are good between MITI and the iron and steel industry (a mature industry) and also between MITI and a number of industries which are still maturing, such as the computer industry. However, the influence of MITI seems to have been weak in the automobile industry and the production of electrical household appliances, which are still in a growth period. The same thing would hold true of the relations between Keidanren and the enterprises in these industries.

If the popular notion of 'Japan Incorporated' were put aside because of the obvious errors it invites, it is still necessary perhaps to supply a macro understanding of the activities of Japan's pluralistic interest groups. The categories developed by Lowi and by Schmitter do not perfectly fit the interest groups examined in this paper. This does not mean that there is no basis for viewing Japan's politics in corporatist terms. In a book edited by Schmitter (1979), Pempel and Tsunekawa have written an essay titled 'Corporatism Without Labor? the Japanese Anomaly'. To be sure, the influence of labour unions in politics, even when acknowledged by politicians and bureaucrats, cannot be described as great (see Table 8.8). But if labour's influence is compared with the influence of the courts, there is not that much difference. Rather, as we have seen, labour's representatives are on some of the councils; the wage decisions resulting from the Spring Wage Offensive and from the setting of the rice price may also be seen as examples of workers being involved in a corporatist framework.

In this regard, one needs to know which interest groups are taken into consideration at the time policy decisions are made. One also needs to think over more carefully the connection between the bureaucratic structure and the government in Japan. At this point, however, we run into the difficulty of measuring influence. However, this problem might be alleviated slightly if we think of the council as one variable in the equation.

If the make-up of the council was decided on the basis of group nominations, if all interests were completely represented, and if decisions in the councils were to take precedence over the national legislative assemblies and the ruling political party, then we might be able to talk of 'corporatism'. If, however, the council is viewed merely as one actor dealing with policy decisions, then it could be said to be closer to the model of interest-group liberalism. Considered in this way, the *shingikai* probably operate more in line with the corporatist model. Still, they are quite far from being the 'pure type'. By having 'men of learning and experience' participate rather than having all council members coming from a particular interest group, room for ambiguity is created. Moreover, a council's 'report' is not a 'decision'; sometimes the administrative organs simply ignore such reports.

Table 8.8 *Influences on Political Decisions (percentages)*

Groups/Organs	Senior bureaucrats	Middle-level bureaucrats	LDP	Opposition
Political parties	47.3	41.9	68.0	43.1
Administrative bureaucracy	45.5	40.3	30.0	41.2
Financial circles and big Business	—	—	—	—
Law courts	—	5.1	—	13.7
Labour unions	—	—	—	—
Interest groups: agricultural groups, medical associations	—	3.1	—	—
Mass media (newspapers, TV)	3.6	3.6	2.0	—
Scholars and intelligentsia	—	—	—	—
Religious groups	—	—	—	—
Citizens' and residents' campaigns	—	0.5	—	—
Others	—	2.0	—	2.0
No answer	3.6	0.5	—	—
Total	100.0	100.0	100.0	100.0
No.	55	196	50	51

Note: 1 The responses were to the question, 'Which of the following do you think has the greatest influence in present-day Japan in deciding the country's political policies? Please choose three and order in terms of their influence from one to three.'
2 The percentage totals (100%) equal the totals for all three choices (i.e., 3N)
Source: Muramatsu (1981), p. 27.

To this must be added one further consideration. Interest groups are not limited to a single channel in communicating their interests to the decision-makers, but have several means available to them. There is also the existence of counteracting interest groups. On this point, the pluralistic tendencies are strong; indeed, the considerable extent to which pluralist interests 'coexist' in the 'marketplace' is probably one of Japan's special characteristics. There are, of course, some notable examples of asymmetry. The Medical Association is not countered by a patients' organization with similar influence. Nor are most producers' groups evenly matched by consumers' groups. The failure to account for the absence of this kind of 'balance' is one deficiency of the pluralist model. Nevertheless, as we have seen above, the relatively weaker sectors (the less-developed regions and declining industries) have been able to do fairly well in obtaining their share of the national budget. When seen as a means of guaranteeing the participation or representation of 'minority' interests, then the administrative measures which provide benefits to the 'weak' in the form of social security and subsidies serve to improve the fit with interest-group theory.

A further problem is the difficulty of finding a link between the LDP and big business on the administrative level. Even if the economically powerful private sectors had received few tangible benefits as far as the general accounts goes, there might still be some who would want to look more carefully at the special accounts and financial investments. Or, it might be possible to consider that big business has received advantages in the way the tax system or the licensing systems are structured. However, the number of licences and approvals in MITI, for example, have decreased along with liberalization. Even 'administrative guidances' (*gyōsei shidō*) seem to have become less important over time. This might be inevitable as infant industries that needed protection at an earlier stage grow successfully and require less protection. Accordingly, it is not at all surprising that Japan's advanced industries with international competitive power have come to consider MITI as no more than an 'information centre'. On the other hand, there are many industries that even today must be protected and nourished in order to survive. Many of these come under the jurisdiction of the Ministry of Agriculture, Forestry and Fisheries, and it may be reasonable to argue that the role of the ministry is relatively important in those industries.

There is also, no doubt, a close connection with the redistributions effected by Japan's political and financial systems. Because Japan is an egalitarian society, it is often argued, the administration aims to promote progressive taxation and the transfer of income to underdeveloped regions and less fortunate industries. However, interest-group theory also provides an explanation by emphasizing the political strength of the economically 'weak'. Such theory emphasizes the importance of the system rather than 'egalitarian feelings' *per se* in accounting for equality. As an ideology which has lulled big business into a false perception that they are unduly benefiting from the system, the general image of big business and 'Japan Incorporated' have perhaps served the interests of the disadvantaged. Nevertheless, these sectors have supported high growth and have received a sufficient distribution of resources from the system over all. Thus it is perhaps natural that they have not complained. Also, even though *amakudari* exists, there are almost no instances in Japan (unlike the situation in the United States) of people who participate directly in public policy-making as a result of reverse *ama-agari* (a movement from the private sector into some organ of the government).

6 Conclusions

Ordinarily, most discussions of Japan's interest groups start with some mention of the 'peculiarly Japanese features' such as the hierarchical principle associated with a 'vertically structured society' (*tate-shakai*) or the extent to which relationships become all-embracing (*marugakae hōshiki*). This chapter has not dealt with problems of internal organization. In regard to the internal make-up of interest groups, however, it is useful to compare them with the analyses made by Olson (1965) or Wilson (1973). A study of the Japan Medical Association and the Agricultural Cooperative would reveal some points in common with the emphases found in the work of Olson, Wilson and others.

A major conclusion from the preceding discussion is that interest groups in Japan are considerably different from the ordinary image of them. At the same time, they provide evidence that influence in the political arena is not necessarily reflected in the marketplace. Also, the discussion of the *shingikai* helped to clarify the process by which some interest groups participate in the policy-making process.

Although in comparison to the way councils seem to function in the Scandinavian countries, it would be difficult to conclude that Japan's advisory councils fit perfectly the corporatist model. Corporatistic aspects might be said to exist within certain defined policy areas such as wage determination. In the private economic sector, where on the whole competition is fierce, there is a strong tendency toward the situation described as interest-group liberalism and away from the corporatist model. One can thus consider Japan to be a democratic parliamentary system which incorporates aspects both of corporatism and of interest-group liberalism.

This chapter has highlighted the linkages between interest groups, the LDP's Policy Affairs Research Council and its divisions (*bukai*), the various standing committees of the Diet, and the various ministries and agencies. Although they are products of the LDP's long term in power, it seems reasonable to expect that changes in the decision-making processes can be discerned by considering carefully changes in these linkages over time.

APPENDICES

Table 8A(1)   *A Typology of* Shingikai

Type of shingikai	*No. of* shingikai
(1) Membership including dietmen	11
(2) Membership including administrative agencies	19
(3) Policy-making type	19
(4) Authorization of agencies' plan	23
(5) *Rinchō* type	4
(6) Interest coordination type	38
(7) Specific technical matter	74
(8) Inactive type	23
(9) Unspecified	4
Total	215

Source: Sone Yasunori (ed.), *Interim Report on Shingikai* (1985).

Table 8A(2) *Classification of Shingikai by Member's Background and by Ministry Affiliation*
A. 1974 (1 April 1974–30 March 1985)

Ministry / Type of membership	Diet members	Tripartite membership	Knowledgeable persons, including scholars	Persons with scholarly experience	Persons representing specific interest groups	(1) Persons with scholarly experience, (2) bureaucrats, and (3) interest-group representations	Others	No appointed members	Not stipulated	Total	Percentage
Prime Minister's Office	18	0	20	25	0	1	3	2	1	70	28.5
Ministry of Justice	0	0	3	0	1	0	2	0	1	7	2.9
Ministry of Foreign Affairs	0	0	1	0	0	0	0	0	0	1	—
Ministry of Finance	0	0	9	6	3	1	0	1	0	20	8.1
Ministry of Education	0	0	2	6	5	4	0	0	1	18	7.3
Ministry of Health and Welfare	0	2	8	4	0	10	1	0	0	25	10.2
Ministry of Agriculture and Forestry and Fisheries	1	0	6	11	1	4	0	0	1	24	9.8
Ministry of International Trade and Industry	0	0	14	14	1	1	0	0	6	36	14.6
Ministry of Transportation	1	0	4	4	0	2	0	0	1	12	4.9
Ministry of Post and Telecommunication	0	0	2	2	0	1	0	0	0	5	2.0
Ministry of Labour	0	5	1	3	5	0	1	0	0	15	6.1
Ministry of Construction	0	0	3	4	0	1	1	0	0	9	3.7
Ministry of Home Affairs	0	0	2	1	0	1	0	0	0	4	1.6
Total	20	7	75	80	16	26	8	3	11	246	100.0
Percentage frequency distribution	(8.1)	(2.9)	(30.5)	(32.5)	(6.5)	(10.6)	(3.3)	(1.2)	(4.5)	(100)	

Source: Gyōsei Kanrichō, *Shingikai Sōran 1975 (A Survey of Shingikai 1975)*.

Table 8B(1) *Classification of Shingikai by Member's Background and by Ministry Affiliation B. 1984 (1 April 1984–30 March 1985)*

Ministry	Diet members	Tripartite membership	Persons with (1) scholarly experience (2) bureaucrats	Persons with scholarly experience	Interest-group representatives	Persons with (1) scholarly experience, (2) bureaucrats, and (3) interest-group representations	Others	No appointed members	Not stipulated	Total	Percentage
Prime Minister's Office	9	0	9	25	0	1	2	2	2	50	23.4
Ministry of Justice	0	0	1	2	1	0	2	0	1	7	3.3
Ministry of Foreign Affairs	0	0	1	1	0	0	0	0	0	2	0.9
Ministry of Finance	0	0	4	10	2	1	0	0	0	17	7.9
Ministry of Education	0	0	1	8	4	1	0	3	0	17	7.9
Ministry of Health and Welfare	0	2	2	9	8	0	0	0	1	22	10.3
Ministry of Agriculture and Forestry and Fisheries	0	0	0	16	2	1	0	2	1	22	10.3
Ministry of International Trade and Industry	0	0	3	21	1	1	0	1	6	33	15.4
Ministry of Transportation	1	0	2	6	0	1	0	1	1	12	5.6
Ministry of Post and Telecommunication	0	0	1	2	1	0	0	0	1	5	2.3
Ministry of Labour	0	5	0	4	5	0	0	0	0	14	6.5
Ministry of Construction	0	0	3	4	1	0	1	0	0	9	4.2
Ministry of Home Affairs	0	0	1	2	0	1	0	0	0	4	1.9
Total	10	7	28	110	25	7	5	9	13	214	100.0
Percentage frequency distribution	(4.7)	(3.3)	(13.1)	(51.4)	(11.7)	(3.3)	(2.3)	(4.2)	(6.1)	(100)	

Source Sōmuchō, *Shingikai Sōran, 1984* (A Survey of *Shingikai* 1984).

References

Almond, Gabriel; and Verba, Sidney
1963 *Civic Culture* (Princeton, NJ: Princeton University Press).
Campbell, John C.
1976 *Contemporary Japanese Budget Politics* (Berkeley and Los Angeles, Cal.: University of California Press).
1979 'The Old People Boom and Japanese Policy Making', *Journal of Japanese Studies*, vol. 5, no. 2, 321–57.
Fukui, Haruhiko
1977 'Studies in Policymaking: a Review of the Literature', in *Policymaking in Contemporary Japan*, edited by T. J. Pempel (Ithaca, NY: Cornell University Press), 22–59.
Gyōsei Kanri-chō [Administrative Management Agency] (ed.)
1979 *Shingikai Sōran* (Conspectus of [Japan's] Administrative Councils) (Tokyo: Ōkurashō Insatsukyoku).
Hashiguchi, Osamu
1977 *Shin Zaisei Jijō* (New Financial Conditions) (Tokyo: Simul Shuppan).
Hashimoto, Ryūtarō
1981 Comments in a round-table discussion, 'Ōki na Seifu ka, Chiisai Seifu ka' (Big Government or Small Government?), *Mita Hyōron*, no. 816 (July), 4–24.
Hirose, Michisada
1981 *Hojokin to Seiken To* (Subsidies and the LDP Government) (Tokyo: Asahi Shinbunsha).
Inoguchi, Takeshi
1983 *Gendai Nihon Seiji Keizai no Kōzu* (The Political Economy of Contemporary Japan) (Tokyo: Tōyō Keizai Shinpōsha).
Ishida, Takeshi
1960 'Wagakuni ni okeru Atsuryoku Dantai no Hassei no Rekishiteki Jōken to Sono Tokushitsu' (The Historical Conditions and Characteristics of the Origins of Pressure Groups in Japan), *The Annals of the Japanese Political Science Association* (Tokyo: Iwanami Shoten), 30–45.
Kaneko, Masashi
1979 'Shingikai Seido to Kokumin Sanka' (The Council System and Citizen Participation), *Hōgaku Seminā*, special issue on *Naikaku to Kanryō* (The Cabinet and the Bureaucracy) (Sept.), 193–203.
Lindbolm, Charles E.
1980 *The Policy-making Process*, 2nd edn (Englewood Cliffs, NJ: Prentice-Hall).

Lijphart, Arend; Pintor, R. L.; and Sone, Yasunori
1986   'The Limited Vote and the Single Nontransferable Vote: Lessons
   from the Japanese and Spanish Examples', in *Electoral Laws and
   Their Consequences*, edited by Bernard Grofman and Arend
   Lijphard (New York: Agathon Press).
Lowi, Theodore
1979   *The End of Liberalism* (New York: Norton).
Muramatsu, Michio
1981a   *Sengo Nihon no Kanryōsei* (Japan's Postwar Bureaucracy)
   (Tokyo: Tōyō Keizai Shinpōsha).
1981b   'Nihongata Puresshā Gurupu no Kenkyū' (Studies of Japanese-
   type Pressure Groups), *Tōyō Keizai* (2–9 May), 76–82.
Muramatsu, Michio; Itō, Mitsutoshi; and Tsujinaka, Yutaka
1986   *Sengo Nihon no Atsuryoku Dantai* (Pressure Groups in Postwar
   Japan) (Tokyo: Tōyō Keizai Shinpōsha).
Nakamura, Akira; and Takeshita, Yuzuru (eds)
1984   *Nihon no Seisaku Katei* (The Japanese Political Process) (Tokyo:
   Azusa Shuppansha).
Nakamura, Kikuo
1975   *Nihon no Seiji Bunka* (Japanese Political Culture) (Kyōto:
   Minerva Shobō).
Noguchi, Yukio
1980   *Zaisei Kiki no Kōzō* (Make-up of Financial Crises) (Tokyo:
   Tōyō Keizai Shinpōsha).
Olson, Mancur
1965   *The Logic of Collective Action* (Cambridge, Mass.: Harvard
   University Press).
Ōtake, Hideo
1979   *Gendai Nihon no Seiji Kenryoku Keizai Kenryoku* (The
   Political–Economic Power of Contemporary Japan) (Tokyo: San-
   ichi Shobō).
Pempel, T. J.; and Tsunekawa, Keiichi
1979   'Corporatism Without Labor? the Japanese Anomaly', in *Trends
   toward Corporatist Intermediation*, edited by Phillippe C. Schmitter
   and Gerhard Lehmbruch (eds) (Beverly Hills and London: Sage
   Publications), 231–70.
Satō, Seizaburō; and Matsuzaki, Tetsuhisa
1986   *Jimintō Seiken* (The LDP Government) (Tokyo: Chūō
   Kōronsha).
Schmitter, Phillippe C.
1974   'Still the Century of Corporatism?', *The Review of Politics*, vol.
   36, no. 1, 85–131.
Sone, Yasunori
1982a   'Japanese Democracy: Ambivalent Views', in *Japan in the*

1980s, edited by Shiratori Rei (Tokyo: Kodansha International), 111–29.

1982b 'Pluralist Democracy and the Contemporary State', *Annals of the Japanese Political Science Association* (Tokyo: Iwanami Shoten), 117–49.

1984 *Kettei no Seijigaku* (The Political Economy of Decision-making) (Tokyo: Yūhikaku).

1986 'Nihon no Seisaku Keisei Ron no Henka' (Changing Patterns of Policy-making in Japan), in *Nihongata Seisaku Kettei no Henyō*, edited by Nakano Minoru (Tokyo: Tōyō Keizai Shinpōsha), 301–19.

Taguchi, Fukuji

1969 *Shakai Shūdan no Seiji Kinō* (The Political Function of Social Groups) (Tokyo: Miraisha).

Tomita, Nobuo; and Sone, Yasunori (eds)

1983 *Sekai Seiji no naka no Nihon Seiji* (Japanese Politics in the World Perspective) (Tokyo: Yūhikaku).

Wilson, James Q.

1973 *Political Organizations* (New York: Basic Books).

Yamaguchi, Yasushi

1982 'Neo-corporatism Ron ni okeru "Corporatism" no Gainen' (Corporatism: Concept in Discussion of Neo-Corporatism), *Shisō*, no. 2, 113–33.

Chapter Nine
Japanese Industrial Relations: an External Perspective

Solomon B. Levine

1 The case of Japan: this world or another

As an 'outsider' who has been viewing industrial relations in Japan close-up for more than thirty years, I feel that the great attention given to a few features of the Japanese industrial relations system has resulted in an oversimplification of the system which has evolved since the end of World War II. Most of the emphasis has been upon such elements as 'life-time employment', 'length-of-service' wages and salaries, company-provided welfare benefits, enterprise level union organization, and worker 'loyalty' to – and hard work in – his company. While there is some truth to these characteristics, they tend to be seen as the only ones that are considered in most descriptions of Japan's industrial relations. A number of others which are just as prominent – indeed, probably more important – are overlooked. This misperception arises not only from stereotypes of Japanese society as a whole, but also from a failure to analyze systems of industrial relations with an adequate frame of reference. The problem is as much one of systematizing analysis as it is the lack of correct facts about contemporary Japan.

As shown in Ōkōchi *et al.* (1973) and in Shirai and Shimada (1978), one begins to realize that there is far more to industrial relations in Japan, as in other countries, than the particular features usually cited as distinctive and unique. In the larger context, lifetime employment, seniority wages, enterprise unionism, company welfare benefits and worker loyalty turn out to be rather selective, perhaps minor, aspects of the total system of industrial relations. Moreover, by focusing on them alone it is impossible to grasp the full scope of the relationships among the actors, the processes for decision-making, and the procedural and substantive rules. All of these – along with forces in the social, political and economic environment – comprise a system of industrial relations.

In other words, exclusive preoccupation with a few alleged features, even if they can be found in some firms, overemphasizes their importance. It is as if in the Australian case the industrial relations system is seen as being only the workings of the conciliation and arbitration commissions with its emphasis on 'comparative wage justice'. Obviously the picture would be incomplete without an analysis of the collective bargaining activities between union and management (cf. Plowman *et al.* 1980). In the American case, to what extent can industrial relations be understood only by reference to the rules and regulations of the National Labor Relations Board or to union–management collective bargaining without attention being paid to the scope and area of collective bargaining itself (cf. Chamberlain *et al.* 1980)? Few would contend that these kinds of limited features, though highly important, would account for virtually all of the systems in Australia and America. Yet in focusing on certain selective aspects, that is precisely what is done in explaining the industrial relations system in Japan.

There is obviously a need for a much broader and more comprehensive approach to the Japanese system than has usually been the case. Viewed from the perspective of industrial-relations system analysis, one might argue that Japan's industrial relations share far more similarities than differences with the systems found in many Western nations. This approach is long overdue, since increasing quantities of data and material have become available, in English as well as in Japanese, to really apply it successfully.[1] At the same time the logic of industrial-relations system analysis itself tends to promote similarities or universals among national industrial relations systems.

A close examination of the supposedly distinctive and particularistic features in the Japanese system does not lend support, either factually or logically, to the view that they are unique. To the extent to which they actually exist, they are the product, as rules and institutions, of the very same set of forces – economic, political, technological, legal, social and cultural – which generate rules and institutions in other countries. No two nations are likely to have the very same set of environmental forces conditioning their industrial relations systems, and one would expect each country to exhibit variations from one another at any given time.

There appears to be wide latitude in the types of relationships and rules which are compatible with the evolution of the industrialization process. Each country does not follow an identical path in developing its system of industrial relations. Over time, industrialization will change the rules and relationships, presumably toward a general convergence among the systems. The path through which a nation's system of industrial relations moves may be just as compatible with economic and industrial growth as the path of any other industrializing society. Although it is frequently claimed that in the Japanese case its supposedly unique features are largely responsible for Japan's outstanding economic and industrial growth in the postwar era, it is still not clear whether any one national industrial relations system is superior to all others in becoming associated with the speed and pace of economic growth and development. In any event, it is unlikely that systems of industrial relations explain why the economies of different nations grow as they do.

This allegation about Japan seems to derive from a preoccupation with the role of traditional cultural values as the only important force explaining economic development. The values usually cited are the Japanese preference for groupism and conservatism rather than individualism, acceptance of vertical authority structures rather than horizontal relationships, status according to age not merit, and the like. However, the picture is more complex. It cannot, for example, explain fluctuations in the pace or direction

1 For a wide variety of recent English-language material on Japanese industrial relations, see *The Japanese Industrial Relations Series*, Japan Institute of Labour, Tokyo. Also see Shirai (1984).

of Japan's development. Nor does it explain sectoral imbalances. Culture is at best only one of the forces at work and probably a minor one, especially as the logic of industrialism – with its emphasis on the universals of science, technology, education, economic rationality, political democracy and social mobility – increasingly overwhelms traditional attitudes and behaviour as industrialization advances.

Even if one accepts that the allegedly unique features of the Japanese industrial relations system are as described, there is room to argue that they are a product of the logic of the industrialization process itself, not an outcome reflecting the force of traditional cultural values. Sugimoto's studies on conflict in modern Japan (1981 and 1982) as well as his work with Mouer (1986) raise serious doubts about early descriptions of what Japan's traditional culture actually was. Not only do they suggest that the cultural values attributed to Japan have little historical basis, they also question whether they exist in present-day Japan. This is not to deny that cultural values have no role to play in Japanese industrial relations. Certainly, they do, as in any national system. But serious questions have emerged as to what they have been and what they have become, so that the degree of their influence is by and large unknown.

Before resorting to a cultural explanation, other forces – economic, technological, political, social – appear to be more powerful than traditional values as explanatory factors. No doubt, lack of familiarity with Japanese history, society, economy and language (at least in comparison to our knowledge about European and North American nations) is a major reason why many have fallen back upon easily understood stereotypes about Japanese culture to 'explain' anything and everything about Japan, including its industrial relations. Actually, the resort to the cultural explanation avoids and obscures the complex analysis which is required to understand fully the other major forces which have been at work. Without a much wider probing, we are bound to miss the universalistic features and persist in singling out the unique aspects and cling to inaccurate stereotypes. The end result is an 'explanation' which focuses on the residual: the unexplainable which is labelled 'culture' rather than on that which has already been explained largely by a number of other commonly cited variables to be mentioned below.

Regardless of one's intellectual orientations, the serious student of Japan's industrial relations will have to confront a massive body of literature, written by Japanese and non-Japanese alike, which emphasizes the importance of culturally unique factors in explaining how work is organized in Japan. This paper begins by presenting a framework for considering any industrial relations system in comparative perspective. To use Befu's terms, it is a starting point, an *etic* checklist against which the *emic* details can be filled in. It then comes back to consider the allegedly unique features associated with Japan's industrial relations. Concluding that the existence of such features is dubious and that their relevance to understanding industrial relations in Japan is limited *even if* we were to conclude that they did exist, the discussion moves on to consider some other aspects of Japan's industrial relations that might more appropriately be considered in constructing a model of Japanese society, at least as it relates to the organization of work.

2 Systematic frameworks and the systems approach: a concept of industrial relations systems

In any modern industrially advanced nation, industrial relations comprise a system which is, at least conceptually, separate from the nation's economy, political arrangements and social structure, but which also cuts across all of these (cf. Dunlop 1958). As a system, industrial relations represent a highly complex combination of many interrelated elements, none of which is meaningfully understood outside the system. An industrial relations system is also a product of history. It is subject to the influence of the changing conditions in the larger society (and even the world). The environmental influences include, of course, variations in the economic conditions which shape the markets for goods, services and labour; changes in technology and organizational arrangements for production; shifts in the distribution of political power and authority that affect the allocation of productive resources; the strengthening and weakening of commonly shared ideological commitments in the population and/or the labour force; and fluctuations in the degree to which cultural values determine or channel people's attitudes and behaviour.

These kinds of forces affect the strategies and tactics of the system's major actors as they deal with one another over time. In the setting of a democratic market-oriented mixed economy, the actors usually include employers and their federations, the workers and their union organizations, and the government and its relevant branches and agencies. Even though the actors may share a consensus regarding the desirability of industrialization, it is highly unlikely that they will agree with one another regarding goals and interests in both the short term and the long run. Thus, while also being characterized by accommodation and cooperation, each industrial relations system exhibits some degree of tension among the actors – and, at times, overt conflict (or the disruption of production).

For the most part, an industrial relations system is characterized by regularities which make it a system. Even though latent tensions may exist, these regularities are usually not defined by disruptions in production. Strikes, lockouts, slowdowns and other types of open conflict usually account for but a fraction of 1 per cent of working time actually performed in an advanced industrial country. The mass media tend to magnify the extent of these 'disturbances'. As a result, the differences among industrialized nations are exaggerated to the extent that attention is focused on these disruptions in production. If, instead, the focus were upon the totality of how industrial relations systems actually and regularly operate, the national systems would probably appear to be much more alike.

The actors deal with one another to generate a huge network of interrelated rules which govern or guide the behaviour of employers and employees in their relationships with one another, the way employees interact among themselves, and the fundamental link between the employee and his or her work. These rules are sometimes fully agreed upon by all actors; at other times they are imposed by one party on the others. The rules are 'hammered out' through a variety of processes: consultation, negotiation, conciliation, mediation and arbitration; legal enactments and court decisions; administrative orders and regulations; and even socially accepted custom. These processes may be carried out on a trilateral, bilateral or unilateral basis. Most national industrial relations systems have examples of all three. Occasionally a system will cease to function temporarily.

The rules are the output of the system, although they themselves may feed back into the system to the extent that they affect the environment in which the system operates (as, for example, when the output seriously affects the distribution of national income or the level of production costs and the prices of goods and services). The rules are both procedural and substantive in nature, and are subject to change as the environmental forces impinge upon the actors, causing them to seek changes in the rules. Certain of the rules, however, tend to become thoroughly institutionalized and persist over long periods of time; they impart to the system a degree of continuing stability. At the same time, while it is usually these institutionalized rules which often receive the greatest attention as characterizing a national system – whether in Australia, in Japan or in the United States – at the same time various other rules are constantly being revised.

One should stress that the notion of there being a national industrial relations system incorporates a set of goals, often conflicting, which the actors are seeking to realize in varying degrees. The system is not necessarily structured to attain economic growth or increased productivity alone. Nor is industrial 'harmony' always a high priority. Many systems are equally concerned with achieving economic, political and social equity, and with providing a sense of participation in decision-making about matters that vitally affect the parties involved.

The industrial relations found in most societies are so complex that it is an abstraction even to talk about a 'national system'. Within each nation there is likely to be a large variety of subsystems, each of which may be different from the others. These occur not only at the industrial level, but also at the workshop level. This is all the more reason why it is inaccurate and misleading to use stereotypes in generalizing about a national system of industrial relations, or to declare that a national system, such as Japan's, is totally unique compared to other national systems. While the comparison of national systems tends to highlight the differences among them, a look at their subsystems, especially at a common industry level, often reveals a large number of cross-cultural similarities. For this reason, comparisons require some systematiz-ation, and the theoretical conceptualization of industrial relations systems presented above provides a useful perspective for consider-ing the Japanese case.

3 How valid are the 'unique' Japanese features?

The allegedly unique features of the Japanese industrial relations system include life-time employment, seniority wages, company welfare, enterprise unionism and worker loyalty. They are largely interrelated and esssentially different facets of the same phenomenon; the literature on them argues that one cannot exist without the other. Accordingly, it is possible to treat them as a single syndrome in discussing their validity.

It should also be noted that this syndrome applies to a minority of the Japanese wage and salary workforce who now number more than 40 million. At most, it is estimated that they extend to no more than one-third of Japan's wage and salary earners; in all likelihood the figure is somewhat less. Except for the statistics on enterprise unionism, we have little accurate data on the other facets. This is true with regard not only to their historical development but also to current practice. No one knows how to measure their prevalence and there are few agreed upon definitions. At best they may be what sociologists have called 'ideal' types – abstractions which exist in our minds but not in reality. In the paragraphs below each of these features is examined more closely.

A   Life-time employment

'*Life-time employment*' is said to occur when a company or enterprise hires an individual directly upon completing school and then retains that person without layoff or discharge for the thirty to forty years' duration of his working career until 'retirement' from the company, and, theoretically, from the labour force. This idea is not uniquely Japanese. In varying degrees the notion of life-time employment has been entertained by workers in other countries who seek employment security through unionization and by management seeking to retain employees in whom they have invested time and money.

If the practice applies in Japan, it is usually found among large-scale organizations in Japan, as is the case elsewhere. It also tends to be a practice confined to male employees, this perhaps being more so in Japan (at least formally) than in other countries. The practice conflicts, of course, with the neo-classical notion in economics that to achieve economic efficiency and employee satisfaction there needs to be a degree of worker mobility from firm to firm, as usually is the case especially in the small and medium-scale company sectors in Japan and in other countries. Given that the external labour market is closed, it is alleged that the opportunity for mobility exists within the firm itself. However, although the law provides protection against termination at will (cf. Hanami 1979), explicit contracts for life-time employment tenure in Japan are rare, just as there are few such contracts in other countries. Moreover, if one measures actual years of service of employees with a single enterprise, the Japanese experience shows it to be no longer than the averages found in other countries (including those with similar demographic characteristics).

Turnover rates from enterprise also indicate that Japanese mobility is about the same as in several West European countries, although as far as we know most of these nations have rates below those of the United States (cf. Cole 1979; Koike 1983a; Levine and Taira 1980). Moreover, in Japan 'retirement' comes much earlier in one's career than it does in most other advanced industrialized nations. In fact, large firms in Japan have implemented a system which makes life-time employment unlikely. The system of compulsory retirement forces separation from the enterprise at the relatively early age of fifty-five to sixty. Moreover, it is not uncommon for many employees to be invited – even strongly encouraged – to resign 'voluntarily' at even earlier ages.

Even if we shift from the notion of 'life-time employment' to the more limiting concept of 'career employment', the facts still are that 'retirees' almost inevitably must seek employment, usually at lower rates of pay, in the small and medium-size sector. Employment rates among older persons in Japan (for example, those aged sixty-five or over) are much higher than in West Europe, Australia and North America.

One should also observe that to the extent long-term employment does obtain in Japan's large-scale firms, the practice is usually accompanied by the presence of 'buffer' groups consisting of temporary workers, part-time workers, subcontract workers and the like. The number of such employees expands and contracts with business conditions. Thus, while protecting the permanent employment of a small number of regular employees, the firms have created, maintained and institutionalized a form of employment which is characterized by high turnover. Even with this cushion, however, some of Japan's largest companies have still laid off regular workers in business downturns. During the economic slowdown beginning with the oil crisis in 1973 and 1974, one could frequently read about such retrenchments in Japan's daily newspapers.

The more closely one looks at the life-time employment concept, the less it seems to be a unique feature with widespread application in Japan. Active external labour markets, and even unemployment, are not absent in Japan, just as they are not absent anywhere else. Also, the practice of long-term employment – as defined by labour turnover rates and average job tenure – can be found in many other societies. These facts, then, cause us seriously to doubt the validity of life-time employment as an important institution, which decisively differentiates or characterizes the organization of work as being peculiarly Japanese.

B Seniority wages

The '*seniority wage*' system is usually defined as a situation in which employees receive regular increments in basic compensation, most often on an annual basis, as long as they remain with the same firm. Thus, it is entwined inextricably with the life-time employment concept. In order for an employee to derive maximum financial consideration – including bonuses, various fringe benefits, a retirement allowance, and a pension – from an employer, he should have to spend his life-time with the same firm. Bound up with the seniority wages ideal is the notion of steady advances in status as one ages and gains experience in the firm. Although the employee's income increases with such promotions up the organizational ladder, they may be nominal. It is not necessary that promotions result in the employee having more authority.

Within the context of life-time employment seniority wages are supposed to be powerful incentives for productive work, although this relationship has not been 'scientifically' tested. It is clear, however, that seniority wages, coupled with life-time employment, provide a rational approach within the Japanese context to rewarding the acquisition and the application of skills which are required only by the employing enterprise. Those employees who are brought into the enterprise on a regular career basis usually begin as unskilled school-leavers, recruited because of their promise and ability to learn and perform tasks diligently, and because of the likelihood that they will fit into work groups and organizational life. From the beginning, they are a highly select group of cohorts. With continuing experience, usually working in a group composed of senior and junior members, they steadily expand their knowledge and skills of the jobs they are assigned. Younger group members constantly learn from the older ones, and the older ones strive to teach the younger ones, so that their value to a dynamic and expanding enterprise lies not only in the jobs or tasks actually performed, but also in the employee's potential performance in the future. Both as group and as individual employees, these persons become highly adaptable to the demands of rapid technological and organizational change; they are often multi-skilled and are easily transferred from one operation to another within the given enterprise.

Such patterns of work mean that the productive value of the regular employee for the firm rises over time with increased work experience. However, because the tasks and jobs within the work group change rapidly, it is difficult to ascertain precisely what that value is at any given time or period for any individual worker. For this reason, it is argued, a general average for the increase in compensation is assumed and is seen as an equitable arrangement both by the employer and the employees. It is not surprising, then, that the 'wage curve' in an enterprise based on age (or length of service, since most regular employees begin at the same age) shows the most rapid gains usually occurring among employees in their early twenties to their mid-forties. That is the period when task and job learning is maximized. The period also parallels the increase in needs arising from marriage and raising a family and in the desire to have a margin for savings, especially to meet costs of living when one is older. If these calculations were done for some other nations, a similar overlapping of learning, earnings and life-cycle needs would probably occur.

Even if one accepts that the preceding paragraph provides an adequate description of the wage mechanism in Japan's large firms, it is an approach to compensation which has little to do with notions of industrial paternalism. It does not flow from non-rational traditions and values such as the practice of reciprocal obligations between superiors and subordinates going back into the feudal period of Japanese history. Rather, it seems to have emerged as a rational response to labour market conditions, in which there was a dire lack of skills and there were few institutions appropriate for training the skilled manpower required to introduce the new and rapidly changing technologies and the concomitant organizations needed for economic and industrial growth. If the seniority wage system is a Japanese solution, it is a solution which was aimed at achieving a massive transition to transform Japan from an agrarian society to an industrial society which had 'caught up with the West'. Under these circumstances, industrial and other modern organizations through which economies of scale could be attained were unable to turn to 'external' labour markets and similar institutions for the skilled manpower and knowledge which was needed. Instead, they had to generate their own human resources *within* their own organizations. To do this enterprises set up an elaborate array of internal training methods on and off the job (Levine and Kawada, 1980: chs V–VIII). Out of this need gradually grew the work-group form of organization at the shop level, the continuous regular employment of a small core of 'key workers', and an array of incentives which included length-of-service compensation and company-level benefits. These practices date essentially from the 1920s, although some examples may be found as early as the 1870s. However, it is only in the postwar period that we can talk about the widespread institutionalization of such practices in a particular set of firms.

It must be stressed again that the seniority wage system, like permanent employment, is found *only* in the large enterprises, public and private. It has not spread to any appreciable degree to the small and medium-scale sectors of the economy. There, for the most part, 'external' labour markets reign, 'internal' training systems hardly exist, and wages and salaries are based more directly on the 'going market value' for the skills employed. Nor does it pertain to the large number of temporary and part-time workers found in most large-scale enterprises.

Even for regular employees in the large-scale enterprises where seniority compensation is supposed to prevail in the most pure form, the system is 'diluted' by a variety of exceptions: group and individual production incentives, various job-related allowances, and promotion based on merit and job content. These elements have resulted from a need to relate to external labour market conditions as well as internal inequities. Not even in Japan, where it is alleged that industrial relations occur within the enterprise, is there an escape from the external forces generated by the general labour market and other aspects of the social milieu.

C Welfare benefits

The highly-touted set of *company-level welfare benefits* in Japan have also been taken frequently as evidence of closed, internalized, enterprise-level industrial relations. Upon close examination (see for example, Koike 1983a) the Japanese case turns out to be nothing unusual. As best as it can be measured, the average level of the monetary value of such benefits – including retirement allowances and pensions, housing, medical care, education, insurance, various kinds of leave, recreation, personnel services and the like – is no higher than that found in most other advanced industrialized economies. This is especially so if we consider the countries of Western Europe. The level is only slightly above that found in America.

Half of the welfare benefits are required by law, principally under the Labour Standards Act adopted in 1947; the remaining benefits provided at the enterprise level are hardly the result of employer paternalism or even generosity; usually they are decided upon through union–management collective bargaining or joint consultation. As occurred with permanent employment and length-of-service compensation, there has been in the postwar period a steady extension of company welfare benefits to the regular blue-collar employees as well as to their white-collar counterparts. Again, this has been primarily in the large-scale enterprises. As Koike (1983a) puts it, there has been a 'white-collarization' of the blue-collar workers. This extension has been the product of labour-union pressure upon management as much as anything else.

In the context of company welfare benefits, one may wonder about the practice of paying large bonuses once or twice a year to all regular employees. In the view of most analysts, however, these are not fringe benefits, but regular, periodical wage payments similar to the monthly wages and salaries which are the base rates for most regular workers in Japan. They too are an important matter for collective bargaining, just like the base monthly rates, and are hardly evidence of some form of employer paternalism or closed family-like companies. That they are recognized as regular, though variable, payments is underlined by the fact that they are officially built into the repayment schemes for many types of loans. Because the amount to be paid as bonuses may fluctuate somewhat, they add flexibility to wage negotiations during the course of the year, and are closely related to the amounts of increases obtained in the bargaining over the 'base-up' in the monthly wage-rate level each spring.

D   Enterprise Unionism

Japan's *enterprise unionism* is often confused with management-dominated or company unionism. However, the enterprise unit is primarily a structural form. Its actions and functions parallel those of unionism elsewhere, whether it be organized on a craft, trade, occupational or industrial basis, or as some mixture of these. Because of the particular economic, technological, political, social, ideological and cultural circumstances of postwar Japan, enterprise unionism emerged, and has remained, as the overwhelming structural basis for the organized labour movement (Levine 1958). It is directed, as unionism is elsewhere, to the security of employment and to advancing the wages and working conditions of its members. Eighty per cent of Japan's 70,000 basic level union organizations and 90 per cent of Japan's 12.5 million union members belong to enterprise-level unions. The great majority are organized in the large-scale public and private sector. The organization rate varies considerably by industry and sector, but is just below 30 per cent of all employees. It should be noted that enterprise unionism is not unique to Japan. Depending on one's definition of the basic unit of union organization, one could argue that perhaps as many as 50 per cent of all American unions have a similar structure.

The majority of enterprise unions in Japan embrace all the regular workers in an enterprise. Blue- and white-collar workers belong to the same enterprise union. Some unions are organized on a plant level, even though the firm may have several plants. Others incorporate employees at all of a firm's several plants.

The logic of this kind of organizational structure was clear from its beginnings in 1945 when General MacArthur and Allied occupation policy called for the rapid unionization of Japan's industrial workers. As one measure for Japan's democratization, unions were seen as a countervailing power against the re-emergence of the oligarchy that had led Japan into the war. Given the prevalence of the internal labour market, described above, effective unionization in most cases had to be at the enterprise level in order to secure employment and provide advancement for workers through the new institutions of collective bargaining and the labour laws. Attempts to organize horizontally in non-existent or weak external labour markets at that time would have doomed the labour movement to an unstable and powerless position in the new social democratic revolution of postwar Japan. Whereas enterprise unionism meant a lack of solidarity for the labour movement as a whole, it proved to be the most effective 'bread and butter' (that is, 'fish and rice') type of organization for forcing management to treat all regular workers equally and equitably within the enterprise itself. Hence, it was attractive both to white-collar and to blue-collar workers within the workplace.

Although the enterprise union may appear to identify closely with the enterprise and may in some cases become prey to management manipulation or become suspect of entering into 'sweetheart' arrangements (which are by no means unique to Japan), it can exert enormous bargaining power *vis-à-vis* the employer. That power can be seen especially when management attempts arbitrarily to discharge or even to lay off regular workers. One explanation for the seemingly low level of work stoppages in Japan, compared with some other countries, may well be the latent power of the enterprise union to compel management to buy peace through assuring employment security and steady advances in compensation and benefits.

Often overlooked in the depiction of enterprise unionism in Japan are the relationships among the enterprise unions themselves. While I will turn to the collective bargaining process more fully below, it is a gross exaggeration to depict union–management relations in Japan as wholly confined within the enterprise. There has been the superficial view, often found in the mass media and popular literature, that the employer and the union in the Japanese company deal with each other in isolation from all other such relationships. Thus, there is the usual reference to 'cultural' explanations emphasizing 'verticalism' or groupism in Japanese society. The assumption, of course, is that units of organization are totally separated from one another and within them there is a hierarchy of tightly knit superior–subordinate relationships that breed intense loyalty to each other. Although there is a modicum of truth in the idea that the enterprise management and the union coalesce in their interests around the continued well-being of the enterprise, neither party is so isolated from their counterparts in other organizational units as to act in such oblivious fashion. As will be noted below, there is much more 'horizontal' coordination than is usually recognized, even of a formal sort through associations and federations, which make Japanese industrial relationships considerably more similar to what exists in other advanced industrialized societies. Within this broader framework, the features which have been singled out for exclusive attention as uniquely Japanese turn out to be less important and less unique than is commonly alleged.

4   What should be emphasized?

The preceding discussion serves to put the common stereotypes of the Japanese system of industrial relations into better perspective. That is an important first step. The next step is to consider numerous other features of equal or even greater importance to our understanding of Japan's industrial relations system at the national level. What are some of these features? In the broader approach to industrial relations systems, four in particular should be emphasized: (1) the highly developed set of laws and legal institutions which have emerged from Japan's postwar social democratic revolution; (2) the labour market structure and labour–management relations in the small and medium-size sector of Japan's industrial economy; (3) the conflicts and disputes that have occurred among organized labour, employers and government around both political and industrial issues; and (4) the role of organized labour and of employer federations in politics as it affects the determination of national economic policies, and especially wage policy. An emphasis on aspects such as these would contribute to balancing the depiction of Japan's industrial relations system. Each is commented on briefly in the paragraphs which follow.

A   Labour law
In the field of *labour law* (cf. Hanami 1979), few countries have developed the comprehensive and detailed legal framework which is found in postwar Japan. Beginning with the Trade Union Act, the Labour Relations Adjustment Act, the Labour Standards Act, the Public Corporation and National Enterprise Labour Relations Adjustment Act, and social security legislation, the legal framework was developed over the years with numerous amendments and supplementary additions as Japan recovered from the wartime

devastation and went on to achieve rapid economic growth and advanced industrialization. For the most part, the basic framework is the product of the reforms initiated by the Allied occupation in the period immediately following Japan's surrender.

More important than the legislation itself, perhaps, is the fact that the laws have been vigorously enforced. The Ministries of Labour and Welfare, among others, as well as such agencies as the labour relations commissions (and even the Japan Institute of Labour in its educational and research activities) have played an important role in assuring that the workers' right to organize unions of their own choosing, their right to engage in collective bargaining, and their right to carry on concerted action including work stoppages (except in the public sector) would be exercised. These bodies have also helped to see that minimal standards of employment would be maintained in a large number of areas. Often overlooked, for example, is the fact that the Labour Standards Law requires employers, including some of the smallest ones, to obtain the reaction of representatives of their employees, even if they are unorganized, before enforcing work rules in the shop. Other prominent examples of regulated behaviour include employment security, health and safety standards, employment of women and minors, minimum wage rates, medical insurance, unemployment compensation, retirement allowances, hours of work, access to leave and holidays. In each case government agencies administer or enforce the rules.

Legislation has served as an important underpinning supporting a vast array of rules which are in place in Japan's system of industrial relations today. The decisions resulting in these provisions are often far removed from the decentralized rule-making at the enterprise level which is emphasized in the conventional treatment of labour–management relations in Japan. They represent a broad social and political concern with equity and individual rights throughout the entire industrial soeicty. Moreover, often there is provision for tripartite consultation and advisory committees with a membership drawn from a wide cross-section of the community. These bodies often play an active role in the interpretation and application of these rules at the enterprise level.

Without recognition of the pervasiveness of this legal framework the analysis of industrial relations in Japan would be sorely deficient. There is nothing particularly unique or secret about this layer of rule-making. The rules in Japan are produced within a democratic framework. Many of the rules, it should also be noted, take their inspiration from the conventions of the International Labour Organization, in which Japan has been an active member for a quarter of a century.

B Small and medium-sized firms in Japan

Also especially neglected in the Japanese case has been the analysis of industrial relations pertaining to *the small and medium-sized firms* which employ at least two-thirds of Japan's non-agricultural labour force. Few of the conditions alleged to be the main features of the Japanese system of industrial relations obtain to any important degree in this sector. There is a dire need for systematic research about industrial relations in the small and medium-sized enterprises,[2] although this is a void that is common to the analysis of industrial relations in many other countries.

The number of small and medium-sized enterprises in Japan runs into the millions. A sizeable proportion consists of one self-employed person and of entrepreneurs who only employ family members. Although this proportion has been steadily declining, the number of small and medium-sized firms has not changed greatly. The existence of this vast sector reflects the 'dualistic' structure of the Japanese economy which became institutionalized in the process of Japan's rapid industrialization.

The characteristics of the labour market and labour relations in Japan's small and medium-size firms are highly diverse, but little resemble those in the large-scale sectors. There is probably much more inter-firm mobility and certainly little evidence of life-time employment, internal training programmes, seniority wages or company welfare benefits. Industrial relations vary according to the level of technology, skill, type of industry, the market and the firm's subcontracting relationship with larger enterprises.

It is also true that few of these small and medium-size firms have been unionized. The unionization rate drops off rapidly as one moves to the smaller enterprises. Where there is unionism, it often takes the form of craft, multiple-shop, or general organization rather than having an enterprise base. On the other hand, the

---

2 One excellent analysis is Koike (1983b). Also see various issues of the English-language monthly, *Japan Labor Bulletin*, which is published by the Japan Institute of Labour, Tokyo.

absence of unionism does not mean unilateral control or traditional paternalism on the part of employers; most of these enterprises are subject to Japan's labour laws, especially the Labour Standards Act. It is not, in my opinion, that workers in these sectors are unaware of their rights to organize. Some of Japan's most troublesome labour disputes occur in the small and medium-size sectors because of the employer's resistance to the efforts of their workers to organize.

The disinterest in formal, legally recognized unionism is probably due less to the difficulties in forming unions than to a belief that unions are not necessary to protect the workers. The chief benefits from wage increases formally bargained collectively in the large-scale sector have tended to 'flow on' to the small- and medium-scale sectors primarily because of competitive pressures in the labour markets. Also, there is undoubtedly a considerable amount of informal collective negotiation within small- and medium-sized enterprises. It is well known that the workers form their own associations or 'friendly clubs' within the small firms for the purpose of presenting a common front to their employer over terms and conditions of work, even though they do not bother to seek to be qualified as legally recognized unions under the procedures provided by the labour-relations commissions. One estimate has found that, if these associations did, in fact, seek to become qualified and certified, the rate of unionization in small firms would probably rise to more than 50 per cent (Koike 1983b: 104). Deterrents to their seeking certification no doubt lie in their ability to obtain improvements without going through the 'red tape' of a labour-relations commission qualifications examination as required by the law for purposes of participating in the selection of labour-relations commission members and commission procedures against employer unfair labour practices.

C   Industrial conflict

Little understood in Japanese industrial relations are the extent and the form of labour–management disputes both in the public and in the private sectors. Overt industrial conflict is not absent in Japan despite the allegations that very little conflict occurs. The long-term record on work days lost until recently shows Japan at the level of France. To be sure, considerable caution must be used in making cross-cultural comparisons because the methods of counting work stoppages and their extent differ from one country to another. The reliability with which the statistics are collected also varies. As in other countries, the actual rates are probably underestimated in Japan. Although the rate of workdays lost has dropped considerably in Japan since 1975 after Japan's rate of economic growth dropped by one-half and the rate of unemployment rose three or four times, it may be predicted that the proportion of stoppages will be on the rise once employment levels stabilize and workers use their organizations to vent frustration and to make their voices heard.

Strike rates in Japan, as elsewhere, are highly variable over time. One should not take short-term trends as indicative of some major change in union–management relationships. Further, conflict may be expressed in ways other than work stoppages, and Japanese unions are as ingenious as unions anywhere in devising tactics and strategies to harass, to pressure and to embarrass employers. The use of the demonstration and even the wearing of 'headbands' and 'armbands' to express protest are among them. Still the highest rates of work stoppages are found among the large-scale firms in the private sector, indicating that union organization is important for carrying out dispute activity (Levine and Taira 1980).

An area of considerable concern within Japan regarding labour–management disputes is the public sector. Here, the unions have been the most militant, the most radical and the most organized. Interestingly, this is true despite their being constrained by laws that seriously restrict their bargaining and strike activities. A long-standing issue in Japan is whether public policy should move in the direction of restoring the right to strike to government employees, a right which was accorded to them (except police, firemen and prison guards) as part of Allied occupation reforms but withdrawn by amendments to the law in the late 1940s and early 1950s following the threat of a general strike which was seen as a challenge to the occupation authorities themselves. Also, it should be noted, this change in policy emerged when the United States sought to rebuild Japan as its most important ally in the Far East as the 'Cold War' began to emerge.

The desire to retrieve the right to strike in Japan's public sector has itself been a major consideration explaining why government employee unions have conducted illegal strikes and protests. Various official commissions and study groups have carefully examined the problem but without any resolution thus far. The entire process has resembled the situation in the United States, where a similar public policy guideline has been debated over the past two decades. In the debates and studies in both countries the questions and issues raised are much the same.

D The political arena

Almost entirely overlooked in Japan's industrial relations system has been the *political role* of organized labour and employer federations. Two major aspects deserve far more attention than they have received because of the usual preoccupation with the enterprise-level relationship. One has to do with the distribution of political power in the governmental sphere. The other has to do with determination of national economic policy, especially in the realm of general wage movements.

It must be remembered that, with the Allied occupation reforms, there was a wholesale shift from oligarchical, elitist political control to democratic competition by sharply opposing political parties. Despite the long sway held by the Liberal Democrats in postwar Japan, the opposition parties – notably the Socialist, Democratic Socialist, Clean Government Party (*Komeitō*), and Communists – have hardly been unimportant. Organized labour has been a staunch supporter of some of the opposition parties. While often sorely divided and unable to overwhelm the ruling Conservative Party, the opposition parties have served to temper government policy in favour of labour. Most fundamentally, they have prevented any amendments to the postwar Constitution which has guaranteed the exercise of basic human and political rights (including labour rights) and they have stood in the way of Japanese remilitarization. The Liberal Democrats have controlled the government at times with only the barest of majorities and would have seriously jeopardized their continuation in power had they blatantly ignored the opposition parties and their organized labour constituents.

On the more practical level of industrial relations, wage determination is hardly a matter confined to the enterprise level. It is largely an affair at the national and industrial level. Organized labour achieves a high degree of coordination among unions, and employers, too, do not act in isolation from one another. The government itself, for fiscal reasons, if nothing else, is also an active participant. These aspects of wage determination are seen mainly in the institution that has emerged since the mid-1950s in the form of the annual Spring Wage Offensive, commonly known as '*shuntō*' or, less commonly, as '*chintō*'. Here, as with other related issues such as the semi-annual bonuses, the retirement allowances and pensions, highly sophisticated strategies to negotiation have been developed and there is wide coordination among the three major actors at the national level. There is also formal multi-employer collective bargaining in the case of the private railways, maritime shipping and still other industries. Informal associations exist in iron and steel, in shipbuilding, in machinery and in electric products (Levine 1984). Key decisions on wages which are made at these levels quickly flow into almost all of the unionized sectors and then onto the non-union sectors. There is also an important linkage between the mediation and arbitration machinery set up for the public sector and negotiations in the private sector. In essence, the whole procedure comprises the making of an annual national wage policy, usually over the course of a few weeks in the months of March, April and May.

In addition to this kind of collective bargaining at the national and industry level, there has also emerged a large set of joint consultation activities at various levels. Not as much is known about this set of activities as should be, but they occur at the national, industrial and enterprise levels. Undoubtedly, however, regularized joint union–management consultation has worked well at the enterprise level in many cases. It probably has served as a means to dispose of worker grievances as they arise, and hence collective agreements do not provide much in terms of formal grievance procedure. Such consultations have also allowed a large amount of information to be exchanged by the parties, and has assisted both parties in narrowing down the issues before engaging in collective bargaining. In the organized sector, joint consultation indicates a reasonable degree of acceptance of unionism at the enterprise level by large-scale employees.

Increasingly, frequent joint consultation has emerged also at the industrial and at the national level, often carried out quite informally with tripartite participation. A notable spread of this activity has been occurring since the late 1960s and has accelerated since the oil crisis in the mid-1970s. Again, this has served not only as an information-sharing process, but also as a means of bridging differences between labour and management over such matters as the amount of the wage increase to be given in the Spring Wage Offensive. A decline in strike activity during *shuntō* in recent years may be attributed in part to the development of joint consultation at these levels. On the other hand, joint consultation has far from displaced collective bargaining itself.

5   Conclusion

Any efforts to corral the emphasis on the stereotypical image of Japanese society and to consider other aspects such as those discussed in the preceding section will serve to provide the observer of Japanese society with a fairly satisfactory view of the complexities of Japan's industrial relations. This is not to suggest that those steps alone will do full justice to depicting the whole of the Japanese system of industrial relations. To go further calls for considerably more research than has been published so far in languages other than Japanese. It would be especially useful if future research sought to incorporate international comparisons.

The aspects I have chosen to bring out seem to indicate that the Japanese system is far more similar to those in other democratic, advanced, market-oriented economies. This does not mean that there can be a wholesale transfer of Japanese industrial relations to other countries or vice versa. However, the system should be examined in its entirety not only for usable ideas but also to gain insights about one's own system.

The tendency to oversimplify the system of industrial relations in Japan is not untypical of the way in which various aspects of modern Japanese society have been commonly treated. This kind of stereotyping seems to occur – whether the focus is politics, economics, social relations or other institutions. Any social institution is highly complex and dynamic; its analysis requires a broader examination and more systematic approach than usually undertaken. Because of its interdisciplinary nature, the study of industrial relations is especially complicated for any country as it deals with a large number of interconnected elements and variables which cut across and draw upon all the social science fields. To grasp the nature of Japanese industrial relations requires no less a comprehensive and systematic treatment than does an understanding of industrial relations in other advanced industrialized societies.

So far, at least in the non-Japanese language literature, such an approach still provides challenges for those seeking to comprehend the institutional arrangements and practices that comprise industrial relations in present-day Japan.

The daily lives of most Japanese, as in other industrially advanced nations, are intimately bound together with work and employing organizations which are at the core of industrialization itself. To characterize their relationships in employment with a few stereotypes of questionable accuracy is to miss by a wide mark the full range of Japanese human experience.

References

Chamberlain, Neil W.; Cullen, Donald E.; and Lewin, David
   1980   *The Labor Sector*, 3rd edn (New York: McGraw Hill). .
Cole, Robert E.
   1979   *Work, Mobility and Participation: a Comparative Study of American and Japanese Industry* (Berkeley, Cal.: University of California Press).
Dunlop, John T.
   1958   *Industrial Relations Systems* (New York: Holt, Rinehart & Winston).
Hanami, Tadashi
   1979   *Labor Law and Industrial Relations in Japan* (Deventer, Netherlands: Kluwer).
Koike, Kazuo
   1983a   'Internal Labor Markets: Workers in Large Firms', in *Contemporary Industrial Relations in Japan*, edited by Taishirō Shirai (Madison, Wis.: University of Wisconsin Press), 29–61.
   1983b   'Workers in Small Firms and Women in Industry', in *Contemporary Industrial Relations in Japan*, edited by Taishirō Shirai (Madison, Wis.: University of Wisconsin Press), 89–115.
Levine, Solomon B.
   1958   *Industrial Relations in Postwar Japan* (Urbana, Ill.: University of Illinois Press).
   1984   'Employers Associations in Japan', in *Employers Association and Industrial Relations: a Comparative Study*, edited by John P. Windmuller and Alan Gladstone (Oxford: Clarendon Press), 318–56.

Levine, Solomon B.; and Kawada, Hisashi
  1980 *Human Resources in Japanese Industrial Development*
  (Princeton, NJ: Princeton University Press).
Levine, Solomon B.; and Taira, Koji
  1980 'Interpreting Industrial Conflict: the Case of Japan', in *Labor
  Relations in Advanced Industrial Societies: Issues and Problems*,
  edited by Benjamin Martin and Everett M. Kassalaw (Washington,
  DC: Carnegie Endowment for International Peace), 61–88.
Mouer, Ross; and Sugimoto, Yoshio
  1986 *Images of Japanese Society* (London: Kegan Paul International).
Ōkōchi, Kazuo; Karsh, Bernard; and Levine, Solomon B. (eds)
  1973 *Worker and Employers in Japan: the Japanese Employment
  Relations System* (Princeton, NJ: Princeton University Press).
Plowman, David; Derry, S.; and Fisher, C.
  1980 *Australian Industrial Relations*, rev. edn (Sydney: McGraw-
  Hill).
Shirai, Taishirō (ed.)
  1983 *Contemporary Industrial Relations in Japan* (Madison, Wis.:
  University of Wisconsin Press).
Shirai, Taishirō; and Shimada, Haruo
  1978 'Japan', in *Labor in the Twentieth Century*, edited by John T.
  Dunlop and Walter Galenson (New York: Academic Press),
  241–322.
Sugimoto, Yoshio
  1981 *Popular Disturbance in Postwar Japan* (Hong Kong: Asian
  Research Service).
  1982 'Japanese Society and Industrial Relations', in *Industrial
  Relations in Japan*, co-authored by Yoshio Sugimoto, Haruo
  Shimada and Solomon B. Levine (Melbourne: Japanese Studies
  Centre), 1–20.

Part Three

Methodological Horizons

Chapter Ten
The *Emic–Etic* Distinction and Its Significance for Japanese Studies

Harumi Befu

1 Introduction

The terms *etic* and *emic* have become part of the standard vocabulary of social science. Although these terms have their intellectual origins in anthropological linguistics, the issues concerning *etic* and *emic* approaches are relevant to the allied social science disciplines. The problems that arise when 'translating' a conceptual framework from one language to another are relevant insofar as these disciplines engage in cross-cultural or comparative research. Because many of the descriptions of Japan are implicitly comparative it is fitting to consider the ramifications of the *emic–etic* distinction and its significance for cross-disciplinary research concerned with understanding Japan both in its own terms and in comparison with other societies. The *emic–etic* distinction concerns not only the question of whether cultures can be compared, but also more fundamental epistemological issues. This chapter explores some major issues raised by the *emic–etic* distinction and identifies some methodological issues which require careful consideration in cross-cultural research.

2   Pike's distinction

The conceptual distinction between *emic* and *etic* was originally formulated by Kenneth L. Pike in a three-volume work (1954, 1955 and 1960) which was revised and published as a single volume in 1967. The two terms were derived from concepts in linguistics, where phon*etics* stands for a universal system of describing the sounds found in the various languages of the world, and phon*emics* refers to the study of the sound system of a given language. Two examples will illustrate the difference between the phonetic and the phonemic approach in linguistics.

In phonetics, a distinction is made between the sound of the aspirated '*p*' as in 'pin' and the sound of the unaspirated '*p*' as in 'stop', and there is a symbol for recording this difference. This is a phonetic distinction. In the English language, however, both these sounds are grouped together as one phoneme (i.e., /*p*/). In other words, English speakers do not subjectively make a distinction between the aspirated and the unaspirated '*p*', although in fact pronounce the '*p*', as in 'pin' and the '*p*' in 'stop' slightly differently. They tend not to be aware of the fact, and both sounds are subjectively grouped together as one and the same sound. The two kinds of '*p*' are said to be 'allophones' of one phoneme. The untutored or casual observer may think that this failure to distinguish between aspirated and unaspirated '*p*' is merely an accident of our writing system, and that the two kinds of '*p*' are in fact distinguished by speakers even though they are written the same way. However, abundant phonological research on English sounds demonstrates that this is not the case. This grouping together of two different kinds of '*p*' has no logical foundation and for our purposes does not need to be explained; it is simply a fact that English-language speakers do not consider the distinction between aspirated and unaspirated '*p*' as significant.

However, when it comes to pronouncing '*l*' and '*r*', it is crucially important for English speakers whether the tip of the tongue touches the area immediately behind the upper teeth (as in the phoneme /*l*/) or whether it curls up slightly without touching the upper palate (as in the phoneme /r/). Although the difference in the sound made in pronouncing 'r' and that in pronouncing 'l' is real and can be verified 'scientifically', the distinction is simply not meaningful to Japanese speakers, and words such as 'lap' and 'wrap' would be heard by Japanese as the 'same' sound. Thus the crucial difference between phonetics and phonemics lies in whether sound description is meant to be merely a description of sound without respect to the 'sense' of the sound held by native speakers of a particular language or to its speech or whether it is to be a system of description which subjectively make sense to the speakers of the language itself.

Pike extended this analytical distinction to non-linguistic cultural phenomena. He used '*etic*' to refer to concepts and systems of classification which could be applied across cultures without reference to the culture's own categories for classifying meaning, and '*emic*' to refer to descriptions of cultural phenomena in terms which make sense to those actually living in a specific culture.

An extended quotation from Pike (1967: 37–9) not only clarifies further the distinction, but also points to its methodological significance:

Units available in advance, versus determined during analysis: Etic units and classifications, based on prior broad sampling or surveys (and studied in training courses) may be available before one begins the analysis of a further particular language or culture. Regardless of how much training one has however, emic units of a language must be determined during the analysis of that language; they must be discovered, not predicted – even though the range of kinds of components of language has restrictions placed upon it by the physiology of the human organism, and these restrictions are to some degree reflected in the events of the observed range of language phenomena.

Creation versus discovery of a system: The etic organization of a world-wide cross-cultural scheme may be created by the analyst. The emic structure of a particular system must, I hold, be discovered. (But here I am assuming a philosophy of science which grants that in the universe some structures occur other than in the mind of the analyst himself. If one adopts a view that no structure of language or culture is present in the universe, except as a theoretical construct created by the analyst, then the paragraph must be restated in a different way, to preserve its usefulness in such a context. Specifically, the linguist who denies structure to a naive sentence or to a sonnet must settle for having his own statements, descriptions, or rules about these phenomena as also being without a publicly available structure or ordering. Linguistic statement comprises a subvariety of language utterance, and hence can have no structure if language has no structure. . . .)

External versus internal view: Descriptions or analyses from the etic standpoint are 'alien' in view, with criteria external to the system. Emic descriptions provide an internal view, with criteria chosen from within the system. They represent to us the view of one familiar with the system and who knows how to function within it himself.

External versus internal plan: An etic system may be set up by criteria or 'logic' plan whose relevance is external to the system being studied. The discovery or setting up of the emic system requires the inclusion of criteria relevant to the internal functioning of the system itself.

Absolute versus relative criteria: The etic criteria may often be considered absolute, or measurable directly. Emic criteria are relative to the internal characteristics of the system, and can be usefully described or measured relative to each other.

Non-integration versus integration: The etic view does not require that every unit be viewed as part of a larger setting. The emic view, however, insists that every unit be seen as somehow distributed and functioning within a larger structural unit or setting, in a hierarchy of units and hierarchy of settings as units.

Sameness and difference as measured versus systemic: Two units are different etically when instrumental measurements can show them to be so. Units are different emically only when they elicit different responses from people acting within the system.

Partial versus total data: Etic data are obtainable early in analysis with partial information. In principle, on the contrary, emic criteria require a knowledge of the total system to which they are relative and from which they ultimately draw their significance.

> Preliminary versus final presentation: Hence, etic data
> provide access into the system – the starting point of
> analysis. They give tentative results, tentative units. The
> final analysis or presentation, however, would be in emic
> units. In the total analysis, the initial etic description
> gradually is refined, and is ultimately – in principle, but
> probably never in practice – replaced by one which is totally
> emic.

Translated into everyday language, *etic* analysis utilizes concepts
or measuring rods which are applicable across cultures. When
concepts such as 'family system', 'urbanization', and the like are
applied cross-culturally, they are used as *etic* concepts. In such
studies it is not important that the people studied in Japan, the
USA, Thailand, Ghana and Australia think of the family in the
same way. To the extent that in all the societies studied there are
social groups which consist of elements that define the concept
(that is, the family) in the same way, we are able to compare them
across cultures.

For Pike and other *emic* analysts such as Goodenough (1970),
however, such research provides only a rough approximation of the
description which is ultimately desired, such as the family system
in each of several cultures. Each system, they would argue, is
culturally unique. It is a subjective experience which is culturally
specific and can be expressed only in *emic* terms. From the
perspective of the *emic* analyst, the *etic* concept of the family
merely enables one to recognize a social unit in its gross and crude
outline, and therefore serves only to provide the social scientist
with a point of departure. This view, then, requires that the *emic*
analyst proceed further to examine the peculiarities of the family
system in each given culture. Here, one discovers that the '*ie*
system' of Japan is vastly different from the 'American family'. It
is this fine-tuned analysis of a given social or cultural unit which
provides meaning to social analysis. For Pike, Goodenough and
other *emic*ists, *etic* analysis merely provides a tool by which one
can arrive at *emic* understanding. By itself, *etic* analysis is not the
objective or goal in learning about other societies or in cross-
cultural research.

In order to understand the functioning of an institution such as
the *ie* system one is necessarily led to analyze its relation to other
subsystems which function within the culture – the economic, the

ecological, the political, the symbolic and so on. It is only by seeing the *ie* system in this total context, the *emic*ist argues, that one can hope to understand the Japanese family system in the *emic* sense. Thus, it is one tenet of the *emic* approach that analysis of a given unit or event is meaningful only if it is done in the context of the larger system of which it is a part, for it is the larger system which gives the unit its peculiar shape and texture. When a given unit is surgically removed from the organic whole of which it is an integral and systemic part, as is often done for the purposes of cross-cultural (*etic*) comparison, it ceases to be a living unit.

3 The *etic–emic* debate

A The *raison d'être* of the *etic* approach

In contrast to the *emic* approach, the proponents of *etic* analysis point out that in linguistics itself (from which Pike derived the concepts), 'language universals' are important phenomena. For example, there are features which are common to all languages (for example, the distinction between vowels and consonants), and there are features of languages which are discoverable only through comparison (such as that there are a finite and relatively small number of phonemes). Greenberg (1957: 86–9) argues that these studies of language universals constitute legitimate social enquiry. They enable us to probe questions concerning the nature of human language, which is a legitimate interest, though quite different from that of describing each specific language. Moreover, such an approach often leads to questions never asked in the analysis of a given language. Why, for example, as Greenberg asks, are there a greater number of historically distinct languages in the world which use prefixing than those which adopt suffixing? Or, why do most languages have around thirty to forty phonemes and not 100 or more? Thus, *etic* analysts would argue, the *etic* approach has its own rationale and its own objectives entirely separate from those of the *emic* approach. Neither can be said to be more legitimate than the other. Nor can either be said to be merely a tool for the other.

Greenberg's arguments are not limited to linguistic phenomena. Cross-cultural research poses questions in many areas which are relevant only as cross-cultural questions. What are the upper and lower limits on the number of kinship terms which will be used in addressing kinsmen and kinswomen? Why in all societies do people seek supernatural answers and solutions to natural questions and problems? One cannot tackle these problems by examining a single case, since the relevance of the problem is cross-cultural. Still, it should be remembered that even in *etic* analysis, the units of analysis must be properly defined so that they can be translated or operationalized into the appropriate *emic* vocabulary which exists in each culture.

B   *Emic*ists' critique of *etic* generalizations

*Emic*ists retort by saying that cultural concepts are unique and that they make sense only in their own cultural context. Accordingly, they argue that any attempt to equate an *emic* concept in one culture with that in another is futile.

Thus, even if a *mikan* is a tangerine, the social meanings of the two words are quite different. For this reason jokes about tangerines which are funny in Japan may not be funny in America.

To take another example, we might consider religion, which is generally regarded as a universal phenomenon by *etic*ists. But what happens when we try to compare views on religion in Japan with views on religion in another culture? In 1980 NHK conducted a survey in Japan and in the USA (NHK Hōsō Yoron Chōsasho 1981). The 'same' questions were asked, as the English version was simply translated from the Japanese version. Question 22 of this questionnaire asks, in the Japanese version, whether the respondent believes in the existence of (1) *kami*, (2) *shigo no sekai*, (3) *tengoku*, (4) *jigoku*, (5) *reikon*, (6) *akuma*. In the English version, these entities are rendered as (1) God, (2) life after death, (3) heaven, (4) hell, (5) a soul, and (6) the devil. One immediately notes that, in the Japanese version, the entity *hotoke* is missing. In asking about the religiosity of Japanese, the omission of a question concerning belief in the existence of *hotoke* is egregious. Also, *tengoku* is meaningful to Japanese Christians, but not to Buddhists who would aspire to go to *gokuraku*, rather than to *tengoku* (which is the Christian heaven). The gross distortions in translation, or in attempts to translate directly (*chokuyaku*) rather than in terms of the meaning (*iyaku*), may perhaps be blamed for part of the problem. But a question remains as to whether by improving the translation, one can indeed discover whether the religiosity of the Japanese is comparable to that of Americans.

For example, even if all Americans believed in God and all Japanese believed in *hotoke*, can we conclude that Americans and Japanese are just as 'religious'? Is belief in *hotoke* the 'same thing' as belief in God? The answer is not likely to be in the affirmative.

C 'Back translation': an *etic*ist solution to linguistic uniqueness

Among certain *etic*ists there is a strong belief that the problem of cultural uniqueness as manifested in *emic* concepts can be overcome by improving translation. Brislin (1976), for example, proposes a method of 'decentering', whereby 'material in one language is changed so that there will be a smooth, natural-sounding version in the second language. The result of decentering contrasts with the awkward, stilted versions common when material in one language is taken as the final content that must be translated with minimal change into another language' (p. 222). Equivalence is achieved by translating questionnaires back and forth between the languages until some kind of neutral statement is constructed which can be translated from one language to the other with a minimal amount of distortion.

D The *emic*ist's first retort

Brislin cites an English sentence (p. 222) which was translated to Chamorro, the native language of Guam and the Marianas Islands: 'I don't find it particularly difficult to get along with loud-mouthed, obnoxious people.' The Chamorro version is not given, but the English language version that finally resulted after 'decentering' is as follows: 'It is not hard for me to talk with people who have a big mouth.' One wonders how the 'decentered' sentences would evolve as the number of languages (that is, the number of comparisons) were increased. Presumably, a study involving ten cultures would require that each question be 'decentered' at least ninety times if the original statement was translated only once from each language into each of the other nine languages. Imagine a questionnaire on religious practices and beliefs administered in fifty different languages, including Japanese, where 'decentered' questions in Japanese would have to be constructed and properly 'decentered' with regard to forty-nine other languages. It seems highly improbable that a Japanese sentence properly 'decentered' in relation to English will also be properly 'decentered' in relation to say, a Hindu language. It is doubtful whether a single Japanese sentence can be found which will be properly 'decentered' for all forty-nine languages.

E The *emic*ist's second retort

*Emic*ists would also argue that Brislin's proposal misses the point about the uniqueness of each language in its semantic domain. No matter how one might rephrase the statement, one cannot eliminate the uniqueness of the meaning inherent in each language. Thus, as long as different languages are used to elicit responses, informants are responding to different stimuli, no matter how similar the statements in the two languages might look in translation.

To give a simple example, the Japanese concept of '*on*' may be translated as '*debt*' or '*indebtedness*' in English. But '*on*' singularly lacks the monetary connotation which the English terms include. '*On*' implies certain social relationships such as the parent–child, teacher–student, or employer–employee relationship, and it evokes a feeling that one is associating with Japan's feudal or traditional values. When Japanese are asked to think of '*on*', they think of all these and more. When Americans think of 'debt', none of these connotations are central, though Americans may have some sense of social indebtedness. Thus, the use of '*on*' in Japanese and 'debt' as its English equivalent would likely lead to erroneous conclusions. Much the same can be said of questionnaires asking about the existence of *kami* in Japanese and about the existence of God in English.

Etic analysts argue that it is possible and meaningful to compare differing concepts between two cultures and to comprehend the similarities and differences. It is highly enlightening, they insist, to know how *on* and indebtedness compare or contrast as concepts in the respective semantic domains. One question *etic*ists ask is whether any concept in one language or culture can be identical semantically to a concept in another language or culture. However, since answers to this question will depend heavily on the use of language and on the social meanings of linguistic expressions, as long as different languages are used in different cultural contexts, the *emic*ists argue that semantic significance will necessarily differ between two languages/cultures.

4   Some further aspects of *etic* analysis

A   The non-linguistic approach of *etic*ists

The *etic*ists' strategy is to transcend this linguistic barrier and work in a domain which is free of interference from semantics. Thus, a category called 'the family' or a concept known as 'stratification' is defined operationally by *etic*ists in such a way as to minimize semantic interpretation. The researcher presumably observes, for example, the agricultural activities of farmers: how long they work the land, how many calories of energy they expend and consume, and how much of which crops they harvest. These are observations of objectively measurable phenomena, and the data can be compared across cultures without *emic* interference. Marvin Harris's proposal (1964) for *etic* investigation is precisely for that type of comparison.

B   *Etic* approach to universals

*Etic*ists are no doubt concerned with universal phenomena and processes. If mankind is one and all *Homo sapiens* share some common characteristics, there should be some common social, cultural and psychological manifestations of that fact. *Etic*ists are driven to prove that hypothesis. But their demonstration seems to run into difficulties. As Geertz has pointed out (1971: ch. 2), we do not see religion in the *etic* sense in every society. What we see is a variety of human experiences which *etic*ists like to characterize as 'religious'. The question is: what licence do they have in grouping everything from Zen meditation through pentecostal speaking in tongues to Balinese cris-stabbing as belonging to one and the same conceptual category called 'religion', except by deciding *a priori* what religion means?

The problem with proving universality is that one exception will ruin the case. Accordingly, any Baconian attempt at generalization from empirical observation to arrive at universals is hopeless. It is enough to remember that there are more cultures which have become extinct in the past million years of human cultural history than those which are now extant. Even if all living cultures share a certain common feature which we abstract as 'religion', we still do not know if this feature was present in the cultures which have become extinct or in those which will come into existence in the future.

C   Implicit *etic*ist imperialism

With its avowed avoidance of language as a means of analyzing data, the *etic* approach must ultimately fail for another reason. *Etic*ists are not Zen philosophers who can make their ultimate point by asking you to stare at a circle; they are necessarily committed to the use of language in its discourse. Harris (1976) recommends for the *etic* approach not to use language and its meaning (that is, verbal testimony of informants) as data to deal with, but instead to rely on direct observation. However, Harris cannot rid himself of some language as a tool of analysis; in fact, language is an essential tool for *etic*ists.

The semantic structure of whatever language that is used as the tool of analysis will necessarily dominate the intellectual processes of *etic* analysis. If English is to be used as the tool of analysis, English concepts like 'behaviour', 'democracy', 'symbols' and 'the individual', with all their implied semantic domains, will be elevated from being mere words to being analytical tools. Even when these terms are very carefully defined, the discourse still remains as a discourse in the English language as long as the defining terms are also in English. While not trusting *emic* definition of words as a basis for classifying data, and therefore shying away from using such descriptive labels, *etic*ists declare that a language can be elevated beyond suspicion and serve as a scientific tool. This author disagrees fundamentally with Pike in this respect. Pike (1954: 37) asserts that etic concepts are available to us *a priori*, whereas *emic* data must be discovered. However, this author would argue that etic concepts too were originally constructed *a posteriori* no less than more recently 'discovered' *emic* concepts.

This example raises the fundamental issue of whether or not there can possibly be a universal *etic* system which transcends the problems discussed thus far. Inasmuch as some language – with all its semantic (*emic*) implications – must be used for *etic* analysis, it seems logically impossible to have a universal, objective (*etic*) framework of analysis which can yield unbiased results from cross-cultural research. Short of inventing a meta-language which transcends the culture-bound limitations of the 'natural' languages, this goal cannot be achieved. But a meta-language of this sort cannot be invented, since its invention and the resultant meta-language must depend on the use of a natural language and will thus be 'contaminated' by that language.

As an example to demonstrate the culture-bound nature of what is, for *etic*ists, seemingly universal, take the concept of the 'individual'. In Western social science, the individual is assumed to be the basic building block of the society. Hamaguchi (1977), however, echoes Hsu (1975) in declaring that the analysis of social phenomena in Japan should not start from the concept of the individual, but instead should begin with relationships between persons because that is how the Japanese conceptualize social phenomena. In short, Hamaguchi argues that the concept of the individual, so important to Western social scientists, is culture-bound. He claims it is not a scientific (*etic*) tool of analysis, but an ethnocentric, Western, *emic* concept misapplied to other cultures as if it were an *etic* concept. He suggests that we leave the concept of the individual as an *emic* concept for the analysis of Western cultures, and that we devise different concepts for analyzing other cultures.

The implications of Hamaguchi's position are vast. If the concept of the individual is culturally bound, then, *mutatis mutandis*, a good many of the other concepts cherished by social scientists (concepts such as 'society', 'social group', 'sovereignty' and 'social stratification', to mention but a few) may also be culturally bound. In short, what Western social scientists are doing is not discovering universal processes applicable across cultures; instead, they are trying to see to what extent Western *emic* concepts can be used as a framework for understanding non-Western social and cultural phenomena. At a rather crude level, for example, one often hears that Japan is not a true democracy. What is often meant is that the Japanese political system diverges from the US system. That is, US democracy is taken as the prototype (that is, the *etic* measuring rod) against which another polity is compared.

As we become more sophisticated and relativistic, we try to avoid such easy pitfalls. Yet, this attempt to create a relativistic concept does not solve the problem as long as one continues to rely on English (or Japanese) in his or her attempts. As long as one's own language is used as the scientific tool, one cannot transcend the problem of non-comparability which *etic*ists criticize *emic*ists for. However, elevating English from being a mere object language for describing ideas in a specific culture to being a meta-language to analyze all other languages and cultures is to arrogate mere English words as God-given truths. The same would also be true of such attempts in any other of the other hundreds of languages which exist. Such attempts represent a kind of intellectual imperialism.

5 *Emic*ists' problem with language

The *emic*ists also have their difficulties. Since words are often the key to identifying and understanding unique cultural concepts, the *emic* approach tends toward the analysis of the meanings of words. Componential analysis of kinship terms, which swept through social anthropology in the 1950s and 1960s, illustrates well the *emic* approach. Kinship terms of a given culture were analyzed into their component 'meanings', which indicated distinctions according to age, generation, sex, collaterality and so on. Each kin term was defined by contrasting the components of one against the components of the other terms.

Later the same basic methodology came to be applied to cultural phenomena other than kinship, and the approach came to be called 'ethnoscience' or 'formal ethnography'. Working out the native systems of classification for colours, plants, and animals became a favourite parlour game of *emic*ists. From these rather rigidly defined categories, *emic*ists moved to less well-defined phenomena which included events such as entering a house or asking for a drink (Frake 1964, 1975).

As Goodenough (1970) suggests, however, the reports written by the *emic* analysts confront a major problem. Ethnographic (that is, *emic*) description is a matter of reporting on the culture of a group in such a way that the reader from another culture (and language) will understand the culture being described. If one were to report on the Truk culture to Americans, as Goodenough did so well, the reporting must be done in English. This requires that Truk cultural concepts be 'translated' and made comprehensible in terms of American cultural concepts.

At this point *emic* analysis is no longer merely a matter of understanding the concepts of another culture on their own terms. Such 'understanding' is only the first necessary step. Such understanding does not become an ethnographic description until it is verbally reported. And this reporting usually is for the benefit of outsiders. Accordingly, reporting must be adjusted according to the language and culture of the audience receiving the report.

Thus, the Japanese concept of vertical relationship would have to be reported to Americans in one way and to Germans in an entirely different way. Reporting it to the Japanese themselves would require still another mode of communication.

If this is the case, the accuracy of ethnographic (that is, *emic*) reporting is questionable in so far as the reporting occurs in different linguistic/cultural contexts. *Emic*ists here seem to run into a solipsistic *cul-de-sac*.

There is an additional problem for the *emic* approach. The best way to understand a cultural concept in its own terms is to understand it entirely in the original language and in the total cultural context. Translation of the concept and its analysis into another language should be avoided since any attempt to characterize a cultural concept in another language is likely to distort the *emic* reality. But since the purpose of ethnographic description is to render a cultural concept understandable to a foreign audience, description must be given in a foreign language. In doing so one must use concepts in the foreign language as descriptors. Even if none of them are regarded as '*etic*' concepts, their use results in implicit comparisons being made. It is not easy, for example, to talk about the Japanese *ie* in English without using such terms as the 'family' or the 'household'. Although one might retain the Japanese term *ie* and dispense with English terms for that particular concept, one must still describe other components of the *ie* and is forced somewhere along the line to resort to expressions like 'father' and 'mother' to identify statuses within the *ie*. Thus, *emic*ists cannot completely get away from the use of English concepts. Even if their goal may be to dispense with *etic* tools entirely, they are still bound by having to use a foreign language to report on the *ie* system, and thus cannot help but introduce distortions into their descriptions. If they cannot rid themselves of the *etic* framework altogether, *emic*ists are in bad straits, for they are in the double bind of suffering from the problems inherent in the *emic* approach and then also from those inherent in the *etic* approach.

There is a further problem with the *emic* approach. Because of their heavy reliance on linguistic data, *emic*ists tend to overlook cultural concepts which are not crystallized into a linguistic expression. One has often heard, for example, Americans say that Japanese do not have the concept of privacy, as evidenced by awkward translations given in Kenkyūsha's *New English–Japanese*

Dictionary. The first translation it gives is *inton*, which in Ken-kyūsha's *Japanese–English Dictionary* back-translates as 'retire-ment', but which might be better rendered as 'hermit-like seclusion'. The second meaning given for 'privacy', in the *New English–Japanese Dictionary* is 'hito me o sakeru koto' (avoidance of being seen by others).

Neither of these two translations is near the mark. Does this mean that Japanese traditionally lacked any sense of privacy? Of course not; the sense of privacy manifested by Japanese families is indeed at least as great as that shown by American families. But the American concept of privacy extends to the handling of documents and records pertaining to a private person. That realm of meaning was not associated with Japanese notions of privacy until the 1970s. Lacking an appropriate expression in their own language, Japanese adopted a transliteration of the English term 'privacy' (*puraibashii*) which they felt corresponded to the Amer-ican concept. No doubt it will not take long before the Japanese term *puraibashii* will assume a life of its own and its meaning will grow and change. There are thus many analyses in which the *emic*ist's focus on linguistic terms has blinded the analyst to non-linguistic phenomena which are none the less culturally important.

6 Other issues

A Prediction

Although one of the aims of the *emic* approach is to predict behaviour, it is often criticized for its inability to predict human behaviour. 'Scientifically minded colleagues' insist that predictions can be made only by constructing a generalized theory of behaviour and then deducing hypotheses in which a particular set of cultural behaviour can be seen as a class fitting that hypothesis. *Emic*ists claim that they specify the particular cultural context in which a given type of behaviour is likely to appear. Once the conditions under which a person calls another by a given kinship term or under which a person requests a drink are specified, for example, one can then predict occurrence of certain behaviour by reference either to the use of kinship terms or to the patterns followed in requesting a drink. While *etic*ists claim that their hypotheses would do the same, *emic*ists argue that their predictions are more accurate because they are able to specify the conditions under which a particular event or behaviour pattern occurs in *culturally meaningful terms* rather than in *etic* terms, which never give a very precise cultural 'fit'.

*Etic*ists may not be able to provide culturally meaningful predictions in a given cultural setting as well as *emic*ists, but they are likely to excel in predicting behaviour which does not depend on verbal symbols. Moreover, only *etic* predictions are possible in cross-cultural comparisons.

B   Generalizations and the *emic*ists' assumption of homogeneity

While *etic*ists are concerned with identifying universal phenomena and with making cross-cultural or multi-cultural generalizations, *emic*ists generalize about whole societies. A basic assumption in the *emic* approach is that cultures are homogenous. *Emic*ists speak of 'colour classification among the x people' or 'how to enter a Yakan house'. In doing so they tend to assume that all members of the culture share a uniform cognitive system (for example, that all Yakans observe the same set of rules regarding entering a house).

This assumption is more tenuous in dealing with more complex and stratified societies, and is a major source of difficulty in many analyses of Japanese society and culture. Of course, this raises the question of representativeness; on what basis are such *emic* features as consensus-oriented decision-making, the emphasis on the group or certain aesthetic concepts (such as *wabi, shibumi* or *mono no aware*) chosen as being typically Japanese? The claim of Japan's uniqueness is often made on the assumption that the Japanese population is homogeneous and that all Japanese equally share features such as those just mentioned. Herein lies a major weakness of the *emic* approach: no culture is completely homogeneous. As a highly industrialized society, Japanese culture is particularly variegated, and one cannot assume that all Japanese share equally all features of 'Japanese culture'. Given the diversity of 100 million Japanese with different educations, with different class backgrounds and with different work experiences, this should not be surprising.

The weakness of the *emic* approach is the strength of the *etic* approach, which is explicit in its use of quantitative analysis to describe a culture. *Etic*ists can define cultural phenomena in terms of means, modes and central tendencies. They are not required to characterize a culture in uniform terms, but can describe internal diversity in statistical terms.

7   The relevance of *emic* and *etic* approaches for the study of Japan

In the light of the the above discussion, how might one make use of *etic* and *emic* approaches in studying Japan? If the preceding summary is correct, neither the *etic* nor *emic* approach is foolproof: both have inescapable methodological shortcomings, which might persuade one not to engage either in purely *etic* or in purely *emic* activities. Such methodological strait-jacketing, however, will not help advance knowledge. Imperfection of any method is as commonly accepted in empirical science as inevitable. As long as we are not engaged in the impossible task of pursuing 'ultimate truths', and as long as we are aware of the imperfections in each approach, we are in a good position to take advantage of both approaches.

Within the framework of *etic* and *emic* analyses, it would appear that the proponents of *Nihon bunkaron* (or *Nihonjinron*) are *emic*ists who have been concerned only with elucidating the unique aspects of Japan. No doubt each culture is unique: *emic*ists have made contributions in elaborating on the nature of the uniqueness of each culture. *Nihonjinron* writers have, as *emic*ists, done just that. Their contributions, in so far as their analysis is correct, should be recognized for what they are. For example, when Doi (1973) shows how the concept of *amae* is used in describing interpersonal relations not only between mother and child but also in many other relations, and how it is related to a series of other concepts (such as *amayakasu, suneru* and *hinekureru*), he is indeed demonstrating the uniqueness of '*amae*' as an *emic* concept.

This fact, however, should not deter us from recognizing the *etic* approach to Japan as an equally valid endeavour. The dependency of children on adults, and particularly on mothers while in their infancy, is a universal phenomenon. The Japanese pattern of this dependency can and should be compared with that in other cultures, which on the one hand would elucidate the differences and unique aspects of the Japanese pattern and on the other would point to those aspects which are common to other cultures.

Let me illustrate with another example: gift-giving, which has ramifications for virtually all aspects of life in Japan (cf. Befu). Gift-giving in Japan falls into one or the other of two categories: formal or informal. The formal gift has a distinct, prescribed kind of wrapping paper called *noshigami*, and is either tied with a special kind of ribbon call *mizuhiki* or has the ribbon printed on the wrapping paper (thereby dispensing with the need of a separate ribbon, a shortcut used with less expensive gifts). Informal gifts by definition have no such trappings. They are, for example, morsels of food that you might take to a neighbour to share, or a cigarette you might offer your friend in a coffee shop. These two categories of gifts are sharply distinguished in Japan. Occasions for giving formal gifts are well prescribed in terms of holidays and important occasions in the life cycle (such as birth, entrance to school, marriage and death). Informal gifts are given on other unprescribed occasions. These two types of gifts correlate with other cultural categories such as *hare/ke*, *ōyake/watakushi*, and *omote/ura*. In other words, formal gifts are given on occasions of *hare* (sacred or religious occasions), and informal gifts on occasions of *ke* (secular occasions). Formal gifts belong to the domain defined as *ōyake* ('the public, or communal'), whereas informal gifts belong to the domain of *watakushi* ('the private'). Formal gifts, with all the trappings of the wrapping paper and ribbon, belong to the *omote* ('front') part of the social life, and informal gifts to the *ura* ('back') part.

Certain changes are taking place in Japan with respect to the meaning of some of these terms, and with these changes, the meaning of the formal/informal gift is also changing. For example, *hare* used to be restricted to holidays or sacred occasions, and a whole life style was associated with it, including special clothes, special food and a basic religious disposition. Also, one did not work on days of *hare*. Formal gift-giving was part and parcel of the set of prescribed activities. As the society became more and more secular in modern times, however, the behavioural patterns associated with *hare* occasions could be found on non-*hare* (that is, *ke*) occasions. Gift-giving has followed the same course, and formal gifts (namely, gifts with the special wrapping and ribbon) are nowadays often given on non-formal and secular occasions as well as on sacred occasions. At the same time, what once was considered sacred (*hare*) is now sometimes not so regarded, the mid-year *chūgen* and the end-of-the year *seibo* are formal gift-giving occasions, but few gift-givers associate such gift-giving with the sacredness of the occasions. Moreover, new secular occasions such as entrance to school have been added to the category as occasions for which formal gift-giving is appropriate. The above ethnographic snippet of gift-giving in Japan is an *emic* rendition of the phenomenon. As a complex of related phenomena and related concepts, and as an integral part of a set of cultural concepts, this analysis makes sense only in *emic* terms.

However, it is, of course, entirely possible to compare gift-giving in Japan with that in another culture. One may compare, for example, the frequency of gift-giving. One may also compare appropriateness of specific gifts for given occasions, considering as criteria the value of gifts for different occasions, and for different kinds of relationships between the giver and the intended receiver. For each of these and other categories of information we can make a point-by-point comparison in an *etic* fashion, and such an analysis might yield information on the relative importance of gift-giving in the two societies in terms of the frequency of gift-giving or the total value of gifts given or received. By analyzing to whom gifts are given and from whom they are received, light might be thrown on the similarities and differences of social relations. The prevalence, for example, of gift-giving between social inequals (as occurs in Japan) might help to indicate the nature of social hierarchy in one society as against that in another society in which such hierarchical gift-giving is absent or much less prevalent. All of this is good, legitimate *etic* analysis.

The illustrations above can be multiplied many times with any number of other social practices and customs. While our understanding of Japan increases as we engage in *emic* analysis and learn of its unique aspects, at the same time *etic* comparisons help us to discover how Japan is part of humanity. Which of the two approaches one would choose depends on the particular problem or topic at hand, and can not be predetermined. Used properly, each can yield significant results and help deepen our understanding of Japan as well as contribute to building social theory.

References

Befu, Harumi
  1984 'Bunka-teki Gainen Toshiteno "Zōtō" no Kōsatsu' (An Analysis of *Zōtō* as a Cultural Concept), in *Nihonjin no Zōtō* (Gift-giving among the Japanese), edited by M. Itō and Y. Kurita (Kyoto: Minerva Shobō), 18–44.
Brislin, Richard W.
  1976 'Comparative Research Methodology: Cross-Cultural Studies', *International Journal of Psychology*, vol. 11, no. 3, 215–29.
  1980 'Translation and Content Analysis of Oral and Written Materials', in *Handbook of Cross-Cultural Psychology*, edited by Harry C. Triandis and John W. Berry, vol. 2. (Boston, Mass.: Allyn & Bacon), 389–444.
Doi, Takeo
  1973 *The Anatomy of Dependence* (Tokyo: Kodansha International).
Frake, Charles O.
  1964 'How to Ask for a Drink in Subanun'. A special issue of *The American Anthropologist* on 'The Ethnography of Communication', edited by John Gumperz and Dell Hymes, vol. 66, no. 6, part 2, 127–32.
  1975 'How to Enter a Yakan House', in *Sociocultural Dimensions of Language Use*, edited by Mary Sanches and Ben G. Blount (New York: Academic Press), 25–40.
Goodenough, Ward H.
  1970 *Description and Comparison in Cultural Anthropology* (Chicago: Aldine).
Greenberg, Joseph
  1957 *Essays in Linguistics* (Chicago, Ill.: University of Chicago Press).
Hamaguchi, Esyun
  1977 *Nihon Rashisa no Saihakken* (Rediscovering the Essence of Japan) (Tokyo: Nihon Keizai Shinbunsha).
Harris, Marvin
  1976 'History and Significance of the Emic–Etic Distinction', in *Annual Review of Anthropology*, edited by Bernard J. Seigal, Alan R. Beals and Stephen A. Tyler, vol. 5, 329–50.
  1964 *The Nature of Cultural Things* (New York: Random House).
  1968 'Emics, Etics, and the New Ethnography', *The Rise of Anthropological Theory* (New York: Crowell), ch. 20.
Hsu, Francis L. K.
  1975 *Iemoto: the Heart of Japan* (New York: Schenkman).
Naroll, Raoul; Michik, Gary L; and Naroll, Frada
  1980 'Holocultural Research Methods', in *Handbook of Cross-*

cultural Psychology, edited by Harry C. Triandis and John W. Berry, vol. 2 (Boston, Mass.: Allyn & Bacon), 479–521.

NHK Hōsō Yoron Chōsasho
1981 *Nichi-Bei Hikaku Chōsa: Kekka no Gaiyō* (A Survey of Americans and Japanese: a Summary of the Results) (Tokyo: Nippon Hōsō Shuppan Kyōkai).

Pelto, Pertti J.
1970 'Units of Observation: Emic and Etic Approaches', in *Anthropological Research: the Structure of Inquiry* (New York: Harper & Row) ch. 4.

Pike, Kenneth
1954 *Language in Relation to a Unified Theory of the Structure of Human Behavior (Part I)*, preliminary edn (Glendale, Cal.: Summer Institute of Linguistics).
1955 *Language in Relation to a Unified Theory of the Structure of Human Behavior (Part II)*, preliminary edn (Glendale, Cal.: Summer Institute of Linguistics.
1960 *Language in Relation to a Unified Theory of the Structure of Human Behavior (Part III)*, preliminary edn (Glendale, Cal.: Summer Institute of Linguistics).
1967 *Language in Relation to a Unified Theory of the Structure of Human Behavior*, 2nd rev. edn (The Hague: Mouton).

Tatje, T. A.
1970 'Problems of Concept Definition for Comparative Studies', in *A Handbook of Method in Cultural Anthropology*, edited by R. Naroll and R. Cohen (New York: Natural History Press), 689–96.

Chapter Eleven

The Role of Typologies in Understanding Japanese Culture and Society: from Linguistics to Social Science*

J. V. Neustupný

1 Introduction

Any system of knowledge is characterized by the search for interdependence among various individual phenomena which together constitute the object of enquiry. In this chapter sets of interdependent phenomena are referred to as 'types'. Since various features of sociocultural processes occur at the same time within the same system, it would be surprising if they were unrelated. However, it is equally unlikely that all structural traits could be

* The author of this chapter is indebted to Ross Mouer and Yoshio Sugimoto for comments which greatly exceed the normal editorial duties. If any omissions or errors remain, they are solely my own responsibility. As far as the main thrust of this paper is concerned, my debt to Vladimír Skalička will be obvious. I wish to dedicate to him this paper which contains little that I have not learned from him.

accounted for by a single general principle. The typological approach to culture and society must take account of both these basic assumptions.

The principle of typology, long discussed in linguistics (cf. Skalička 1979; C. Lehmann 1983), is not alien to social science. In a paper presented at the 1977 meeting of the American Anthropological Society, Harumi Befu (1980) outlined an 'alternative model' of Japanese society. His framework was built around three components. The first was the 'group model' which prevailed in the 1950s. In Befu's system it remains restricted to ideology. Second was the 'exchange model', applicable to social behaviour. The third component was the '*seishin* model', used to account for an individual's motivation to act in a particular way (Befu 1980).

Each of Befu's components claims in fact the existence of a different *general principle* which underlies the multiplicity of behaviour in each area: the group principle in ideology, the exchange principle in social behaviour, and the *seishin* principle in the individual's motivation. Each of these principles is seen as governing, in its own area of applicability, a number of features. This, clearly, represents a typological approach, an attempt to establish the interdependence of various socio-cultural features. In addition to each of the components containing a 'type' in the sense of this chapter, the three components are conceived as related and often going hand-in-hand. For instance, an individual claiming to act in the interests of a group (as prescribed by the ideological component) can at the same time actually serve his own self-interests (that is, exchange resources he desires for other resources), with the stress created in the situation being resolved through the individual's previous training in endurance (namely, the *seishin* component). In this example the three general principles coincide in the same behaviour. However, if it is true that the three components are interrelated, one can posit the existence of another, more general, higher-level principle which governs all three components. All three components can thus be considered as a single set of interrelated features, a 'type'. The fact that the general principles do not determine in detail all features of each component should not worry us. Many principles of conduct are not categorically binding: they apply in a variable way, sometimes dependent on particular conditions, sometimes not (cf. Labov 1972).

Sugimoto and Mouer combined Befu's second component with

a consistent regard for variation, translated the framework into a sociological idiom and further developed it (Sugimoto and Mouer 1982, Mouer and Sugimoto 1986). They also provided a list of resources (income, power, information and prestige) and variables, called 'agents of stratification' (such as gender, age, residence, education, industry, occupation and size of enterprise) which are seen as accounting for the distribution of resources. Individuals or groups maintain their access to resources by exercising control in four different ways: through coercion, through utilitarian manipulation, through distortion, or the management of symbols. The basic principle of self-interest which leads individuals to establish or to maintain control over resources is similar to Befu's exchange model. The Sugimoto and Mouer model assumes thus the existence of a broad (typological) principle which governs a large number of social processes.

Both Befu's and Sugimoto and Mouer's models provide frameworks of considerable usefulness for those who wish to develop further the contemporary paradigm of the study of Japan (cf. Neustupný 1982a). Moreover, although the proponents of these models do not explicitly state the fact, they show an interest in questions concerning the interdependence of socio-cultural traits, and hence in the nature of *typology*.

Since typology has frequently been equated with holism, this claim may seem to be contradicted by Mouer and Sugimoto's frequent anti-holistic statements. However, I believe that their attack is directed against particular types of holistic schemes and does not concern the typological principle as such. In *Images of Japanese Society* (1986) the term 'holism' is used to refer to 'an approach which assumes that societies represent the major cognitive unit for analysis, that they have goals, ends and purposes which form the dominant components of the mechanism accounting for individual motivation, and that they are characterized by a high degree of consensus which means that variants in behavior may best be understood as "deviant behavior"' (Mouer and Sugimoto 1986: 22).

The approach discussed in this chapter differs significantly from the concept of holism as set up by Sugimoto and Mouer. First, typology assumes that there are networks of features which are governed by the same general principle, but does not imply that *all* features of a culture or a society are governed in this way. The tendency to establish Japan as a totality, to paint an all-embracing portrait of Japanese culture and society in a single colour, is absent from the typological approach. Second, the general principle which governs a type frequently generates new principles and rules of a lower order, and socio-cultural features. However, the way in which a principle works itself out in concrete terms is shaped by a number of factors. One certainly cannot speak of the most general principle as a 'goal' towards which the whole of the system will or should drift. Typology is free of teleology of any kind. Third, rather than explaining variation in behaviour as 'deviant behavior', contemporary typologies accept the coexistence of a number of types within a single system. It is the existence of these various 'types' that leads to variation and conflict.

Of course, it is necessary to admit that some historical typologies happened to be holistic in the sense described by Mouer and Sugimoto. However, not all typologies are holistic in this sense. While rejecting theories of Japanese society which are holistic in trying to explain *all* phenomena with one single principle, we must – as Sugimoto and Mouer argue – be careful not to lose the positive, while refuting the negative features of such theories.

In this chapter I wish to develop in some detail a number of ideas which seem to be implied but not explicitly discussed in many anthropological and sociological approaches to Japan. It should be noted that while the starting point was anthropology for Befu and sociology for Mouer and Sugimoto, my own approach derives unequivocally from my experience in the study of communication and social aspects of language (cf. Neustupný 1978: ch. I). In linguistics the typological method was applied in the pre-structural (cf. Horne 1966), structural (cf. Skalička 1979; Greenberg 1957) as well as post-structural (cf. C. Lehmann 1983) periods. Obviously, many of my examples will be drawn from areas close to my own analytical work, while issues in social science which are more remote from my interests will remain less developed.

2   The nature of typology

The key concept in this chapter is 'typology'. To understand this concept it is useful to start with a full discussion of its major component, the 'type'.

347

A   The concept of type

The term 'type' will be used to refer to a set of socio-cultural features which are interconnected because they have been generated by a similar set of general principles. The 'group principle' mentioned above in connection with Befu's model, can be seen as a very general principle generating a number of socio-cultural features. Schematically, we can represent the type as a tree diagram in which each higher node is a principle of a more general order, while each lower node represents a less general principle:

Figure 11.1   *Hierarchy of Interrelated Principles and Features*

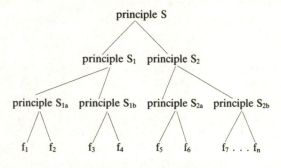

Features $f_1 \ldots f_n$ are related because all of them are interconnected within the same hierarchy of interrelated principles. The difference between principles of varying level of generality (for example, S, S_1, S_{1a}) will be discussed later in this chapter.

Since no society can consist of completely unrelated components, the existence of types can be posited as a socio-cultural universal. Notice that type as conceived in this chapter is a fact that can be fully defined within a single system: it can be exploited for comparative studies, but does not depend on a comparison between two or more systems. For instance, we can claim that a set of certain features of a Japanese religion are interrelated and constitute a type, but this fact is not dependent on comparison having been made with other religions. Also, types are often thought of as classificatory devices. However, type as it is defined here is not basically a tool for classification. Some types can be used for classification (for example, types such as 'agglutination' or 'modern society' have often been used in this way). Yet, types serve mainly as devices which explain the generation of individual rules and features, variation and conflict. Typology is primarily not a tool for comparison or classification.

B Universal and particular types

There are obviously types that are 'universal'. They apply in all human societies. In other words, there are configurations of features which all derive from the same universal formula. Here two examples are presented from linguistics and from social science.

1 *The 'sound language' type.* In the case of language, a number of features are derived from the principle of 'sound language' – in other words, from the fact that natural languages primarily use the acoustic medium. However, this principle, in its turn, is determined by the fact that language (1) is an extensive set of means (that is, not just a few signals), and (2) is primarily used in the production process (in which hands and feet are occupied in a non-communicative activity). From the principle of 'sound language' a number of more specific principles can be deduced. A sound language operates on (1) the principle of 'linearity' (namely, arrangement of symbols basically in one line), while communication through pictures can use a two-dimensional space; (2) the principle of 'recurrence' (the use of a limited number of components or symbols – a completely different symbol for each idea would be unfeasible); and (3) the principle of 'arbitrariness' (using symbols which do not resemble objects or ideas, since most objects and ideas cannot be imitated in sound). Because of the presence of these principles language has rules for splitting discourse into sentences, sentences into words, words into morphemes, and so on.

Many features of language, though not all, can be brought into explicit relationship in this way. The 'sound-language type' explains why we find so many similarities between spoken languages throughout human society.

2 *The 'self-interest' type.* As an example of a non-linguistic universal type we can use a set of Japanese socio-cultural features all derived from the general principle of 'self-interest' (Befu 1977, 1980, 1981; Sugimoto and Mouer 1982; Mouer and Sugimoto 1986). The powerful formula of 'self-interest' seems to account for a large number of facts in Japanese society, and in all other human societies. As examples of how this principle is applied, Sugimoto and Mouer cite overseas travel in groups (the cheapest and most convenient form of travel), overtime work (leading to promotion), and gift giving (1982: 217). Obviously, self-interest is not the only factor present, but it is definitely a guiding principle. A tree

Figure 11.2 *A Tree Diagram of the 'Self-Interest' Type*

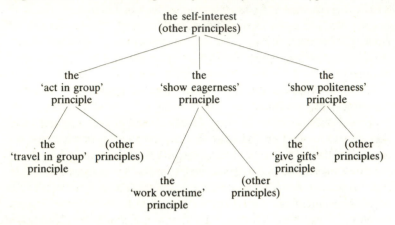

diagram of the 'self-interest type' can be represented as shown in Figure 11.2.

Like the notion of 'sound language', the principle of 'self-interest' can be defined as a universal principle which operates in all human societies and thus constitutes a 'universal' type. On the other hand, types which derive from formulas specific to particular societies or groups of societies may be referred to as 'particular' types. Examples of 'particular' types will be given in the forthcoming discussion. Types which have been developed to explain Japanese society as such are, of course, particular types. The distinction between universal and particular typologies is of importance for further development of the typological approach.

C   Personnel and texture types

Another way of classifying typologies is to consider whether the typology concerns particular groups of participants. It can be claimed, for instance, that an individual is characterized by a set of interrelated features, or that a 'social class' (that is, a certain grouping of personnel) is so characterized. In these cases we can speak of 'personnel types'.

However, my principal concern in this chapter is types which are not bound to any particular category of personnel but to the structure or, as I shall call it, the 'texture' of a culture or society. In the past such configurations have frequently been referred to as types with labels such as 'shame culture' (Benedict), 'vertical society' (Nakane) or 'contextual society' (Hamaguchi). Each of these types has been portrayed as consisting of a large number of features distributed over a variety of processes. These typologies do not refer to the properties of particular categories of personnel. Emphasis here is on explaining a large variety of features which make up the texture of a culture or society. Types of this kind can be called 'textural types'.

Textural types were in considerable disrepute in linguistics as well as in sociology of the structuralist period, and partly continue to be mistrusted by contemporary social scientists who have retained features of structuralistic methodology in their approach. The strong mistrust of some social scientists for theory made it impossible for them to accept anything more than a descriptive account of 'the facts'. Explanatory principles such as typological ones were out of fashion. Of course, it must be admitted that many textural types, apart from violating the particularistic anti-typological trends of structural social science, were simply bad typologies. When I say 'bad typologies', I refer to the fact that the general principles which were assumed to operate in the system in question were erroneously established. The principles alleged to be central to the society were not really there and could not, therefore, explain the phenomena they were supposed to explain. They also functioned, as emphasized by Sugimoto and Mouer (1979), Kawamura (1980), Hata and Smith (1983) and others, to support particular ideological aims. In the next few paragraphs I wish to consider briefly two examples of personnel and two of textural types.

1 *Personnel types: Bernstein's restricted and elaborated codes.* The first example of a personnel typology will be taken from the work of Basil Bernstein. Bernstein is known as the proposer of the distinction between 'restricted' and 'elaborated' codes of speech through which certain classes of speakers can be characterized. Speakers who appear in social relationships 'based upon a common, extensive set of closely shared identifications and expectations' (Bernstein 1966: 128) possess the restricted code. Those who appear in less predictable social relationships develop the elaborated code. According to Bernstein, all classes of the contemporary British society possess the restricted code, while only the middle class and associated strata are likely to have developed the elaborated code. This theory results in distinguishing between two

types of personnel: the R (restricted code only) speakers and the ER (elaborated and restricted code) speakers.

In Bernstein's typologies the degree of predictability of social relationships is the highest-level principle. In the case of the R-type the predictability is high and the less general socio-linguistic principles developed on this basis are:

(1) the importance of social position or status in networks,
(2) the orientation towards extra-verbal channels,
(3) the choice of routine combinations of linguistic means rather than selection and organization of individual elements, and
(4) de-emphasizing of individual differences (Bernstein 1966: 128).[1]

As a result of these strategies the networks of an R-type speaker will be closed; his vocabulary will remain narrow; the meanings conveyed are likely to be concrete, or narrative, and sometimes highly condensed; speech is likely to be fast and fluent.

On the other hand, the ER-type speakers (who use both elaborated and restricted codes) also communicate, in addition to the R-type situations, under conditions of less predictability. Here social status recedes into background while the individual's communicative needs are maximized. The basic principles concern the selection and organization of verbal means into explicit messages. Networks broaden; the speaker's vocabulary is enriched and the syntactic structure of sentences becomes more sophisticated; speech is slower and self-correction assumes a special importance as the speaker aims to achieve more precision.[2]

It is not my aim in this chapter to evaluate individual typologies. Doubts have been expressed concerning the validity of most typological schemes, either because of their weak empirical basis, or because of the tendency, already mentioned, of most social scientists educated in the structuralistic paradigms to despise the

1 It should be noted that a variety of this R-type seems to be present in Japanese communication, but does not necessarily characterize the 'lower than middle class'. This paper does not aim at resolving whether this R-type is a personnel type or some other type in Japanese society.
2 There is an enormous amount of literature on the theory of elaborated and restricted codes. For a fuller discussion of the points made here cf. Robinson 1972.

principle of typologies and to treat all facts of society as mutually independent. Bernstein's theory has been attacked mainly because of the claim by some supporters that the R-type acted as a determinant of certain negatively evaluated cognition processes in working class children. Nevertheless, whatever the validity of the theory may be, there is not doubt that in the R-type as well as in the ER-type we have to do with a set of more general principles which govern more particular principles, with particular features appearing as the consequence of the latter. In other words, Bernstein's two types are types in the sense described above. They are personnel types because they are concerned with the sorting of particular groups of personnel within the societies involved.

2 *Personnel typologies in the Sugimoto and Mouer framework.* Most typologies available in social psychology and sociology, from personality types to the Marxist social class, belong to the category of 'personnel' types (Kubíčková 1969). The Sugimoto and Mouer framework also contains 'personnel typologies'. With regard to the distribution of resources, individuals are seen as falling into one of four levels of configuration, each of them having a plurality of types (Sugimoto and Mouer 1982: 237–40; and Mouer and Sugimoto 1986: 318–19). The levels and types are:

(a) the statistical grouping level (e.g., containing the 'urban dweller' type);
(b) the social grouping level (containing, e.g., the 'OL girl' type);
(c) the social stratum level (e.g., the 'female' type); and
(d) the social class level (the 'ruling class' type, the 'masses' type, etc.).

Sugimoto and Mouer distinguish among these levels by reference to the extent to which 'members' of a particular grouping possess roughly similar amounts of resources, and their shared consciousness and sub-culture is at a certain level of development (that is, they share certain patterns of thought and behaviour). The most general principle here concerns the degree of control which one has over resources. The degree of control determines more detailed common principles (attitudes to culture, thought and so forth), and these in turn govern more detailed rules of conduct – for instance, particular modes for the organization of communication). Some personnel types may be universal, but the majority are specific to particular (types of) societies. Among Sugimoto and Mouer's types, the 'urban dweller' type obviously exists only in societies which have achieved a certain degree of urbanization and is therefore not universal. Neither could universality be claimed for the 'female' type, which has undergone significant historical changes, and may be considerably weakened in the not so distant future.

3 *Textural types in linguistics: grammatical typologies.* In linguistics the 'grammatical types' provide the most widely known examples of textural types and for a long period provided the basic support of linguistic typology in general. Languages have been assumed to contain such types as isolation, inflection (sometimes called 'fusion', cf. Comrie 1981: 41), agglutination, polysynthesis, and others.

For instance, a very general textural principle of the inflectional type is a high degree of cohesion of the linguistic unit usually called the word. On one hand the existence of the word is indisputable; on the other, the word does not easily split into clearly definable smaller units. The inflectional type operates in languages such as Latin or Russian, though, of course, these languages are shaped by other principles as well. From the broad general principle we can derive a number of lower-level principles, for example:

(a) a sentence consists of a definable number of highly inter-dependent words;
(b) a word carries both a lexical meaning (such as, 'car') and one or more grammatical meanings (for instance, 'singular', 'subject', etc.);
(c) the segmentation of the word into smaller units is not essential; . . .
(n) . . .

These principles, in their turn, account for a number of characteristics of individual grammatical rules of particular languages. For instance, in classical Latin

(a) The word order is relatively free, though normally it is subject–object–verb.

(b) A noun consists of a stem and an ending. The ending carries, as a rule, the number meaning (singular/plural) and the case meaning (nominative/genitive).

(c) Endings are highly homonymical. The nominal ending -a, depending on the category of the stem it follows, has the following meanings:

(1) singular/nominative

(2) plural/nominative

. . . .

Though not presented in this form and hindered by a number of false beliefs, grammatical typology formed an important component of pre-structural linguistics (cf. Horne 1966) and was retained and developed by some post-structurally-minded linguists during the structural period (cf. Skalička 1979, Greenberg 1957). These typologies were texture typologies and, because of the isolationism (emphasis on 'immanence') of structural linguistics, their application was normally limited to grammar or, more narrowly still, to the morphological subsystem of grammar. However, it is obvious that the network of interdependent features is wider. For instance, one can talk about isolating, agglutinative (and so on) phonologies (Neustupný 1978: ch. 7), incorporate the system of writing, and certainly go as far as to some formal properties of poetry (such as the presence or absence and character of rhyme [cf. Neustupný 1980]).

In contemporary grammar the typological way of thinking has been revived (for example, W. Lehmann 1972, C. Lehmann 1983), even if the current emphasis is on sets of interrelated features of lesser extension than the traditional grammatical types. Kuno (1973: ch. 1), for instance, presented an interesting 'minor' (relatively unextensive) typology of this kind for Japanese. He claims, for instance, that the subject–object–verb word order in Japanese is firstly connected with the position of relative clauses before the modified noun; secondly, with the fact that when deletion of an identical word takes place, it is the first occurrence of the word which is deleted; thirdly, with the abundance of postpositions, suffixes and particles (rather than prepositions and prefixes); and fourthly, with the existence of so-called sentence final particles. Kuno hesitated, however, to move beyond this set of features in the direction of the more extensively conceived classical typologies.

4 *Textural typologies in social sciences*. As far as Japanese culture and society is concerned, Befu's account of the group model (which, let me remind the reader, has a limited though real validity in his system) certainly represents an example of typological thinking. In my formalization the most general principle which governs the whole model is the cohesion of the social group. The more specific principles are:

(1) hierarchy within the group,
(2) emotional bonds between members, and
(3) high degree of conformity and loyalty (Befu 1980).

A number of more detailed rules of social conduct can be derived from these principles.

Sugimoto and Mouer have consistently criticized the popular textural typologies of Japanese society such as presented by Nakane or Doi. As I mentioned above, this criticism may be correct as far as it affects the specific typologies, but does not affect the typological principle as such. As already the few examples above show, the authors themselves do use the typological principle in general. Moreover, in Sugimoto and Mouer (1982) a further example, this time of a 'minor' (relatively unextensive) textural typology, can be identified. This is when the authors speak of the general principle of 'reverence for the West' (Sugimoto and Mouer 1982: 247) which is connected with the following phenomena:

(1) displaying Western-looking mannequins in Japanese department stores,
(2) weekly magazines and sports magazines emphasizing in their photo section pictures of white athletes,
(3) presenting large breasts as ideal of feminine beauty, and
(4) including only English and no Asian language in curricula of the compulsory school education in Japan.

The example seems to indicate that in principle typologizing is compatible with Sugimoto and Mouer's framework. Moreover, it also suggests that the typological approach is a necessity if we wish to understand how Japanese society works. Admittedly, the principle of 'reverence for the West' may serve, as Sugimoto and Mouer point out, as a symbolic means of control within Japanese society. The next question then must be: why is it 'reverence for the West' and not something else – such as reverence for China – which fulfils the control function? Is there a connection with some other more general principle within Japanese society? What is the structure of the whole network of interdependencies? What role is fulfilled within this structure by the 'reverence for the West' principle? (Is it, for instance, irreplaceable or only marginal to the whole?)

In other words, a consistent typological approach to all facets of Japanese culture and society is required. Interrelations and determinants, sets of mutually supportive features need to be established. There is no doubt that the typological theory can still be considerably improved. However, once developed, it will become an indispensable tool of social science research about Japan.

3   Toward better typologies of culture and society

In the past many textural typologies simply listed a number of features that happened to occur in a model system under consideration. Features which appeared present in American or British society of the twentieth century but which were absent in the nineteenth century were 'modern'. This was usually sufficient to assume that the occurrence was not accidental, and that some (further unspecified) interrelatedness of the features existed. The criteria on which one decided that a configuration of features constituted a type were seldom discussed in explicit detail.

In the case of types established in this purely empirical way it was difficult to explain why features of different types frequently coexisted within a single system. Also, typologists could not easily explain why and how a type changed. Frequently, the type was *de facto* conceived as a 'permanent' type which had always been there and would continue to be there. Accordingly, questions about change were never asked.

Moreover, nobody could say for certain why typologies were needed in the first place. It seemed that human interaction could be accounted for without such an abstract construct. In view of the pioneering role that linguistics has played in the development of typology it will be of interest to note that the transformational generative grammar of the 1960s developed complicated systems of rules which promised to generate language without reference to anything that would even resemble the traditional grammatical typologies.

Today we accept that typologies must be developed in more rigorous ways than in the past. Concepts such as 'determinants' or 'strategies' (cf. Brown and Levinson 1978, Goody 1978) are available to assist in this task. And a dynamic view of society does not merely tolerate but directly demands tools such as typologies which provide a possibility of a dynamic approach to the study of society.

The following discussion considers some issues of the typological method with special reference to the needs of Japanese studies.

A Structure of the typological network

I suggest that the type should be considered as a set of interrelated features generated by principles of varying degrees of generality. So far the term 'principle' has been used as an overall term. It is now useful to consider more carefully a terminology for principles of varying degrees of generality. In my view the number of steps to be distinguished is not a very important issue. In reality there are probably no discrete steps. Yet, the division is an important heuristic device, necessary for talking about the structure of the typological network of interdependencies, in which some principles are more general than others. When we are comparing the level of generality of two or more principles there is a need for some kind of scale, and I shall suggest that the following set of categories might provide a starting point:

1 *Determinants*. Determinants are the most general principles. They describe social processes which affect a very large number of less general principles. I assume that among the determinants one can count, for example, particular pattern of production, economic or geographical factors of primary importance, and so on. (As noted above, these determinants 'determine' only the selection of *some* socio-cultural features and do not, therefore, constitute a strict deterministic system.)

2 *Maxims*. The next level of general principles can be called maxims. They affect a wide range of behaviour, but are not as general as determinants. Examples might include the principle of emphasizing the individual, the principle of independence from other societies, and so forth. The term 'maxim' was first used by

Grice (1975) in his study of broad conversational postulates.

3 *Strategies*. Strategies are specific to some particular areas of interaction. One speaks normally of strategies of communication, economic policy strategies, and so on. Our concept of strategies owes much to Brown and Levinson's 'politeness strategies' (1978). A politeness strategy is, for instance, 'seek agreement', 'be optimistic', 'apologize', 'understate', 'be vague' (1978). This level of patterning has hardly ever been systematically discussed in the study of culture and society. The level of generality of strategies differs substantially from that of 'determinants' and 'maxims' on one hand and 'ordinary rules' on the other. I believe that it is expedient to keep a different name for each of these levels, rather than always to speak simply of 'more general' or 'more specific' strategies.[3]

4 *Ordinary rules*. Ordinary rules govern a number of features of segments of interaction. In linguistics the concept of rules has perhaps been elaborated in more detail than in any other discipline. There is a set of rules for forming the past tense, for the position of the hands while bowing, and many other processes of communication. It is immaterial whether members of a culture are aware of the existence of a rule and whether it has been explicitly formulated and/or discussed. Most linguistic rules (and certainly most socio-cultural rules in general) are used without any consciousness on the part of their users.

Outside language there are sets of ordinary rules for the preparation of individual dishes (which are in turn governed by more general strategies of cooking), behaviour of drivers or pedestrians in the city traffic (underlain by a set of more general strategies) and for handling legal relationships, such as the treatment of relatives in matters of inheritance. However, it can be legitimately asked whether all levels of patterning exist in all categories of non-communicative interaction. It may be that the principles operating within, say, the family or public domain are sometimes restricted to determinants, maxims and strategies.

Rules are determined by strategies, and this is particularly important in the case of newly established or reformulated rules. However, such determination does not necessarily concern detail. No set of grammatical strategies can account for all details of the

---

3 The term 'strategy' has also been employed in a similar way by Wunderlich (1981).

formation of the Japanese past tense. There is always a residuum which remains to be specified in the rule. Hence, the level of ordinary rules, wherever it exists, cannot be dispensed with. Traditional linguistics *had to* develop those complicated systems of rules when accounting for the generation of sentences. As linguistics shows, there are more and less general rules, but what linguists speak about does not usually reach the level of generality of strategies. In their preoccupation with rules linguists completely omitted from their accounts any higher-level principles. The result was a static system which could not explain how rules themselves were generated, and contained no mechanism for the explication of change. One could also argue that principles more general than ordinary rules were excluded precisely to make the texture of language appear static and invariable.

5 *Listing rules*. Ordinary rules are not the last category of principles. Ordinary rules have the form of 'for all *x y*'. But there are exceptions. For instance the 'regular' past tense of the Japanese verb *iku*, 'to go', should be *iita* (like *kiku* becoming *kiita*), but it is *itta*. Listing (or, perhaps, 'singular') rules specify all behaviour that concerns one particular item. Again, a listing rule that leads to the derivation *iku*, 'to go' *itta* 'went' – cannot be fully accounted for on the basis of principles of a higher order (whether strategies or ordinary rules). There is a residuum that must simply be listed. In the case of *iku*, 'to go', it is the information that the listing rule (always) affects that particular lexical item and not other items. In non-communicative behaviour the definition of electoral districts is usually formulated on the basis of some kind of listing. There may be strategies and rules which serve as a guideline in setting up an electoral division, but they cannot decide whether a particular block of houses will belong to a particular district.

Should social interaction be conceived as a static system with no variation or internal conflict, as was often the case with the structuralist social science, one could indeed manage with ordinary rules and listing rules. However, since society is in a continuous process of change, more than rules are needed. New listing rules, new ordinary rules, new strategies and maxims must constantly be produced. The more general principles provide guidance for the creation of new principles of lower degree of generality and for the change and recreation of existing ones. No dynamic model of social interaction can therefore manage without a full account of all existing general principles within the system under investigation.

Notice that in the proposed system normally *several* principles of a higher rank contribute to the formation of a principle of a lower rank. Seldom are rules derived from a single maxim or strategy. The rules of overseas group travel by members of Japanese society cannot be explained by their group consciousness alone: however, neither will the pursuit of self-interest nor any other single general principle account for the entire complex behaviour known as the 'Japanese group tour'.

It must be accepted that principles intersect, and that actual social processes derive from this complicated interaction of general principles of varying kind and order. For example, the maxim of individualization (which is characteristic of the 'modern' social type) can clash within the same system with a group-dependence maxim (deriving from a more traditional social type), the result being decided by a number of other principles operating at the moment in the system. This is how conflict and variation in culture and society develop.

As explained above, a type consists of a set of interrelated principles of varying generality which generate a set of features of socio-cultural processes. Because classical typologies did not have an explicitly defined hierarchy of principles (with the more general principles to explain the more specific ones), they were of a basically static character.

B   One or more types within a system?

In the past it was common for the use of the typological approach to stop with the establishment of *one single type*. Linguists spoke of Japanese being an agglutinative language, and historians wrote of Japan as being a traditional *or* modern society. However, systems can normally only be described by reference to a number of different types, all present in the system. It is necessary to postulate that the Japanese language contains, to a varying extent, the agglutinative type as well as the inflectional and isolating types. In the same way – as already suggested above – it is necessary to concede that Japanese society is not completely modern or traditional; it contains the early modern, the modern and the post-modern (or contemporary) types at one and the same time.

The major focus when describing the nature of Japanese society should then be not on whether it is traditional, modern or post-modern, but on identifying sections and subsystems which might contain predominantly one or another type, or which might comprise several types. The perspective of a comparative typological study *within the same society* is perhaps one of the most exciting perspectives provided by theories which utilize the typological approach. The theory of the Japanese society in the 1960s which suggested that Japan could best be understood as having a 'dual structure', however much it may have failed our requirements of rigour and elaboration, focused attention on a very interesting and important aspect of Japanese society.

In one of my earlier publications (Neustupný 1978: ch. 6) I developed in some detail the typologically unorthodox suggestion that the system of Japanese declension (noun + particle) was more agglutinative, while the conjugation of the verb and, in particular, the system of Japanese numerals showed more inflectional features. In other words, I claimed that there were several grammatical types present in Japanese grammar and that they interacted to produce the grammatical system. It was interesting to see that such interaction was not restricted to the area of morphology in the narrow sense of the word, but extended to accentual behaviour as well. The resulting picture revealed that to a surprising degree individual subsystems of language were sensitive to the presence of various grammatical types. The situation seems to be similar with regard to other kinds of social processes.

The particular network of types within a particular part of society and within the society as a whole can be called the 'typological profile' of that part or of the society as a whole. The typological profile of Japanese society should specify not merely the types present but also assess their relative weight and inter-relationship.

C   Major and minor types

The distinction between major and minor types is one of degree. A 'major type' is an extensive set of interrelated features which normally operates throughout an area, or in several areas of a culture or society. The term refers thus to a type which covers a large number of various socio-cultural facts. Types such as 'feudalism', 'modern society' or 'agglutination' are major types. On the other hand, a 'minor type' concerns only a relatively small set of features. A network of features deriving from the principle of 'reverence for the West' mentioned above (Sugimoto and Mouer

1982) is a minor type – unless it can be connected with a large variety of other conduct. An example of a minor type derived by Kuno from the subject–object–verb word order strategy was quoted above in our discussion of textural grammatical typologies.

The contemporary trend of paying attention to minor types is a positive development and should be welcomed. Minor types lend themselves more easily to a detailed analysis and as such can serve as a basis on which the typological theory and method can be developed further. The greater the number of the minor types which have been identified, the clearer it becomes that in their turn they, too, are mutually interrelated and are constituents of the same major type.

One of the fundamental problems of typologies of the past was the attempt of their proponents to apply the major types too categorically, as if they could account for all phenomena in the area concerned in a totally obligatory way. Such sweeping generalizations contributed to the impression shared by many social scientists that major types were stiff constructs defiling social reality and that they should be avoided whenever a dynamic approach to society was desired. However, major types defined in terms of general principles such as determinants, maxims or strategies – in other words, as trends rather than fixed sets of obligatory characteristics – are useful tools for understanding the dynamic character of society.

D Categories of textural types

An extensive classification of types is beyond our present competence. The study of minor types is particularly underdeveloped. Some categories were already mentioned above, in particular the distinctions between *universal* and *particular* types on one hand, and the distinction between *personnel* and *textural* types on the other. As far as textural types are concerned, at least three categories must be distinguished: developmental types, interaction types and common denominator types.[4] The relationship between

---

4 Five categories were identified in my earlier classification of linguistic types (cf. Neustupný 1978: ch. 5). It now seems to me that some could be collapsed, with three categories (developmental, interactional and common denominator) remaining.

Table 11.1 *A Typology of Types*

	Particular	*Universal*
Personnel	Bernstein's types . . . /Social Stratum/Social Class	
Textural		
1. Developmental	. . ./Early Modern/ Modern/Post-Modern	
2. Interactional	Islamic/Sinic/. . . American/. . .	
3. Common denominator	Agglutinative/Isolation/ Inflectional/ . . .	
?		Sound Language Self-Interest Reverence for the West . . .

all these categories is shown in Table 11.1. Each of the three categories of textural types is examined below.

1 *Developmental types.* The maxims of developmental types are the most general principles of developmental stages of social change such as the early modern, modern or post-modern (post-industrial or contemporary) stage. In Japanese studies the notion of 'modernization' which was used in the Princeton series has, in my understanding, never been examined as a typological problem. When I speak here of modernization, I am indebted to Marxist sociology, which has always retained a strong typological interest (cf. Hall 1985).

The question of developmental types cannot be avoided if we wish to capture the dynamics of contemporary Japanese society. The central importance of the social group, which seems to be utilized as the general principle of what I have called the 'early modern' type (cf. Neustupný 1978: 147) cannot be rejected for a major part of Japan's modern social history. Although I am in sympathy with the war against the 'ideology of the group-orientation', I would also emphasize that a categorical and complete denial of the principle in any possible shape or form would run against all we know of social change, not merely in Japan but elsewhere as well. The development from the early modern type to the modern type is a universal fact, valid for all societies. Moreover, if it is true that the early modern type was present in Japanese society twenty years ago, it would be most surprising not to find traces of it even today.

The question is not so much whether the early modern type and modern type exist in present-day Japanese society; rather, attention should be focused on identifying the social strata and subsystems in which they exist, and on ascertaining the extent to which and the processes by which the early modern type has been replaced by the more 'individualistic' modern type. Moreover, we should ask what is the process of the growth of the post-modern (or contemporary) type (cf. Neustupný 1978 and 1982b), with its strategies of return to the problems of variation and conflict. It would be regrettable if we turned to the study of resident movements, environmental movements or minority movements without considering, at the same time, their implications for the broad typological changes within Japanese society.

2 *Interactional types*. The general principles of alliance generate interactional types. Interaction can lead to the influence of one system on another (one-way interaction) or to mutual influence (two-way interaction). Elsewhere (1978: ch. 5), I referred to the former as 'interferential types' (giving the Islamic or Sinic type as examples) and to the latter as 'areal types' (for example, the Balcanic Area, or the Indian Area; cf. also Haarmann 1976). I would now prefer to reconsider these as two extreme points on a continuous scale.

The importance of interactional types for the study of Japanese society is obvious. At the international level Japan moved after the Meiji period from its traditional reliance on China to an alliance with the Western world, and the theories of Japan's Westernization have flourished ever since. Where the growth of the modern type seemed to be clearly connected to internal developments, observers repeatedly referred to the force of the Western influence. Even the development of the Japanese family was frequently explained as being part of the process of Westernization.

Extensive sets of typological interdependencies deriving from the principle of alliance with particular foreign societies have always existed in Japan. It is necessary to give them full and systematic attention. Unless more careful consideration is given to how the American type in contemporary Japan is defined the existence and development of the type and its relation to conflict within the society cannot be solved. Before we can discuss these issues we need to know which of the similarities between America and Japan (some features of the education system, importance of technology, and so on) are components of the interactional type, and which are due to other factors, such as developmental types.

At the national (as opposed to the international) level the concept of interactional interference is useful in considering virtually all social issues. To what extent, for instance, does the life style of the middle class influence other classes? How does this influence combine with other factors (such as the dynamics involved in shifting from one developmental type to another) to shape the life style of other than middle-class Japanese?

3 *Common denominator types.* The third set of typological principles of basic importance are those which underlie common denominator types. The matter is that in some social subsystems a more-or-less arbitrary choice has to be made among a limited number of general principles for the construction of the subsystem; once a choice is made, the selected principle is applied widely. With developmental types or interactional types it was relatively easy to identify the determinants; however, it is not easy – if possible at all – to establish what introduces the common denominator type (or types) into the system in question.

The most typical example of the common denominator types are the grammatical types, such as agglutination, inflection, isolation, polysynthesis and others. Various attempts have been made in the past to explain on the basis of social features the selection of a particular grammatical type in a language. For instance, Otto Jespersen believed that, with proceeding modernization of societies, languages tended to become more analytical (isolational – that is, similar to contemporary English). It has now generally been accepted that arguments which try to connect grammatical types with social development are untenable. Rather, it would be argued that the 'decision' of a community to adopt one type of grammar or another is arbitrary. However, after the selection has been made, the network of typological connections is established easily and can spread widely. Features established in this way usually support each other (cf. Skalička 1979). Of course, these interrelationships do not determine all elements within the system. One grammatical type can coexist with another, and many features of languages cannot be explained by reference to any major type.

Although several grammatical types can be identified in Japanese, the dominant type is definitely the agglutinative type. The principle of agglutination applies in Japanese morphology, lexicon, phonology; it significantly affects the Japanese system of writing and even extends to some formal aspects of literature (for example, the euphonic patterns of Japanese poetry, cf. Neustupný 1978 and 1980).

Outside the sphere of language, common denominator types, at least minor ones, seem to operate in areas which are highly formalized, without being at the same time determined in detail by outside factors. With reference to Japanese law, Smith (1981) speaks of 'structural inhibitions' which account for facts such as the role of conciliation, the character of the jury system and the character of criminal litigation. These 'structural inhibitions' seem to explain many aspects of legal organization better than any social factors. It is not unlikely that we have a 'common denominator type' here.

4 Application I: the Japanese reference system

Two applications of the typological approach outlined in the preceding sections are briefly introduced in the paragraphs below. The first application concerns the way persons are referred to within the Japanese system of communication. Although space does not allow for a full analysis of the reference system itself, the discussion does illustrate the usefulness of the approach and the directions in which typologically oriented research ought to be developed.

Anthropologists and socio-linguists since the late 1950s (cf. Befu and Norbeck 1958, Fischer 1964, Passin 1966, and Suzuki 1984, to name only a few pioneers) have intensively studied the way Japanese refer to self and others. The general conclusion seems to be that pronouns (of which a considerable number exists) are used much less than in English or in other European languages, while kinship terms, names and titles are applied much more frequently.

In this context it is interesting to ask whether the reference system is connected with other facts of Japanese culture and society with which it would form a typological configuration – that is, a type. In terms of the definitions given above, this question concerns a particular (that is, not universal) textural typology. If the Japanese reference system can be understood as a component of a major type, would the type be primarily developmental, interferential or denominatory? To what extent is the reference system formed by an overlapping of several types?

A Rules and strategies

The reference system consists of a large number of 'ordinary rules', such as the following rules for a lower primary schoolgirl addressing her father:

Rule 1: Address [father]   →   KINSHIP TERM
Rule 2: KINSHIP TERM   → *papa*
                                           otōsan
                                           otōchan
                                           tōchan
Rule 2a: [+urban, +salaried, +nuclear]   Var→ *papa*
Rule 2b: [+urban, +salaried, −nuclear]   Var→ *otōsan*
Rule 2c: [+urban, +self-employed]   Var→ *otōchan*
Rule 2d: [−urban]   Var→ *tōchan*
Rule 3 : [family f_n]   → *papa*

These rules are based on Peng and Maruyama's analysis (1975) of data from a number of strata of Japanese society. While Rule 1 and Rule 2 are categorical (applied in 100 per cent under normal circumstances), Rules 2a–2d are variable (indicated by 'Var' before the transcription arrow): they do not apply consistently (cf. Labov 1972). Rule 3 is one of the many 'listing rules'; it confirms for each family that one particular rule out of 2a–2d applies. The aim here is not to test the formal structure or empirical adequacy of these rules; rather, I shall attempt to show how the rules can be accounted for by reference to types.

Rule 1 can be connected with a strategy that prescribes, under certain circumstances, the use of kinship terms for reference to members of one's family. In English the same strategy applies, but only in third person reference ('my father did . . .') or in a direct appeal to the addressee ('Daddy, what do you think?'). In Japanese this strategy is used widely in reference to self (first person), addressee (second person) and third person, even if only when the referent is a senior family member. I shall refer to this strategy as the Senior-Kinterm Strategy. Differences in the application of this strategy in English and in Japanese may prove meaningful for its typological assessment.

Rule 2 seems to derive from a strategy that selects a child's point of view as the basis for reference terms to be used in the family. I shall call this the Junior-Pivot Strategy. The implication here is that the family is a cohesive social group, in which the youngest child (normally a boy) is the central participant. The same strategy is also applied in other rules, such as the optional rule of using *boku* as 2nd person reference to small boys, in rules of conducting casual conversation (a child, if present, tends to become the pivot), or in rules that legitimize (verbal) aggression by children against older members of the family (Fischer 1970).

However, Rule 2 can also be interpreted as simply representing the point of view of the speaker: the referent is father in relation to the girl in question. Let us call the strategy which underlies such interpretation the Speaker-Pivot Strategy. A possibility of the same rule deriving from two or more strategies is typologically significant: if the strategies are members of different types, the rule can survive even if one of the types is weakened or removed.

Rule 2a can be considered to derive from the previous three strategies. In addition, it may be the result of simultaneous application of a Borrowing Strategy. The terms *papa* and *mama*, are still marked as loan words in Japanese. If they are used, this may be because the speaker wants to use loan words (is applying the Borrowing Strategy). Apart from this, Rule 2a perhaps also serves as a means (strategy) of neutralizing the *otōsan/ otōchan/tōchan* opposition. In other words, the use of *papa* does not involve the *-san/-chan* or *o-/zero* choice. Because such a choice implies communication about the type of relationship between the daughter and the father (that is, distance between them), this strategy can be called the Distance-Avoidance Strategy.

In Rule 2b two strategies seem to be identifiable. One is a strategy leading to emotionally neutral though polite language, resulting in the use of *-san* and the prefix *o-*. This can be called the Formality Strategy. An alternative account is provided by a Standardization Strategy. The form *otōsan* is the most strongly textbook-like of the whole set and may be used in order to make the speaker's language sound more Standard.

Finally, in Rule 2c and Rule 2d the suffix *-chan* is the result of an Intimacy Strategy and the presence of *o-* in Rule 2c and its absence in Rule 2d can be explained by the application or absence of what we can call a Refinement Strategy.

B Maxims

In the above analysis I have listed nine strategies which govern the rules 1–3 of reference as well as a large number of other

Table 11.2 *Some Japanese Reference Strategies*

Name	Content
1 Senior-Kinterm	'refer to senior family members with a kinship term'
2 Junior-Pivot	'take the point of view of the youngest child (boy) in the family'
3 Speaker-Pivot	'take the point of view of the speaker'
4 Borrowing	'borrow a term from a modern foreign system'
5 Distance-Avoidance	'avoid communication of distance'
6 Formality	'use formal language'
7 Standardization	'use standard language'
8 Intimacy	'communicate solidarity'
9 Refinement	'always be polite'

rules. These strategies can be summarized as in Table 11.2. The next question to be asked is whether these strategies can be related to any more general strategies or other general principles operating in the Japanese language.

The Senior-Kinterm Strategy emphasizes the importance of hierarchy in family networks. As such it may be related to a more general Hierarchy Strategy which, in turn, can be explained as deriving from the maxim of Group-Dependence of the early modern type. However, this is but one possibility; before we can accept such connection as a fact, it is necessary to find evidence of its existence.

How can evidence be found? Several steps may be helpful.

1 *Social structure analysis.* It is unlikely that the Senior-Kinterm Strategy would form a part of the early modern type, if this type were absent in Japanese of the early modern period.

2 *Correction processes.* If rules governed by the strategy in question are being weakened or removed as a consequence of a demonstrable trend away from the early modern principle, then

the strategy may be assumed to be related to the early modern type. The gradual increase in the frequency with which the urban middle class uses the expressions *papa* and *mama* (Peng and Maruyama 1975) – in other words, corrects towards *papa* and *mama* – indicates that being a member of the urban middle class is a significant consideration affecting the choice of the strategy involved.

3 *Attitudes.* Even if no correction takes place, the attitudes of native speakers such as 'this is old-fashioned' or 'I don't like this expression' (in the case of speakers with a clearly modern life style) become an important consideration.

4 *Analogy.* Historical processes in other languages can be taken into account and provide evidence that a connection between two or more principles exists. If a strategy is uniformly introduced in a number of communication systems at the point of their entry into the modern era, it is worth considering whether the introduction of the same strategy in the communication system under examination is not connected with the modern type.

Let us now examine, from this point of view, the interdependence of the strategies of reference as given above. In the case of the Senior-Kinterm Strategy, its compatibility with maxims of the modern communications systems is attested by an analogy from European languages. As already mentioned, in certain environments 'father' was commonly used as an address term in European languages throughout the modern period (and continues to be used even today) without much evidence of attempts at correction. Although the width of application in Japanese is much greater, I have no clear evidence of correction here either and the only attitudinal testimony concerns a case of reciprocal kinterm usage (*otōsan – okāsan*) by elderly parents of a teenage girl, a usage extending to situations in which the daughter is not present. This usage has been marked as 'old-fashioned' by a number of speakers.[5] No systematic research into the attitudes of native speakers or into their correction of reference terms in discourse has been conducted. However, I believe that such research will reveal, in the future, at least partial connection of this strategy with the maxims of modernization.

5 The usage has variously been assessed by observers as reflecting the fact (1) that the parents were fairly aged, (2) that the father had been a *nisei* (that is, lacked experience in Japanese situations), and (3) that the mother came from one of Japan's rural areas.

As far as the other strategies are concerned, the Junior-Pivot and perhaps the Formality Strategies seem to me to be potentially related to early modern maxims. The former because it implies a cohesive hierarchically oriented social group, the latter because it seems to be connected with the unemotional hierarchical character of the early modern *bushi*-type family. I possess evidence from interviews with native speakers that they have negative attitudes towards both the Junior-Pivot Strategy and the Formality Strategy, in the latter case based on a comparison of *otōsan* (negatively evaluated) with *papa* (neutral).

On the other hand the Speaker-Pivot Strategy treats the speaker as an individual and as such can probably be connected with the modern-type maxims. The same seems to be true about the Borrowing Strategy (alliance with the modern world) and Distance Avoidance Strategy (a refusal to recognize hierarchy in networks). The Standardization Strategy may well be modern (connected with the role of education in modern society), while the Intimacy and Refinement Strategies appear to be typologically neutral. Although the evidence gathered so far concerns attitudes and is not sufficient in itself, it nevertheless demonstrates the potential usefulness of investigating further in this direction.

C Discussion

It is too early to draw conclusions without further empirical data. Nevertheless, it seems that both the early modern and modern types are operating in the Japanese reference system.

The result is conflict and variation. It appears that there is a considerable amount of variation within the reference system. The use of kinship terms (*oniisan*, *oneesan*) rather than given names when referring to older siblings reflects this kind of conflict.

Other aspects of the language with which we are more familiar than with the reference system confirm these findings. For instance, in the Japanese honorific system, regrouping of features which can be connected with the early modern type has either been completed or is well under way, while some clearly modern strategies are being strengthened (cf. Neustupný 1978: ch. 10). Furthermore, other types such as the interaction type and the grammatical type appear to be playing an important role in the restructuring of the system.

Linguists of the structuralist schools tended to believe that language was immune to conflicts which were affecting other parts of society. It is now becoming clear that this assumption was incorrect: the developmental types of language are certain to assume an important role in future linguistics.

5 Application II: the Westernization of Japanese culture

The second application draws from suggestions presented in Befu's paper *Civilization and Culture: Japan in Search of Identity* (1984). Befu notes (p. 63), following Umesao, that 'from the early days of modern Japan, dress in the "public" sphere was defined as "Western". As a consequence, "Japanese" style clothing came to be confined more and more to "private" areas of life.' He goes on to describe the Japanese orientation to food, shelter, furnishings and, to some extent, music in the same terms. It seems that we can speak here again of a type, a network of features extending over a relatively wide area of Japanese culture, all connected with a single general principle of 'Westernization'.

A Rules and strategies

Reference to Westernization can be found in many rules which constitute Japanese culture. I have already spoken of the principle of 'reverence for the West' as suggested by Sugimoto and Mouer; under the heading of 'interactional type', other related facts were also mentioned.

I assume that Japanese culture contains systems of rules (ordinary rules) which specify in detail the procedures to be followed when using dress, food and so on. These rules constitute in culture what corresponds to the traditional grammar of language within linguistics.

Each of the rules can be connected with a number of strategies, some of them particular, some universal. Among the particular strategies the Borrowing Strategy ('borrow from a modern foreign system') – mentioned above in my discussion of the reference system – operates and contributes to the shaping of a number of rules. The weight of the strategy among other strategies may vary: what Befu suggests is that the Borrowing Strategy is very important. Many rules are more or less shaped by this strategy. Of course, we know that the rules for clothing, food, shelter and art, which

Befu has in mind, are not completely borrowed rules, even in the public sphere. For instance, Japanese pictures (*nihonga*) may be used in public buildings, the colour scheme of designs may be non-Western, some Japanese food (such as *tenpura*) may be served at public banquets. Also, even if all objects may be of Western origin, they may be used in significantly non-Western ways. Although slippers are unequivocally a Western object, the Japanese practice of changing into one's slippers in the office area is not acceptable in most Western offices.

We must also note a number of instances in which the rules seem to call for the opposite – namely, the use of Western patterns in the private sphere and of traditional Japanese patterns in the public sphere. For example, the official ideology of imperial Japan was certainly not Western at all. As far as language is concerned, loan words in Japanese are used in private domains to a considerable extent, whereas the official (administrative and legal) idiom has always refrained from the use of foreign loans. These examples clearly suggest that other strategies must also be taken into consideration. In saying this I am not suggesting that the Borrowing Strategy is of little importance. It is highly significant, but simply cannot explain all situations.

B   Maxims

Where does the Borrowing Strategy come from? Is it an independent principle which is self-supporting and self-regenerating (something like the general principles responsible for the 'common denominator types' mentioned above), or is it connected with other strategies within the same system? In the latter case, what are the maxims (and possibly the determinants) under which it could be placed?

I believe that the occurrence of the Borrowing Strategy can be interconnected with at least four general maxims. The first is the maxim of alliance with the Developed World. This implies dissociation from the earlier pre-modern alliance with China and assures the necessary in-flow of modern information. The alliance serves both practical functions (such as facilitating communication) and the symbolic function (for example, symbolizing the nation's modernization). This maxim is an important factor promoting borrowing but does not by itself account for the whole process.

Second is the maxim of Modernizing Development. Western

institutions are suitable for an industrializing society, and their introduction is consistent with the more general principle of modernization, present in post-Meiji Japan. In other words, borrowing takes place as a part of Japan's economic, social, political and cultural processes.

The third is the maxim of Modernizing Individualization. Here I am referring to the equality of the individual – understandably, within the limits of a modernizing society. Seating provides one example. In a traditional Japanese setting some people sit on a *zabuton* and others, normally with lower social status, on *tatami*; when chairs are used each participant occupies one chair, normally identical with the other chairs (except for the chairman's chair which may be used to communicate the differential status of its occupier – the pre-modern character of the exception is then obvious).

Fourth is the maxim of Modern Unity. The acceptance of Western institutions erases regional and other differences which stand in the way of the creation of centralized national markets, and so on.

Each of these four maxims is a general principle which can be accommodated under the more general principle of modernization. The Westernization type (an interactional type) is therefore a sub-type within the modernization type (a developmental type). Indeed, for many members of the Japanese culture Westernization and modernization have always been synonymous. Until at least the 1960s the most strongly modern strata of the Japanese society very positively valued the Westernization type and saw the Japanese Indigenous type in very negative terms.

On the other hand, it is obvious that the modern type covers an area which is much more extensive than the area of the Westernization type. For example, from this perspective we can see changes in the family in a new light. The modernization of the family is no longer the result of the Alliance maxim; that is, it is not an instance of Westernization.

Another issue which deserves closer examination is the extent to which the Borrowing Strategy can operate independently from the modernization principle. With regard to the Japanese language, purely structural factors (for instance, the absence of a suitable indigenous word formation formula) seem to have been at work. One of the reasons why so many loan words have entered modern Japanese vocabulary is the fact that new words cannot be easily formed from purely Japanese elements and new Sino-Japanese compounds consisting of two characters are also strongly constrained.

C   Discussion

Why did the relatively sharp distinction between the public and the private sphere appear in the first place, and why has it gradually lost its significance over time?

The Westernization type was initially in conflict with the traditional Japanese Indigenous type. We should not be surprised that the Westernization type was most prominent in those areas of culture and society which were of greatest importance for the bureaucratic/entrepreneurial establishment: at the national macro-level. In a previous study of the modernization of the Japanese language (Neustupný 1978: ch. 9), I described two different phases in the modernization process: macro-modernization and micro-modernization. The same distinction can be drawn not only in the area of language, but for culture and society in general. Westernization proceeds in the public 'macro' area first, and then advances slowly over time to displace the Japanese type in the private 'micro' area.

The history of the Westernization type is thus largely isomorphic with the history of Japanese modernization except that, as mentioned above, modernization was a much more encompassing process. The spread of the Westernization type went hand in hand with modernization. Why Japan experienced virtually no strong wave of cultural purism (Neustupný, forthcoming) – apart from some beginnings during the war – remains to be explained; the explanation is likely to be through a set of principles and rules operating at the same time as the Westernization type. The Westernization type gradually expanded to cover the private domains as well, but has never completely replaced the Japanese Indigenous type.

Today, with the modernization process virtually complete, the conflict between the two is not felt as strongly as it used to be. Although there are still some pre-modern overtones present in the Japanese Indigenous type, on the whole the two types have lost their original connection with the 'modernizing' and 'pre-modern' general principles. Consequently, Westernization in Japan today is a matter completely different from Westernization in the Meiji period, in the 1930s, or immediately after World War II.

The typological approach allows us to assess in an efficient and dynamic way problems which have confronted Japanese studies ever since the discipline came into being.

6 Conclusion: Japanese society as a dynamic system of types

The framework advocated in this paper can be applied to any society. Societies contain a large number of intersecting typological principles which serve to organize various mutually interrelated features. The relative importance of individual typological principles and of the types they define is constantly changing. Although some types, in particular the common denominator types, seem to change more slowly than others, none remains constant within any society over an indefinite period of time. This is true with regard to Japan as with regard to any other society.

Students of Japanese society must take full account of this fact. Certain general typological principles have a universal character. Some types, such as the developmental types, can be found in a large number of societies, but there may be others which are characteristic of Japanese society alone. The identification of networks of interrelated features which derive from the same general principle or strategy and are, therefore, mutually supporting should be the goal of those seeking to build models of Japanese society.

As long as the general principles and strategies which shape social interaction within Japanese society are not explicitly identified, we will at best end up with nothing more than a static picture. The study of the interdependence of various strata and subsystems of Japanese society in which shared principles, strategies and rules play an important role, is of equal importance. To account for fixed categories and to classify them is relatively easy in a non-typological framework; however, to explain on-going *processes* is virtually impossible if the only tools available to us are ordinary or listing rules. Conflict normally involves a clash or competition between two or more types, as occurs between the modern and the contemporary type. Here again typologies are badly needed. Finally, we need to realize that the variation we are interested in is variation in the types, not variation in individual unrelated features. It would be naïve to account for socio-economic or any other category of variation without considering each stratum or a subsystem as potentially characterized by differing types.

References

Befu, Harumi
    1977 'Power in the Great White Tower', in *The Anthropology of Power*, edited by R. D. Fogelson and R. M. Adams (New York: Academic Press), 77–87.
    1980 'The Group Model of Japanese Society and an Alternative', *Rice University Studies*, 66/1, 169–87.
    1982 'A Critique of the Group Model of Japanese Society', in *Japanese Society, Reappraisals and New Directions*, edited by Y. Sugimoto and R. Mouer. Special issue of *Social Analysis* 5–6 (Dec. 1980), 29–43.
    1984 'Civilization and Culture: Japan in Search of Identity', *Senri Ethnological Studies*, 16, 59–75.
Befu, Harumi; and Norbeck, E.
    1958 'Japanese Usages of Terms of Relationship', *Southwestern Journal of Anthropology*, 14, 66–86.
Bernstein, B.
    1966 'Elaborated and Restricted Codes: an Outline', in *Explorations in Sociolinguistics*, edited by S. Lieberson (Bloomington, Ind.: Indiana University Press), 126–33.
Brown, P.; and Levinson, S.
    1978 'Universals in Language Use: Politeness Phenomena', in *Questions and Politeness*, edited by E. N. Goody (Cambridge: Cambridge University Press), 56–324.
Comrie, B.
    1981 *Language Universals and Linguistic Typology* (Oxford: Blackwell).
Fischer, J. L.
    1964 'Words for Self and Others in Some Japanese Families', *American Anthropologist*, 66/6, Part 2, 115–26.
    1970 'Linguistic Socialization: Japan and the United States', in

Families in East and West, edited by R. Hill and R. König (The Hague: Mouton), 107–19.

Goody, E. N. (ed.)
1978 *Questions and Politeness* (Cambridge: Cambridge University Press).

Greenberg, J. H.
1957 'The Nature and Uses of Linguistic Typologies', *International Journal of American Linguistics*, 23, 68–77.

Grice, H. P.
1975 'Logic and Conversation', in *Speech Acts (Syntax and Semantics 3)*, edited by P. Cole and J. L. Morgan (New York: Academic Press), 41–58.

Haarmann, H.
1976 *Aspekte der Arealtypologie* (Tübingen: Gunter Narr).

Hall, S.
1985 'Signification, Representation, Ideology: Althusser and Post-Structuralist Debates', *Critical Studies in Mass Communication*, 2, 91–114.

Hata, H.; and Smith, W.
1983 'Nakane's *Japanese Society* as Utopian Thought', *Journal of Contemporary Asia*, 13/3, 361–88.

Horn, K. M.
1966 *Language Typology* (Washington, DC: Georgetown University Press).

Kawamura, N.
1980 'The Historical Background of Arguments Emphasizing the Uniqueness of Japanese Society', in *Japanese Society, Reappraisals and New Directions*, edited by Y. Sugimoto and R. Mouer as a special issue of *Social Analysis*, 5–6 (Dec. 1980), 44–62.

Kubíčková, M.
1969 *Typologická metoda v sociologii a společenských vědách* (Prague: Universita Karlova).

Kuno, Susumu
1973 *The Structure of Japanese* (Cambridge, Mass.: The MIT Press).

Labov, W.
1972 *Sociolinguistic Patterns* (Philadelphia, Pa.: University of Pennsylvania Press).

Lehmann, Ch.
1983 'The Present State of Linguistic Typology', in *Proceedings of the XIIIth International Congress of Linguists* (Tokyo), 950–6.

Lehmann, W. P.
1972 'Converging Theories in Linguistics', *Language*, 48, 266–75.

Mouer, R.; and Sugimoto, Y.
1986 *Images of Japanese Society* (London: Kegan Paul International).

Neustupný, J. V.
  1978   *Post-Structural Approaches to Language* (Tokyo: University of
    Tokyo Press).
  1980   'Japanese Language and Japanese Literature', paper presented
    at the Third National Conference of the Asian Studies Association
    of Australia, Griffith University, Brisbane (24–29 Aug.).
  1981   'Gaikokujin Bamen no Kenkyū to Nihongo Kyōiku', *Nihongo
    Kyōiku*, 45, 30–40.
  1982a 'On Paradigms in Japanese Studies', in *Japanese Society,
    Reappraisals and New Directions*, edited by Y. Sugimoto and R.
    Mouer. Special issue of *Social Analysis*, 5–6 (Dec. 1980), 20–8.
  1982b *Gaikokujin to no kommyunikeeshon* (Tokyo: Iwanami
    Shoten).
  Forthcoming 'Language Purism as a Type of Language Correction',
    to be published in *The Politics of Language Purism*, edited by B.
    Jernudd and M. Shapiro.
Passin, H.
  1966   'Intra-familial Linguistic Usage in Japan', *Monumenta
    Nipponica*, 21, 97–113.
Peng, F. C. C.; and Maruyama, Taeko.
  1975   'Sociolinguistic Patterns of Japanese Kinship Behaviour', in
    Language in Japanese Society, edited by F. C. C. Peng (Tokyo:
    University of Tokyo Press), 91–128.
Robinson, W. P.
  1972   *Language and Social Behaviour* (Harmondsworth: Penguin
    Books).
Skalička, V.
  1979   *Typologische Studien* (Wiesbaden: Vieweg).
Smith, M.
  1981   *Law in Japanese Society*. Inaugural Lecture of the Japanese
    Studies Centre (Melbourne) (7 July).
Sugimoto, Y.; and Mouer, R.
  1979   'Kutabare Japanorojii: Nihonjin Dōshitsuron no Hōhōron-teki
    Mondaiten', *Gendai no Me*, 20/6, 134–45.
  1982   *Nihonjin wa 'nihonteki' ka* (Tokyo: Tōyō keizai shinpōsha).
Suzuki, Takao
  1984   *Words in Context* (Tokyo: Kodansha Intl.) (Originally published
    as *Japanese and the Japanese*, 1978.)
Wunderlich, D.
  1981   'Linguistic Strategies', in *A Festschrift for Native Speaker*, edited
    by F. Coulmas (The Hague: Mouton), 279–96.

Index

Page numbers with *f* refer to figures, with *t* to tables. Textual matter may occur on the same pages.

Abegglen, James C. 230
Achenbaum, W. Andrew 87
advertising 185
Advisory Council on Population
    Problems 187
advisory councils 262, 263, 277–82,
    289
    ad hoc councils 263
    aims 278
    bureaucrats' appraisals of 278–9
    classification by members'
        backgrounds 291t, 292t
    political influence of corporations
        280–1
    roles of 278, 279
    selection of members 279–80
    types of 290t
age
    age-based conflict 233–4
        see also New Liberal Club split
    inequalities 10
    see also lifecourse
Agricultural Cooperative 289
agriculture, subsidies 274–5
Agune, Noboru 266t
Akutagawa Prize 173
All-Japan Pearl Culture Fishing
    Industry Cooperative
    Federation 281
Allan, G. A. 136, 142, 144

Allport, Gordon W. 73
altruism 60, 161, 194
amae see dependency
amakudari 268, 271, 289
Amanuma, Kaoru 5
ancestors 83
    ancestor worship 215–16
    social exchange and 41–2
anti-establishment movements 4
    regulating activities of
        academicians 25
anti-pollution movements 4
anti-Semitism 22
Aoshima Yukio 265
Asano, Ken-ichi 182
Association for the Advancement of
    Japanese Pearls 281
Atsumi, Reiko 11, 40, 130–53
Austin, Lewis 230
Australia–Japan Economic Research
    Centre 26
Australian mateship 136
Australian society 16t, 17f
authoritarian personality 3
Avon Grand Prize 174
awards 171, 172t, 173–4
    industrial 172–3
    literary 173–4
    sports 174

Index

Babchuk, N. 142, 143
balanced exchange *see* social
    exchange, balanced
Basabe, Fernando M. 191
Basic Survey of the Wage Structure,
    The 107, 112
Bates, A. P. 142, 143
Befu, Harumi 2, 9, 10, 11, 15, 18,
    23, 39–66, 160, 300, 323–43, 345,
    347, 349, 356, 367, 373
behaviour
  assumption of variations 160
  at work 94–129
    decision making 96, 97t
    democracy *see* industrial
        democracy
    flexibility 101
    international comparisons 95–
        100
    see also employment: quality-
        control circles
  constrained conflict behaviour 241
  consumer behaviour 189–90
    conspicuous consumption 174–5
  deference 240–1
  Japanese group tour 361
  prediction 337–8
  rules and 44
Bell, Robert R. 136, 142, 143
Benedict, Ruth 88, 170, 230, 350
Bengtson, Vern L. 80
Bernstein, Basil 351–3
big business *see* corporations
biographies *see* lifecourse
Blau, Peter M. 40
BLL *see* Buraku Liberation League
    (BLL)
blood type personality 21
blue-collar workers
  age-wage international
      comparison 108, 109f
  white collarization
    labour turnover 111–12, 113f,
        114
    wages 111
    welfare benefits 308
bonuses 308, 317
borrowing 138–9
Bott, E. 142, 144
Brandes, Stanley H. 133, 134, 137,
    138, 140, 141
brandism 175
bribery 50, 54–6
Brim, Orville G. Jr. 85

Brinton, Mary C. 2
Brislin, Richard W. 330
Brown, Keith 81
Brown, P. 358, 359
Buddhism 191
  meditation 86
Buraku Liberation League (BLL)
    234–5, 248–9, 250, 251
burakumin conflict 234–5
  basis of 237
  escalation and de-escalation 249–
      50, 251
  higher status third parties 243–4
  initiation of 246, 247, 248–9, 250
  manifestation of 242
  termination of 251–2, 253, 255
bureaucracy 260
  HOC candidates from 267–8, 269t
  LDP, big business and bureaucracy
      alliance 260, 271, 290
  power 57–8
Burridge, Kenelm 73
Buruma, Ian 22
businesses, big *see* corporations

Campbell, John C. 274
career
  in lifecourse 75
  long-range view of 79
Caudill, William 84
Central Association for the
    Prevention of Labour
    Accidents 173
Central Bank for Agriculture and
    Forestry 281
Central Bank for Commercial and
    Industrial Associations 281
Central Social Insurance and Medical
    Care Council 280
Chalmers, W. E. 120
Chamberlain, Neil W. *et al.* 297
charity 60
China
  friendship in pre-revolutionary
      142
  Japanese contempt for 20–1
chōnin class 148–9
Chrysanthemum and the Sword, The
    (Benedict) 88
citizen movements 4
civilization 7–8, 13
Clark, Rodney C. 186
class *see* social class

Clean Government Party *see* Komeitō
Cohen, Yehudi A. 133, 137, 138, 139
Cole, Robert E. 230, 304
Coleman, James S. 235, 236
Coleman, Samuel C. 76
collective bargaining *see* industrial relations
community interest 195
commuters 76
company unions 104, 217
company welfare benefits 296, 297, 308–9
    international comparisons 96
Comrie, B. 354
concreteness, social exchange 48, 49f
conflict
    age-based 233–4
        see also New Liberal Club split
    awareness process 239
    caste-based 234–5
        see also burakumin conflict
    consciousness-raising process 242–3, 244–5
    constrained conflict behaviour 241
    deference behaviour 240–1
    gender-based conflict 233
        see also tea-pourers conflict
    higher status third parties 243–4, 255
    industrial relations *see* industrial relations
    lack of institutionalized channels for resolution 253
    leaders 242, 243–4, 254, 255
    low levels of 3
    renegotiation of relations 12
    stages of 235–54
        escalation and de-escalation 249–51
        initiation 245–9
        manifestation 238–45
        objective bases 236–8
        termination 251–4
    status-based 228–58
        democratic ideologies and 229–31
        methodology 233–5
        non-economic issues 231–2
        see also stratification
    subcultures within Japan 15–16
    theories 4
    unstated grievances 244–5
    use of deprecatory terms 250–1

consensus model 2, 3, 160
    criticism of national stereotypes 5
    ie or *mura*-type approach 5–6
    non-visible forms of control criticisms 4
Conservative Party 316
conspicuous consumption 174–5
consultation 125
consultative councils *see* advisory councils
consumption
    brandism 175
    conspicuous 174–5
    consumer behaviour 189–90
    product differentiation 189–90
contextualism 6–7
    collective action and 10
    interpersonal 9
control 11
    non-visible forms 4
    see also power relations
Cook, Theodore F. Jr. 78
copyrighting 183
corporate bodies, social exchange and 42
corporate images 185–6
corporations 277
    contribution to LDP 275
    Emperor system and 212, 213, 214, 216–17
    finance from private sources 272
    LDP, big business and bureaucracy alliance 260, 271, 290
    political influence of 280–1
    support for small interest groups 270
    use of family ideology 216–17
corporatism 279, 282–9
Coser, Lewis A. 235, 236
Council on the Pearl Industry 281
Crystal Always (Tanaka) 175
culture
    cross-cultural comparisons 14–15
    cultural imperialism 15
    cultural relativism 3, 5, 15
    culturally bound concepts 333–4
    emic homogeneity assumption 338–9
    friendship and 141–5
    ideology and 11, 161
    in lifecourse 73
    industrial relations and 298–300
    national 3, 4, 5
    subcultures within Japan 15–16

Index

culture – *cont.*
  subsumed to civilization 7–8
  Westernization of 373–7
  see also emic-etic distinction

Dahrendorf, Ralf 164
Dale, Peter 2, 5, 22
Dator, James Allen 191
decision making, at work 96, 97t
defence related expenditure 273t,
  274
deference behaviour 240–1
deities, social exchange and 41–2
Demming Award 174
democracy
  at work *see* industrial democracy
  Japanese form 6
Democratic Socialist Party 266t, 316
dependability growth 80–4
dependency 7, 339
Derber, Milton 120
Di Palmer, Guiseppe 235
Doi, Takeo 5, 7, 81, 85, 132, 339,
  356
Dore, Ronald P. 14, 178
Douglas, Mary 240
Dower, John 6, 22
dōzoku lineage groups 206–7, 215
Du Bois, Cola 133, 137
Dunlop, John T. 300

Edelman, Murray 252
education
  acquisition of knowledge 183–4
  control in discussions of 4
  gender segregation in 146
  information-based rewards 178–9
  life-time 184
  miscellaneous schools (*kakushu
    gakkō*) 182
  moral 184
  status and 175–6
  see also on the job training
Eisenstadt, S. N. 140
Ejiri, Hiroshi 175, 189
Elder, Glen H. Jr. 73
elitism 261
Embree, John F. 83, 135
emic-etic distinction 323–43
  back translation 330
  culturally bound concepts 333–4
  decentering 330–1
  emic concepts 15, 16, 17, 23, 27,
    300

  homogeneity assumption 338–9
  language problems 335–7
  etic concepts 15, 16, 17, 23, 300,
    328–9
  generalizations 329–30, 332,
    338
  non-linguistic approach 332–5
  universals 332
  kinship terms 328–9, 335
  Pike's distinction 324–8
  prediction of behaviour 337–8
  relevance to study of Japan 339–
    41
  uniqueness of meaning in each
    language 331
  views on religion 329–30
Emperor system 4–5, 11–12, 20
  head of original main family 211–
    12, 224
  order of succession 213f
  status hierarchy 177
  use by corporations 212, 216–17
  women's movement and 4, 12
employee housing 96
employment
  breadth of career 115–16
  democracy at work *see* industrial
    democracy
  enterprise unionism *see* enterprise
    unions
  flexibility 101
  incentives and rewards *see*
    industrial relations: rewards
  industrial democracy 98, 99t
  industrial relations *see* industrial
    relations
  job definitions 100–1
  length of service 111–12, 113f, 114
  life-time employment 100, 112,
    113f, 223, 296, 297, 303–5
  mobility
    cost of changing firms 122–3
    internal labour markets 122–4
    job transfers 114–15
    turnover 111–12, 113f, 114
  on the job training 106, 112, 114,
    116, 307
  promotion 115, 116–17
  security 97, 98t
  seniority wages *see* seniority wage
  skill notions of 102–17
  unionism *see* unions
  see also behaviour, at work: quality-
    control circles

empty nest 77–8
enterprise unions 10, 100, 104, 223, 296, 297, 309–11
  coordination among unions 310–11, 316–17
  'sweetheart' arrangements 310
enterprises *see* corporations
enterprisism 10
entertainment, overlapping rewards 186
Erikson, Erik H. 85
ethnicity, inequalities 10
ethnography 335
ethnoscience 335
etic concepts *see emic-etic* distinction
Etō Akira 269t
Etō, Jun 20
European Community 100, 107
examinations, status and 176
exchange model *see* social exchange model
expressivity 44–51, 52, 58–61

family allowances 96
family businesses 148–9
family planning 76–7
family *see* household system
fascism, 'friendly' 4
feminists *see* women's movement
Fifteen Years' War 21, 22
fiscal management
  defence related expenditure 273t, 274
  general accounts budgets 272, 273t
  industrial economy 273t, 274–5
  interest groups and 272–7
  local tax grants 273t
  public deficit 275
  public works expenditure 273t
  reforms needed 275–6
  resistance to reforms 276–7
  social security expenditure 273t, 274
Fischer, J. L. 367, 369
Flanagan, Scott C. 231
flexibility 101
Foa, Uriel 48, 49
Ford Foundation 25
fortune telling 191
Foster, Brian L. 133, 134, 138, 139, 141
Foster, George M. 41
Frake, Charles O. 335
Freeman, Jo 245

Fried, Morton H. 142
friendly fascism 4
friendship 11, 130–53
  advice 139
  American men and women friends 139, 143
  among elite Indonesian men 133, 139, 140
  Australian mateship 136
  casual friends 134, 137, 138
  changes in 132
  definition 130
  economic assistance 138–9
  emotional friendships 137
  emotional support 139
  English working class 144
  essential properties
    affectivity versus instrumentality 137–8
    durability 139–41
    equality of relationship 133–4
    intimacy and confidence 134–5
    mutual obligations and duties 138–9
    voluntary nature of 136
  exclusive friends 137
  expedient friendships 137
  formal friends 134
  formed through school or college 135
  friends of trust 134
  future of, in Japan 145–9
  gender segregation 144, 145–6
  housewives 135, 143–4, 146–7
  intensive shared experiences 135
  Japanese merchant class 148–9
  openness 134
  pre-revolutionary China 142
  pseudo-kinship and fictive kinship relations 140
  relevancy rules 139–40
  self-employed people 148–9
  shared by husband and wife 142–3
  socio-cultural variables and 141–5
  termination 139–41
  Thai 141–2
  timing of 82–3
  true friendship and friendly relations 134
  tsukiai 134–5, 136, 137, 147
  valued in culture 132
Fujioka, Wakao 189
Fukaya, Masashi 146

Index

Fukui, Haruhiko 260, 261
Fukuma Tomoyuki 266t
Fukutake, Tadashi 2, 190
Fukuzawa, Yukichi 244
Fulbright Fellowship 25
funding Japanese studies 24–6
  Japanese sources 26
funeral ceremony 215
fungibles 164, 184–7
Fuse, Tetsuji *et al.* 2

Garner, Roberta Ash 22
Geertz, Clifford 73, 332
Gelya, Frank 73
Genda, Minoru 269t
gender inequalities 10
gender segregation
  education 146
  friendship 144, 145–6
  role 145–6, 147–8
gender-based conflict 233
  see also tea-pourers conflict
Genji, Keita 77
geographic inequalities 10
gerontology *see* lifecourse
gift giving 190–1, 340–1
Gill, Robin 2
Gilmore, David 134, 137, 138, 139,
  141
Glazer, Nathan 2
Gluck, Carol 2
Goffman, Erving 240
Goodenough, Ward H. 327, 335
Goody, E. N. 358
Gordon, Milton 164
government *see* bureaucracy
Grant Study (Harvard) 72
Greenberg, J. H. 347, 355
Greenberg, Joseph 328
Greentopia activities 178
Grice, H. P. 359
Grossberg, John B. 79
group model 3, 160, 345, 356
  dependability growth and 81
  lifecourse and 69
  subjectivity growth and 75–6
groupism 13, 59, 62, 100–2, 219, 222,
  298
  see also interest groups
Gusfield, Joseph R. 229
Gyōsei Kanrichō 278

Haarmann, H. 365

Hakuhōdō Seikatsu Sōgō Kenkyūjo
  189
Hall, Ivan P. 5
Hall, S. 364
Hallowell, A. Irving 73
Hamaguchi, Eshun 2, 5, 6–7, 158,
  177, 334, 351
Hanami, Tadashi 304, 311
Hane, Mikiso 158
Hareven, Tamara 73
Harris, Marvin 332, 333
Harrison Prescott Eddy Medal 174
Hasegawa, Keitarō 20
Hashiguchi, Osamu 271
Hashimoto, Ryūtarō 276
Hashimoto, Shigeru 40
Hata, H. 351
Hata Yutaka 265
Hatoyama Iichirō 265, 269t
Hayakawa, Kōichi 40
health 187–9
  industrial accidents 188
  medical services and income
    188–9
Hendry, Joy 5
Henry, Kules 80
Hidaka, Rokurō 4
Hidaka Incident 25
Higuchi, Kiyoyuki 179
Hill, Reuben 73
Hino, Hideitsu 188
Hitachi Group 266
holism 346–7
  see also typology
Homans, George C. 42
Honigmann, John J. 141
Horne, K. M. 347, 355
Hosojima, Izumi 239
Hosokawa, Migiwa 178, 188
House of Councillors 262
  candidates from bureaucracy 267–
    8, 269t
  candidates' support groups 265,
    266t, 267
  interest groups and 261, 262,
    264–71
  successful candidates 265
House of Representatives 264
household system 11–12
  ancestor worship 215–16
  compound families 205, 206f, 213
  conjugal families 205, 206f
  dōzoku lineage groups 206–8, 210,
    215

household system – *cont.*
Emperor and 212, 213, 214, 216–17, 224
families during the war 210–12
family as ideology 216–17
geneological continuity 223
ie shakai 222–4, 225f
landlords 209, 214
modernization and 202–27
patrilineal descent 214
postwar continuities 212–14
postwar families, structural continuities 215–16
pre-Meiji family 205–8
prewar family 209–10
stem families 205, 206f, 213, 214
vertical relationships and class 217–21
housewives *see* friendship: gender segregation
housing, employee 96
Hsu, Francis L. K. 87, 334

Ichikawa, Fusae 265
ideology, culture and 11, 161
ie approach 5–6
ie shakai 222–4, 225f
Ike, Nobutaka 231
Ikeda, Masayuki 2
Imperial Rescript on Education 178
imperial system *see* Emperor system
incentives 121–8
income, as reward 162, 163t, 164
indebtedness *see* reciprocity
individuals
as analysis unit 6, 7, 8
culturally bound concept 334
in social exchange 41
Japanese conception of 39
long-term planning 69
western use of 219, 222
Indonesian men, friendship 133, 139, 140
industrial accidents 188
industrial democracy 98, 99t
consultations 120, 121t
higher management authority 120, 122t
international comparison 119–21
loyal insubordination 120, 121t
rotation 118
workshop practices 117–19
industrial economy 273t, 274–5

industrial relations 2, 12–13, 100, 296–320
buffer groups 304–5
collective bargaining 308, 310–11, 316–17
company welfare benefits 296, 297, 308–9
conflict 314–16
demonstrations 315
international comparisons 99
media focus on 301
public sector 315
right to strike 315–16
strikes 315
consultation 125, 317
coordination among unions 310–11, 316–17
culture and 298–300
enterprise unions *see* enterprise unions
incentives and rewards 121–8
careers structuring 121–4
production incentives 307
role of unions 124–6
joint consultation activities 317
labour law 311–13
life-time employment 296, 297, 303–5
mobility 304
political role 316–18
retirement 304
rules governing 301–2
seniority wages *see* seniority wage
small and medium-sized firms 313–14
supposed uniqueness of Japan 296–7, 298, 303–11
systematic framework and systems approach 300–2
training 307
wage determination 316–18
worker loyalty 296, 297
Industrial Revolution 87
industrialism 10
inequality 10–11
see also stratification
influence, power relations and 11
information society 177–8
information-based rewards 162, 163t, 164
acquisition of knowledge 183–4
importance of education 178–9
information as consumer good 181–3

information-based rewards – *cont.*
  instrumental information 180–1
  knowledge and 177–84
  privacy and right to know 182–3
Inglehart, Ronald 231
innovation
  incentives and rewards 121–2,
    123
  necessary discretion for 118–19
Inoue, Takashi 269t
instrumentality
  in social exchange 44–51, 58–61
insubordination, loyal 120
intelligence 179
intelligent cities 178
interest groups 259–95
  advisory councils *see* advisory
    councils
  corporatism 279, 282–9
  counteracting groups 287–8
  economic expenditures and
    resource distribution 261,
    262–3, 272–7
  fiscal management *see* fiscal
    management
  House of Councillors
    candidates from bureaucracy
      267–8, 269t
    candidates' support groups 265,
      266t, 267
    national constituency and 261,
      262, 264–71
  influence of
    on political decisions 286, 287t
    self-appraisals 281
  international comparison of
    membership 284t
  LDP, big business and bureaucracy
    alliance 260, 271, 290
  liberalism 261, 282–9
  pluralism 283–4
  year of formation 284, 285t
  see also groupism: self-interest
intermediate organization, and social
  exchange *see* social exchange
internal labour markets 122–4
International Centre for Japanese
  Studies 20, 24–5, 26
International Labour Organization
  313
internationalization 8, 17–27
  Japanese contempt for Asian
    countries 20–1
  racism and nationalization 20–3

reciprocity 18
recurrent change 22
intra-societal dynamics 15
Inuzuka, Sen 40
Irokawa, Daikichi 4, 12
Ishida, Takeshi 260
Ishikawa, Kaoru 101
Itagaki, Tadashi 266t
Itano, Shigenobu 269t
Itō, Ikuo 266t
Itō, Shuntarō 8, 177–8
Itō, Zen-ichi 177
Iwami, Kazuhiko 22
Iwao, Sumiko 243

Jacobs, J. B. 133
Japan Airlines Scholarships 26
Japan Chamber of Commerce and
  Industry 276–7
Japan Communist Party 234, 250,
  265, 316
Japan Council of Organizations for
  Young Workers 173, 186
Japan Dental Federation 266t, 267
Japan Essayists' Grand Prize 173
Japan External Trade Organization
  281
Japan Federation for Industrial
  Safety 173
Japan Federation of Employers'
  Associations 216
Japan Foundation 26
Japan Foundation Prize 174
Japan Friendship Award 174
Japan Grand Record Prize 174
Japan Incorporated 12, 260, 272,
  284, 286, 288–9
  change to internationalization 17–
    27
Japan Institute of Labour 177, 312
Japan International, change from
  Japan Incorporated 17–27
Japan Labor Bulletin 313
Japan Medical Association 266t,
  267, 274, 287, 289
Japan Pearl Exporting Union 281
Japan Socialist Party 243, 266t
Japan War Bereavement
  Association 266t, 267
Japan-bashing 20
Japanese studies
  funding 24–6
  official interpretation 24–5

job rotation 118
Johnson, Chalmers 5, 193

Kajiki, Matazō 267
Kajiwara, Kiyoshi 269t
Kamata, Satoshi 4
Kan, Takayuki 4–5
Kanebō Misesu Juvenile Literary
    Prize 173
Kaneko, Masashi 279
kanjinshugi see contextualism 6
Kanō, Miyoko 4, 12
Karachi Plan 178
Karatani, Michikazu 266t
Kasuya, Terumi 266t
Katayama, Jin-ichi 266t
Katō, Shūichi 22, 86
Kawada, Hisashi 178, 307
Kawamura, Nozomu 2, 5, 9, 11–12,
    202–27, 351
Kawanishi, Hirosuke 2, 10
Kenkyūsha's *New English–Japanese
    Dictionary* 336–7
KICA Prize 174
Kikuchi, Kan 82–3
kinship terms 328–9, 335
Kobayashi Kuniji 267
Kogawa, Tetsuo 10, 122
Koike, Kazuo 9–10, 94–129, 158,
    180, 184, 304, 308, 313, 314
Kokuritsu Minzoku Hakubutsan *see*
    National Museum of Ethnology
kokusaika see internationalization
Komeitō 265, 267, 316
Kōno, Yōhei 239, 241, 242, 246, 247–
    8, 250
Koschmann, J. Vistor 158
Krauss, Ellis S. 77
Kriesberg, Louis 235, 236
Kubíčková, M. 353
Kubota, Masao 22
Kumon, Shunpei 5, 222
Kuno, Osamu 2
Kuno, Susumu 355
Kurihara, Akira 4
Kurth, S. B. 133, 134, 138
Kusatsu, Osamu 84
Kuypers, J. A. 80
Kyōto school academics 20
kyūdan 249, 255

labour law 311–13
Labour Ministry *see* Ministry of
    Labour

Labour Relations Adjustment Act
    311
Labour Standards Act 308, 311, 312,
    314
Labov, W. 345, 368
landlords 209, 214
Langness, L. L. 73
language 15, 23
    see also emic-etic distinction:
        typology
Larson, Margali Sarfatti 176
lay-offs
    anti-seniority principle 123–4
    seniority principle 123
Lebra, Takie 40, 41, 79
Lebra, T. S. 135
Lehmann, C. 345, 347, 355
Lehmann, Jean-Pierre 2
Lehmann, W. 355
Lenski, Gerhard 164, 168
Lévi-Strauss, Claude 42
Levine, Robert A. 73, 79
Levine, Solomon B. 12–13, 178, 296–
    320
Levinson, Daniel J. 143
Levinson, S. 358, 359
Lewis, Robert A. 143
Liberal Democratic Party 20, 62,
    263, 266t, 316
    alliance with big business and
        bureaucracy 260, 271, 290
    contribution by big business 275
    Policy Affairs Research Council
        270–1, 290
    split *see* New Liberal Club split
    Taxation System Investigation
        Committee 282
liberalism, interest group liberalism
    261, 282–9, 289
licensing, status and 176
life cycle notion 9
life-time education 184
life-time employment 100, 112, 113f,
    223, 296, 297, 303–5
lifecourse 67–93
    age as obsolescence 87
    age classes 67–8
    age identity stabilizing 85
    age norms 73
    ageing 69
    career 75
    changing views on 68
    'convoy of social support' 80–4
    cultural schedules 73

lifecourse – *cont.*
  dependability growth 80–4
  empty nest 77–8
  family planning 76–7
  Galilean view 87–8
  gerontology 71, 87
  group model and 69
  human relationships development
      80–4
  individual and person 72–3
  individual synchronization of
      development arcs 77
  Japanese long time scale 69, 78,
      83, 86–7
  mass longevity concerns 88
  mastery of self 84–7
  optimistic outlook 70
  patterns in growth and
      development 71–2
  personal philosophy of life 84–7
  role dedication and ability to
      change 77–8
  self as agent of development 71
  subjectivity growth 75–9
  timing of biographies 67–70
  timing of friendships 82–3
  timing of life events 72–5
  unscheduled crises 73–4
Lifton, Robert J. 86
Lindbolm, Charles E. 277
linguistics *see* typology
living national treasures 171
local tax grants 273t
long-term planning 10
longevity 187
loss of face 170
Lowe, John C. 73
Lowi, Theodore 261, 282–3, 286
loyal insubordination 120, 121t
Lummis, C. Douglas 2, 4

McCormack, Gavan 4, 25
MacDougall, John J. 133, 139, 140
Maeda, Hajime 216
Mainichi Publication Culture Prize
    173
Mainichi Shinbunsha Seijibu 234
management
  affective relationships 53–4
  authority of higher management
      120, 122t
  corporate image 185–6
  dissemination of 23–4
  information required by 181

union participation 125
women's absence from 186
Mannari, Hiroshi 18
manuals 119
marriage ceremony 216
martial arts 86
Marumo, Shigesada 266t
Maruyama, Masao 211
Maruyama, Taeko 368, 371
Marx, Karl 167, 168
Matsumoto, Eiichi 266t
Matsuura, Isao 269t
Mattessich, Paul 73
maxims *see* typology, maxims
media terminals 178
Meguro, Kesajirō 266t
Meiji Restoration modernization
    203–4
merchant class 148–9
meta-*nihonjinron* 2–3
methodology 14–15
Military Pensioners Federation 266t,
    267
Mills, C. Wright 23
Milton, T. 120
Minami, Hiroshi 2
Minear, Richard 2
Ministry of Agriculture, Forestry and
    Fisheries 267, 269t, 288
  Council on the Pearl Industry 281
  Greentopia activities 178
  Rice Price Council 281
Ministry of Communications,
    Teletopia Project 178
Ministry of Construction, intelligent
    cities 178
Ministry of Education 24, 26
Ministry of Finance 270, 271
Ministry of Foreign Affairs 243, 268
Ministry of International Trade 260
Ministry of Labour 102, 107, 112,
    312
  awards 172–3
  Women's Bureau 147
Ministry of Posts and
    Telecommunications 271
Ministry of Transport, media
    terminals design 178
Ministry of Welfare 312
  Division of Statistical Information
      187, 188
Minobe, Ryōkichi 265
minorities 186–7
Mishima, Yukio 74, 81

MITI 268, 285, 288
  Industrial Structure Council 280
  New Media Community Concept
    178
Mitsui Scholarships 26
Miyata, Teru 265
Miyazaki, Masahiro 22
mobility 304
modernization 24
  of household system *see* household
    system
  theories 3, 14
  typology and Westernization 373–
    7
Mombushō Scholarships 26
Monopoly Corporation 268
Moore, Joan W. 73
Mori, Arinori 244
Morioka, Kiyomi 191
Morita, Akio 5
Morris, Ivon 86
Morsbach, G. 79
Morsbach, Helmut 79
motivation 121–8, 161
Mouer, Ross 1–35, 157–201, 299,
    345–6, 347, 349, 351, 353–4, 356,
    362–3, 373
Mukai Nagatoshi 266t
mura approach 5–6
Murakami, Masakuni 266t
Murakami, Yasusuke 215, 222, 232
Muramatsu, Michio 278, 281–2
Murofushi, Shigenobu 174
music appreciation 191–2
mutual understanding industry 5

Naegele, Kaspar D. 134, 139, 140
Nagoya, Tokimasa 2
Naitō, Kunji 2
Najita, Tetsuo 158
Naka, Kaoru 171
Nakane, Chie 5, 7, 217–21, 230, 255,
    351, 356
Nakano, Kōichi 174
Nakasone, Prime Minister 21, 179
Nakayama, Chinatsu 265
Nakayama, Ichirō 6, 178
Naoki Prize 173
Narumo, Shūichi 185
national culture 3, 4, 5
National Federation of Fishermen
    281
national interest 195
National Museum of Ethnology 7

nationalism
  contempt for Asian countries 20–1
  re-emergence of 20
  uniqueness of character 21–2
  see also neo-nationalism: racism
neo-nationalism 4, 19–20
  providing self-justification 21
  see also nationalism
Neugarten, Bernice 73, 74, 80, 85
Neustupný, J. V. 2, 16, 160, 344–80
New Liberal Club
  basis of conflict 237
  escalation and de-escalation 250
  initiation of conflict 246, 247–8
  manifestation of conflict 239, 241
  split 233–4
  termination of conflict 251
New Media Community Concept
    (MITI) 178
Newspaper Week (1986) 183
NHK Public Opinion Research
    Institute 190, 191
nihonjinron see consensus model
Nishikawa, Kiyoshi 186
Nishioka, Takeo 241
Nita, Michio 125
Nobel Prizes 174
Noda, Tetsu 266t
Noguchi, Yukio 272, 275
Nomura Sōgō Kenkyūsho 2
Norbeck, E. 367

Oakland-Berkeley growth study 72
occupation 20, 231
  inequalities 10
Ogawa, Yō-ichi 4
Ohira, Prime Minister 223
Okabe Saburō 267, 268, 269t, 270t
Okada, Gō 185
Okada, Hiroshi 266t
Okaki, C. 79
Okamoto, Hideaki 185
Okamoto, Yasuo 101
Ōkōchi, Kazuo 120, 297
Olson, Mancur 289
Olympic Games (Tokyo) 174
'On the Conduct of Lord Tadanao'
    (Kikuchi) 82–3
on the job training 106, 112, 114,
    116, 184, 307
Ono, Tsuneo 13
Order of Aquira Azteca 174
organizations 13
  concentration of power 218, 221

Orita, Yoshirō 185
Osada, Yūji 269t
Osagari Jirō Prize 173
Oyama, Hiroshi 4
Ogawara Taichirō 269t

Pachinko Culture Award 174
Paine, Robert 133, 134, 137, 139, 140
Parsons, Talcott 168
particularism 48, 49f
Passages (Gail Sheehy) 73
Passin, Herbert 178, 367
patrilineal descent 214
Pelzel, John C. 83
Pempel, T. J. 262, 286
Peng, F. C. C. 368, 371
personal relationships
    tsukiai 130, 134–5, 136, 137, 147
    see also conflict: friendship:
        stratification
Pharr, Susan 10, 12, 77, 146, 158, 228–58
Pike, Kenneth L. 324–8, 333
Piker, S. 133, 140, 141
Pitt-Rivers, J. 140
planning, long-term 10
Plath, David W. 9, 10, 67–93, 135, 158
Pleck, J. 139, 143
Plowman, David *et al.* 297
pluralism 261, 283–4
politics
    influence of corporations 280–1
    role of organized labour and
        employers 316–18
    see also interest groups
Post Office 271
power
    as reward 162, 163t, 164
    in social exchange 57–8
    influence and 11
    of organizations 218, 221
    political 12
    relations 11, 12
    see also control
prestige *see* status
Prime Minister's Office 192
    Bureau of Commendations 172
    Youth Policy Office 145, 146
Princeton series 25
production process
    knowledge of 105–6, 116
    technical knowledge of 117

production workers *see* behaviour, at
    work
professionalizing 176
Project on Human Potential
    (Harvard) 70
promotion 115
    from within 116–17
proverbs 185
    intelligence in 179–80
    status in 170
Provisional Council on Educational
    Reform 184
Public Corporation and National
    Enterprise Labour Relations
    Adjustment Act 311
public deficit 275
Public Opinion Research Centre 179
Public Opinion Research Unit of
    Sankei newspaper company 190
public works expenditure 273t

qualifications 175–6
quality-control circles 9–10, 101–2
    as large-firm phenomena 102–4
    democracy in *see* industrial
        democracy
    effectiveness of 102, 103t
    necessary conditions for 104–5
        technical knowledge 105–6, 116, 117
    notions of skill 102–17
    prevalence of 102, 103t

racism 5, 20–1
    anti-Semitism 22
Rape of Nanking 21
reading 179
reciprocity 18, 43, 161
Red–White Song Competition 174
Reich, Michael 86
Reischauer, Edwin 5
relationships *see* friendship: personal
    relationships: stratification
religion
    emic-etic distinction 329–30
    religious practices 191
Research Institute for the Science of
    Labour 188
retirement 304
reverence for West 356–7
rewards 162, 163t, 164
    awards 171, 172t, 173–4, 186
    fungibility 164, 184–7
    income 162, 163t, 164

rewards – *cont.*
    information-based *see* information-
        based rewards
    minorities and 186–7
    power 162, 163t, 164
    prestige *see* status
    status *see* status
Rice Price Council 281
Riley, Matilda W. 73
Robinson, W. P. 352
Rohlen, Thomas P. 86–7, 132, 145,
    146, 230, 234
role gender differentiation 145–6,
    147–8
rotation of jobs 118
Roth, Julius 73, 75

Sabata, Toyoyuki 21
Sahlins, Marshall 50–1
Saitō, Eizaburō 265
Salamon, Sonya Blank 135, 142, 143,
    144, 147
sampling 157–8
Sangyō Kōzō no Chōki Bijon 280
Santō, Akiko 265, 266
Sapporo Winter Olympics 174
Sasameyuki (Tanizaki) 74
Satō, Seizaburō 5, 222
savings 272
Schelling, Thomas 236
Schmitter, Phillippe C. 283, 286
Schneider, David M. 42
scholarships 26
Schooler, Carmi 84
Sea of Fertility, The (Mishima) 74
seishin model 345
Sekiguchi, Keizō 266t
self-interest 9, 160–1, 194, 346
    interpersonal relations 10
    linking with group activity 9–10
    motivation 161
    rewards *see* rewards
    type 349, 350f
    see also interest groups
selfhood *see* individuals: lifecourse
seniority wage 100, 106–8, 223, 296,
    297, 305–7
    blue collar workers 108, 109f
    older workers' wage drop off 109
    white collar workers 110f, 111
    white collarization 108–11
shame 170
Sheehy, Gail 73

Shimada, Haruo 2, 297
Shimada, Sei-ichi 181
Shimizul, Ikutarō 2
Shinbori, Michiya 2, 25
shingikai see advisory councils
Shintoism 191
Shirai, Taishirō 297
Shiroi Kyotō (Yamazaki Toyoko)
    54–5, 60, 62
Skalička, V. 345, 355, 366
skills, enterprise specific 122
Skinner, Kenneth A. 76
Smith, Eugene 182–3
Smith, M. 367
Smith, Robert 11, 135, 139
Smith, W. 351
social class 167, 168t, 169–70
    vertical relationships and 217–21
social conflict *see* conflict
social exchange 9, 39–66, 345
    balanced 10, 50–6, 61
    bribery 50, 54–6
    charity and altruism 60, 161, 194
    concreteness 48, 49f
    corporate bodies 42
    customary rules of exchange 43
    deities and ancestors 41–2
    exchange resource 40
    expressivity 44–51, 52, 58–61
    generalized 10, 50–1, 61
    horizontal 56
    ideals and behaviour 44
    imaginary alters 42
    individuals 41
    instrumentality 44–51, 58–61
    intermediate organization and
        51–4
        affective relationships 53
        expressive solidarity 52
    modelling interpersonal relations
        40
    particularism 48, 49f
    power in 57–8
    reciprocity 18, 43
    social and cultural contexts 40–1
    social inequalities in 11
    society and 42–3
    strategies of 43–4
    unbalanced and negative exchange
        11
    vertical 56–7
social inequality *see* inequality:
    stratification
social security expenditure 273t, 274

Index

Socialist Party 234, 316
society, social exchange and 42–3
Society for the Comparative Study of
    Civilizations 7
soft-authoritarianism 4
Sōmūchō, Seishōnen Taisaku Honbu
    145
Sone, Yasunori 10, 11, 12, 259–95
Sony 217
sound language type 349
sports
    overlapping rewards 186
    status and awards 174
Spring Wage Offensive 317, 318
status 162, 163t, 164, 170–7
    awards 171–4
    based conflict *see* conflict
    conspicuous consumption 174–5
    inconsistency 164
    popularity 177
    prestige 162, 163t, 164
    professionalizing 176
    qualifications 175–6
    shame and loss of face 170
    see also rewards
strategies *see* typology, strategies
stratification 157–201
    agents of 165–6, 168t, 169, 186,
        346
    assumptions of model 160–1
        self-interest 160–1
        variation of behaviour 160
        volition shaping 161
    behaviour differentiation
        consumer behaviour 189–90
        health 187–9
        interpersonal relationships
            190–1
        music appreciation 191–2
        religious practices 191
    information and *see* information-
        based rewards
    model 15
        social inequalities in 11
    multi-dimensional model 159–70
    objective and subjective aspects
        169
    rewards *see* rewards
    social class and 167, 168t, 169–70
    source of social tension and
        conflict 158–9
    status and prestige *see* status
    vertical and horizontal 7, 218–21
    see also conflict, status-based

strikes *see* industrial relations,
    conflicts
subcultures 15–16
Sugimoto, Yoshio 1–35, 157–201,
    299, 345–6, 347, 349, 351, 353–
    4, 356, 362–3, 373
sumō, prizes for 174
Suntory Arts Prize 173
Suntory Foundation 26
Survey of Industrial Injuries 188
*Survey of Labour-Management
    Communications, The* 102
*Survey on Industrial Safety and
    Health* 188
Suzuki, Akira 192
Suzuki, Kazumi 266t
Suzuki, Takao 367

Tabuchi, Tetsuya 266t
Taguchi, Fukuji 260
Taira, Kōji 315
Taiwan, friendship in 133
Takabatake, Michitoshi 4
Takamiyama (sumō wrestler) 186
Takano, Norinari 4
Takeda, Kiyoko 5
Takezawa, Shin-ichi 95, 119–20
Tanaka, Sōji 185
Tanizaki, Jun-ichi 74
tateshakai see relationships, vertical
    and horizontal
taxation 275
    Taxation System Investigation
        Committee 282
Tazawa, Tomoharu 266t
Tea Aesthetic 86
tea-pourers conflict 233
    basis of 237
    deference behaviour 240–1
    initiation of 245, 246
    leaders 242, 243
    termination of 251, 252, 253
technical knowledge, QC circles
    and 105–6, 116
Teletopia Project 178
Terman study of gifted children 72
Time-Life Books 5
Toyota Foundation 26
trade surpluses 23
Trade Union Act 311
training 307
    see also education: on the job
        training
Tsuda, Kōzō 211

tsukiai 11, 130, 147
  economic assistance and 138–9
  friendship and 134–5, 136, 137
Tsukishima, Kenzō 2
Tsunekawa, Keiichi 262, 286
Tsunoda, Tadanobu 21, 179
Tsuratani, Taketsugu 229, 230
Tsuruda, Naofumi 180
Tsurumi, Kazuko 86
Tsurumi, Shunsuke 4
typology 344–80
  concept of type 348
  dual structure 361–2
  holism 346–7
  Japanese reference system
    application 367–73
  Japanese society as dynamic system
    of types 377–8
  major and minor types 362–3
  maxims 358–9, 370–2, 374–6
    alliance 374, 375
    Group-dependence 370–1
    interdependence of reference
      strategies 371–2
    Modern Unity 375
    Modernizing Development
      374–5
    Modernizing Individualism 375
  nature of 347–57
  network structure 358–61
    determinants 358
    listing rules 360–1
    maxims 358–9, 370–2, 374–6
    ordinary rules 359–60, 368–70,
      373–4
    strategies 359, 368–70, 373–4
  personnel type 350, 351–4
    Bernstein's restricted and
      elaborated codes 351–3
    Sugimoto and Mouer
      framework 353–4
  rules 359–61, 368–70, 373–4
  self-interest type 349, 350f
  sound language type 349
  strategies 359, 368–70, 373–4
    Borrowing Strategy 369, 372,
      373–4, 375
    Distance-Avoidance Strategy
      369, 372
    Formality Strategy 369, 372
    Hierarchy Strategy 370
    Intimacy Strategy 369, 372
    Junior-Pivot Strategy 369, 372
    politeness strategies 359

    Refinement Strategy 370, 372
    Senior-Kinterm Strategy 368–9,
      370, 371
    Speaker-Pivot Strategy 369, 372
    Standardization Strategy 369,
      372
  textural types 350–1, 354–7
    areal types 365
    categories of 363–4
    common denominator types
      366–7
    developmental 364–5
    in linguistics 354–5
    in social science 356–7
    interactional types 365–6
    interferential types 365
  Westernization of culture
    application 373–7

Ueyama, Shunpei 20
Umehara, Takeshi 20
Umesao, Tadao 7
unions 10, 98–9, 102, 103t, 104
  company unions 104, 217
  distributive shares 125
  enterprise unions *see* enterprise
    unions
  expressing views to management
    124–5
  job transfers 114–15
  participation in management 125
  promotion and 115
  seniority principle 123
  support for House of Councillors
    candidates 266
  weakness in Japan 104
  workshop innovation
    implementations 126
Uno, Masami 22
urbanization 215

Van Tassel, David D. 87
Vogel, Ezra F. 5, 142, 146, 178, 230
Vogel, Suzanne 77–8, 146

Wada, Ryūko 177
Wada Shizuo 266t
Wagatsuma, Hiroshi 86
Wage Structure Survey (EC) 100
wages
  determination 316–18
  international comparisons 96
  seniority *see* seniority wage
Ward, Robert E. 15

Index

Watsuji, Tetsurō 222
Webber, Jonathon 5
Weber, Max 58, 231
Weinberg, S. Kirson 142
welfare *see* company welfare benefits
Wessolowski, W. 164
Westernization 203, 204
  reverence for West 356–7
  typology and 373–7
  see also household system,
    modernization and
White, Robert W. 85
white collarization 308
  seniority wage as result of 108–11
white-collar workers 138–9
Whitehill, Arthur M. Jr. 95, 119–20
Wilson, James Q. 289
Wimberley, Howard 142, 146, 148
Wolf, E. R. 137, 138
women's movement
  emperor and 4, 12
  see also tea-pourers conflict

work *see* behaviour, at work:
  employment
workshop practices, industrial
  democracy 117–19
World Exhibition (Osaka) 174
Wunderlich, D. 359

Yamagishi, Toshio 2
Yamaguchi, Toshio 241
Yamaguchi, Yasushi 261
Yamaguchi, Yoshiko 265
Yamamoto, Haruyoshi 2, 5
Yamamoto, K. 79
Yamazaki, Masakazu 189
Yamazaki, Toyoko 54–5, 60, 62
Yano, Tōru 8, 20
Yasuoka, Masahiro 181
Yōka High School *see burakumin*
  conflict
Yoshida, Shōin 74
Young Workers' Welfare Law 173
Yuan, Ying-ying 137, 139, 144